Saints with Slingshots

Daily Devotions for the Slightly Tarnished But Perpetually Forgiven Christian

by

Meg Blaine Corrigan

Published by Create Space
www.createspace.com

All Scripture quotations are from the *Holy Bible*, New *International Version*©, as it appears on www.biblegateway.com .

ISBN 10: 978-1517164737
ISBN 13: 1517164737

Cover Design by Fuzion Print
Cover Artwork by Meg Blaine Corrigan
Author Photos by Portrait Innovations

Copyright© 2015 Meg Blaine Corrigan. No portion of this book may be reproduced, stored in a retrieval system or transmitted in any form—electronic, mechanical or other means without written consent of the author except in the case of brief quotations embodied in critical articles and reviews. All rights reserved.

Note: These Christian devotions are intended for the spiritual enrichment of the reader and do not necessarily reflect the doctrine of any specific Christian church. The author's words are her own interpretation of the sources cited.

For additional copies of this book, to inquire about quantity discounts, or for more information about the author, go to www.MegCorrigan.com .

Other titles by this author available at www.Amazon.com :
Then I Am Strong: Moving From My Mother's Daughter to God's Child
Perils of a Polynesian Percussionist

PRAISE FOR SAINTS WITH SLINGSHOTS

I've found a great deal of comfort in Meg's devotions. Stephanie Landsem, author *The Living Water Series: The Well, The Thief, The Tomb*

Meg's messages are short, sweet and to the point. They ignite my day. I love the vitality and eagerness she expresses. Kathi Holmes, author, *I Stand With Courage: One Woman's Journey to Conquer Paralysis*

Meg's devotions are thought provoking and well written. Ruth Bachman, author, *Growing Through the Narrow Spots*

I am so grateful for your daily dose of straight speaking, solid faith and love. Stephanie Sorensen, Author, *Madoula: A Story Tour of Birth*

I love the history and connections Meg's devotions make. They bring the gospels ALIVE for me! They penetrate right to the heart. Sheila Krejce, M Ed HRD, Sheila K Training, Inc.

It can take so long for some people to realize their worth. Meg's devotions are making a profound difference for those who read them. Blessings! Cathy Platenberg, Best Light Image Video Production and Digital Cinema

Once again, today's devotion nailed it! A good reminder to SLOW DOWN AND LISTEN TO HIM! It's not only FREE – it's FREE-ING! Meg is so gifted in putting her thoughts into words. Joleen Amberg, Blog Follower

Meg is doing a wonderful job, making the Bible come to life. Sharon Dornfeld, Blog Follower

Meg is very astute and writes with sound evangelical Lutheran insights. David Olsen, Friend, Part-Time Theologian

Meg's daily devotionals bring me back to realizing God is in control, because He created everything. Janine Stusinski, Friend

I am so grateful for your daily dose of straight speaking, solid faith and love. Stephanie Sorensen, Author, *Madoula: A Story Tour of Birth*

I love the history and connections Meg's devotions make. They bring the gospels ALIVE for me! They penetrate right to the heart. Sheila Krejce, M Ed HRD, Sheila K Training, Inc.

It can take so long for some people to realize their worth. Meg's devotions are making a profound difference for those who read them. Blessings! Cathy Plantenberg, Best Light Image Video Production and Digital Cinema

Meg is doing a wonderful job, making the Bible come to life. Sharon Dornfeld, Blog Follower

I have really needed and appreciated Meg's devotions. Nicole Fende, author, *How to Be a Finance Rock Star: The Small Business Owner's Ticket to Multiplatinum Products*

Meg finds inspiration EVERYWHERE. Diane Keyes, author, *This Sold House: Staging Your Home To Sell In Today's Market* and *Spirit of the Snow People*

FOREWORD

The "power of the story" is evident in Meg Corrigan's devotions, which address the spiritual challenges and opportunities common to human existence. In her own inimitable way, she draws from a wellspring of professional and personal life experiences, as well as from a variety of literary resources, both ancient and modern, to share with her audience the experiences and realities that have shaped her spiritual life. As a consequence, she concomitantly touches and stirs the hearts, minds, spirits, and lives of her readers.

Employing her own understanding of the biblical witness as a foundation for each of her meditations, she probes both the ecstasies and constraints of life's encounters endemic to our existence. She then weaves together an ornate tapestry utilizing the deep and rich reservoir of history, tradition, humor, art, poetry and imagination to illuminate the meaning of the holy in our existence as the people of God. The multi-colored threads of love, grace, forgiveness and mercy are woven in such a way as to inspire the reader with the "good news" of the gospel message.

Each meditation serves to probe, guide, challenge and stretch the reader in her or his spiritual imagination. Meg writes in such a manner that one can vicariously enter into the personal experiences which have provided her life with meaning and purpose. As a result, she touches the heart and the spirit of the reader who is able to identify, recognize and utilize each message.

These brief but powerful and poignant reflections emanate from Meg's vivid imagination and creativity. She provides the reader with a cool, refreshing and invigorating experience that will both nurture and nourish her or his life. This is a precious gift, as we struggle to make meaning in a world that is concurrently beset by beauty, pain and mystery. Take the time to read carefully, meditate prayerfully, and benefit practically from Meg's honesty, insight, and wisdom.

Robert H. Albers, PhD, Distinguished Visiting Professor of Pastoral Theology (Retired), United Theological Seminary, New Brighton, Minnesota

ACKNOWLEDGEMENTS

Where do I begin thanking the people who helped make this book possible? I appreciate the loyalty of my blog followers from all over the world, your comments, and your support. Thanks to all my friends and relatives who also followed the blog, cheered me on, and gave me ideas for entries. Special thanks to my "guest writers:" Nikki Abramson, Nadia Giordana, Diane Keyes, Sheila Krejci, Mary MacFarlane, Diana Merkl, Katie Sluss, and Gloria and Onno VanDemmeltraadt. Your entries gave the book variety and spark, not to mention giving me a bit of a writing break.

Special thanks to my proof readers, Kathi Holmes, Stephanie Sorenson, and Gloria VanDemmeltraadt, formatter Nicole Fende, and blog technical advisor Tai Goodwin Kastens. To Ann Aubitz of Fuzion Print: thank you for your patient assistance in designing the book cover, and for gracefully riding all the waves of change I kept sending your way. All are members of Women of Words (WOW), our amazing women's writers' group.

The book would not be what it is without the help of my friend and mentor, Bob Albers. Bob, thank you for reading every single one of my blog posts. Thanks, too, for sending me heartfelt and challenging comments about each topic. We had quite a discourse during this past year, and as I said a couple of times, I felt like I had just been through every one of your seminary classes by the time it was over. Your insights and encouragement for my efforts meant more than you know.

To my loving husband, my self-professed "number one fan," thank you for putting up with me being "in the zone" for months while I lived and breathed the devotions I was writing. You will be glad to have your wife back now, but you must know how much I appreciate your unfailing love and support. You have known all along how much this project meant to me, and you got out of my way and let me run with it. I love you!

And to my Lord and Master, Jesus Christ, Who sustained me, prodded me, filled me with His marvelous Spirit, and gave me the very words to write: thank You for loving me and walking with me each day of this journey. You are the reason for these devotions.

INTRODUCTION

For surely I know the plans I have for you, says the Lord, plans for your welfare and not for harm, to give you a future with hope. Jeremiah 29:11

When I launched my daily devotions blog on January 1, 2015, I had no idea where God was taking me. I was simply led to begin writing what was on my heart. I quickly learned that the commitment of writing a *daily* blog post was more than I had bargained for. It appeared easy, to write four hundred words or less a day about any topic of my choosing, speaking my mind about how God moved and worked in my life and the lives of countless others whom I knew personally or had knowledge of through books, magazines, news articles, and the Internet. (As they say in the writing field, "To steal from one source is called plagiarism; to steal from many sources is called research.") God was faithful and gave me ideas every day—often so many ideas, it was a bit overwhelming. By year's end, I had a list of over five hundred ideas, more than enough for a year's worth of entries. In the beginning, I stayed about six weeks ahead of the blog publishing dates, cranking out lots of material. Then six weeks dwindled to a month, then two weeks, and at one point, I ground down to where I was writing a blog post due in three days. That was stressful.

A few weeks into the process, people began writing to me and asking me to put the blogs in writing, to publish a devotional book at the end of the year. I was elated when people liked what I was doing, and I set about writing *all three hundred sixty six blog*s (including one for February 29, since the book would be a "perpetual calendar") by October 1, in order to publish the book in time for Christmas. During the last few intense weeks of writing, there were many prayers to God asking why He had led me to do this project. But the ideas kept coming, compelling me to write.

Along the way, I learned an unfathomable amount about myself, my God, the Bible, and the opinions and perspective of innumerable other writers before me. To say I grew in the Lord would be an understatement. Many days, I felt like I was seated at the feet of the Master with His knowledge, power and love flowing into my being like the Living Water of which Jesus spoke. The process became all-encompassing; I ate, slept, and breathed God's word for nine months, and I could feel myself expanding and putting on "the mind of Christ." I experienced the phenomenon of "praying without ceasing:" I was listening to God throughout the day and dreaming about God at night. I had never been as in tune with His will as I felt during the months I was writing.

Some have asked about the title. The blog was called *Brilliant Resilience*, which came about because many have commented on my resilience after the assault which nearly ended my life. Since many of the blogs contain humor (or at least my estimation of what is humorous), I decided to change the title for the book to *Saints with Slingshots*. When I was in college, my mother gave me a set of handmade angel Christmas ornaments with ceramic faces and felt robes and wings and wire halos. One of the angels was named Butch, and he was posed with a mischievous look on his face, aiming a tiny slingshot out at the world. Butch reminds me that, no matter how sweet we all may try to appear, we are, after all, sinners. The subtitle, *Daily Devotions for the Slightly Tarnished But Perpetually Forgiven Christian* sums up our state of affairs with our Lord.

So here it is: my heartfelt gift to my current followers, and to all who don't yet know me. I realize I am no Biblical scholar, and I hope my words speak to the hearts of my readers. Each Scripture passage has been chosen to best fit the topic in the day's devotion. I always recommend that readers use the "rule of five:" read at least *five* verses before and *five* verses after a specific verse so the context of each verse is fully understood. Any Scripture verse cannot stand alone, but must be studied in depth for the words to come alive. I pray that my devotions make the Word of God come alive for each of my readers.

Many Blessings,
Meg (and Butch)

For Patrick

January

January 1

NEW YEAR'S REVOLUTION

I am making all things new. Revelation 21:5

I often think we should not make New Year's *resolutions*, but rather be intent on carrying out a New Year's *revolution*. While this word often conjures up thoughts of violence, Webster also defines *revolution* as "a sudden, extreme, or complete change in the way people live, work, etc." Wouldn't it be great if, every single year, we could recommit our entire beings to following Jesus Christ, obeying God's commandments, and allowing the Holy Spirit to dwell in us richly?

We have discussed this in my Bible study group at church. We came to the conclusion that this type of "all in" devotion to Christ could best be followed if we all lived in a monastery. Not a particularly practical plan for most of us! But there is another way to join this "revolution": we can ask God each and every day to help us to follow Him to the best of our ability *just for that day*. The Bible says God's mercies are "new every morning" (Lamentation 3:22-23). As long as we are faithful to ask God's forgiveness for our sins, we can forget about yesterday. He removes our sins "as far as the east is from the west" (Psalm 103:12), and makes us "white as snow" (Isaiah 1:18). Through His amazing, undeserved grace, we can move on and spend another day walking with Him. I want to be part of that "revolution."

God of Morning Mercies, thank you for forgiving my sins when I ask You to. Because of Your gracious act of sending Your only Son to die on a cross for me, I can live each day as part of Your radical army of peace. Amen

January 2

MASTERPIECE OR FAKE?

I am the way, the truth and the life. No one comes to the Father except through Me. **John 14:6**

What if you went to a famous art museum because you heard there would be a famous painting on display. You found the painting and were standing there admiring how beautiful it was, when a museum employee came up and unceremoniously removed the name plate beside the painting and replaced it with one which said the work was actually done by an artist you had never heard of! You watched as the employee went to another painting that you had just passed by without even noticing and put the first name plate up next to that painting. A couple of minutes ago, you thought the first painting was a masterpiece. Now you are thinking you were deceived.

How easily in this life we are deceived by things that catch our eye. We sometimes get caught thinking, "If only I can have a nicer house, newer car, or better job, I will be content." We ignore the image of Christ we see in other people and in each of God's marvelous creations, and we focus on what is only temporary. Today's society—indeed, society for centuries—has wooed us with ideas and things that take our focus away from the One Who created the earth and everything in it. We would do well to shift our focus daily back to Jesus, Who is "the way, the truth and the life." It is in the Master that we will find a true masterpiece.

Great God of the universe, thank You for all the beautiful things you have created and for the many wonderful things you have enabled people to create. Remind us daily that we may appreciate the things of earth, but the most important thing we need to do is to prepare ourselves for eternity. Amen

January 3

PULLING OUR LOAD

Take My yoke upon you, and learn from Me; for I am gentle and humble at heart, and you will find rest for your souls. For My yoke is easy and My burden is light. **Matthew 11:29-30**

When my father was a boy in the early part of the last century, his family had a couple of horses that pulled a wagon for their very large family to ride in. On Sunday mornings, rain or shine, my grandparents and various ones of their thirteen children would pile into the wagon and travel along the rural roads of northeast Missouri to the little church in the town of Bible Grove. The horses, Sadie and Henry, had differing ideas about how to do their job.

Sadie, the younger mare, had an aversion to hard work. With the entire family in that wagon, the task of pulling them was too much for her. She lagged back and let Henry, the old gelding, do most of the work. My grandfather would slap the reigns against Sadie's rump, and she'd resign herself to her task for a while. But soon enough, she'd slow down again and let Henry put forth most of the effort.

Jesus said He would be there when our burdens become too great for us. During times when we don't think we can put one foot in front of the other, or make difficult decisions, or endure one more minute of physical or emotional pain, He is there not only to help us, but to take the load completely from us. If we rely on our own strength, times of trial will weigh us down. But if we rely on His strength, we find that we are more than capable of pressing on to a better place. That place may be acceptance of a situation or complete freedom from worry. Or it may just be realizing that God truly is our strength and our deliverer.

Oh, Great God, You are our "load bearer" and You are always ready to come to our aid when the load becomes too much for us to carry. Help us to know when that time comes, and to turn to You for help. Amen

January 4

SELF-CONFIDENCE OR GOD CONFIDENCE?

It is better to take refuge in the Lord than to put confidence in mortals. **Psalm 118:8**

As a youth, I lived in Colorado, and worked at the Cave of the Winds in Manitou Springs during the summer. Most of the employees were young people like me, and we had a lot of fun together. There was one young man, however, who did not seem to like me. He showed his disdain for me every time he saw me, which I found unnerving. I asked some of the others if they knew why he felt this way, but all I heard was that everyone knew he did not like me. No one could (or would) give me a reason.

Although I did not know Christ at the time, this young man's aversion to me didn't bother me greatly. I had not been popular in my high school, and I was having the time of my life with all of my other new friends. But through the years, I've thought about this young man and his puzzling treatment of me. Now that I am a follower of Christ, it has occurred to me that I have had this exact same disdain for some people in my life for no good reason. I have repeatedly been convicted to do my best to treat *all* the people I meet with equal love and compassion. Other people's opinion of me—and mine of them—pales in comparison to knowing that we are loved and valued by God. He cares about each of His creations, from the tiniest insect to those of us created in His image. Jesus said, "Do not be afraid; you are of more value than many sparrows" (Matthew 10:31b). If I am to truly "put on Christ" (Romans 13:14), I would do well to value others too.

Loving Lord, help me to see that You made all creatures, including me. No matter how annoying others may seem to me at any given moment, You are loving that person at that same moment. Teach me to see the love You have for others, and to know that You love me too. Amen

January 5

RUN FOR COVER!

The name of the Lord is a strong tower; the righteous run into it and are safe. Proverbs 18:10

My father was an Air Force colonel, stationed at what was then Ent Air Force Base in Colorado Springs, Colorado. When I was about ten years old, my mother once took my sister and me to visit my father at the Air Defense Command when he was serving as Officer of the Day. This meant that he was in charge of a team of people who watched the brand new Distant Early Warning Line, or DEW Line, a system of radar stations in northern Canada, Alaska, the Faroe Islands, Greenland and Iceland. The DEW Line was set up to detect incoming Soviet bombers during the Cold War, between the years of 1957 and the late 1980s. It was the most advanced radar system available at a time when the United States military was vigilant about watching for potential Soviet activity.

After my father gave us a tour of the facility, which included a huge electronic map showing US planes and other aircraft in our airspace, I became agitated. "What happens if you see too many Russian planes on the map?" I asked my dad. With a big grin that assured me he was joking, my father answered, "Find the sergeant on duty and run for cover!"

As Christians, there are many times in life we may feel like running for cover. But God is always there for us, serving as our "distant early warning line" and providing us with a strong tower of protection. Even though our lives may feel like a war zone, God will be there to guide us through the worst of times and keep us in His loving care.

Father of Peace and Strength, make Yourself known to us in our times of distress. Show us the way to Your "strong tower," so that we may feel Your protection and love. Amen

January 6

IMMOVABLE GOD

He will not let your foot be moved; He who keeps you will not slumber. **Psalm 121:3**

I once heard a story about an old farmer who was driving into town with his wife in their timeworn pickup truck. The wife was in a particularly bad mood and was scolding her husband.

"I don't know why you can't be a little nicer around the house! You just seem so preoccupied with your own troubles. You never seem to notice mine!" She was practically crying now, huddled by the passenger side window. "And another thing: you used to put your arm around me when we were in the truck driving someplace, and you haven't done that in years!"

The old farmer regarded his wife for a moment, and then said, "Well, Bessie, I ain't moved."

There are times when we feel that God is far away, that He just can't be bothered about our own petty concerns. Satan loves to trick us into believing this. But the Bible tells us that God "ain't moved." It is we who have drifted away from Him or forgotten to listen for His voice when we are agitated or afraid. He longs to have us seek Him and He is always waiting for us to talk to Him, no matter how small or insignificant our concern might seem to us.

Almighty Father, give us confidence in knowing that You are always watching over us, every hour of every day. Let us trust You completely, knowing that You never sleep and You will not allow us to be moved from Your side. Amen

January 7

SNOW BIG DEAL

Have you entered the storehouses of the snow, or have you seen the storehouses of the hail, which I have reserved for the time of trouble, for the day of battle and war? Job 38:22-23

Before winter comes to our home state of Minnesota, the Department of Transportation and county and local agencies begin stockpiling sand, salt and chemicals to lay down on the roads and highways, in order to keep travelers safe and reduce the number of vehicle collisions. The news stations interview government officials who assure the citizens that there will be enough sand, salt and chemicals—and enough money in the budget—to get us through yet another winter. Depending on weather conditions, however, chemicals may be rendered ineffective if temperatures are too high or too low, sand and salt supplies may run out, and money may become an issue before the end of the season. In truth, we may not be prepared for weather surprises.

God asked Job if he really understands what it takes to run the world! God, not man, is in charge of "the storehouses laden with snow," and whether we need to drive someplace or not, He will decide if we get two inches or twelve, glare ice or powder. We try to be prudent in this life and be prepared; indeed, God wants us to practice discernment. But in spite of all the Dopplear radar and well-trained meteorologists, we will never know exactly what the weather will do. We must trust God to carry us safely through all of life's "storms."

Lord of Snow and Sun, keep us safe in whatever climate we reside. Help us have a healthy respect for nature, but also to trust You completely to see us through life's storms, including the white, fluffy ones. Amen

January 8

GOD HAS NOT LEFT THE BUILDING

Jesus answered him, "Very truly, I tell you, no one can see the kingdom of God without being born from above." John 3:3

Today is Elvis Presley's birthday. Many called him "the King of Rock and Roll," or just "the King." Most agree he was one of the most influential people in the history of modern music. Some followers refused to accept his untimely death at the age of forty-two. To this day, Presley's Graceland estate in Memphis, Tennessee, serves as a monument to this legendary figure. Adoring fans still mourn his death.

For the Christian, there is only one King. He is the Lord Jesus Christ. Scripture tells us that the coming of Christ was predicted by many Old Testament prophets (Isaiah 9:6). The wise men from the east followed a star to find His birthplace (Matthew 2:1-2). This baby King was born in a humble stable with a manger for a bed (Luke 2:16), but he grew up to be the Savior for all mankind (John 14:6). All who believe in Him will receive eternal life (Mark 10:30). Jesus, not a rock and roll singer, deserves our humble adoration and faithfulness. He will never leave us or forsake us. He will never die. Wherever you find yourself, Jesus has not left the building.

King of Kings, rule in our lives as only You can do. Humble us and call us to Your sacred work here on earth. Let us not be swayed by earthly "kings" and "superstars." They are empty idols. You are our one true God and Father. Amen

January 9

LISTEN UP!

The Lord God has given me the tongue of a teacher, that I may know how to sustain the weary with a word. Morning by morning he wakens— wakens my ear to listen as those who are taught. Isaiah 50:4

People have said they believe I have a natural ability to teach, although I'm not sure I feel that qualified. As a retired college counselor, I have limited experience teaching in a classroom, but I have always noticed that when I learn something new, my immediate desire is to share it with someone else. I think I got this from my father, who hungered for knowledge until the day he died. I also inherited his interest in history, in touring museums and visiting national monuments, and ferreting out information about subjects that interest me.

Because of my curiosity about life, I've had some wonderful experiences through the years. I have also had some very traumatic times during which I might not have been thinking, "This is cool! I need to share this with others!" But thanks be to God, I have also learned that the manner in which I got through these difficult times can be of interest to others. Lessons of hard-earned wisdom, along with encouragement, can go a long way to "sustain the weary with a word." God wants all of us to share what we know with others who are struggling—and the best thing we can share is our knowledge of the redeeming and merciful love of Christ.

Jehovah Raah, God the Shepherd, thank you for walking with me through my "valleys of death's shadow," and for bringing me into the light of Your marvelous love and grace. You have sustained me in my darkest hour, so I am compelled to help others in their earthly struggles. Amen

January 10

BOGO

To the exiles...who have been chosen and destined by God the Father and sanctified by the Spirit to be obedient to Jesus Christ and to be sprinkled with his blood: May grace and peace be yours in abundance.
I Peter 1:1-2

An interesting acronym in many grocery ads is BOGO, which means "Buy One, Get One." How enticing it is to see some of my favorite products appear in a deal like that! It's almost impossible to resist the urge to jump in my car and drive directly to that store to stock up on sixteen kinds of pasta or dozens of cans of tomato soup.

But there's another deal I am offered every day and I am pleased to accept: BOG2F. That is, "Buy One, Get Two Free," the amazing "deal" we get when we accept Jesus as our Lord and Savior. Not only do we get the Person of Jesus Christ as our friend, protector and guide, but He throws in his Dad, the Creator of the Universe, and the Holy Spirit, who helps us remember why we wanted all this in the first place.

All of this is included in the deal: "(God) destined us for adoption as His children through Jesus Christ, according to the good pleasure of His will" (Ephesians 1:5). "In (Christ) we have redemption through his blood, the forgiveness of our trespasses, according to the riches of His grace that He lavished on us" (Ephesians 1:7-8). Besides that, "(God) has made known to us the mystery of His will" (Ephesians1:9) through the Holy Spirit. Now that's what I call marketing!

Triune God, I am in awe that all three of You are in my life! I have three wonderful and distinct Companions Who love me desperately and guide me moment by moment as I walk this earthly path. Thank You for Your abundant grace and mercy. Amen

January 11

HUMAN NOISES

I call heaven and earth to witness against you today that I have set before you life and death, blessings and curses. Choose life so that you and your descendants may live. **Deuteronomy 30:19**

I dread taking my car into the dealership when I think something is wrong. I am the least mechanical person I know, and I am never able to give an accurate description of what I believe is going on. I say things like, "The engine goes 'boing boing,'" or, "There's a thumping noise somewhere on the back passenger side of the vehicle." I know I sound silly, and I am invariably met with strange looks from the service representatives. I am certain they are thinking "This woman is clueless and there is probably nothing wrong with her car at all." I want to be responsible about taking care of my vehicle, so I continue to have this conversation whenever I have a concern. Once in a while, something turns out to be very wrong and I'm glad I persisted. Most often, however, I have overreacted and my car is fine.

Imagine what God must think when we come to Him completely worked up over something over which He has complete control (which is everything). We lament that something is wrong in our lives, but often we are not sure what. Many times, whatever we think the problem is may be something we brought about by our own actions or inactions, or by not knowing the best course of action at a particular time. But God listens to our "noises," large and small, diagnoses our problem, and sends His Spirit to guide us in the right direction. He never regards us as though we are silly or foolish, and if we but ask, He is always ready to forgive us our shortcomings and help us start over once again. As it says in Deuteronomy 30:19, each day God tells us, "Choose life!"

Master Fixer, hear my human cries for help and come to my rescue! Relieve my anxieties about the cares of this life, and set me on a course that is in keeping with Your will and Your way. Amen

January 12

GET OUT OF JAIL FREE CARD

Peter followed (the angel) out of the prison, but he had no idea that what the angel was doing was really happening; he thought he was seeing a vision. Acts 12:9

It seems like an impossible story to believe: after Jesus death, resurrection, and ascension back to heaven, Peter gets himself thrown in a Roman jail for telling people about Christ. Peter was being guarded by "four squads of four soldiers each" (Acts 12:4), waiting out the Passover before he was to be tried by the evil King Herod. Here Peter was, bound in chains, sleeping between two soldiers, "when an angel of the Lord appeared in a bright light. "Quick!" the angel said, and Peter's chains just fell right off his hands. Then, the angel takes Peter out of the jail without anybody even noticing or trying to stop them. (Acts 12:6-7)

How can people say the Bible is boring? The Bible is pure magic, and more exciting that any Hollywood action film! And the best part is, these things really happened. And if we care to look, miracles are still happening every day. You may not have seen anything quite as dramatic as Peter's angel-assisted, death defying escape from King Herod, but our God continues to show us His majesty and power every day. From a spectacular sunset to the miracle of human and animal birth, we see the Divine all around us. People cross paths at just the right time, modern Good Samaritans help strangers, homeless shelters find funding to stay open one more year, and abused children find safe and loving foster homes. Let's remember Peter's "Get Out of Jail Free Card," and look for everyday miracles in our own lives.

Great God of Broken Chains, free us from our complacency and help us see Your sovereignty and grace each and every ordinary day. *Amen*

January 13

ONLY ONE?

One of (the ten lepers), when he saw that he was healed, came back, praising God in a loud voice. He threw himself at Jesus' feet and thanked Him—and he was a Samaritan. Luke 17:15-16

My husband and I spent some time on the island of Moloka'i, Hawaii, to tour the Kalaupapa Leprosy Settlement and National Historic Park. Leprosy, or Hansen's Disease, was discovered among the population of Hawaii in the 1860s, and at that time, there was no cure. The Hawaiian government exiled all adults and children found to have the disease, forcibly removing them from family, friends and society to the north side of the island of Molokai. Conditions were deplorable, and most of the "patients" died without the comfort of loving family or adequate medical care. The steepest, most foreboding cliffs in the world shelter the former two leper settlements of Kalaupapa and Kalawao, making it almost impossible for anyone to escape. Even today, the only access is by plane, boat or mule. The exile was enforced until a cure was discovered in the 1940s. A few former patients and their descendants still live in the area.

In Jesus time, there was no cure for leprosy either—except the healing power of Christ himself. In Luke 17, Jesus cures ten lepers, but only one returns to thank Him. How like them we all are, that when miracles occur in our daily lives, we just go about our business without considering the divine intervention we might have just received! Today, people with debilitating and incurable diseases may not be "healed," but these patients may know Christ's compassionate care through other people who take the time to show God's love to them. As Christians, we must take God's great commission seriously, show His love to those in need, and always, always be the one who comes back to give Him thanks and praise.

Healer of every illness, make me one who comes back to thank You when You move in my life or in the life of someone I know and care about. Banish my complacency in life and make me appreciative of the miracles You perform each and every day. Amen

January 14

DAILY BREAD IS SO…DAILY

Give us this day our daily bread. **Matthew 6:11**

I love food! I'm not sure I would call myself addicted to food, but I certainly love to eat, especially sweets. And the older I get, the harder it seems to watch what I eat. I read recently that the average American eats about a hundred and twenty-five pounds of sugar a year! That is like eating a whole person. If we lined up that many sugar cubes or cups of sugar, most of us would be repulsed. But in small amounts and over time, it is much easier to consume that much sugar.

I've often thought how people in Biblical times walked everywhere, ate sparse diets, and did more manual labor than most of us do today. In the prayer that He gave His disciples, Jesus prayed, "Give us today our daily bread." He didn't pray for eighty foot buffet tables laden with rich, fattening foods. He didn't pray for us to consume a whole week's worth of meals in one sitting. And He certainly didn't ask God to give each of us a hundred and twenty-five pounds of sugar each year!

Jesus knew the importance of taking care of our bodies, which are the temple of the Holy Spirit (1 Corinthians 6:19-20). He knew how destructive it is for us to eat too much. So He simply prayed for His Father to give each of us enough for one day at a time. Good advice to follow!

Jesus, Bread of Life, feed us just what we need: a daily supply of nutrients and a never-ending source of love, grace, and forgiveness. Amen

January 15

PRAYER PRIME: HE DELIVERS

When you ask, you do not receive, because you ask with wrong motives, that you may spend what you get on your pleasures.
James 4:3

When my grandson was about five years old, his mother got a new laptop on which she placed some orders through Amazon Prime, the service that delivers with one click on the keyboard. The little guy watched his mother carefully and followed the steps he had observed when she wasn't watching. A few days later, a brand new Kindle Fire electronic reader was delivered to the door. My daughter had not ordered the device, and quickly figured out what had happened. The child's innocence had gotten him into a tight spot and his mom was not pleased.

In today's world, it is so easy to "get stuff" that sometimes we don't even think about what we are doing. But James reminds us that, if we ask God for something, we need to ask with the right motives (i.e., in God's will). This can be difficult when we ask for something we cannot imagine God denying. Heal this child. Keep this soldier safe. Bless this marriage and make it work. Why wouldn't God want to say "yes" to each of those requests? It's hard to understand that God is in control, and that, even though our requests seem well-intentioned on our part, He knows the plans He has for each of us, and those plans are part of His grand design. We ought to pray instead, as Jesus did, "Thy will be done" (Matthew 6:10). God wants us to make our concerns known to Him, but the ultimate outcome is in His hands.

God of All Good Things, teach us to pray in total faith that Your will is far superior to ours. And help us trust You when our prayers are not answered the way we expect. Amen

January 16

REPENT, THEN TAKE A NAP

This is what the Sovereign Lord, the Holy One of Israel, says: "In repentance and rest is your salvation, in quietness and trust is your strength, but you would have none of it." **Isaiah 30:15**

When I was a child, Billy next door used to bully me. I was minding my own business one day, playing Sheba of the Jungle in the tree in our front yard. My parents were gone, and our nanny was inside the house, so I was not being closely supervised. Suddenly, Billy caught hold of my foot and started to pull me down from the tree. I wrestled loose, and broke off a small branch, threatening to throw it at Billy if he didn't stop bothering me. He persisted, and knowing that I could not hit the broad side of a barn with a shotgun, I threw the branch. Amazingly, it hit its mark and split Billy's forehead open like a melon.

Billy ran into his house, and moments later, he and his mom came rushing out and got into their car, presumably to take him to the emergency room. I climbed down from the tree and went through the most painful ten minutes of my childhood before going inside and 'fessing up to the nanny.
Repentance is painful! Many tears were shed. I was exhausted. Although all was eventually made right (apology from me to Billy, lecture from my father), I had a hard lesson in what guilt feels like. Then I took a nap.

God told the Israelites that repentance and rest go together, but so do quietness and strength. If we demonstrate more of the latter, we may not experience as much of the former. Bullying is tough on kids and is not overlooked today as it was when I was young—and this is good. But the mature Christian remembers that God keeps us "in perfect peace" if we keep our minds focused on Him (Isaiah 26:3).

God of Second (and Third and Fourth) Chances, be patient with us when we refuse to admit we have failed You. Thank You for opening Your arms wide to welcome us when we finally come to You for forgiveness. Amen

January 17

JUST DROPPING BY

Whenever you enter a house, first say, "May peace be on this house!" And if a peace-loving person is there, your peace will remain on him, but if not, it will return to you. **Luke 10:5-6**

I read an article about some of Europe's queens in medieval times. If the queen did not like one of her kingdom's noblemen or his wife, she would send word that she was coming to visit. The lord and lady would set about getting ready for the queen's visit, sometimes spending great amounts of money to make their household suitable for such a distinguished visitor. Once the queen arrived, she would remain in that house until the host and hostess were essentially bankrupt, and the she would return to her castle. This was an unkind but very effective method for rendering the lord and lady powerless.

After Jesus had trained the original twelve disciples, he sent out seventy-two more men to visit places where he planned to go next. The new disciples were given the instructions to take nothing with them and to greet no one on the road" (Luke 10:4). They were to stay in a home where peace was evident. These men were to heal diseases, cast out demons, and preach God's word, all in Jesus' name and with His power. Later, the King of kings would be visiting each of those same towns to bring them everlasting life and peace, forgiveness for their sins, and a new type of kingdom on earth, not based on material wealth but on God's abiding presence in their daily lives.

We as fellow Christians want to see the Good Word flourish, and hospitality is one way of doing that. Let's be good hosts and hostesses when God's workers come calling.

God of Good News, help us to spread Your love wherever we go. We may not perform the same kind of miracles that Your early followers did, but if each one reaches one, we can make a difference. Amen

January 18

FAR OFF? FAR OUT!

So he got up and went to his father. But while he was still a long way off, his father saw him and was filled with compassion for him; he ran to his son, threw his arms around him and kissed him. **Luke 15:20**

In the story of the Prodigal Son, Jesus told about a man who gave his two sons their inheritance while he was still living. One son dutifully stayed at home and worked with his father as a show of respect. But the other son left immediately, squandered his money until he was starving and homeless, and then decided to return to his father and beg his forgiveness. The son hoped only that his father would give him a servant's position, and certainly didn't expect to be reinstated as a son. After all he had done wrong.

This story, of course, is an analogy for believers slipping away from their faith and then repenting and returning to God. What always strikes me about the way things go in this tale is that the father (God) sees the son (wayward Christian) while he is "still a long way off." In the parable, the father is so excited, he runs to meet the son, throws his arms around him, bestows his own robe and ring on the boy and throws a huge party (much to the dismay of the "loyal" son, but that's another story). The picture I have here is that God sees us when we are at our lowest, maybe just deciding we have messed up, and maybe just thinking we'll see what God would do it we turned back to Him. Surprise! As long as God's children have been sinning (which is since Eve ate the apple), God is watching to see when our hearts turn. And He doesn't wait for us to come groveling (although sometimes maybe we should). God picks us up, gives us a big hug, says, "I forgive you, My child. Let's try again!"

Now that's far out!

God of Compassion, thank You for Your willingness to take us back into Your loving arms when we stray. Help me not to stray in the first place. Amen

January 19

I AM WHO I AM

God said to Moses, "I am who I am. This is what you are to say to the Israelites: 'I Am has sent Me to you.'" **Exodus 3:14**

Popeye was a popular cartoon character in the 1930s. Popeye was a rough and tumble sailor, who sang the theme song:

I'm Popeye the Sailor Man/I'm Popeye the Sailor Man,
I am who I am/And that's all that I am/I'm Popeye the Sailor Man!

Popeye was known to be strong, supposedly because he ate lots of spinach. He had a girlfriend named Olive Oil and an adversary named Brutus. Popeye may have been popular with kids of all ages in an earlier era, but today, he might be thought of as somewhat of a self-centered braggart! When he sang, "I am what I am, and that's all that I am," he was declaring to the world that people could take him or leave him, but he wasn't going to change to please anybody, even Olive Oil.

The Old Testament tells of another Who claimed, "I am Who I am." When Moses asked the Lord how he should explain to the Israelites about the conversations he and God were having, the exact words, "I am Who I am" were given to him. Jesus referred to himself using these same words in John 8:58. Popeye's creators may have made him appear to be strong and unchanging, but God already had that market cornered. God is omnipotent (all powerful), omniscient (all knowing), omnipresent (present in all places at all times), and "omni-loving" (my made-up word for "loving His children always, no matter what!). God probably likes spinach too (after all, He invented it!), but unlike Popeye, God doesn't need a vegetable to perform His mighty deeds.

Lord of all Creation, it humbles me to think, with all Your power and wisdom, You still take time to listen to my tiny prayers. Help me to remember always that You are with me wherever I go, twenty-four/seven. Amen

January 20

GOD'S REHAB LAB

Therefore, if anyone is in Christ, the new creation has come: The old has gone, the new is here! **2 Corinthians 5:17**

HGTV's Nicole Curtis is known as the "Rehab Addict." She restores historic houses to their original magnificent condition, with careful consideration to every bygone detail. On one episode, she was searching for dozens of identical light fixtures in an historic design to use throughout one mansion. Her attention to every tiny element of the house's design sets her apart from other "house flippers" who often cut corners and pay no attention to a structure's original "bones." The enthusiasm Curtis shows in preserving these wonderful historic homes makes me want to go out and buy an old relic and start rehabbing!

God doesn't cut corners when He creates a "new creature" in His faithful children. He tells us to take off our "old self with its practices," and "put on the new self, which is being renewed in the image of its Creator" (Colossians 3:9-10). He helps us clean up our lives and our attitudes, and he patiently waits while we are trying on our new selves. He works with us until we are comfortable with Him and with our own transformation. And He helps us see how our transformation has made us into His children, holy and blameless, saved and free. What a rehab job that is!

Great God, the Architect of my faith, I pray that you will continue to "rehab" me and change me into Your most glorious vision of what I can become. Help me to yield to you as you spiff up my life and my attitude. Amen

January 21

PAYING IT FORWARD

Praise be to the God and Father of our Lord Jesus Christ, the Father of compassion and the God of all comfort, who comforts us in all our troubles, so that we can comfort those in any trouble with the comfort we ourselves receive from God. **2 Corinthians 1:3-4**

In the year 2000, a movie was released called *Pay It Forward*, based on the novel of the same name by Catherine Ryan Hyde. Haley Joel Osment plays Trevor, a boy who has been given a school assignment to create a project that will change the world. Undaunted by the magnitude of the task, Trevor begins a chain of good deeds in his community. Instead of "paying it back" to the person who was kind to them, people are asked to "pay it forward": to do something worthwhile for another person. As the plot develops with many twists and turns, a whole community is transformed into caring and compassionate souls who form unlikely bonds with their neighbors and even their adversaries.

In 2 Corinthians 1:4, the Apostle Paul asks the people of Corinth to recognize the compassion and comfort God bestows on them, and then pass that comfort on—pay it forward—to others who are suffering. A powerful tenant of the Christian faith is that we *cannot* repay what Christ did for us when he went to the cross as the once-for-all sacrifice for our sins. Christ does not want us to pay Him back; He wants us to "pay it forward" by loving and forgiving our fellow human beings. What a movement Christ began with His powerful statement of love and grace! Let's keep the project going!

Jesus, we thank You for taking our place on the cross and dying for our sins. Enable us to see opportunities for us to carry Your work forward by showing love and compassion for a hurting world. Amen

January 22

THE LEAST OF THESE

"Then the righteous will answer him, 'Lord, when did we see You hungry and feed You, or thirsty and give You something to drink? When did we see You a stranger and invite You in, or needing clothes and clothe You? When did we see You sick or in prison and go to visit You?' The King will reply, 'Truly I tell you, whatever you did for one of the least of these brothers and sisters of Mine, you did for Me.'"
Matthew 25:37-39

I lead a Bible study and weight management program called First Place 4 Health at our church. The program is based on placing Christ first in our lives and enhancing spiritual growth in all four areas of our being: mental, physical, emotional and spiritual. I was skeptical at first. I had participated in several other weight loss programs, and I longed for something more meaningful than just eating sensibly, exercising and tracking my food intake. But the idea that Christ cared whether I was at my optimal weight and ate enough vegetables to feed a third world country? I wasn't buying it.

Then, I read the passage in Matthew 25, where Jesus tells His disciples that He had been hungry, thirsty, lonely and ill, and they (the disciples) had come to His aid. The disciples said they didn't remember doing these things. But Christ said, "Whatever you did for one of the least of these brothers and sisters of Mine, you did for Me." And then it hit me: I am "one of the least of these!" When I take good care of my body—God's "temple"—I am taking care of Christ Himself! It's not a matter of vanity. When I eat right, stay active and focus on God's holy word, I grow closer to becoming the person He wants me to be. I serve God and my fellow human beings more effectively when I am operating at optimal level. Now that's a diet I can live with!

God of the hungry and poor of spirit, stir in me the desire to live only for You, and to serve only You. Grant that I may keep that focus until the day You call me home, so that You will one day say, "Well done, good and faithful servant." (Matthew 25:21). Amen

January 23

GOD WITHOUT BORDERS

And this gospel of the kingdom will be preached in the whole world as a testimony to all nations. Matthew 24:14

Doctors Without Borders (Médecins Sans Frontières) is a French-founded (now international) non-governmental organization known for its humanitarian projects in war-torn regions and developing countries facing health crises. "Humanitarian action is more than simple generosity," said James Orbinski, the organization's president at the time it won the Nobel Peace Prize in 1999. "It claims to build spaces of normalcy in the space of what is abnormal."

We ask, "What is normal?" In God's view, "normal" is what He intended humankind to be: first and foremost, His beloved children who live each day with the intention of following God's ways with integrity and in good faith. The prophet Micah summed it up perfectly: He has shown you, O mortal, what is good. And what does the Lord require of you? To act justly and to love mercy and to walk humbly with your God (Micah 6:8). Of course, we are human, and we are unable to do all of this on our own. We need God's help, which is why He sent His only Son Jesus Christ to die on a cross for our sins. In sending Jesus, God's plan was to "build spaces of normalcy in the space of what was abnormal," namely, a fallen world. Believing in His Son frees us from all the messiness of this world and daily gives us another chance, if we confess our sins and ask for forgiveness. We can be "normal" no matter how dysfunctional our lives may be, if we simply look to Jesus.

God of the Normal and Dysfunctional, Disenfranchised and Marginalized and all the other creatures on this planet, be patient with us as we navigate our way through this strained and broken world. Grant us strength and perseverance for the journey and aid us in doing the next right thing. Amen

January 24

I'M GRATEFUL!

Therefore let us be grateful for receiving a kingdom that cannot be shaken, and thus let us offer to God acceptable worship, with reverence and awe. **Hebrews 12:8**

The pastor who married my husband and me had an unexpected daily greeting. When people asked him how he was, he would respond, "I'm grateful!" Most people thought he was saying, "I'm great." That is a standard greeting in our society. They were caught off guard and often asked the pastor to repeat himself. That was exactly what the pastor wanted. He could then relate what he was especially thankful for that day. My husband picked up this pastor's unique response and has had many interesting conversations with people he meets.

In contrast, I once had a co-worker who had experienced much tragedy in his life. His response, when asked how he was doing, was to say under his breath, "Doesn't matter," and then he would hurry away. One day, I caught him by the arm and gently said, "It matters to me." The look on his face was priceless, and this brief exchange fostered a caring friendship between us until I moved away. I often think of the man and hope his attitude about life has improved.

God wants us to share our blessings with others, not just the big events in our lives like the birth of a child or a new job. He wants us to show our gratitude for the tasty hamburger we ate for lunch and the surprise email we got from an old friend. Sharing our gratitude with others is catching; soon others are telling us about the blessings in their lives too. Next time somebody asks you how you are doing, say, "I'm grateful!" It might surprise you where that answer will lead.

Holy Father, You shower us with untold blessings every day. Help us to be conscious of them and also tell others about them. Cause us to begin a contagious conversation about Your goodness. Amen

January 25

WASHABLE MARKERS

Then the Lord said to Moses, "Come up to Me on the mountain and be there; and I will give you tablets of stone, and the law and commandments which I have written, that you may teach them." **Exodus 24:12**

Parents of young children around the world will agree that one of the best inventions in recent years has been washable markers. Kids love to draw and color, and when they are very small, they don't distinguish between what is an acceptable place to create their works (their own paper, tablets and coloring books) and what is not (walls, furniture, household pets and their own clothing and faces). Parents now have the choice of purchasing art supplies that can be washed away. Their biggest task nowadays is to keep the adult (indelible) writing instruments locked up and allow their children to use only the kind that can be removed.

Sometimes people think God's commandments are written in washable markers. We choose which commandments we want to follow and erase the others (in our minds, at least). Most of us don't murder or steal, but if we really examined the other eight commandments, we find that we do sometimes break them, or at least function "outside the lines" of what God originally set forth as undisputable law. We salivate when we see someone else's new car (Commandment 10); we slip and use the Lord's name in vane (Commandment 4); we allow ourselves to be overly focused on money, status, power, *insert-idol-here* (Commandment 5). God doesn't want us to wash away any part of His commandments. That's why they are written in stone!

Almighty, All-Powerful God, touch up those laws You wrote so long ago and fill our hearts and minds with them. Cause us to think before we break—or try to erase—them. Amen

January 26

I BELIEVE! HELP!

When the spirit saw Jesus, it immediately threw the boy into a convulsion. He fell to the ground and rolled around, foaming at the mouth. Jesus asked the boy's father, "How long has he been like this?" "From childhood," he answered. "... if you can do anything, take pity on us and help us." "'If you can'?" said Jesus. "Everything is possible for one who believes." Immediately the boy's father exclaimed, "I do believe; help me overcome my unbelief!" **Mark 9:20-24**

When one of my daughters was in high school, she developed an eating disorder. Back then, I was not familiar with the signs and symptoms of this potentially deadly condition. Though I had been trained as a counselor, I did not recognize what was happening until my daughter was well into the patterns of both anorexia and bulimia. I knew this wasn't "demon possession;" my daughter needed support and counseling. Her first inpatient treatment failed, and I was desperate to find some help. She was away at college, and I did not know how bad things were getting.

As I walked near our home one day, I prayed heartily for answers from God to help my girl. Though I was not familiar with the passage, Mark 9:24 came to me as a clear message: "I do believe; help me overcome my unbelief!" Later, when I looked it up, I was amazed that the passage was about a parent asking Jesus to heal his child. I gained renewed strength to search for a different program for my daughter. She received the counseling she needed from some very skilled mental health professionals and was able to deal effectively with the disorder. She is now happily married with four beautiful children.

Gentle Healer, come to the aid of those with eating disorders and other mental health challenges. These people are Your children and need Your healing touch for distresses most of us cannot understand or fathom. You know, Lord, what they need. Amen

January 27

SEE THE WORDS

Our message of the gospel came to you not in word only, but also in power and in the Holy Spirit and with full conviction.
1 Thessalonians 1:5

When I became a Christian, I was overwhelmed. Suddenly, I had a completely new purpose in life, and I felt as if the entire world was waiting for me to spread the Good News I had just learned. A believing friend Martin Luther called this, "swallowing the Holy Spirit, feathers and all." It's been said that new Christians should be locked up for six months until they "learned the program."

Now that I've been following Christ for several decades, I look back on what I must have been like in the beginning. I wouldn't exactly say that I was an "in your face" Christian, but I certainly did utilize every opportunity to let people know about Jesus! I wanted everyone to share in this unspeakable peace and joy that I had found. I still feel that way today. But I have learned over the years that sometimes people need to see Jesus in action in my life rather than listen to me explain about Him. Edgar Guest put it so well in one of his songs: "I'd rather see a sermon than hear one any day." Sometimes, it's the little things we say and do that make the most difference in other people's lives. And most of the time, we will never know how our words and action affect those around us. We plant the seed, God causes the growth.

God of All Growth, let me be the seed planter for You in this troubled world. Let my words be Your words, and let them fall on fertile soil so that You may grow them into something wonderful. Amen

January 28

GOD DOESN'T MAKE RAT RODS

So God created mankind in His own image, in the image of God He created them; male and female He created them. **Genesis 1:27**

According to Wikipedia, Rat Rods are a style of hot rod or custom automobile built to imitate or exaggerate "traditional" hot rods, or period-correct restorations of original hot rods built in the 1940s, '50s and '60s. Some people think Rat Rods are built of junk parts. Pat Ganahl, a rat rod enthusiast and writer, is quoted in the Wikipedia article: "What I personally call Rat Rods, (is) a positive term... They're artistic, fun, and sensational reinterpretations of late-'40s/early-'50s hot rodding as a culture that includes music, clothing, hairstyles, and tattoos. The cars are low, loud, chopped...with giant rear tires, lots of carburetors, open pipes, and tall gearshifts." Rat Rods are easy to recognize because they are so outlandish in appearance and noise. If you've seen one, you know this!

Although God did give "rat rodders" the talent to create these crazy vehicles, He stands firm in how people are created: in His image. The Bible doesn't say God created us to be "sensational reinterpretations" of Himself, and certainly we are not built of "junk parts!" First Corinthians 6:19 says that our bodies are "temples of the Holy Spirit," Who lives in those who believe in Jesus Christ. Some of us may be "low and loud," and our clothing and hairstyles vary, but we are all God's children, created to love and worship Him.

Next time you see—and hear—a Rat Rod, thank God by making a joyful noise to the Lord!

God of the Rat Rodders, cause me to know that I am created in Your image and my purpose is to do Your will, whether it be "traditional" or "on the edge." Amen

January 29

WOULD GOD EAT LUTEFISK?

Then a voice told him, "Get up, Peter. Kill and eat." "Surely not, Lord!" Peter replied. "I have never eaten anything impure or unclean." Acts 10:13-14

In the Midwestern part of the United States, particularly my home state of Minnesota and neighboring Wisconsin, a strange phenomenon occurs at least annually. Lutefisk dinners are held—and widely attended—in Lutheran church basements and Scandinavian cultural centers. "Lutefisk—codfish (fisk) preserved in lye (lut)—is both a delicacy and a tradition among Scandinavian-Americans," reports Smithsonian.com, "who serve the chemical-soaked, gelatinous fish with a warm and friendly smile. Lutefisk, or lutfisk in Swedish, is a traditional dish in Norway, Sweden, and parts of Finland."

I have never eaten—nor do I intend to try—lutefisk. I cannot even stand the smell of it! But many a bitter-cold night in our area, people line up outside for hours at fire halls and service clubs waiting to get in to eat the stuff. Now, I know God created everything in this world, and He told Peter that all food is suitable for consumption, not just foods allowable for the ancient Jews (Acts 11:9 "Do not call anything impure that God has made clean."). But when I get to heaven, one of the questions I'm going to ask Him is, "Why lutefisk?" Don't get me wrong: I love food, and I'm the first to line up for a good old-fashioned church supper. But when it comes to this particular dish, I cannot go there. I'm not in the line for lutefisk; I'm in the line that sells the tee shirts that say, "Lutefisk: Just Say No!"

God of Tasty Morsels, thank You that You gave each of us varying tastes in this life. You allow us to be unique, even though we are all created in Your image. Help us celebrate one another's differences. Amen

January 30

REBORN OR WELL-WORN?

Jesus replied, "Very truly I tell you, no one can see the kingdom of God unless they are born again." John 3:3

I consider myself to be "reborn:" I was not a believer, and now I am. When I became a "new creation" in Christ, I began to wonder what the difference was between people who were raised in the church and had always known Christ, and people like me who floated around in a daze until the day I laid down my life for Him. A Christian friend had a wonderful explanation.

"If a horse, or foal, is born on a ranch," she said, "and raised by a caring person, the horse learns to trust her owner in 'baby steps.' First, the owner feeds and waters the foal, then puts a halter on her. Soon, a blanket follows, along with a saddle and bridle. When the horse is old enough, the owner gets on her back and teaches her to carry his weight and obey his commands. The horse doesn't know exactly when she gave her will to her master, but she definitely has decided to trust him with her very being.

"A wild horse who wanders into that same owner's corral one day would have a totally different experience. When the owner 'breaks' the wild horse, different techniques are used—great patience, 'listening' to what the horse is telling you, understanding what this horse is thinking (perhaps she fears you want to eat her for dinner!), gaining her trust. But it is very clear to both human and horse exactly when the will of the horse became that of the master."

My love for horses made this example especially meaningful. I understood that being "born again" in Christ could happen in degrees while being raised in a Christian home. And I could surely relate to the concept that I needed to be "broken" before I was suitable to be one of the King's kids!

Master of All Creatures, thank You for Your precious gift of unending grace and abiding love. I am so glad I wandered into Your corral! Amen

January 31

WHAT WOULD ELLIE DO?

Jesus replied: "'Love the Lord your God with all your heart and with all your soul and with all your mind.' This is the first and greatest commandment. And the second is like it: 'Love your neighbor as yourself.' All the Law and the Prophets hang on these two commandments." Matthew 22:37-40

My mother-in-law, Ellie Corrigan, was an exceptional person. She died at age 80 of an unexpected, avoidable illness, and the entire family was devastated. Those first, raw days after she was gone, we needed some comic relief. We missed being able to ask for her advice about practically everything. We joked about having bracelets made that said, "WWED?" What Would Ellie Do? Our joke brought tears of joy in remembering all the times she had dispensed wise and comforting words to each of us. Six hundred people attended her wake. The officiating pastor said, "Ellie prayed for each and every person gathered here tonight."

The text of Matthew 22:37-40 were words that Ellie Corrigan lived by. She showed her love for the Lord in many ways, like taking and giving communion, attending her church and helping with various events there, and visiting the sanctuary almost daily to pray for others. There was never a day that went by that Ellie did not demonstrate God's love to family, friend, neighbor or stranger. Her kind words and gentle spirit were a blessing to all who knew her. We miss her greatly, but we know she is one of those "great cloud of witnesses" (Hebrews 12:1) who surround us daily with unseen love.

God of Wisdom and Care, help us never to forget the wonderful people who have touched our earthly lives in special ways as Ellie did. Thank You for putting people like them in our lives, and thank You for taking good care of our departed loved ones until we see them again. Amen

February

February 1

ANAM CARA

The soul of Jonathan was knit to the soul of David, and Jonathan loved him as his own soul. **1 Samuel 18:1**

In Celtic spiritual tradition, an *anam cara* is a connecting and bonding of two souls, creating an open and trusting friendship. A brief definition of *anam cara* is "soul friend." Catholic priest and Irish poet John O'Donahue describes anam cara this way: "You are joined in an ancient and eternal union with humanity that cuts across all barriers of time, convention, philosophy and definition. When you are blessed with an *anam cara*, the Irish believe, you have arrived at that most sacred place: home."

In the Bible, David and Jonathon had an *anam cara* relationship. Although Jonathan's father, Saul, hated David and sought to kill him, Jonathan supported David and helped him hide from Saul. When Jonathan was killed in battle, David grieved deeply and wrote the moving "Song of the Bow" (2 Samuel 1:18-27), which is still a revered passage in the Jewish tradition today.

I recently gave a bracelet inscribed with the words *Anam Cara* to my closest girlfriend, Barb. I am blessed to have had her as my friend for many years; she knows just about everything there is to know about me and loves me anyway! Together, we share a bond that must be nurtured by God, because we can clearly see His divine involvement whenever we get together. I thank God daily for my friendship with Barb. She has helped me grow as a Christian and has always been there when I need a shoulder to cry on or a foot to kick me in the rear.

Do you have an *anam cara* friend? Tell that person today how much she or he means to you, and thank God for him or her in your life!

God of Anam Cara Friendships, help us see our "soul friends" in this life and honor them in special ways. Bless them this day and every day for helping us walk closely with You. Amen

February 2

IMAGINE THAT!

The word of the LORD came to me: "Son of man, prophesy against the prophets of Israel who are now prophesying. Say to those who prophesy out of their own imagination: 'Hear the word of the LORD!'" Ezekiel 13:1-2

Have you ever tried to share your faith with an "all-inclusive believer?" You know, the people who seem to pick and choose what they believe, mixing many religions and philosophies into a big pot of soup that makes it unclear exactly what principles might be at the center of their "faith." Christians are called to love and action, to show our concern for others in advance of any expounding of our own beliefs. Jesus modeled this when he fed the five thousand and cured the diseases of many, often *before* He did any preaching. And perhaps our job sometimes is just to listen to others tell us what they believe and then share what we believe, leaving the "heavy lifting" to the Holy Spirit.

The most difficult part for me, when encountering the "all-inclusive believer," is when I have to walk away and let the situation be. I know other folks who might stick with it, determined to "evangelize" the other person into belief in Christ. I am not one of those folks. But I do believe that we can sincerely plant the seed, let the Holy Spirit do the watering, and perhaps a change will take place. In Romans 14:11, we read, *It is written: "As surely as I live," says the Lord, "every knee will bow before me; every tongue will acknowledge God."* Until that day, it's our job to keep praying and loving our fellow men and women, no matter what they believe.

Great God of All Mankind, we await the day when every knee will bow before you and every tongue confess that You are Lord. Stir us to prayer and not judgment when we believe differently than others. Amen

February 3

COLOR ME BLOWN AWAY!

And the one who sat there had the appearance of jasper and ruby. A rainbow that shone like an emerald encircled the throne. **Revelation 4:3**

I love color! When I was an art major in undergraduate school, I was amazed, and still am, at the names of colors in the products in an art supply store. Cerulean blue…puce…periwinkle… The people who name nail polish and paint shades have endless imagination. Basic white latex becomes "Moonlit Ivory." Women wear shocking pink polish named "Oh, Baby!"

Recently in our Bibles study, we were talking about what to expect heaven to be like. One person said we will spend all of our time praising God. Others said we will have wings to fly around, and we'll be singing constantly. I said I expect to forget all about the questions I thought I might ask God when I finally get to see Him, because I'll be so amazed that I won't even care why I could never get my closets cleaned out, or what He was thinking when He invented the mosquito.

One woman in our group sat pensively for a few minutes and finally said, "There could be colors we've never seen before." That really made me think. Has God created more colors than what the human eye can see? Does He design the back side of a rainbow with another whole spectrum of shades we've never known? Is the underside of an ocean wave a different kind of gray/blue than we could ever imagine? And in the darkest forest on this planet, are there shadows of green we cannot detect, even with a human-invented infrared camera?

God created all things in this world and outside of this world. How can we doubt that He may have plenty of surprises for us when we arrive at His heavenly home?

Creator God, thank You for all the beauty in this world. It is impossible to imagine what a feast for the eyes awaits us in heaven, if our is only the appetizer. Amen

February 4

NEVER GIVE UP!

***Forgetting what is behind and straining toward what is ahead, I press on toward the goal to win the prize for which God has called me heavenward in Christ Jesus.* Philippians 3:13-14**

At a Minnesota Bass Nation banquet, my husband and I heard professional angler, Mike Iaconelli. This young man hails from New Jersey and learned to fish from his uncle. He started a competitive bass club, eventually leading him to win the Bass Nation competition, the Bass Master Classic, and B.A.S.S. Angler of the Year. Since then, Iaconelli has gained much media attention.

Iaconelli told a story about winning the Bass Master Classic with the last fish of the last cast of the day. The camera man in his boat kept telling this highly energetic and emotional fisherman that they needed to head back to the weigh-in immediately if they were to make it in time for Iaconelli not qualify. Not having had a particularly good day, Iaconelli made one more cast and brought in a huge bass, which not only won him the tournament, but was also the biggest fish of the tournament. After that day, Iaconelli developed a motto: "Never Give Up," which he now has posted in several places in his boat and everywhere else including his website.

The apostle Paul wrote many passages in his letters using sports analogies. Great athletes from football to fishing must have perseverance to keep on trying to get better and better at their sport. Whether we are into physical sports or not, Paul's reference to what it takes for athletic excellence is good for us to hear. The biggest supporter in the stands of our lives is the great High Priest Who intercedes for us when the going gets tough. His advice to believers for generations has always been, "Never give up!"

Encouraging God, cheer us on when we are discouraged and give us strength when we are spent. When following You is our goal, we know we are never without a coach or a team mate in this race called life. Amen

February 5

WHICH WAY?

Jesus answered, "I am the way and the truth and the life. No one comes to the Father except through me." John 14:6

Last month while we visited the Hawaiian island of Maui, we drove to the top of Haleakala Mountain to view the spectacular sunrise. The temperature was 40 degrees, and the winds were blowing forty miles per hour, which made it feel like 25 degrees. Because it was crowded outside and very cold, we decided to wait inside the visitor center. I watched a father try to explain a three-dimensional topographical map to his son of about four years old.

"We are here," the father said, pointing to the red X on the map. "And this is east, west, north and south." The boy looked puzzled, apparently not fully able to "see" the map in relation to where he was actually standing. But he was concentrating very hard, wanting to please his daddy. Finally, the father asked, "Now, which way do you think the sun will come up?"

The little guy hesitated for a moment, and then said, "All the way up?"

Jesus came all the way *down* for you and me. Even though we as human beings have continued to sin since Eve shared her apple treat with Adam, Jesus came down to us in order that He might die on a cross to take our sins away. Sometimes we are just like the little boy with the topographical map: we don't "see" where we are in relation to where God wants us to be. But if we believe that He loved us enough to die for us, and if we trust Him to lead us, we can say each day, "I am here, and You are here with me, Lord, and we will walk this road together."

Lord, go before me and lead me in righteous paths according to Your will. Let me not become discouraged if I don't understand Your map, but grant that I may trust You to guide me where You want me to go. Amen

February 6

THE ELEVENTH COMMANDMENT

For I am not ashamed of the gospel, because it is the power of God that brings salvation to everyone who believes: first to the Jew, then to the Gentile. **Romans 1:16**

Have you heard of the 11th Commandment: Thou Shalt Not Should? People are always saying, "I should do this," or "I shouldn't have done that." We get all hung up on what we don't do right, causing a lot of shame and guilt.

What's the difference between *shame* and *guilt?* Guilt is about what we do, knowingly or unknowingly, that has the cause or effect of hurting someone else. Forgetting a birthday or an anniversary. Gossiping about a person. Losing our temper. If we take responsibility, apologies hopefully are accepted; everyone feels better.

Shame is something we allow to happen to us, perhaps the result of how we were brought up, or feelings of perceived personal failure. Our families of origin may have certain "rules" or "customs which, if not adhered to, may be viewed as dishonorable or improper. When we aren't conforming to these learned ways of doing things, we may feel ashamed, which in turn may limit us in how we are able to interact with others.

But Jesus took our guilt and our shame to the cross with Him, and we can be free from our guilt and shame if we confess our shortcomings to God and ask for His forgiveness. As Christians, we can eliminate the 11th Commandment—thou shalt not should—from our vocabulary. We still need to be responsible for our actions and seek to make amends with those we harm in some way—that's part of walking daily in God's path. But thanks be to our gracious God that He throws all of our transgressions into the deep, deep sea. And *no fishing*!

God of Grace and Forgiveness, thank You that we no longer need to say, "I should have." Help us do the right thing when we miss the mark, and then to move on in Your loving care. Amen

February 7

THE POWER OF PRAYER

Therefore confess your sins to each other and pray for each other so that you may be healed. The prayer of a righteous person is powerful and effective. **James 5:16**

Have you ever wondered why God seems to ignore your most fervent prayers when it's so obvious to you that He should answer them immediately, just the way you requested? There is no time in life when we feel more powerless as when we feel God has left us empty handed.

The Bible says "the prayer of a righteous person is powerful and effective." Author Annie Dillard wrote: "Does anyone have the foggiest idea what sort of power we so blithely invoke?....We as the church are children playing on the floor with chemistry sets, mixing up a batch of TNT to kill a Sunday morning....We should all be wearing crash helmets...life preservers...signal flares...lash us to our pews."

Count how many electrical outlets in your home are not being used. You *believe* that each of those outlets has the capability of producing more energy, but you don't think you *need* to plug that many things into the wall. You might even blow a circuit if you tried, depending on what you plugged in. But God will never blow a circuit! And if we truly believe that God is in charge and doing a pretty good job of running the universe, we can continue to pray *that His will be done* until the day we finally see Him face to face.

Let's not let earthly circumstances hinder our desire to talk to God. He knows our limitations, but He also wants us to keep on telling Him what's on our minds. And we can also cling to the promise in Romans 8:28 that "all things God work for the good of those who love him, who have been called according to his purpose."

Father of Light and light sockets, stir me to continue in fervent prayer to You that I may know You are indeed listening and working things out for Your good and the good of all humankind. Amen

February 8

PUT THE FUN BACK IN DYSFUNCTION

Trust in the Lord with all your heart and lean not on your own understanding. **Proverbs 3:5**

Many of us live in less than ideal situations. The people in our lives may not always say or do the things we would like them to do. Whether it is a rebellious teenager, an alcoholic spouse, a power-hungry boss, or a meddling mother-in-law, we sometimes have to deal with difficult people. It's easy to think we can control that difficult person by what we say and do.

Trying to control or even predict the outcome of someone else's behavior is not a particularly good use of my time. It wastes my energy, frustrates me, and probably raises my blood pressure. While I don't always take my own advice, I am learning to allow other people in my life to make their own mistakes and to be responsible for their actions and behavior (to whatever degree they choose or are able). This may not seem to solve the problem at the time, but the peace of mind I have later far outweighs the frustration of running headlong into someone else's nightmare.

The most obvious way to stay out of other people's business is to trust God. Our faith is based on the confidence that God is in control, not us. When we accept the premise that God loves the difficult person as much as He loves any of us, we are better able to step back and allow Him to do the heavy lifting. And sometimes, a difficult person needs to find her own way back to God and a more agreeable life. In the words of St. Francis of Sales, "God does not deprive us of His love; we deprive Him of our cooperation. God would never reject (us) if (we) had not first rejected His love." It's important to keep on loving the people who drive us crazy, and to "work out (our own) salvation with fear and trembling" (Philippians 2:12).

God of the Best and the Worst of Us, we pray for patience and compassion for difficult people because their actions tell a deeper story. Cause us to love them in a special way, with an open heart and a smile that they may see You shining through us. Amen

February 9

IN PIECES, LET US PRAY TO THE LORD

Jesus said to the woman, "Your faith has saved you; go in peace." Luke 7:50

I once vowed that I could die happy when I had my closets cleaned out. My husband would concur that I am one of the most disorganized people in the world. I save everything, "just in case." I scour thrift stores for that one perfect treasure, but bring home many imperfect things as well. My "in box" in our home office overflows until it spills onto the floor. Archaeologists would find many buried treasures in my basement.

Now that I am retired, I am trying to mend my ways. I truly believe there is an organized person inside of me screaming to get out, one who wants to alphabetize her magazines on the coffee table (or throw them out as soon as she has read them). And I am enlisting God's help to do this. "What's that," you say, "you're asking *God* to help you get organized?" Who better than Him, Who created a perfectly ordered universe that continues to operate pretty well even while humankind is trying to destroy it?

What I'm really asking God to do is to make my "pieces" into "peace." It's a no-brainer that I don't *need* all the "stuff." But what is more important is that I stress out about the "stuff" instead of concentrating on God. Jesus says we are either "all in" or we're not, we either listen to God's voice or we don't (1 John 4:6). Collecting earthly things to the point where it worries us is idolatry, and like they say, you can't take it with you. I think God wrote the mantra, "Reduce, reuse, recycle," and I'm trying to do my part. The less "stuff" that clutters my life, the more room there is for Jesus.

Great God of the Ordered Universe, please take away my desire to be surrounded by material things. Grant that I may find Your peace amid the clutter and let go of all but Your saving grace. Amen

February 10

BREATHE

And with that he breathed on them and said, "Receive the Holy Spirit." John 20:22

I once read that we should try to stay close enough to Jesus to hear Him breathing. The image of that comforts me, causes me to think about a living Jesus Christ Who is truly present in our lives every day. When I think about hearing Christ's act of breathing, it brings me to a sacred place, a place where He and I can have an intimate conversation with no interruptions, even though (and this is the miraculous part) He may be having the same type of talk with many other people in this world at the same time, maybe even while He's moving mountains and healing the sick and calming people who were freaked out a moment ago. Jesus, the Divine Multitasker!

And then I think about how I try to multitask myself, and probably do a poor job of getting anything done well because my mind is like a computer with seventy-five tabs open at the same time all day long! That's exactly why we need quiet time. We can't hear Jesus breathing if our minds are scattered a thousand other places. We can't be in tune with the beating of His heart unless we take time apart from our daily activities to find sanctuary in His presence. And Jesus knows this too. He longs for us to intentionally set aside a place and time when we are focused on Him wholly, shutting out everything else except what we bring before Him.

Spend some time quietly before God today and see what happens. God longs for each of us to do this, and to make it a daily habit.

All-Present God, stir us to find the time and the place to meet You personally each day. Rescue us from the frenzy that seems to overshadow Your presence, and teach us to make fellowship with You our anchor in a stormy sea. Amen

February 11

DUCK AND COVER

For you have been my refuge, a strong tower against the foe. Psalm 61:3

I grew up during the Cold War, the period of time of political and military tension between Western and Eastern nations following World War II. In those days, school kids watched a movie called "Duck and Cover," which showed smiling teachers assisting children in crouching below their little wooden desks with their hands over their heads, as if this action would have done anything at all to protect them from the nuclear war that everyone feared in those days.

Today's schools and colleges all have to have "safety plans." Whether the threat is fire or weather or the greatly feared school shooters prowling about, campuses everywhere are mandated to have a strategy for keeping their students safe. We live in a world where natural disasters and man-made tragedies are a reality. But those who put their trust in Jesus Christ know that He sustains us in good times and bad. Like the bumper sticker says, "KNOW GOD KNOW PEACE; NO GOD NO PEACE.

Creator of All Living Things, protect our children from harm, and sharpen our memory of the wonderful blessings we have, including those very children. Grant us peace in a broken world, and let us be ever thankful for all You do for us. Amen

February 12

TENDERLY CRADLED IN FREE FALL

Whoever dwells in the shelter of the Most High will rest in the shadow of the Almighty. **Psalm 91:1**

Kayla Mueller, 26, the Arizona aid worker held captive by the terrorist group ISIS was confirmed dead on February 10, 2015 by her family. In August 2013, Kayla was returning from a Spanish Doctors Without Borders facility at Allepo, Syria, when she was reportedly captured. Following the brutal murder of Jordanian hostage, airstrikes targeting ISIS activities were increased, apparently resulting in Kayla's death.

In her short life, Kayla did more for humanitarian efforts in the United States and abroad than would have been thought humanly possible. Her work was possible through God's power, not her own. In a 2014 letter to her parents, this selfless girl wrote, "I remember Mom always telling me that all in all in the end the only one you really have is God. I have come to a place in experience where, in every sense of the word, I have surrendered myself to our creator (because) literally there was no else … (and) by God (and) by your prayers I have felt tenderly cradled in freefall."

Kayla was the embodiment of the selfless use of her God-given gifts in the service of others (1 Peter 4:10, Ephesians 2:10). Kayla knew how broken this world was, but she wasn't afraid to go where God sent her. As for Kayla's captors, John 5:29 says, *Those who have done what is good will rise to live, and those who have done what is evil will rise to be condemned.* The world poises to react in some way to ISIS, but God will have the final word.

God of Peace, renew in us a sense of hope when we hear what evil still stalks the earth. Grant our world leaders wisdom in dealing with this ever-present threat of terrorism, and watch over all who join this battle. Hold Kayla's family in Your loving arms and help them to know You are doing the same for their precious child. Amen

February 13

PRAYERS THAT WORK

Confess your trespasses to one another, and pray for one another, that you may be healed. The effective, fervent prayer of a righteous man avails much. **James 5:16 (NKJ)**

Have you ever experienced a time when you could say you have "travailed in prayer." To "travail" means to toil, or labor hard at a task. Synonyms are agony, anguish and torment. As we pray through those situations that seem hopeless from a human perspective, we may literally *beg* God to make a change for ourselves or another. And not having hope that things will change can literally make us sick at heart (Proverbs 13:12).

I have a little book called *Prayers That Avail Much*, published in 1980 by Word Ministries, Inc. The word "avail" in the title, is the opposite of "travail." "Avail" means to produce or result in a benefit or advantage. Prayers that "avail much" get results. The premise of this book is that we must "allow the Holy Spirit to make the Word a reality in our hearts." If we are not steeped in God's Holy Scriptures, we really do not know how to pray; we may be sincere in our requests, but unless we are in tune with God's will, we may find ourselves continuing to agonize in prayer.

James reminds us in today's Scripture that, in order for our prayers to be effective, to "avail," we must also strive to be righteous. So many conditions! But wait! Christ took care of all this for us! Romans 5:19 says that through our faith in Christ, we are made righteous. Just like that. Next time you are "travailing" in prayer, remember that Christ is the intermediary between us and God. We truly have this Great High Priest interceding for us whenever we turn to Him for help. And Jesus not only "avails;" He rules!

Blessed Jesus, stir me up in prayer and teach me to petition fervently, while knowing that You are beside me, interceding, always leading. Amen

February 14

LOVE

Whoever does not love does not know God, because God is love. 1 John 4:8

Our church used to dedicate a Sunday morning to addiction recovery. As a special musical offering, I sang a song entitled "Hold On" by Nicole Nordeman. The lyrics depict people who are at the end of their rope, whether from addiction, depression, illness, poor choices, or other devastating occurrences. The chorus says, "Love will find you." Nordeman uses "Love" interchangeably with "God," at one point saying, "To hang between two thieves in the darkness/Love must believe you are worth it."

I was asked by church staff to change the lyrics of the song to say "God" instead of "Love." It was felt people would not understand the words were meant to be interchangeable. I complied…except on the last stanza. I believed it was important to sing at least part of the song as written, to honor the songwriter and to demonstrate that God is indeed Love.

While my actions might have been a bit rebellious, I still believe the lyrics are most impactful as written. Anyone who has ever stood on the edge of the cliff, literally or figuratively, and wondered if there would be a tomorrow—if there would be any shred of hope that life could go on—but found the strength to try one more day—those people know what it means to trust God. Those who have been to hell and back because of their own choices or the cruel choices of another can tell you that Hope lives in one outreached hand, two smiling eyes, and three words, God Is Love.

This Valentine's Day, instead of the candy hearts and paper greeting cards, give someone a different gift: the gift of friendship, the gift of caring, the gift of encouragement. Show them that God Is Love.

Gracious God of All Love, be my valentine, and help me to be a living valentine to someone new this day. Thank You for creating love, for perpetuating love, and for sending Love to hang between those two thieves, for me. Amen

February 15

AWAKENINGS

May he strengthen your hearts so that you will be blameless and holy in the presence of our God and Father when our Lord Jesus comes with all his holy ones. **1 Thessalonians 3:13**

A 1990 movie called "Awakenings," was based on a memoir of the same title written by Oliver Sacks. Sacks was a British neurologist, but the character is fictionalized as an American physician named Malcolm Sayer, played by Robin Williams. In both the book and the movie, the setting is a hospital ward of catatonic patients who survived an early 20th century epidemic of *encephalitis lethargica*. The drug L-Dopa is found to benefit the patients, causing them to "awaken" from their unresponsive state after many years. Most returned to their previously productive personalities, enjoying life for the first time since the epidemic. Sadly, the story goes on to reveal that the effects of the L-Dopa do not last. The patients watch as their fellow sufferers, one by one, return to their withdrawn state.

But in the end, another kind of "awakening" occurs, as the hospital staff have begun to treat the patients with a new respect and to appreciate the afflicted as people and not just lifeless bodies. Patient care improves and staff morale rises, even though the task still remains the same: to care for their unresponsive charges.

The lesson to be learned here, or course, is that God looks upon each one of us as "blameless and holy," no matter our lot in this life. God's eyes are the kindest kind of prism, making all human beings equal in His sight. Though we will never be able to see our fellow earth-travelers exactly as God sees them, we can learn from Him that imperfections can be overlooked and sins can be forgiven. And the cost to us for His marvelous prism-love is just to believe in His Son and His atoning death on a cross.

God of Rose-Colored Glasses, aid us in seeing others as You see them, as children of the Living God, blameless and holy, saved and free. Amen

February 16

CLEANING FISH

"Come, follow me," Jesus said, "and I will make you fishers of men."
Matthew 4:19

I have a friend who sends me funny emails, and today he sent "Christian One-Liners." The one that caught my eye (pun intended) said, "Fish for people: you catch 'em, God cleans 'em." Since I am a sometimes a nervous evangelist, this idea appeals to me. Plus, sharing Christ, like cleaning fish, can sometimes get messy.

One thing I have discovered is the more I *know* about God's Word, the easier it is to talk about it. While much of faith is just that, *faith*, skeptical people want real answers. I can't tell someone I believe in God's promises if I can't relate a few of them from Scripture. Jesus redemptive work on the cross may sound ghastly to someone who can't understand we are all sinners. Paul says in 1 Corinthians 1:18 "the message of the cross is foolishness to those who are perishing, but to us who are being saved it is the power of God." It is our responsibility as ambassadors of Christ to be prepared to share that "power of God," through our own stories. But we also must be prepared to back up our personal faith experience with sound Biblical insight as to why we believe.

Witnessing for Christ doesn't have to be so scary if we just follow God's lead! We can do our best to get folks *interested* in the Gospel ("catch 'em") and let God show them the way to their own redemption ("clean 'em").

Faithful Father, sometimes "cleaning" Your fish can seem like an unpleasant experience for us. Help us to do our part in "reeling in" some prospects for Your kingdom, and we will trust You to work on the "cleaning" part. Amen

February 17

SHALL WE GATHER AT THE RIVER?

In those days John the Baptist came, preaching in the wilderness of Judea and saying, "Repent, for the kingdom of heaven has come near." Matthew 3:1

Barbara Kingsolver's best-selling novel, *The Poisonwood Bible*, should be required reading for all seminary students today! Kingsolver's tale of the zealous missionary, Nathan Price takes place in 1959. Price, his wife and four daughters move from ultra-conservative Georgia to the Belgian Congo. Price had an agenda: to get everybody baptized. But the locals knew perfectly well that the river into which Price was attempting to dunk their children was infested with crocodiles! The tale continues with much roaring and screaming in the name of evangelism, until Price's wife and the three daughters who *didn't* die from a snake bite leave the old bugger to his own devices.

Whew! Did it really used to be like that? Heaven help the heathen, is what I say! Where did these early missionaries ever get the idea that this approach would bring forth the kingdom of God? Certainly not in the Bible I read today! My introduction to Jesus Christ was of a much gentler nature. I was told all I had to do was believe Jesus Christ is the Son of God, and that God sent Him to live among us in order to die for our sins. This plan struck me as crazy *until I chose to believe it*.

All of this causes me to consider the people in my life who are where I used to be: lost. Our job is *not* to rush in and throw these folks in the river. It's to *witness* to them with our lives and our actions and maybe some well-chosen rhetoric if the opportunity presents itself. How hard it is to remember that others often want to see our faith in action more than they want to hear about it.

Father of Light, help us shed some light in this dark world! Let us not be stumbling blocks to those who are struggling by rushing to judgment as to what they need. Help us remember to pray first, talk later. Amen

February 18

CONSIDER THE SOURCE

(Thomas) said to them, "Unless I see the nail marks in His hands and put my finger where the nails were, and put my hand into His side, I will not believe." John 20:25

One Sunday afternoon years ago, I was sketching scenery near a mountain park not far from my home in Colorado, unaware that the people in the park were packing up and leaving. Suddenly, a strange man wearing a mask jumped from behind a rock brandishing a gun. He sexually assaulted me and then intended to shackle me to a tree with a large chain. Instinctively, I shouted at the man, "In the name of God, don't do this!" Surprisingly, the man's eyes softened for just a moment, like a little boy who got caught with his hand in the cookie jar. A complete transformation occurred when I had invoked the name of a God in whom I did not believe at that time. The man then hit me with the chain and knocked me down. And then he fled.

Suffering for years from this traumatic experience, I could not understand what it all meant. God pursued me until I finally laid down my life for Him. That's when I began to heal. The ensuing journey has led me places I never dared to hope I would go. I wrote a book about God's unfailing love, grace and compassion. I speak to groups about my experience, and help other victims of trauma in their healing. I was *believed* to be a credible source to others because of my first-hand experience.

Jesus' disciple Thomas is mostly remembered for his denial that Christ could have risen from the dead. Even the very men with whom Thomas had just spent three years were not able to convince Thomas of what they had seen. Thomas wanted to see and hear Christ himself. Many people want to hear something from the source or they won't accept it. Someone may need to hear your story, so tell it!

Gracious God, Your Word is life to us; Your Word is a living, moving force that can change the world. Help us to find our own voices to share our word and Your Word to make a difference in the life of even one of Your precious children. Amen

February 19

I'VE GOT YOUR BACK

For he will command his angels concerning you to guard you in all your ways. **Psalm 91:11**

Three cheers for Robert McDonald! The 2014 Secretary of Veterans Affairs appointee is a man with a plan. As part of President Obama and the VA's goal of ending Veteran homelessness by the end of 2015, McDonald participated first-hand in the Point In Time (PIT) count of all homeless persons in Los Angeles in January 2015. "There is no question that the goal to end Veteran homelessness is within reach," said Secretary McDonald. "Ending Veteran homelessness in America is … about helping communities...house every (homeless) Veteran… today and…in the future." The January 2014 PIT Los Angeles Count revealed a 33-percent decline in homelessness among Veterans since 2010. Similar counts are being done all over the nation.

On a national newscast the day of the February PIT count, McDonald spoke with homeless veterans on camera, facing down his worst fear. He said he doesn't want to find someone on the street that he served with, one who "had his back" in combat. He stated the takes his job with the VA seriously: he wants the homeless vets to know he now has *their* back.

The VA has had some bad press in recent years, and rightfully so. But at the core of all the accusations is still a face, a life, a story. If we care at all about furthering God's kingdom here on earth, we would do well to pray for these men and women who served selflessly only to be left to fend for themselves when they got home. God bless the veterans, and may Robert McDonald lead us to a better place in history.

Oh, God, when You hung on that cross, You felt all of the pain and anguish that all of Your people have suffered and are suffering and will suffer. Comfort those who feel abandoned and help these good men and women who served our country return to happy, healthy and productive lives. Amen

February 20

WHAT'S UP WITH THAT, LORD?

(Joseph said,) "It was not you who sent me here, but God. He made me father to Pharaoh, lord of his entire household and ruler of all Egypt." Genesis 45:8

Recently, I was supposed to attend a Christian women's weekend retreat where I would be one of the speakers. I spent a great deal of time preparing for my talk. I worked on the content, timing, delivery, and a detailed Power Point presentation for days, right up until the evening before the event.

The next morning, I awoke feeling terrible. A trip to my clinic revealed that I had a bad case of influenza, which meant I had to cancel out on the entire retreat. Someone else stepped in and gave my talk. I really wondered why God had allowed me to go through all of the preparation for the weekend. I knew He didn't want me there to give everyone else the flu. And being exhausted from attending the retreat would surely have delayed me getting well.

So I wondered, why did I get the flu? Didn't God like my speech? But then I thought about all the times in the Bible where God's people took detours. Joseph's brothers sold him into slavery only to find Joseph later in a position of great authority with the ability to help his family *and* all of Israel (Genesis 45:4-8). Esther was also a slave who was given an opportunity to speak up on behalf of her people (Esther 4:14). And another Joseph thought he was marrying a simple village girl, but soon found himself parenting the Son of God (Matthew 1:20). God knows what He's doing. We just have to trust Him and follow His lead.

God of Endless Opportunities, we know that You work all things together for the good of those who love You. Fill us with faith and remove all doubt that You always have our best interests in mind. Amen

February 21

WE ARE THE DARKNESS

In Him was life, and that life was the light of all mankind. The light shines in the darkness, and the darkness has not overcome it. John 1:4-5

Okay, so I'm not dark *all* the time. And before I learned that sin is…well, disappointing God, I would have said I was a "good" person. But the truth is, whatever is not pleasing to God *is* sin, and we need to continually remind ourselves of that if we want to live in true fellowship with Him every day.

So do I have this down? No way! I go through an average day letting lots of things "slip." I think, "Slow drivers are idiots and fast drivers are maniacs." Sometimes I tell the people in my life how I *really* feel when I'm upset. If I say I'll pray for someone, did I really mean *every day*? And I've been known to tell a white lie now and then if I am pretty sure I can get away with it. (What, you've never done that????)

Wow, that was painful! I just wrote down several things that exposed me as a true sinner, and I'm going to post it on the Internet so everyone can read it. Maybe I'd better hit the "undo" button… But wait, Life doesn't have an "undo" button. It's up to us to "undo," or repent, from the things we've done that might (probably will) bother God. I can stop criticizing other drivers, soften my words, keep my promises, tell the truth. That wasn't so hard, now was it?

Aren't you glad that God came into the world so His light can shine on our darkness? And the best part is, He forgives us when we ask Him and He gives us a second chance to walk in that light. Praise God! Hallelujah!

Thank You, Gracious God, for lighting up my life and the lives of all of Your children. Help us to turn to You in repentance when we step out of that light. Amen

February 22

THE STILL, SMALL VICE

And after the earthquake a fire, but the Lord was not in the fire; and after the fire a still small voice. **1 Kings 19:12**

No, it's not a typo. We have all been guilty of "the still, small vice:" that little, niggling *sin-that's-not-really-a-sin*. The one we think we are getting away with or that we don't even realize or remember we've committed. The one we think God won't notice, that we probably don't need to worry about. Or do we?

I know I fail my Lord every day, in big (huge!) ways and small. I'm human, and it's impossible for me to know all the things I may say or do that grieve God. I'm eternally thankful He is a forgiving God, for where would I be if He wasn't? So how do we reconcile those sins we don't even think about? For me, the answer lies in asking God to forgive *all* my sins, those I know about and those I don't remember (or pretend I don't remember). If we are God's children and He is our Father, then He as a parent knows the human spirit can be broken by too much guilt. A child who is constantly told she is wrong about everything has a hard time growing into a confident person who can make intelligent, discerning decisions throughout her life. God knows this.

There is an old saying: "Don't sweat the small stuff (p.s.: it's all small stuff)." Sin is sin. Of course God wants us to 'fess up when we have hurt someone or done something that clearly is not His will. But let's remember He is a loving Father Who wants us to learn and grow in His love every day. If we give Him our hearts, God can be trusted to hear those sins we confess and to help us recall the ones we leave unconfessed. And He loves us anyway.

God of Unfailing Compassion, know that I want to do Your will. Help me in my time of confusion to reach for Your hand to guide me in all I do. Amen

February 23

GET THE BOAT!

Because of the crowd he told his disciples to have a small boat ready for him, to keep the people from crowding him. **Mark 3:9**

On our recent vacation, the airline had a new safety video that was quite entertaining. In the segment showing passengers how to use the oxygen masks "in the unlikely event" they would be needed, a man correctly put his own mask on before assisting his young daughter. Then the daughter placed a mask on her dolly in the seat next to hers. The instructions were cleverly presented, and as always, the more mature or able-bodied passenger makes sure his own mask is in place before assisting someone who needs help. We cannot help another passenger with the oxygen device if we ourselves are not properly oxygenated.

Jesus knew this was true with any type of help He was to render. The third chapter of Mark finds Jesus in the early part of His ministry, healing the withered hand of a man. People began to press in on Him with needs of their own, but Jesus asked the disciples to "get the boat," so they could make their escape. The fully-human Jesus knew He needed to take care of Himself and his new disciples if He was going to have the energy to meet the demands of His ministry. He modeled this behavior for us; we need to make sure we are not taking on so much in our lives that we have no time or energy to serve God. As the saying goes, "The devil loves a busy Christian." So remember it's okay to "get the boat" if you need to escape into the restful arms of Jesus for some rest and renewal!

Jesus, we are so glad You modeled perfect behavior for us! Help us see the practical lessons You shared during Your ministry, as well as the life-changing acts of kindness You showed the people You met. Amen

February 24

LEAVE THE LIGHT ON

When Jesus spoke again to the people, he said, "I am the light of the world. Whoever follows me will never walk in darkness, but will have the light of life." John 8:12

A popular motel chain has a slogan, "We'll leave the light on." The voice in the ad is saying the motel isn't anything fancy, just like coming home to Grandma's, reasonably priced, not a lot of frills, and the people at this motel are around all the time leaving on a light to guide you there. The chain has done well with this warm and cozy image, and I get a chuckle out of the ad every time I hear it.

Jesus "leaves a light on" in the souls of all His believers. But what does this really mean? Like Abraham Lincoln once said, "People are about as happy as they want to be." So how much does happiness depend on our own attitude and how much does it depend on the work of Christ within us? It seems pretty clear to me happiness depends on both the indwelling Christ (who moved in and turned the light on the minute we believed) and our own acceptance of Christ in our lives (daily acknowledgement of that light within us, which is the Holy Spirit). Simple enough, but it takes practice. Just like the motel's ad campaign, we need some reminders to let Christ's light show through us. Whether it's reading a daily devotion, listening to Christian music, studying the Bible, or viewing God's ever-present display of natural wonders, the little holy things we include in our daily life can make us sparkle with the love of Christ even on the days we might be a little down ourselves. So next time you hear that ad campaign for the motel we all know about, remember Whose light is on in *your* world!

Rainbow-Maker, Keeper of the Sun and the Moon and the Stars, create a sense of wonder in us minute by minute. Let us never forget that You are the Light of the World, and the Light in our hearts. Amen

February 25

THE SHACK IS BACK

Then you will know the truth, and the truth will set you free. John 8:32

Wm. Paul Young's iconic 2007 novel, *The Shack*, tied my brain in knots! The story is about Mack Phillip's, an ordinary guy whose young daughter was abducted and never seen again. Evidence found in an abandoned shack in the Oregon wilderness points to the child having been brutally murdered. A few years afterwards, Mack receives a note, presumably from God, asking him to come to that very shack, the embodiment of what Mack calls *The Great Sadness*. The cabin, as it turns out, has been transformed and occupied by Love Himself.

"Everything is about (Jesus)," Mack is told. "And freedom is a process that happens inside a relationship with Him." This relationship, and the freedom that accompanies it, is the answer Mack seeks. But Mack's pain and sense of loss is not appeased until he understands how profoundly and perfectly healed his daughter is now that she is in heaven. Jesus tells Mack, "When the light shines into the place where (fear) lives inside you," it can no longer have the same power over you.

Reading about this was an "aha" moment for me. I have faced down the barrel of a gun and lived to tell about it, but it has truly been through God's grace that I have healed and reached a place of peace in my daily life. The story in *The Shack* helped to alleviate my "survivor's guilt;" if I have been able to heal in *this* life through the love of God, then I can know those who have *not* survived brutal attacks like mine are experiencing a far greater healing in the arms of the One Who holds them now.

All-Powerful God, Your grace has transformed me from a sorrowful wanderer to a joyous follower of Your Word and Your ways. I pray that other survivors of violence may find their way to You and through You, and that those who do not survive now know Your ultimate healing. Amen

February 26

DOWNSIZING

You shall have no other gods before me. **Deuteronomy 5:7**

We are "downsizing" at our house. Well, I should say my husband is downsizing. I am taking one last leisurely trip down Memory Lane, holding each piece of "stuff" tenderly before making the painstaking decision whether or not I can let it go. My husband doesn't think I'm serious about this project. He calls me a "pack rat" when he simply doesn't see the importance of me keeping things "just in case." I took my shoes off the other night and he put them on EBay.

The bottom line is that most of us in our country get hung up on possessions. God wants us to enjoy this life but He definitely doesn't want us hopelessly distracted by "things." When the material baggage we collect takes on more importance than the Creator Himself, that's idolatry. And the Bible is very clear we "shall have no other gods before" God. Period.

I lived in a thirty-three foot travel trailer when I was younger, and I am fascinated by the tiny house movement going on right now. My husband says we could move to a tiny house if he could have a huge shed for his "boy toys." We are working out this plan for our "golden years." But one thing is for sure: as we grow older, we both find ourselves focusing more on our relationships, with each other, the ones we love and care about, and our God. When God is our focus, any house is His.

Father of All Creation, walk with us through our lives and temper our desire for material things. Help us to put You first at all times, no matter how much or how little we possess in this life. Amen

February 27

FACES OF WAR, FACES OF PEACE

From my youth I have suffered and been close to death; I have borne your terrors and am in despair. **Psalm 88:15**

She was a tiny Cambodian woman, dressed in simple American clothes. The determination in her eyes that haunts me even today. Her English As A Second Language teacher brought her to the college's counseling office to see me in the spring of 1990. This woman whom I will call Ponleak (which means *strength* or *endurance*) had witnessed the brutal murder of her husband and her two oldest children by Communist leader Pol Pot's merciless soldiers during the Kmer Rouge in the late 1970s. An American soldier met Ponleak and her three remaining children in a refugee camp and brought her and her family back to the United States. He married her and together they raised her children to become successful members of American society.

There was only one problem: the American soldier beat Ponleak daily and treated her as his slave. Now, she stood in my office saying she wanted to go to a women's shelter. Her children had all moved away, and she wanted to live out her life alone, in peace and freedom.

I was—and still am—astounded at what the human spirit can endure. This woman had seen so much hatred and evil and cruelty, and yet she still had the will to seek her independence and regain her dignity. To know the depths of despair that Ponleak had known and have the will to go on was almost more than I could take in. As I was assisting her, I thought of King David in all of his trials, a confessed sinner who still trusted God to see him through. Ponleak had done nothing to bring on her misfortunes, and I was humbled beyond words to be assisting her in her purposeful and most sacred journey.

God of Healing, when will there be an end to war and danger and fear? Those of us who trust in You know a peace others may never feel. Aid us in raising prayers for their safety and security in this dispirited world. Amen

February 28

DON'T TRY THIS AT HOME!

Jesus said to them, "Surely you will quote this proverb to me: 'Physician, heal yourself!'" Luke 4:23

Once, when my husband and I were visiting Telluride, Colorado, we heard about George Balderston, a doctor who removed his own appendix in 1949. A Huff Post article says Balderston performed the surgery "to get a first-hand reaction of a patient to local anesthesia....to study post-operative effects." Some Telluride residents insist Balderston was offended when a patient called him a "butcher," and completed the self-surgery to prove him wrong. The good doctor reportedly used no mirrors and finished the procedure in forty-five minutes, returning to work after two days. Balderston's operation is said to be the first and only of its kind in Colorado.

The idea of performing "self-surgery" sounds preposterous to most of us. But we think nothing of becoming impatient with "God's timing" and snatching our lives back out of His hands when we think we can take care of things better/faster/easier than He can! We as humans constantly want to "fix" things on our own, rather than waiting for God's good plan to unfold. God gave all of us our talents, from ditch digging to brain surgury, and He wants us to use our talents to help make this world a better place. But He also wants us to come to Him for wisdom and guidance using those talents.

It takes a lot of trust to let somebody cut into your body and perform even a minor procedure! If the surgeon suddenly said, "Here's the scalpel, Honey, go for it," I would surely freak out. Thanks be to God there are men and women who have the skills to take care of us when we need an operation. And thanks be to God He is always there, unfolding His plans throughout our lives.

Lord, You have been called The Great Physician, and we know all healing comes through Your hand. Guide us in making wise decisions about our earthly health, and guide those who treat us for the diseases we encounter. Amen

February 29

A LEAP OF FAITH

"Where were you when I laid the earth's foundation? Tell me, if you understand. Who marked off its dimensions? Surely you know! Who stretched a measuring line across it? Job 38:4-5

My Grandmother Birdie Mae Rollins was born on February 29, 1872. Because she only had a birthday every four years, the family joked that Birdie got married at age three, and had her eight children when she was four, four and a half, five, five and a half, six, six and half, seven and seven and a half.

A year is defined as the time it takes for the Earth to orbit around the sun once. It takes the Earth about 365 ¼ days to make one entire orbit around the sun (a day is one rotation around the Earth's axis). By adding one extra day about every four years, the Earth is in the same point of its orbit at the same time of the calendar year each year. I often wonder what God thinks of these human contrivances. It must amuse God that we as humans have to be so "organized" in His world, which is already perfectly organized and has been since He declared it all "good."

In the book named for him, Job found his friends had lots of ideas about why he was suffering, but in the end the truth revealed itself. God had "allowed" Satan to mess with Job because God knew Job would never renounce Him. Most of us would hope we'd never be put to the test the way Job was, but can any of us truly say we understand God's intentions? The Lord told the prophet Isaiah, "My thoughts are not your thoughts, neither are your ways my ways." So while we as humans can easily justify our attempts to organize this world, let's all remember just Who put it all into orbit in the first place.

Creator God, we marvel at Your works, which are too magnificent for us to understand. Grant us a peace in which we can simply worship You for all You have created, without having to alter it in some way to suit our human purposes. Amen

March

March 1

CHOCOLATE OVERLOAD!

You prepare a table before me in the presence of my enemies. **Psalm 23:5**

In 2002, I was being laid off from my job at the end of spring semester in a two-year college. There had been a "hostile takeover" of new administrators whose "vision" turned the college upside down. That winter, my father was dying fifteen hundred miles away. I had no sick leave or vacation time left, and "bereavement leave" could not be used while he was still alive. I feared if I went to see him I might lose my union rights to claim another position. I was trying to finish out the school year with professionalism and integrity, but staff morale and workplace climate were deteriorating rapidly.

During a sleepless night, I saw verse five of Psalm 23 as if for the first time: *You prepare a table before me in the presence of my enemies.* It hit me: God didn't want me to suffer through this "season" of my life! He wanted me to pull up a chair and indulge in a banquet of His blessings while chaos rained down all around me! I still had to work out my contract until the end of the school year, and unfortunately, my father died before I was able to see him again. I adopted a different attitude about my circumstances. I interpreted the "table before me" part of the Psalm to mean unlimited chocolate, which didn't help my waistline. But I kept reciting that verse over and over again whenever the situation at work got out of hand, and the same verse helped me get through my father's funeral and moving my mother closer to my husband and me.

God will give us a guiding verse if we stay aware as we study His Word. What is your guiding verse this week?

Shepherd of Our Hearts, walk with us and grant us special sight to find our special verses in Your Word. Let us "see with new eyes" the words You want us to hold close and savor. Amen

March 2

RUB-A-DUB-DUB

And this water symbolizes baptism that now saves you also—not the removal of dirt from the body but the pledge of a clear conscience toward God. It saves you by the resurrection of Jesus Christ. **1 Peter 3:21**

Rub-a-dub-dub/Three men in a tub/And who do you think they be?
The butcher, the baker/The candlestick-maker/Turn 'em out, knaves all three!

If you remember this 1846 English nursery rhyme, you are dating yourself! I was reminded of the jingle when I read today's Scripture passage, which makes the distinction between a *bath*, which keeps our physical bodies clean and *baptism*, which ushers us into the family of God.

A knave is a *dishonest man, deceitful fellow, most likely of humble position.* They are just the type of guys Jesus would have loved to have met. Perfect candidates for a spiritual overhaul! And although the phrase "cleanliness is next to godliness" doesn't actually appear in Scripture, it is well-known in the mental health field that letting one's physical appearance go is a sign of serious personality concerns. So this butcher, baker and candlestick-maker might have been delighted to run into the Savior when their little tub ran aground. Maybe another nursery rhyme could be written:

Rub-a-dub-dub,
Sinners in a tub,
How can they all be so mean?

The fibber, the con man,
One in the KK Klan,
The Savior will make them all clean!

Father, You sent Jesus to take away our sins and make us all clean. Help us to walk daily in remembrance of our baptism, that sacred ceremony in which our sins were washed away and we became Your children. Amen

March 3

ROOMS

My Father's house has many rooms; if that were not so, would I have told you that I am going there to prepare a place for you? John 14:2

How many rooms does your home have? We have more than we need. We have rooms for everything you can think of: one to sleep in and three more of those, in case we have company, plus one for an office. We have a room to cook in, with a space to eat if the cooking works out, plus a separate space for formal meals. A living room and a family room give us places to lounge and entertain. We have three bathrooms, one we never use. There are little rooms called closets that store the stuff we need and lots of stuff we don't need. And our heated garage, my husband's "man cave," where he stores his big toys to use in the summer and mostly look at in the winter.

My favorite space in our house is my *room for improvement*. It's not a whole room, just a corner of our living room where I sit every morning with my coffee, two Bibles, my Bible study and devotions books, a thesaurus and my laptop, before my day gets crazy. I still my mind and spend quality time with God. I wasn't able to do this when I worked full-time, but now I am retired. I cherish and protect this time and space.

A *room for improvement* can take many forms: your vehicle in traffic, the doctor's office while you are waiting. It could be a garden or a lake or a country lane. You could be folding clothes or changing the oil in your car in your *room for improvement*. The time and place doesn't matter to God, as long as we meet Him there to learn and to grow in His love and His Word. He waits for us every day, all day, and He is ecstatic when we say, "Here I am, Lord! What shall we talk about today?"

Father of All Good Gifts, thank You for the physical spaces we call home, and watch over all those whose living conditions are less comfortable than ours. Help us make time to come into our room for improvement *each day, and to guard our time with You for the treasure it is. Amen*

March 4

WHAT'S SO SOCIAL ABOUT A GADGET?

What then shall we say, brothers and sisters? When you come together, each of you has a hymn, or a word of instruction, a revelation, a tongue or an interpretation. Everything must be done so that the church may be built up. 1 Corinthians 14:26

Social media is hard for me. As an author, speaker and trainer, I am told that I need to have an "Internet platform," which I describe as a three-dimensional resume in Technicolor on steroids. People say I must have a secure email account, a website, a LinkedIn account, a Facebook presence (all of which I do). To be successful in today's world, I should be Tweeting, putting stuff on Pinterest, and using a whole host of other electronic communication tools, all to get the word out that I want to come and share my faith story with people face to face. Seems kind of ironic to me!

I often wonder what God thinks of the Internet. He gave people the intelligence to come up with all the technology (whether those people believe He even exists or not), but as with many things, what humans do with God-given talents can be quite diverse! I imagine God is pleased for people to have this wonderful resource to learn about things, but that it makes Him sad when people choose electronics over relationships. The number of "friends" we have on Facebook will never take the place of a personal conversation between two or three of those people. The body of Christ can use media to get the word out about events in the church, but the Bible tells us corporate worship and personal mission are still necessary to do God's work. The task, as I see it, is to utilize these technological resources wisely, but not neglect the impact personal contact has on spreading the Gospel of Christ. Next time you click "like" on Facebook, remember to "like" God with a little prayer.

God of Wisdom, enlighten us about the responsible use of technology, protect the innocent who navigate the Internet, and help us to continue to build personal relationships that further Your kingdom on earth. Amen

March 5

WARNING LABELS

You, Lord, will keep the needy safe and will protect us forever from the wicked. Psalm 12:7

Remove Child Before Folding, The 101 Stupidest, Silliest and Wackiest Warning Labels Ever, is a book by Bob Dorigo Jones. The publication offers some explanation as to why modern society is so fraught with these alarming notifications: because of lawyers seeing dollar signs. NBC Nightly News reporter Tom Brokaw said, "We are the world's most litigious society (which) has given rise to a whole new form of literature: the warning label."

We've seen fish hooks that warn, "Harmful If Swallowed," and sleeping pills that suggest "May Cause Drowsiness." I saw a TV ad saying, "Do not take this medication if you are allergic to the medication or any of its ingredients." The people in the ad were skipping through meadows of daisies, smiling and living large, probably because they were just actors.

What if the Bible had a warning label? "Do not read if you do not want to believe." "Text contained herein is divinely inspired and could cause human inspiration." How about, "Do not use this product without the consent of the Holy Spirit Who lives in you whether you know it or not?" And "Words contained in this book are not necessarily the opinion of all the peoples of the earth, although We the Editors believe they should be."

It's a fun exercise, and might be a good one for Sunday school kids or confirmation students. But one thing is for sure: God does not create, design, or dispense anything for which He might later need a lawyer. He is the lawyer, and He doesn't see dollar signs. He sees His precious children, desires only the best for them, and loves them all.

Father, it is a dangerous world we have created, and humans seem to make it more dangerous all the time. Surround us with Your angels and protect us from those who seek profit over safety. Amen

March 6

RANK AND PRIVILEGE

For all have sinned and fall short of the glory of God. **Romans 3:22**

Members of Alcoholics Anonymous have a saying when they meet: "The highest rank here is drunk." Once an AA member walks through that door, she or he is equal to all the others present. Each are "one drink away" from a slip-up, needing to "work the program" one day—even one hour or one minute—at a time. Changing their lifestyle is paramount to success: where and with whom they spend their time can mean the difference between victory over their addiction and sudden return to the compulsion.

Christians have one rank too: sinner. We cannot fully follow Christ if we are not willing to accept the fact that each of us has sinned, and will continue to sin. It's part of our human nature, just like the shape of our noses and the color of our eyes. So what can we do about this sin condition? The plan seems simple: just have Jesus spend a little time on earth and then allow Himself to be nailed to a cross and hang there until He dies for our sins.

Wait, *WHAT?!?* That's not a plan! That's awful! Why can't we just try not to sin and save Him all that trouble? We must remember that God's ways are not our ways (Isaiah 55:8), and to think we might have a better idea is restricting God only to human behavior. Secondly, when Adam and Eve committed the "original sin," God promised them that He would one day provide the perfect sacrifice to atone for their sin (Genesis 3:15). So a whole lot of lambs lost their lives, but when the time was right, God sent Jesus to take the place of the lambs and other animals. *"God made Him (Christ), who knew no sin, to be sin for us that we might become the righteousness of God in Him"* (2 Corinthians 5:21). Aren't you glad that Christ gave you the privilege to live forgiven because of His sacrifice? Jesus is the only One who deserves a rank in this world: He is King!

Praise You, Lord Jesus! You are my redeemer, and although it's hard to understand the plan, I am so blessed that You sacrificed Yourself for my freedom! Amen

March 7

THE CLEAN PLATE CLUB

Do not let the sun go down while you are still angry. **Ephesians 4:26**

Several years ago, my husband and I were fortunate enough to be adopted by two baby Basset Hounds. Bayfield was the firstborn of the litter, a handsome specimen of manhood. Though low-slung and jowly, he is a regal dog. He exercises restraint and dignity, except when it's walk time, when his nine-year-old body becomes a riotous mess of leaping fur and slobber.

His sister, Beulah, outweighs her brother by at least ten pounds. She is slow and exceedingly lazy. Though she's the runt of the litter she has a ferocious appetite, eating anything left in her path, especially her brother's food. When she gives him the "stink eye," this normally stately male "Hound Hunger Games," and it takes constant supervision to keep both dogs happy. If there ever was a Canine Clean Plate Club, Beulah would be president. Beulah's other favorite dining spot is the pile of dead and decomposing grass at the back of our property, earning her the nickname, "Cow Face."

We love our dogs to absolute distraction, and we believe they love each other. The Bible says God loved animals too, because He chose to save them over the not-so-faithful people on earth at the time of the flood. But I think Bayfield and Beulah teach us a lesson about relationships. There is a lot of give-and-take between these two, and yet they always bed down together at night. They forgive each other, and most of all they forgive my husband and me when it's too cold or we're too busy to go for that walk. They are comforted by our mere presence, and a pat on the head goes a long way to ushering each of them into a long and peaceful nap. Someone once said that we should all aspire to be the person our pets think we are. Wouldn't that be a wonderful challenge for us Christians?

God of All Living Creatures, thank You for the blessing of animals. Teach us to take time to observe them and learn from them, for they are truly one of Your nicest creations. Amen

March 8

ONE PERSON'S HOPE, ANOTHER'S FREEDOM

Always be prepared to give an answer to everyone who asks you to give the reason for the hope that you have. **1 Peter 3:15**

Trudy Baltazar had never met him, but she had a clear message from God that she was supposed to help St. Paul resident Koua Fong Lee. Lee was driving home from church with his family in 2006 when his car suddenly accelerated, hitting and killing three people. Lee was sent to prison...until complaints surfaced of "sudden unintended acceleration" in the same type of vehicle. These reports never resulted in a recall. Enter Baltazar, with a God-driven motivation that would put the most seasoned activists to shame.

Trudy held two rallies for Koua, networked with hundreds of other supporters, raised awareness with media, and eventually was caught on camera hugging Koua leaving prison, fully exonerated of the "crime." Baltazar wasn't done yet. She followed Koua's case through the stormy civil trial. Koua struggles with the jury's decision to assign forty per cent of the "blame" to him in the civil trial. As a Laotian refugee, the difference between the criminal and civil trials in this country is not clear to him. But the case has opened the door for other wrongly-imprisoned drivers.

In her book, *A Road to Freedom: Strangers Restore Justice for an Innocent Man*, Baltazar insists her passion for this case was born out of her own pain having been abused as a child. One word about Baltazar stood out for me: *hope*. In following God's lead to help a stranger in need, Baltazar faced down her own demons and created hope for both herself and Koua. Trudy has grown in the Lord's grace and power while being instrumental in restoring freedom and trust in humanity to Koua. How many others of us might follow God's lead as she did to step out in faith for another human being?

Almighty God, Your power can move mountains, whether they be made of rock or injustice. Bless this selfless woman and the man she helped, and walk with them as they continue in Your path of righteousness. Amen

March 9

EVEN THE DEMONS BELIEVE

You believe that there is one God. Good! Even the demons believe that—and shudder. James 2:19

"I'm a believer." If we want to make this statement become more than a line from an old Monkey's song, we had better pay attention to what James is saying in the second chapter of his letter to his own church, the Jewish Christians. And since James is Jesus' little brother, he grew up with the Guy and got to witness His superpowers firsthand every day. So Mother Mary says to Jesus one day, "Hon, go see why Your little brother is crying instead of napping." "Okay, Mom," He says, and goes over to James' little pallet. Jesus shouts, "OUT!!" And all these little demons come scurrying out from under the pallet like the law is after them. Which is true. And James gives his Bro' a high five and goes back to sleep. Little Jamie was a believer before he even lost his baby teeth.

But now, the all-grown-up James is saying, "So you believe in Jesus? No big deal! Even the demons under your bed believe, but you've got to do more! You've got to *act out your faith!*" A recurring theme here is that faith without works is dead. Once we accept that Jesus is Lord of our lives, we have to move on from there and do something about it. Merely *thinking* we belong to Christ is vastly different from having a burning passion to share that truth with everyone we meet, whether by telling them or showing them. Jesus said, "Go and make disciples of all nations, baptizing them in the name of the Father and of the Son and of the Holy Spirit, and teaching them to obey everything I have commanded you" (Matthew 28:19-20). Brother James is telling us nap time is over!

Jesus, Redeemer and Friend, walk with us as we share the best news of our lives with those we meet! And if among those we meet are demons, scatter them or sanctify them, whichever is Your will! Amen

March 10

MANURE HAPPENS!

"'Sir,' the man replied, 'leave it alone for one more year, and I'll dig around it and fertilize it.'" Luke 13:8

I never knew the Bible says God gives us…well, *manure*! But here it is, in the 13th chapter of Luke! The parable is about of the vineyard owner with a fig tree that isn't producing. He is about to cut the fig tree down, but the vine dresser says, "Wait a little while, and I'll dig around it and put some…*manure* on it, and we'll see what happens." Now any gardener worth her veggies knows that…*manure* is a very good thing to mix into the soil around a plant that isn't thriving. My friend Diane raises sheep and keeps the "primo stuff" (ten years old or older) for her own gardens. Perks her plants right up.

So what does this parable about…*manure* really mean? God owns the vineyard and Jesus tends it and we are the fig tree that isn't producing fruit. I get that. I also understand the parable is referencing Christ's desire to bring us all into fellowship with Him and is willing to work with us when we are going through a bad season. But should I be reading anything into the part about the…*manure*? Could it be that while we are wandering around not doing much to edify the kingdom of God, we might *step into something unpleasant that makes us grow*, like the plants in Diane's gardens? Or could it be the real lesson here is that this little fig tree was intentionally planted by God and nurtured by Jesus, and they both want the tree to hurry up and produce figs before it's too late?

God offers us unlimited opportunities to further His kingdom on earth. He wants us to take advantage of those opportunities, whether we're in sitting in jail or in a Jacuzzi, in the mountains or in Madagascar. And if we have to step in some…*manure* along the way, it's only going to help us grow!

Great Vinedresser, prune me and dig around me and put anything on me that will help me improve Your kingdom on earth. May I grow into the best ambassador for Christ that I can be! Amen

March 11

LOVE STORY

All the prophets testify about Him that everyone who believes in Him receives forgiveness of sins through his name. **Acts 10:42**

Love Story is a 1970 tragic, romantic motion picture, derived from the book of the same name, both written by Erich Segal. Ali MacGraw plays Jenny, a working-class student at Harvard who meets family-fortune heir Oliver, played by Ryan O'Neal. The two fall in love and marry, in spite of Oliver's father cutting him out of the family inheritance for his perceived poor choice of a partner. But Ali finds out she is terminally ill, and the plot takes a sorrowful turn (some might agree with me that perhaps it already had).

The "buzz phrase" between these two ill-fated lovers in the movie was "Love is never having to say you're sorry." It seemed like an entire generation swallowed that line and made it the Relationship Mantra of the Seventies. I thought it was pretty stupid then, but what did I know? I was only twenty-three years old and pretty oblivious to the way relationships should go.

Then I met Jesus, and realized the statement was not only ridiculous, it was un-Biblical! Christianity is based on the fact that we all *should* say we're sorry as soon and as often as we discover we have failed our Lord. Jesus came to earth, lived as a fully-human man, had a seemingly too-short career as a preacher, and then went to the cross so that we could be forgiven for our sins. Our motto as Christians should be "Love is God providing a way for us to be sanctified, once for all." Indeed, Love is God!

Love Story may have touched the hearts of many a romantic in 1970, but God's Love Story is real, powerful, reliable, and last forever.

Father of Love, You created romance and relationships, and You gave us writers to tell stories about those things. Hold us in Your embrace so that we can view the things of this world without wavering from Your true Word. Amen

March 12

TIME AND SPACE

Then he said to them all: "Whoever wants to be my disciple must deny themselves and take up their cross daily and follow me." Luke 9:23

When I worked as a college counselor, my colleagues and I would jokingly ask, "What is that student taking up?" The reply: "Time and space." Some students had no clear career goal, or even a clue what they'd liked to do. Some students would even have a "flat profile" on career inventories: they couldn't even choose which of two activities would be more interesting. These students were a lot of work for us counselors. They could take "general" courses which would work for most degree programs. But even that could waste time and money. If a career path was eventually chosen requiring specific courses, the student might find herself spending longer in college than mom and dad preferred or financial aid would cover.

Jesus is the Quintessential Career Counselor: He gives us clear direction: "Deny yourself, take up (your) cross and follow Me." Our "cross" is whatever burdens us or slows us down, an indifferent attitude or a physical impairment, financial difficulties or an overburden of responsibilities. Christ says to bring it along for the trip and work on it while you move forward. You can't spend much time really walking with God without beginning to view your own situation in a different light. Christian pastor and author Chuck Swindoll says, "We have a choice every day regarding the attitude we will embrace for that day. We cannot change the inevitable. The only thing we can do is play on the one string we have, and that is our attitude." Jesus will help us with that. The Bible will help us with that. Hanging around other Christians will help us with that. And here's the thing: whether you love your job flipping burgers or hate your job flipping houses, you can still find fulfillment in your life in Christ, the most satisfying "career" of them all.

God of All Creation, create in me a burning desire to take up my personal cross and follow You. Help me to see how my attitude towards my life can change for the better in serving You. Amen

March 13

VOICES FROM GOD

***Afterward Jesus appeared in a different form to two of them while they were walking in the country.* Mark 16:12**

Joan of Arcadia was a television drama series that ran from 2003 until 2005. The title comes from Joan of Arc, a 15th century French woman who saw visions of saints. The television Joan, played by Amber Tamblyn, promises God she would do anything for Him if He let her now paralyzed older brother survive a car crash. God begins to appear to Joan as different people: a geeky little girl, a Goth boy with spiked hair, a frumpy old lady, and an handsome young man. Joan tells no one about God's appearances except her Jewish friend, "Amazing" Grace (Mary Steenburgen). The tasks God asks Joan to are entertaining and end in a life lesson.

People talking to God is called prayer, but God talking to people is called insanity. But what if God spoke—and even appeared—directly to us in everyday circumstances? Perhaps He does! The men on the road to Emmaus didn't recognize Jesus when He walked with them (Luke 24). After Jesus revealed Himself to these two in the breaking of the bread, the men realized their "hearts burned within" them when they first met Jesus and heard Him explain Scripture. Would God's presence be so powerful we could feel it surging through our minds and bodies, even if we didn't know what it was?

God's words may come to us through other regular, ordinary people. Our words can bless each other as well. "Do not forget to show hospitality to strangers, for by so doing some people have entertained angels without knowing it" (Hebrews 13:2) We don't have to do anything fancy to have God's pure love move between us. We just have to pay attention to the opportunities presenting themselves *every single day* to "be" Jesus to someone else, or allow someone to "be" Jesus to us. No televisions script needed.

Omnipresent God, You DO speak to us every day, even if we can't "see" You. Stir us to listen closely for Your life-giving words, and to share them with others. Amen

March 14

SCIENCE GONE AWRY

Let my vindication come from you; may your eyes see what is right.
Psalm 17:2

Henrietta Lacks was an African-American woman who was completely unaware that cells from her cancerous tumor were cultured by a physician named George Otto Gey. In 1951, Lacks felt a "knot" inside of her, eventually leading her to John Hopkins Hospital in Baltimore, Maryland, the only hospital to treat blacks at the time. While she was in the hospital, two samples of Lack's cervix were removed, a healthy part and a cancerous part, without her knowledge or permission. These cells eventually became the HeLa "immortal" cell line, still used today in biomedical research. Lacks died later that year, but her family didn't find out about the cells being taken until Rebecca Skloot began researching the case for a revealing book she published in 2010 (*The Immortal Life of Henrietta Lacks*, Crown Publishers).

Lacks' poorly educated relatives were confused about what all of this meant. Some family members thought Henrietta herself was somehow being kept alive at John Hopkins, that her entire body was being subjected to medical experiments. One of Lack's daughters helped put together Skloot's book, but died herself before her mother's story was published. Millions were made from the sale of Henrietta's cells, but the family got little money.

Henrietta's amazingly "fertile" cells have done much good for others, but the way in which they were procured was wrong. This must make God sad. As the saying goes, "The only thing necessary for evil to prevail is for good (people) to do nothing." We as Christians in a fallen world have a responsibility to help those who are vulnerable, by our love, our actions and our prayers.

God of Creation, we know people would still be living in the Dark Ages if not for scientific research and advances. But when new technologies are pursued for financial gain and not for Your kingdom, things spin out of control. Save us from bad people who use good things solely to their own advantage. Amen

March 15

BEHIND IN MY WORK

(Jesus) rebuked Peter. "Get behind me, Satan!" he said. "You do not have in mind the concerns of God, but merely human concerns." Mark 8:33

The disciples didn't want to think about what Jesus was saying in Mark 8:32. Jesus asked His boys, "Who do people say I am?" Peter said, "You are the Messiah." Jesus gave him a high five, and then He went on to the not-too-popular topic of His imminent suffering, death and resurrection. The disciples missed the *resurrection* part altogether (hell-OOOOO?). Peter, whom Jesus had just praised, grabbed Jesus and told Him to cork it. And Jesus started calling Peter Satan! Now the boys were really confused.

Do you only live in the *shadow* of Christ's cross, lamenting what an awful world you've been dumped into, and finding nothing good in Christ's unthinkable act of redemption? Or do you blast open that tomb of doubt and sorrow and celebrate the resurrected Lord and all the promises that come with Him being alive and well and living in your heart? Peter didn't have all the pieces of the puzzle: he certainly wasn't in a place where he could *trust* Jesus completely. He knew who He was—Messiah, *God With Us*— but he hadn't yet placed *all* of his trust in that Messiah, or he wouldn't have questioned Jesus' explanation about the looming events.

What about those of us who live now, not having seen Jesus walk among us, talk to us about mysteries and promises and a kingdom without a fancy human ruler wearing purple velvet and crown jewels? Are we so different? Can we, too, cry, *"Get thee behind me, Satan,"* and move from doubt to assurance that Jesus *did* rise from the dead and He *lives* in our lives today? Now that's an Easter blessing I can really celebrate!

Jesus, Our Humble King, the people misunderstood You, scorned You, tortured You, and they put You to death because You were different. But You have the last Word, and that Word is living and moving in our fractured world still. Praise Your Holy Name! Amen

March 16

WRITE TO EXCITE!

So is my word that goes out from my mouth: It will not return to me empty, but will accomplish what I desire and achieve the purpose for which I sent it. **Isaiah 55:11**

My friend Stephanie Landsem knows how to make Bible characters come alive. Author of three Biblical fiction books, Landsem tells the "back story" of the people Jesus touched during His short but momentous ministry. Landsem began her book series with the tale of the Samaritan woman at the well, moved on to the thief who hung on the cross next to the Savior, and her newest novel, *The Tomb, A Novel of Martha*, was released March of 2015. The Library Journal Starred Review said of *The Tomb*, "Landsem's sympathetic and poignant portrait of a familiar Biblical figure is a well-crafted tale of strength, hope, and love."

What strikes me about Landsem's work is her ability to reach back in time and write as though she walked among these Bible characters. She mostly leaves Jesus out of the narrative, never embellishing what the Bible reports about His activities and the words He spoke. But as each of her characters is touched by Jesus' healing presence, Landsem allows a fresh, new story to unfold. As I read her books, I find myself transported back in time, as though I too am traveling the dusty paths of ancient towns and villages, struggling with my own concerns along with the people in these fascinating "back stories." Landsem does with her books what a good preacher does in a sermon: she makes these tales so personal that I cannot help but sit up and take notice—and that notice changes how I look at the stories and the people Jesus touched. I imagine that's exactly what both a skilled preacher and Stephanie Landsem have set out to do.

Father, You have spoken to us in Your Living Word and given us rich stories to illuminate our lives. Thank You for giving us people who continue to light the way for us to understand all that Your Word has to say. Amen

March 17

ST. PATRICK AND THE SNAKES

And these signs will accompany those who believe: in My name, they will cast out demons; they will speak in new tongues. They will pick up snakes with their hands; and when they drink deadly poison, it will not hurt them at all; they will place their hands on sick people, and they will get well. **Mark 16:17-18**

St. Patrick's Day, which is celebrated worldwide on March 17, honors St. Patrick, the Christian missionary who supposedly rid Ireland of snakes during the fifth century A.D. But according to the official National Geographic website, this is an unlikely legend. Ireland is one of only a handful of places worldwide that is and always has been "a snake-free zone," suggesting the tale is allegorical. Serpents are symbols of evil in the Judeo-Christian tradition, so St. Patrick's dramatic act of snake eradication might more accurately be interpreted as a metaphor for his Christian influence.

According to the English standard Version Study Bible, today's passage from Mark, above, is questioned by some Biblical scholars; some believe verses 9 through 20 in Mark 16 were added at a later date and may not have been penned by Mark. Nowhere else in the New Testament does Jesus command the disciples to "pick up snakes with their hands…and drink deadly poison." But indisputably, throughout the New Testament, Jesus and His disciples were protected from all kinds of harm. Perhaps this passage is also meant to point the disciples—and us—to complete trust in the Almighty to protect those who go forth in His name to carry His message.

Please don't start picking up snakes and drinking poison in the name of Jesus! But remember God's promise to the psalmist: He "will command his angels concerning you to guard you in all your ways." If we trust Him, our God can be trusted to drive the metaphorical snakes out of our lives.

Father God, we know that You make all things work for good for those who follow You. Open our hearts and minds so we know that You are with us always. Amen

March 18

WHO YOU GONNA SERVE?

As for me and my house, we will serve the Lord. **Joshua 20:15**

In the March 2015 issue of AARP Magazine, Bob Dylan, at seventy-three, talked about his life, career and his album, *Shadows In The Night*, I've always thought Dylan was spot on with his *own* song lyrics when it came to describing life, but like many fans, didn't know much about the man.

I bought an album by Christian recording artist Nicole Nordeman, which includes the moving song, *Gotta Serve Somebody*. That song seemed to be written from the heart of someone who had...well, been around more than young Nordeman. I read that the song was written by Bob Dylan in 1979, during a period when Dylan had become a reborn Christian and even *preached* to thousands of his adoring concert fans. His personal faith has since retreated back to his private life, but I found this particular song riveting. I think I played it about sixty times in a row.

Gotta Serve Somebody was indeed written by someone with plenty of of personal angst under his belt. Dylan had been in a serious motorcycle accident in 1966, after which he went into seclusion for almost ten years. He accepted Christ and spent quality time with his family. The song says, "You might be a rock 'n' roll addict prancing on the stage/You might have drugs at your command, women in a cage...But you're gonna have to serve somebody, yes indeed/You're gonna have to serve somebody/Well, it may be the devil or it may be the Lord/But you're gonna have to serve somebody." Dylan's lyrics brought me up short and refreshed my memory once again. Whether I encounter rock stars or ordinary people on the street, I need God's reminder daily that He is in charge of other people's hearts.

Lord, You said You'd walk through the valley with us, and You do that with every person who asks You to. Convict my heart again that I have no idea what other people believe. Only You know their hearts. Amen

March 19

A KING ON A DONKEY?

Jesus found a young donkey and sat on it, as it is written: "Do not be afraid, Daughter of Zion; see, your king is coming, seated on a donkey's colt." John 12:14

It would have made so much more sense to the onlookers, that day we now call Palm Sunday, if Jesus had ridden in on a spirited white stallion, dressed in fine purple robes wearing a bejeweled crown. The people viewed His entry into Jerusalem as triumphant. Everyone thought Jesus had come to bring instant delivery from the Romans, but He didn't look like much of a conqueror with His simple cloak and working man's hands. The Old Testament prophesied this: "Your King is coming to you, righteous and having salvation is He, humble and mounted on a donkey…" (Zechariah 9:9). But the people seemed to have forgotten that prophesy.

But Jesus' popularity was not to last. Within five days, many of those same followers would be crying, "Crucify Him!" Prophets predicted this too (Isaiah 6:10). How could this have been part of God's plan? The very ones who were starting to "get it" about Jesus were going to turn on Him now and send Him to a painful death?

I shouted "Crucify Him!" once. Many of us did, as a "dramatic statement" during the reading of Scripture at a Good Friday service many years ago. Several of us rose, one at a time, and demanded the release of Barabbas, then we jumped up in unison and cried, "Crucify Him!" at the top of our lungs. We startled the congregation, but more importantly, we startled ourselves. What a strange feeling to be making that statement, with such conviction, even though it was all for show. The experience gave me a knot in my stomach and a feeling of acute guilt, and I still sometimes recall that visceral response when I know I have deeply failed my Lord. How tenderly He comes to me with love and mercy when I return to Him. He always forgives my momentary but frequent transgressions.

Humble King, we called You a fake when You were there to save us all. Praise You for Your everlasting love and forgiveness. Amen

March 20

SURPRISE PARTY!

Then Judas, the one who would betray him, said, "Surely you don't mean me, Rabbi?" Jesus answered, "You have said so." Matthew 26:25

Jesus was full of surprises. The disciples weren't expecting to hear what He revealed at the Last Supper. They were having a nice, quiet supper planned and carried out for their beloved Teacher. But then Jesus started blowing their minds, saying, "the Son of Man goes as it is written of him" (Mark 14:21). Judas would "betray" Him, they were told, although no one but Judas knew what that meant. Jesus called the bread His "body," and the wine His blood. He even washed the disciples' feet. Bold, hot-headed Peter refused, then relented and allowed this humble act of love. And off they go to the Garden of Gethsemane to pray.

Isn't this just like our lives? We pad along on our routine activities, never thinking our lives could be changed forever—or ended—in the blink of an eye. We as believers trust our God to see us through whatever comes our way in this life, and we believe we will see Him face to face when this life ends. In a way, we are blessed that we did *not* walk with Christ when He traveled this dimension called Earth. Unlike the disciples, we didn't have to watch helplessly as the events of "Holy Week" unfolded. We didn't watch with human eyes, as Judas did *indeed* betray Him, and the soldiers dragged Him off and tortured Him. We weren't in the crowd who yelled, Crucify Him!" We weren't at Calgary when they murdered him and let Him die a slow and agonizing death. All the bleeding was over by the time we got here.

This year, let's reflect on the meaning of Good Friday. The end which became a beginning, the sorrowful event which resulted in the most important news in the world: the resurrection of Jesus Christ on Easter morning.

Eternal God, Father, Son and Holy Spirit, shake us from our complacency like You shook the earth on Easter morning. Amen

March 21

TRUTH IS STRANGER THAN FICTION

Jesus answered, "I am the way and the truth and the life. No one comes to the Father except through me." **John 14:6**

As an author, I have written one memoir and one novel, but I've decided I like writing fiction better. Fiction is way more fun because you get to sit around in your pajamas all day, drink coffee and make stuff up. If you decide your main character has a big nose, that's your decision. Romance? No problem. Superhero, wealthy, good-looking, whatever you want, you can make it happen. It helps to have a plot. Oh, and your characters can't sue you, which is not always true with non-fiction.

When I was in college, I didn't read much fiction, unless you consider the examples in our Case Study class for my counseling major. But those really bordered more on fantasy, or maybe science fiction. Ordinary people couldn't possibly have that many issues. After I completed my master's program, I became a Christian, and then I devoured many inspirational works to learn more about faith in God. And of course, I read the Bible.

The Bible has been called a lot of things: a bunch of fables or allegories, a history book, and many more names. Scoffers and nonbelievers think God's Word can't be true because it is too preposterous to be real. We as Christians believe the Bible *is* God, and the words contained in its pages are *indeed* real. They are God-inspired, living, breathing, and moving inside of us. The Lord told Isaiah as the rain and snow water the earth and make it flourish. "So is My Word that goes out from my mouth: It will not return to me empty, but will accomplish what I desire and achieve the purpose for which I sent it." Human authors want their words to be read and enjoyed, and also found useful or entertaining. God's Word is much more powerful: His Word has the power to change lives, nations, and the world itself.

Almighty Father, You created in humans the ability to communicate in many ways. Help us stay the course to spread Your love in all we say, write and do. Amen

March 22

GET YOUR GOAT!

Truly I tell you, anyone who gives you a cup of water in my name because you belong to the Messiah will certainly not lose their reward. Mark 9:41

As a social worker in the 1970s in rural Minnesota, I had a tough client, an old farmer I'll call Jerome. He lived on an ancient farm site and raised a variety of animals—chickens, ducks, a couple of cows, goats—none of which were particularly well cared for. Jerome had recently lost his wife, and the county stepped in to help. There was a county health nurse and a couple of paraprofessional aides, and me, the "psycho-social" worker, each of us visiting Jerome at different times. All of us were female. But Jerome was belligerent and yelled at us, even groping some of those who helped with his personal care. Eventually, Jerome's entire "team" requested an audience with the county board. I trembled as we presented our case: discontinue all services to Jerome unless he could treat us with respect. I was dumfounded when the board members agree. We immediately terminated Jerome's case.

A few short weeks later, a young single mother came to her county worker, saying her newborn baby was allergic to her breast milk, any type of formula, and anything the doctors could come up with, except goat's milk. The worker asked if I knew anyone who raised goats. Jerome came to mind, but there were so many barriers… Fast forward a week later, when I dropped in at Jerome's farm out of curiosity and found Jerome cradling the baby while the young mother milked his goats. The two hit it off the minute they met. Jerome was lonely and grieving and barely able to care for his animals. The young mother was more than willing to help him with his chores in exchange for the milk her child so desperately needed to grow and thrive.

Isn't it wonderful how God hooks us up with just the right person at just the right time? It was a miracle for crabby Jerome and a desperate young mom!

God of Grace and Compassion, help us see places in Your world where we can give that cup of water. Amen

March 23

THE CURTAIN

And when Jesus had cried out again in a loud voice, He gave up his spirit. At that moment the curtain of the temple was torn in two from top to bottom. **Matthew 27:50-51**

One thing I love about writing this blog is getting to do a little research when I'm puzzled. I wondered why Jesus "giving up His spirit" was linked in Scripture to the tearing of the curtain in the temple. Hebrews 9:1-9 tells us a "veil" separated the area of the temple known as the "Holy of Holies," the earthly dwelling place of God's presence. Only the high priest was allowed to go beyond this curtain into the presence of God, and then only once a year (Exodus 30:10; Hebrews 9:7). It was clear that man's sin separated him from God (Isaiah 59:1-2), and the priest was responsible for passing through the curtain to make restitution.

This "veil" was no Walmart café curtain! First century historian, Josephus, recorded the veil was four inches thick and horses tied to each side could not pull the veil apart. And yet, the moment when Christ died on the cross, the curtain was completely torn in two! Another significant factor about this amazing event is the link between Christ's body being broken—in essence, *torn*—and the curtain being opened. Paul says, "We have confidence to enter the Most Holy Place by the blood of Jesus, by *a new and living way opened for us through the curtain*, that is, *His body*" (Hebrews 10:19-20, emphasis mine). Jesus not only died as atonement for the sins of humankind, but His selfless act ushered all who believe *directly into God's presence*. The curtain made of cloth was destroyed; in its place, we have Jesus Christ, the Son of God, walking boldly with us into firsthand fellowship with the Father. I imagine all who understood what the temple veil stood for were quaking in their boots. No wonder the centurion at Calvary said, "Surely this man was the Son of God!" (Mark 15:29)

Atoning King of Kings, thank You for going to the cross for my sins. You have opened the way for all believers to come into the presence of the Most High God. Amen

March 24

MULTIPLE GUESS TEST

Now when Jesus saw the crowds, He went up on a mountainside and sat down. His disciples came to Him, and He began to teach them. Matthew 5:1

When I was counseling at a two-year college in the early 1990s, I helped a student from Ukraine, a former Soviet republic, preparing to take a math entrance exam at our school, to determine which level courses were appropriate for him. In the study booklet, he showed me a page filled with multiple choice questions. He thought he had the wrong booklet, and I assured him that he had the correct study guide. He said, "In Russia, we don't guess. We learn the math *without* the answers." This was a grim reminder of why, over many years, Russian kids have performed better in math and science than kids in our nation. This Ukrainian guy was actually a math whiz and could have taught most of our courses himself!

What if Jesus' disciples wanted the things Jesus was teaching them to be presented in a more "student friendly" manner? So, after the Sermon on the Mount, Simon Peter might have said, "Are we supposed to know this?" And Andrew said, "Do we have to write this down?" James wanted to know if there would be a test, and Phillip didn't have any paper. Bartholomew's pencil was broken. John asked, "Did the other disciples have this same assignment?" Matthew needed to go to the bathroom, and Judas said, "What's this got to do with real life, anyway?" The little children, who had been allowed to sit on Jesus' lap during the lecture, asked when they could go for recess. A Pharisee came up and challenged Jesus to show the syllabus for His course and asked if it contained appropriate evaluation techniques, the policy on cheating, and details on how to find Jesus after class. Jesus' mom said, "Don't forget to make your language all-inclusive, Sweetie."

And Jesus wept.

Holy Teacher, deliver us from complacency when we hear Your Words over and over. These are the Words of Life, and You have promised to save us from testing! Amen

March 25

BLOOD PRESSURE: GETTING IT UP, GIVING IT UP

One of the soldiers pierced Jesus' side with a spear, bringing a sudden flow of blood and water. John 19:34

I have hypertension which is "controlled" with medication. But there was one time when *high* blood pressure was not my problem.

I needed a "revision" of my original total hip surgery eighteen months earlier. My hip implant was recalled, like an automobile when the accelerator sticks or the air bags won't deploy. I was sick for the year and a half I had the implant in, but until the body part company recalled their product, no one could figure out what was wrong with me. After the surgery, as the team was moving me to my hospital bed, I heard one of them say, "BP 80 over 40." Half asleep, I rose up off the bed and exclaimed, *"What did you say?"* I had lost a lot of blood during the procedure, and had a difficult first night. The next day, I was the lucky recipient of two units of transfused blood. I was never in danger of losing my life, but it was a scary experience.

The gospel accounts indicate that Jesus died less than six hours after He was nailed to the cross, much sooner than the expected twenty-four hours or more. This raises the question, how did His life on earth actually end? He had been brutally beaten, and nails were used to secure Him to the cross, whereas other condemned prisoners were tied to their crosses. So He might have lost a lot of blood, which normally leads first to unconsciousness, then gradual death. The gospels indicate that Jesus was fully conscious, even talking to His mother and brother, and to the Father. John reported, Jesus said, "It is finished," and bowed His regal head and gave up the fight (John 19:30). All of this has left Bible scholars—and me—to wonder if Jesus "chose" the moment of His death by stopping His own heart as part of this mysterious plan to save the world.

O Sacred Son of God, You took such unspeakable punishment for my sins! If I had been there, I could not have stood to watch. Thank You for Your unimaginable sacrifice. Amen

March 26

DETAILS AT TEN

Then you will know the truth, and the truth will set you free. John 8:32

Canadian pop singer Ann Murray, popular during the 1970s, recorded a song called *A Little Good News*. The lyrics detailed a typical day in which we hear a lot of bad news. How nice it would be to turn on the television and hear the words of the chorus:

Nobody robbed a liquor store on the lower part of town/Nobody OD'd, nobody burned a single building down/Nobody fired a shot in anger...nobody had to die in vain
We sure could use a little good news today

As Christians, we know the true Good News comes from the gospel of Jesus Christ. "Gospel" means "truth," and nothing is more true to believers than Jesus' life on earth and death on a cross. Skeptics say Christ's story could not have happened the way the Bible says because there is no proof, that all the "eye witnesses" would have been dead before the New Testament was written. Twentieth century biblical archaeologist William Albright concluded the biblical accounts of history were largely accurate. John A. T. Robinson, a contemporary of Albright, discovered that other scholars he had respected had not been honest with evidence purported to show when New Testament books were written. Robinson concluded that *all* New Testament writings were written by AD 45, in time for eye witnesses to still be alive to write them. And what we know about those eye witnesses is they believed strongly enough in what they said had actually happened, they were willing to—and in many cases did—die for those beliefs.

It sure would be wonderful if we could tune in for "details at ten" and hear the *true and important* account about Jesus!

Lord Jesus, we believe in You and we believe the accounts recorded in the Bible of the mighty deeds You did when you walked the earth. Help us to endure the bad news and focus on the good. Amen

March 27

REDUCED TO RUBBLE

For dust you are and to dust you shall return. **Genesis 3:19**

In 2012, my husband and I made a trip to my home state of Colorado. The deep greens and browns of the mountain ranges, some with snow caps, the clear, cold streams, and the jewel-toned turquois sky were all just as I remembered. But while we were traveling around the state, each place we left suddenly succumbed to sweeping forest fires. We broke camp one morning in Rocky Mountain National Park and by nightfall, there was a raging blaze not far from our campsite. As we left Colorado Springs, the Waldo Canyon fire was just beginning, causing the evacuation of 32,000 area residents. Treasure, Weber, Flagstaff, and Ironing Board were names given to other Colorado fires that June, reducing the gorgeous scenery to rubble.

Ash Wednesday is the first day of the season of Lent, when ashes are applied to people's foreheads in the sign of a cross, to signify an inner repentance. When Adam and Eve committed the original sin by eating the forbidden fruit, God told them they had come from dust (ashes) and would return there (Genesis 3:19). Today's imposition of ashes is a reminder of our sinfulness and mortality, and our need to repent. The sign of the cross on the forehead signifies the good news that Jesus Christ brought through His crucifixion: there is forgiveness of all sins for those who accept Christ.

Even though they are devastating, forest fires are part of God's plan too. The intense heat from the fires breaks open the seeds on the forest floor, promoting new life out of what appears to be destroyed forever. How like God's way this is: from the ashes of sin, sorrow and destruction, we can rise into the life and love of the Savior Who chose to die for us, even though we were undeserving. God's grace makes a way where there appears to be no way.

Atoning Father, grant that we may be made new in the sacrifice of Your Son. Help us see new life in our ashes and hope in the sign of the cross. Amen

March 28

BLANK PAGE

Now the earth was formless and empty, darkness was over the surface of the deep, and the Spirit of God was hovering over the waters. **Genesis 1:2**

My son-in-law is an architect, and I have a degree in interior design. We both like to create things. We once had a lively discussion at an art fair about the excitement we each have when we consider a blank page—sketch pad, water color paper, canvas—before embarking on some sort of artistic creation. My daughter, whose gifts do not include art, gave us a puzzled look while her husband and I talked about that moment when the wheels in our brains start turning as we decide how to begin a new "masterpiece."

I imagine the angels watched God as He poised above the "formless and empty" void that would soon be called "Earth." The Spirit of God "was hovering over the waters," with a divinely detailed idea in His mind. He raised His mighty arms and began to "paint" the world as we know it into existence. God created light and darkness and separated the waters from the dry land. Vegetation came next, followed by a great light for daytime and a "lesser" light for night. Sea creatures and living things on the land followed, and on the sixth day, God created man. *Then God blessed the seventh day and made it holy, because on it He rested from all the work of creating that He had done* (Genesis 2:3). Artists know the feeling of completing a work of art with one's own hands is a very satisfying sensation indeed!

Even if you only draw stick people, there is something you do that, when it's completed, gives you a great sense of fulfillment. Whatever that is, the next time you finish, take a moment to thank God for His wonderful creation and the talents which you possess. You'll feel even better in the act of gratitude, and God can say of your work, "It is good."

Creator God, You have given each of us talents that we may not use or appreciate. Shine Your loving light on the things we do and make to Your glory, and give us the confidence to keep on keeping on. Amen

March 29

EVICTION NOTICE

Early on the first day of the week, while it was still dark, Mary Magdalene went to the tomb and saw that the stone had been removed from the entrance. **John 20:1**

When I think about that first Easter morning, my mind gets all wonky. After the crucifixion, Joseph the Arimathean had gone "boldly to Pilate and asked for (some translations say "craved") the body of Jesus" (John 19:38). He was a high council member but a secret follower of Jesus and took a huge risk. Pilate' guards so none of Jesus' followers would steal His body and claim He rose from the dead (Matthew 27:65-66).

Those guards took off when a violent earthquake hit and an angel rolled the stone away (Matthew 28:2). Mary Magdalene and "the other Mary" found the tomb empty at dawn (Luke 24:1). Jesus appeared just then. "Greetings," He said, like they just had seen each other a half hour ago. He told the women not to be afraid, and to go tell the others.

What was Jesus thinking while He was in that tomb? Alone and cold, and wrapped up like the dead body everyone thought He was, at what point did He say, "Well, that's enough of this! I think it's time to rock the world!" You'd think He'd be a little under the weather after all He'd just been through. But He could heal everybody else, so He could certainly pull Himself together. He even took time to fold the shroud that had been wrapped around Him. (His mother must have been so proud!) Was He hiding behind a Joshua tree when the angel spoke to the women, so He could surprise them with the Good News, the turning point for all of mankind? We'll never know what was going through Jesus' mind that day, but we know He went through it all to save us from our own sin-sick selves.

Atoning Savior, this Easter season, grant that each of us can grasp at least part of the magnitude of the sacrifice You made for us! Thank You for Your loving grace that made all of this happen. Amen

March 30

CALVARY OR CAVALRY?

***When Jesus' followers saw what was going to happen, they said, "Lord, should we strike with our swords?" And one of them struck the servant of the high priest, cutting off his right ear.* Luke 22:49-50**

I once read a Good Friday devotion about Mount *Calvary*, but there was a typo, and instead it read, Mount *Cavalry*. The word "cavalry" was mistakenly associated with Jesus' betrayal and arrest, trial, and sacrifice on the cross. Perhaps the writer thought someone should have charged in and saved Jesus! His disciples were willing to come to His defense when Judas led the soldiers to Him. One even chopped off the ear of the high priest's servant. Knowing what was coming, Jesus took compassion on the servant and healed his ear instantly, telling His disciples not to become violent.

What might I have done if I had been there with Jesus that night? *I wouldn't have fallen asleep!* It should have been so obvious to these men who were so close to Jesus that He was in great distress, praying so hard He sweat blood. But I'm not much of a night owl, and any kind of stress just wears me out. So maybe I *would* have slept while Christ prayed. I am *certain* I would have been outraged at Judas forsaking Jesus the way he did (Mark 14:44)! *I would never do that!* But would I later have stood with Peter, more concerned with warming my hands over a courtyard fire than standing up for the Man Who loved me like no other (Luke 22:57)? It is so easy to say we would have defended Christ—*led the cavalry to Calgary*—but would we really have had the strength to take action to save our Friend, even if it meant to die trying?

Jesus knew His followers would betray Him, but He went to that cross anyway. And now He is the One Who leads the Heavenly Cavalry, doing battle with the forces of evil in our lives every day.

King Jesus, thank You for charging in and keeping me safe from the enemies of spiritual warfare. Keep me vigilant each day when the enemy comes prowling like a hungry lion. Amen

March 31

WASH, RINSE, REPEAT

Though your sins are like scarlet, they shall be as white as snow; though they are red as crimson, they shall be like wool. Isaiah 1:18

I intensely dislike housework more than almost anything else in life! Housework is so *endless!* I vacuum and mop, and five minutes later, there is dog hair all over the floor. I wash, dry and fold clothes and the laundry basket miraculously fills up again. Dishes can all be organized in their proper cupboards and suddenly, there is another sink full. While I'm on my way to dress for company, I discover dust an inch thick in a place I hadn't even noticed before. My "to do" pile grows exponentially while my "nice and pretty" house continues its march into oblivion.

My sins are like this too. Just when I think I have a handle on gossip, something unplanned slips out of my mouth. I think I have my use of four-letter words under control when a driver cuts me off and I blurt out an expletive. My sunny attitude guides me into a leadership role, but then I suffer from a serious attack of self-doubt, making me think I should be laying low instead of modeling for others how to live a Christian life.

In Frank Peretti's 2003 novel *This Present Darkness*, angels and demons engage in lively spiritual warfare, affecting the lives of the book's characters. This novel was a major player in my early understanding of "the powers of this dark world and…the spiritual forces of evil in the heavenly realms" (Ephesians 6:12). Peter tells us, *Be alert and of sober mind. Your enemy the devil prowls around like a roaring lion looking for someone to devour* (1 Peter 5:8). This same passage tells us about the "armor" God provides us to fight off Satan, enabling us to walk in God's light. When we do mess up, God promises to "wash, rinse and repeat" *every time* until our sins are "white as snow."

Healing Father, help us to be ready for Satan's attacks and to use all the tools You have given us to thwart his influence on our lives. Amen

April

April 1

GRACE AT THE CAPITOL

But he said to me, "My grace is sufficient for you, for my power is made perfect in weakness." Therefore I will boast all the more gladly about my weaknesses, so that Christ's power may rest on me.
2 Corinthians 12:9

Each year, an Action Day is held at the Minnesota State Capitol. Many concerns are represented, domestic and sexual violence among them. I attend for my own continued healing and to support others and to speak to legislators about the need for increased funding for crime victims' services.

Last year, I brought along my beloved Teddy bear, Amazing Grace, who was given to me by the El Paso County Sheriff's Department when I visited them on the fortieth anniversary of the assault on a mountain in their Colorado jurisdiction. In addition to this soft and cuddly stuffed animal, I received an official apology for the unconscionable treatment I received in 1972. I also was escorted by three officers, packing heat, in a department vehicle to the place where the assault occurred. Although the assailant was never found, I experienced profound peace as I walked off that mountain the second time, holy and blameless, saved and free.

The assault was a turning point in my life. It took years for me to realize I was not at fault for the assault, and God loved me immeasurably and delivered me from a sure death in order that I might help other trauma victims. The Israelites took forty years to make a two-week trip to get from Egypt to the Promised Land. God knew they were "a stiff-necked people," and He led them around in the wilderness until He felt they were ready to listen to Him. I would not change anything about the order of events in my life because I know I am right where God wants me to be: in His loving arms and willing to listen.

Saving Father, this broken world is full of sorrow and pain. Forgive those who have wronged us and help us use our memories to stay safe. Amen

April 2

UNCONDITIONAL POSITIVE REGARD

There is no fear in love. But perfect love drives out fear, because fear has to do with punishment. The one who fears is not made perfect in love. 1 John 4:18

In counseling training, I learned about Carl Rogers, a twentieth century American Psychologist who developed the "person-centered" approach to psychotherapy. Rogers was noted for *unconditional positive regard*. He said, "The individual has within him or herself vast resources for self-understanding, for altering her or his self-concept, attitudes, and self-directed behavior." In other words, it is up to us to choose whether we will approach others with love, or with built-in baggage.

Countless people have benefited from Rogers' psychotherapy techniques by learning to accept themselves and take responsibility for what they do and say. But didn't Jesus have this theory down pat long before Rogers was ever born? In fact, one of Rogers' protégés David G. Meyer gave a distinctly Christian spin in describing Rogers' method: "This is an attitude of *grace…* that values us even knowing our failings… a profound relief to drop our pretenses, *confess* our worst feelings, and discover that we are *still accepted*" (italics mine). Sounds a whole lot like what Jesus said.

Jesus told the accusers of the alleged adulterous, *"Let any one of you who is without sin be the first to throw a stone"* (John 8:7). He used His own saliva to wipe the blind man's eyes, but when the man said the people looked like "trees walking around," Jesus touched his eyes a second time until he saw more clearly (Mark 8:22-15). Jesus touched and healed countless lepers—the "untouchables"—without a second thought. And He will touch and heal each of us, even while knowing all about our shortcomings. Now *that's* "unconditional positive regard!"

Healing Jesus, You are the Personification of "all-inclusive." Help us to do our best to get that concept right while we walk this earth. And praise You that You approach us, always, with "unconditional positive regard," also known as Divine Love. Amen

April 3

THIS WAY OUT

No temptation has overtaken you except what is common to mankind. And God is faithful; He will not let you be tempted beyond what you can bear. But when you are tempted, He will also provide a way out so that you can endure it. **1 Corinthians 10:13**

When I was a teenager in Colorado, I worked a summer job in the gift shop at the Cave of the Winds. Only the boys were allowed to be cave guides because of an old mining law prohibiting females from working underground. But the law didn't say we couldn't date each other, which we did with great abandon. At the end of each summer, a year-end employees' party was held, during which we got to explore the cave on our own, hopefully with a cute guy as our date.

Invariably, someone (most likely male) would turn out all the lights in the cave to scare the others (most likely female). The darkness was total and all-encompassing; it would have been impossible to find the way out.

God tells us that we are never alone in the dark of sin. When faced with temptation, we can always find a morally right solution if we call on Him. Because of our human frailty, that "way out" may not appear to be clear at first. But if we are rooted and grounded in God's Word, through prayer and studying the Scriptures, our tender minds will quickly be able to call up an honorable response. We won't always get it right, but God appreciates our efforts towards living a holy, balanced life. Forgiveness is ours if we ask, and repentance is especially sweet to the Lord if we learn from our mistakes.

The next time the lights go out in your life and you find yourself on the brink of disappointing God, remember that you hold His hand in the dark, and He will turn the lights on in the cave of your distress.

Abiding Father, take me by the hand when I am walking through dark shadows. Steer me in the way You want me to go, and imprint on my mind the lessons Christ came to teach us. Amen

April 4

JOHN THREE SIXTEEN

For God so loved the world that he gave His one and only Son, that whoever believes in Him shall not perish but have eternal life. For God did not send His Son into the world to condemn the world, but to save the world through Him. **John 3:16-17**

In my novel, *Perils of a Polynesian Percussionist*, I have a character named John Three Sixteen. John plays steel guitar in a Hawaiian revue band, but more importantly, he serves as the moral compass for the odd assortment of musicians traveling with the show. The character idea came from a very vocal but perhaps misguided man who used to dress in sackcloth and walk the Las Vegas Strip carrying a sign that said "Repent! The time is near!" In my novel, John Three Sixteen has a gentler approach, seeking quiet moments when he might impart the Word of God to others over coffee.

The oft-quoted words of John 3:16 have been called "the Gospel in a nutshell." The concept that God loved "the world" and not just the people of Israel was news to the Jews! They had always been God's "chosen people," but the idea that God was now including *all people* in His amazing love had to have upset the Pharisee's apple cart. In this verse, we see that *whoever believes in (this Son) shall not perish but have eternal life.* Not only can *anybody* claim this promise, but those who do will enjoy endless blessings in *this* life *and eternally* in heaven when this life is over.

But the *next* verse, John 3:17, is equally important in telling the story of Christ's redemptive work on earth. The Bible makes it clear that Jesus is God's Son, born both fully human and fully divine. Plus, Jesus is God's delegate to carry His message of love and grace, *not* judgment. Jesus comes to *save the world*, not to find blame in us. Jesus doesn't carry a sign like the guy on the Vegas Strip. Jesus *is* the sign. He is "the way, the truth and the life" (John 14:6).

Jesus, Redeemer, praise You for coming into this fallen world of human frailty, and for caring enough to offer salvation to anyone who believes in You. Amen

April 5

DON'T STRAIN YOUR BRAIN!

But we have the mind of Christ. **1 Corinthians 2:16**

In a *Reader's Digest Magazine* article, I recently learned that a study at the University of Rochester supplies evidence to support the theory that the brain needs sleep. Apparently, the brain performs maintenance on itself during sleep, casting out the "junk" that builds up in brain cells during the day *as a by-product of thinking*. Without enough sleep, our noggin clogs up and actual *chemical waste* accumulates. This "garbage collection" may cause an increased risk of several types of dementia, including Alzheimer's disease.

But wait, did the study say *garbage* accumulates from *thinking*? Is there any difference in the "garbage" we gather if we think about positive things as opposed to negative? Do practicing Christians amass as much "brain trash" as, say, deranged terrorists hoping to obliterate everyone in their path?

The Bible certainly has plenty to say about how we care for our brains. How to "have the mind of Christ" is laid out conveniently in a number of helpful passages. Paul states that, when I am "crucified with Christ," it is no longer I who live in this earthly vessel, but Christ Who lives in me.

As for rest, Genesis 2:2 states even God took a breather after He created the world. He made that seventh day holy, to be observed by us forever. In Mark 6:31, Jesus tells His disciples, "Come with me by yourselves to a quiet place and get some rest." The God Who built our brains knows what is needed to keep them humming along at optimal level. So what's it going to take for you to do what your mother always told you to do, "Get some rest?" Your brain and your mom will be happy. God will too.

Restoring Savior, help us to slow down and live quietly in Your beautiful world! Our modern ways have caused many of us to neglect the peace and beauty You provide for us, even on our busiest days. Remind us again of the value of resting in Your loving embrace. Amen

April 6

SLIGHTLY TARNISHED

All have sinned and fall short of the glory of God. **Romans 3:23**

My friend and college roommate, Jan had a long and hard labor with her first son, and was transported to a bigger hospital in the middle of the ordeal. The experience was quite overwhelming for this new mom. When it was over, she just wanted to rest and could not deal with the idea that her son was not doing well. Some neighbors she hardly knew offered to pray for the baby. She responded, "Yeah, sure, whatever." When her son made a miraculous recovery, Jan gave God the credit and never turned back.

When Jan's first child was about four years old, the band in which I played drums went to my home town, Colorado Springs, Colorado, where Jan and her family lived. They came to hear us perform, and as I predicted, Jan stuck a religious tract under my nose and started trying to "convert" me. "I'm not a sinner!" I shrieked at her. "I've never robbed a bank or murdered anybody. I don't need your Jesus!" Jan shrank back in dismay (I can still see her face) and never mentioned Jesus to me again. It was years before I "hit bottom" and realized I needed Jesus in my life too.

Through the years, I've learned that for me, being a Christian is more about "attraction" rather than "promotion" (to borrow one of the Alcoholics Anonymous' Twelve Traditions). I can comfortably use the word "saved," but I'm more likely to say I was lost and then found. I know I cannot be strong by myself, but it is with God's strength that I face each new challenge in my life. Pride of self has gradually been replaced by contentment in becoming who God wants me to be. Most importantly, I now know that I am a sinner, but that Christ has paid the full price for my sin, rendering me holy and blameless before God.

Compassionate Lord, thank You for answering the fervent prayer of those who love You. Help each of us to carry Your message in whatever fashion You wish, and let that message change other's lives like it has ours. Amen

April 7

THE WRITING ON THE WALL

Suddenly the fingers of a human hand appeared and wrote on the plaster of the wall, near the lampstand in the royal palace. The king watched the hand as it wrote. **Daniel 5:5-6**

In 1992, I visited "new" Berlin. Soviet troops were being withdrawn from what had been "East Berlin," the post-WWII communist-controlled portion of the city established from 1949 until two years after my visit. The occupying Soviets "goose-stepped" through the city as we tourists gawked. Checkpoint Charlie, crossing point between the East (communist) and West (free) portions of the city, was still staffed by Allied and Russian soldiers.

Berlin was trying hard to establish a post-Cold War economy, and tourism was on the list of new ventures. Our hotel was a run-down former barracks for troops and their families. Small, double-occupancy rooms featured bare linoleum floors, a mid-twentieth century bath, and a huge armoire in place of a closet. Hidden plumbing fixtures had supplied water to a single-wall kitchenette. The twin iron cots had springs under lumpy mattresses, but on each pillow, the hotel staff had placed a green peppermint candy.

We also saw the Berlin Wall, built in 1961 to stop emigration from East to West. Many were gunned down while attempting to escape the oppression in the East. Now, the great human spirit had risen with a paint brush to squelch all memory of those evil days. Still mostly intact when I visited, the entire barrier was covered with graffiti in many languages, declaring sweet freedom in all the colors of the rainbow. This brightly embellished barricade reminded me of another wall in the book of Daniel. Both walls foretold the end of cruel oppression and the coming of a better life under new rulers (Daniel 5:22-30). The Berlin story encourages us that God is faithful to His people and will have the last word over human oppression.

God of Freedom, we know You want all Your people on earth to dwell in peace with no worries of oppression. Until that day comes, sustain us with Your Word and Your grace. Amen

April 8

BELL IN MY HEART

For I am not ashamed of the gospel, because it is the power of God that brings salvation to everyone who believes. **Romans 1:16**

One summer in college, I took a Romantic Literature course. I memorized this line: "Your name is like a bell inside my heart. I would tear my body to pieces just to hear the sound of it one time." I was in love, once again, with some guy who didn't stand the test of time (I had a number of those in my youth), but I never forgot this poignant, love-struck line. I can't remember what book or author it was from, and could not find the source in my mother's 1923 copy of Bartlett's Familiar Quotations or by "Googling" it.

How many of us have had these impermanent romances? The fleeting, here-today-gone-next-semester kind of romances capture our attention, but perhaps not our hearts in a lasting way. And if and when we finally are blessed to find "the right one," most of us can't wait to have everyone meet this new, golden "love interest." Our parents, siblings, best friends, coworkers, the barista we buy our morning coffee from, all hear us say with a huge grin, "I just can't wait for you to meet him/her!" I did this exact thing when I met my husband Patrick—and I was forty-nine years old!

Are we as bold about wanting those we know to hear about the God Who lives inside of us every day? We believe He is "the right one" for us, our Best Friend, our Mentor and Guide, the Author and Finisher of our faith (Hebrews 12:2 KJV). Why don't we "talk him up" like we do other important things and people in our lives? Paul says in Romans 1:16 that he's not ashamed to share the gospel, because he saw God's power first hand when he was blinded on the road to Damascus, and then redeemed and declared fit to serve God. Who wouldn't want that ending for a love story?

All Powerful God, inspire me daily to share Your Word with those I meet. I don't want You ever to be ashamed of me, so please keep me from being ashamed of You. Amen

April 9

TAKE THAT, SATAN!

I saw Satan fall from heaven like lightning. **Luke 10:18**

It was only for a few seconds I saw his eyes change. The man who had just raped me stood holding a chain with which he intended to shackle me to a tree and leave me in a mountain forest in Colorado. I cried, "In the name of God, don't do this!" I watched those eyes change beneath his bandana. Those eyes—the eyes of Satan—suddenly became soft and timid. But Satan reared his ugly head again and the eyes grew dark again. "Don't talk about God!" the man screamed, as he knocked me to the ground. Then he turned and ran down the mountain, escaping on a motorcycle I heard in the distance.

In Luke 10, Jesus commissioned "seventy-two others" besides His twelve, sending them out to the villages and roadways "like lambs among wolves," to heal the sick and bring peace to those who would accept it. When they returned, overjoyed at all they were able to accomplish in His name, Jesus told them He had watched in His mind's eye as they caused "Satan to fall from heaven like lightning."

Did I momentarily cast Satan out of the rapist that awful day on a Colorado mountain? I didn't even believe in God at that time, and yet it seemed that just invoking God's name was enough to throw the man off guard, most likely saving my life. Do you believe you have the power to "overcome all the authority of the enemy?" (Luke 10:19) I pray none of my readers will ever have to endure an assault as I did, but I believe with all my heart, if I could change the course of a life-threatening event in my own life, other believers are able to do the same too.

April is Sexual Assault Awareness Month. Please be mindful of others who might be vulnerable and take appropriate action if possible to help potential victims.

All-Powerful God, save us from earthly trials and embolden us to use Your power as You intended for us to do. Amen

April 10

EAR WORMS

Fix these words of Mine in your hearts and minds; tie them as symbols on your hands and bind them on your foreheads. **Deuteronomy 11:18**

Have you ever had a song running through your head and you just can't stop it? The phenomenon is called an "ear worm" and can make you feel like you literally have a brain parasite. There is a physiological reason for these tunes taking over our minds, actions and conversations. The "ear worm" becomes embedded in a "phonological loop," a short-term memory system in the auditory cortex which stores a small amount of aural information such as the chorus of a song. Songs appear to remain in the short-term memory for longer than other data—like commercial jingles that haunt you even though you can't remember what the ad was for!

I know a woman whose worst "ear worm" is "Happy Trails," the old Roy Rogers theme song. She can be hung up on that song for weeks if she hears it, and her friends tease her by singing it to her whenever they part company. (You're singing, "Happy Trails to yoooooooou, until we meet again…" just from hearing me mention this, right?)

I love all kinds of music, but I listen mostly to contemporary Christian songs. If I have to have an "ear worm," I mind it less if it has an uplifting message. I'd rather be stuck with an Amy Grant tune than to be captivated by something by the Rolling Stones. Maybe the Holy Spirit places "ear worms" in my brain (and I don't mean the Rolling Stones song!). Sometimes I even wake up singing "Amazing Grace" or some other well-known hymn. In today's Scripture selection, Deuteronomy 11:18, God is telling us that He wants us to "embed" His words in our hearts and minds, and to affix them to our hands and foreheads. Maybe God even invented the "ear worm" as a way to bring His Word to our minds!

Father, You know what is best for us. Fill our minds with good things so we remember all You want to teach us. Amen

April 11

A CHILE PEPPER MOMENT

How beautiful on the mountains are the feet of those who bring good news, who proclaim peace, who bring good tidings, who proclaim salvation, who say to Zion, "Your God reigns!" Isaiah 52:7

Rushing around the supermarket, I stopped at the fresh chile bin to buy some *anchos* and *poblanos* for a mildly spicy dish Mexican dish. She was standing there too, looking puzzled. "Do you know anything about fresh chiles?" she asked me. "Yes," I replied, "I lived in New Mexico and I cook with chiles all the time." Thus began a conversation which somehow led to the fact that we both came from difficult homes, and were continuing the healing process into our adulthoods. We met for coffee a few days later and I listened as this woman poured out her heart to me. I was happy to listen; I'd been there too. She said it helped to talk to me. Soon it was clear our acquaintance was just "for a season," and not meant to last forever.

Fellow Christian author and friend Mary Treacy O'Keefe has written two books compiling stories of people who heed hunches and nudges, dreams and rainbows, believing that they are somehow directed to another person for a reason. In *Thin Places* and *Meant-To-Be Moments: Discovering What We Are Called to Do and Be*, O'Keefe chronicles stories of people motivated by serendipity. They believe that "hosts" of beings—angels, departed saints and even God Himself—are out there to help us discover a whole new way to respond to others.

How often are we open to God's direction if it comes in unexpected ways? Are we willing to allow God to work *through* us, not just *in* us? What exciting service adventures await God's beloved as we travel this road called life!

Empowering Father, we know the peace we have felt when others have shown us Your love. Help us to be those people with the beautiful feet that Isaiah 52:7 tells about. Amen

April 12

THE PEOPLE IN YOUR NEIGHBORHOOD

Love the Lord your God with all your heart and with all your soul and with all your strength and with all your mind; and, Love your neighbor as yourself. Luke 10:27

Fred McFeely Rogers fell in love with puppets as a child, and graduated magna cum laude with a degree in music composition. He began hosting children's television programs, which led him to obtain a divinity degree. The Presbyterian Church asked him to continue to serve children and families through television. *Mr. Roger's Neighborhood* was born in 1968 and ran until 2001, shortly before Rogers death. In his later years, he said, "I went into television because I hated it so, and I thought there's some way of using this fabulous instrument to nurture those who would watch and listen."

And listen and watch we did. Mr. Rogers had a gentle way of bringing the message of God to children and adults alike, through the 200-plus songs he wrote. His endearing puppets inhabited his "Neighborhood of Make Believe." King Friday XIII, Queen Sara Saturday (named after his wife), and Henrietta Pussycat "helped" Rogers learn how things worked or were made and took "field trips" to various sites in the "neighborhood." No "preaching" went on, but Rogers' endearing persona, his "sneakers" and his cardigan sweater allowed viewers to rest and reflect on all that is good.

Today's television is "loud and proud." If something isn't being blown up on an action/adventure series, or the news media isn't bringing us "the worst of the worst," today's viewer might be bored. Even Biblical fiction in recent years focuses more on the bloody and violent than on love. Is it too late to have a "Mr. Rogers Neighborhood"? I believe God still wants us to have a quiet experience, a "Sabbath rest," which happens only when we sit back, turn off the noise of today's world, and listen quietly to God's beauty and love. Sneakers and cardigans are optional.

Father of Peace, guide us in our quest for personal peace and quiet, and let our efforts spill over onto those we cherish. Amen

April 13

WAITING IMPATIENTLY

Those who wait for the Lord shall renew their strength, they shall mount up with wings like eagles, they shall run and not be weary, they shall walk and not faint. Isaiah 40:31

It's trying to be spring here in Minnesota, the Land of the Frozen Chosen. Avid gardeners wait all winter since our growing season here is so short. We can't plant tender seedlings until the middle of May, when all chance of frost is gone. We are naturally impatient because we've only got a certain number of weeks before Old Man Winter whistles his sinister tune and blows frigid winds over our garden plots and hanging pots. I even have an impatient sign in my veggie garden that screams, "Grow, Damn It!"

Sometimes we are impatient waiting for the Lord to act as quickly as *we* think He should. We try to will God to work faster, even knowing His timing is perfect. "Hurry, God!" we cry. God must be yukking it up in His big easy chair in heaven, while he sips a leisurely cup of coffee and says to His angels, "This is going to take a *little* more time than My child on earth has in mind."

We are like northern gardeners, yanking up a plant and saying, "Grow, damn it!" before we've even given the sun and the rain and the worms and *God* time to produce a healthy outcome! God already knows the results of our requests anyway, but it's up to Him to reveal it to us "in the fullness of time." When we ask God for something without *first asking that His will be done*, we are interfering with a perfect process which is not ours to mess with. Let's pray instead for patience, trust and faith that God is in control. Because, guess what? He is.

Father of Eternity, You invented time and it is Yours to manage, not ours. Temper our impatience and strengthen us in our trust that You know the right time for all things to happen. Amen

April 14

THESE DREAMS

Daniel went in to the king and asked for time, so that he might interpret the dream for him. **Daniel 2:16**

"These dreams go on when I close my eyes/Every second of the night I live another life/These dreams that sleep when it's cold outside/Every moment I'm awake the further I'm away." So go the 1986 lyrics of a song recorded by the rock group Heart. The song tells of a woman descending into a fantasy world whenever she falls asleep. Reality and make-believe cannot be distinguished from each other. She wants to "hide away from the pain."

I have suffered from nightmares since I was assaulted at gun point at age twenty-five. I found the Heart song's lyrics described exactly how I felt when I descended into my "dream world." My dreams were never about the assault, but were disturbing nonetheless. I have dreamed the senior center calls to tell me my mother has come back to life and I must resume caring for her immediately. It was my fault she died the first time. Many disasters have visited my dreams, from flaming car accidents to Apocalyptic-type wars. "Get the net," you must be saying by now! "This girl needs some serious therapy!" Either that, or you think I should call an exorcist.

I have chosen a different way to deal with my nightmares. I have decided to trust God. I do not know where these dreams come from, but I know whether I am awake or asleep, God will take good care of me. I don't profess to have supernatural powers like Daniel, to interpret these dreams as he did for King Nebuchadnezzar. But the point of this whole story of Daniel and the king's dream is that Daniel gave one hundred per cent of the glory for the solution of the puzzle to the One True God (Daniel 4:24). God honored Daniel's humility and protected him, and God will do the same for me, no matter how wacky my dreams may be.

Lord of Peace, grant that I may be comforted by Your enduring love. Whether I wake or sleep, watch over me and hold me in Your loving arms. Amen

April 15

COMMUNITY

Day by day, as they spent much time together in the temple, they broke bread at home and ate their food with glad and generous hearts. Acts 2:46

"Waits at the window, wearing the face that she keeps in a jar by the door. Who is it for?" These lyrics from Paul McCartney's song, "Eleanor Rigby," speak of a profoundly lonely woman who "lives in a dream." Does the face in the jar hide her sadness, and from whom is she hiding? Poor Eleanor is so isolated, when she dies, her name dies with her. An equally isolated priest, Father McKenzie, apparently officiates at Eleanor's burial, but neither he nor she has garnered any support for the occasion. Father McKenzie's parish, if indeed he has one, seems to be completely devoid of congregants. "All the lonely people," the lyrics wail, "where do they all belong?"

A visiting pastor and a very wise man named Tim Hackbarth told our congregation recently that "isolation grows out of mistrust, but community grows out of integrity." Pastor Hackbarth's words set my mind to spinning about people who are marginalized in our society. Like Eleanor Rigby.

In Bible times, there wasn't much these "fringe dwellers" could expect from society, except perhaps a few morsels of food from those who had plenty. Today, a great fear has gripped the land that someone "different" might be dangerous. Indeed they might, but are we willing to brave at least some situations to show the love of God to another? Can we risk a smile, a hand, a dollar bill? Are there Eleanor Rigbys and Father McKenzies in your life, and can you reach out to them today? Can you show them the Gospel message with some small act of kindness? Jesus calls us to carry His message to the ends of the earth. Let's start with the edge of our comfort zones.

Father of Compassion, stir us to walk with You in integrity within our houses and in places we frequent. Protect us as we do Your work and help us identify those people whom You want us to include in our community. Amen

April 16

RETIRED? FROM WHAT?

His master said to him, "Well done, good and trustworthy servant; you have been trustworthy in a few things, I will put you in charge of many things; enter into the joy of your master." Matthew 25:21

While I was working at my job, I thought I knew what retirement would be like. I would sleep late, eat breakfast with my husband, read good books for hours, garden in the summer, cross-country ski in the winter. The grandchildren, who would all live in our neighborhood, would come to our house after school for milk and cookies. There would be nice, long trips in the winter to warm places like Florida and Hawaii. In the summer, we'd take the dogs and go to the lake where we would do more sleeping, reading and eating, along with fishing and hiking in the bucolic woods.

What was I thinking? My writing "career" involves speaking engagements, meetings, and "networking" activities. Breakfast together might happen once a week. Only one of our kids lives nearby. But *their* kids are in so many activities, the parents have considered starting a taxi company. The dogs have gotten old faster than we did, and they hate riding in the car. I've had so many joint surgeries, I don't trust myself to get on my old skis, fearing I would fall down and freeze to death on the spot. My once-gorgeous gardens have succumbed to neglect, weeds and canine plundering. We are blessed with enough money to get by, but not to tour the world in grand fashion.

There is one thing I have done more of than I expected, and that is to spend time with God. All year, I've gotten up early to write these devotions. Then, I read and study the Bible and pray. I attend a Bible study, and play drums and sing in a contemporary worship group at church. And I always look for opportunities to encourage other survivors of violence, sharing with them the hope I find in my Living Lord. I'm not retired; I'm rewired!

God of Renewal, I sometimes felt "used up" when I worked, but now I want You to "use me up" for Your glory! Give me unexpected energy to serve You in my later years. Amen

April 17

DIRTY UNDERWEAR

Then I went to the Euphrates, and dug, and I took the loincloth from the place where I had hidden it. But now the loincloth was ruined; it was good for nothing. **Jeremiah 13:7**

Did you know God wants to be closer to us than our underwear? Jeremiah is doing his best to be a good prophet, but things aren't going well and he begins to wonder about God's effectiveness. Jeremiah believes that Judah is a ruined nation, doomed in his eyes and probably God's. No hope is offered here for the people, who are having a love affair with the gods of Babylonia.

God tells Jeremiah to buy some fancy underwear, a linen loincloth normally worn only by priests and nobility (Leviticus 16:4). The prophet is instructed to put the new loincloth on, keeping it pure. He parades around with his new lingerie under his prophet ensemble, creating quite a stir. Then God tells him take the new loincloth off, and stuff it in a rock cleft with the mud and the weeds. Some days later, Jeremiah is instructed to go back and get the loincloth out of the muck, and naturally, it's ruined (Jeremiah 13:1-11).

This parable proclaims God wants His people as close to His heart as divinely possible. We know our bodies are temples of God, inhabited by the Holy Spirit (1 Corinthians 6:19-20). God wants not just our bodies to be wholly devoted to Him, but our minds and hearts as well. It's not difficult to imagine the people of Jeremiah's day worshiping "foreign" gods; we do it all the time today. Money, fame, beauty, power, "me-me-me"—and the list goes on and on. When we seek after these things at the expense of our true and right relationship with God, it's like we are taking God's closeness (the new, clean and pure loincloth) and messing it up (cramming it into the muddy cleft) with our selfish desires. Don't trade some fleeting, earthly "treasure" for God's shiny new love, grace and forgiveness. And be sure to wash your underwear once in a while too.

Patient God, deliver us from our obsession with earthly things that do not last. Help us see the eternal value in our heartfelt obedience to You. Amen

April 18

GOD'S THEME PARKS

Who has measured the waters in the hollow of his hand and marked off the heavens with a span, enclosed the dust of the earth in a measure, and weighed the mountains in scales and the hills in a balance? **Isaiah 40:12**

Why do parents insist on introducing their children to the particular curiosities of manmade theme parks over touring God's natural wonders? What is the fascination of a life-size mouse roaming around a plastic park created for the sole purpose of separating families from their hard-earned cash so their children can momentarily pretend to be princesses or pirates? The last time my husband and I toured a certain theme park, he called it "The Line King," because all we did was wait in line.

I know I'm skating on thin ice with all you mouse-worshipers. But what about all the stuff that was here long before there were animated mice and long-eared, dimwitted dogs? What about all the places to explore just because they are so incredibly, naturally *beautiful*?

"But the kids want to be *entertained*," you cry. Yes, they do, and today's society clearly dictates just *how* that's supposed to happen. Many kids today think they need to be in a constant state of ecstasy or life simply is not worth living. From their sugar-coated cereal breakfasts to their way-past-normal bedtimes at night, a constant "buzz" must surround them or they yelp, "Not fair! Tommy (or Insert-Name-Here) is allowed to (Insert Activity Here)!"

Let's take time to show our children God's creation. Instead of "buying in" (literally) to the manmade wonders of *this* world, let's start reinforcing God's handiwork as the miracle it is. After all, this is just a preview. The *real* excitement is in our eternal home with Jesus and His cast of characters.

Lord, You gave us the most wonderful "theme park" that will ever be, and that "theme" is Your magnificence. Thank You. Amen

April 19

WHO WOULD YOU CHOOSE?

Jesus said, "You have now seen Him; in fact, He is the One speaking with you." John 19:37

If you could meet anyone, living or dead, who would it be? Many would choose a loved one who died and is greatly missed. Others would pick a famous person in history, like Abraham Lincoln or Mahatma Gandhi. Some might go for Elvis Presley or Leonard Nemoy of *Star Trek* fame. Children might like to meet someone like Dr. Seuss or *Muppets* creator Jim Henson.

I would want to meet Jesus, to sit with Him quietly in some olive grove and listen to His life-giving words. If I could speak at all, I would first ask why He had to die such a horrible death. Wasn't there an easier way? And He would say, no, not really. It took a shocking event to rid us of our complacency. I would ask Him about the people I am praying for, friends and relatives and world leaders and even the bad guys. "What's up with the terrorists, Jesus?" I would venture. How would He answer *that????*

I might ask why I'm unable to organize my office or balance my checkbook, little things that bug me, but never seem to capture my full attention. Should we sell our house? Maybe Jesus could give me some advice on our investments, small as they are. "You can't take it with you," He would say with a smile.

The conversation between Jesus and me could go on forever! When the question about who you'd want to meet is asked, nobody ever says how long the visit will last. But guess what? I can talk with Jesus every day, as long as I want to talk. "Unceasingly" was the word Paul used. And when I get to heaven and have God's ear for eternity, my worries from this world won't even enter into the conversation.

Abiding Christ, thank You for Your ever present love and grace. Help me be so tuned in to You that I can feel You in my heart. Amen

April 20

DYSFUNCTIONAL FAMILY SURVIVORS

See, I have engraved you on the palms of My hands; your walls are ever before Me. Isaiah 49:16

In a cartoon entitled "Functional Family Convention," one lonely guy sits in a huge auditorium. For generations most families have had some issues, large or small. We have legions of "family therapists" who make a good living helping relatives live together better, if indeed those families have the financial means and the mindset to use these services.

I am a survivor of a dysfunctional family and a retired counselor. The problem is across the board: people from every ethnic, economic and educational group often find their families in crisis. Those who profess to have a strong belief system are not immune to troubles. My parents came from humble Christian backgrounds. When my Air Force father, was assigned to the American Embassy in Ottawa, Ontario, neither he nor my mother was prepared for the awaiting high society. Mother began her morning with ten o'clock sherry parties, followed by wine with lunch and cocktails at the Officer's Club. Evening brought a round of parties, where champagne and cocktails flowed unceasingly. Soon, my previously tea-totaling mother became an alcoholic, creating a demon that haunted her throughout her long and unhappy life. The Air Force frowned on officers having "personal problems," and our family sank into total codependency.

Accepting Christ in my twenties was the first major step to healing for me. Knowing God loved me *no matter what* strengthened my belief that a better life was possible. My mantra became, "Don't confuse the life around you with the *life force* within you." If my name is engraved on the palms of God's mighty hands, I am freed from my past because I don't live there anymore!

Gracious Father, there is so much sadness and hurt in this world. I know it is because of human frailty and sin, but I pray You will reveal Yourself in a profound way to each person who reads this and give them hope. Amen

April 21

BURNING HEARTS

As they talked and discussed these things with each other, Jesus Himself came up and walked along with them; but they were kept from recognizing Him. Luke 24:15-16

I love the story of Jesus on the road to Emmaus. The story simultaneously fills me with mystery and enlightenment. Jesus is enjoying Himself after being cooped up in that tomb for three days, and He decides to have some fun with these two hapless travelers. The men don't recognize Him when He joins them on the road and says, "What's shakin'?" The men are amazed this fellow Traveler could be so uninformed. Jesus plays along and lets the fellows tell Him the whole story, which of course is about Him.

Still not 'fessing up to Who He is, Jesus tells the travelers "the back story," from the Prophets' predictions to these recent events. Even though the two guys *still* don't recognize the Christ, they ask Him to join them for a meal at an inn. This is the really cool part: Jesus breaks the bread, and *voila!* The two men's eyes are opened and they realize just Who their dinner companion is. "Didn't our hearts burn within us?" they ask each other later (Luke 24:32). Well, *yeah!* I suppose *something* was going on, with all that Christ-Light bouncing around!

A few days before, Jesus had held this same ritual with His disciples. He said, "This bread is My body, broken for you," and, "This wine is My blood, shed for you." Until I read and studied the passage about the road to Emmaus, it never occurred to me each time I partake of the wine and the bread I am "recognizing" Jesus again. It's easy to forget what He "looks" like, when I'm tearing around living my crazy-busy life and generally ignoring my spiritual self. But now, each time I accept the wafer and the cup, I breathe deeply and remember that the Eucharist is there to remind me at what great price Jesus purchased me and made me whole.

Jesus, Light of Life, burn within our hearts and help us "recognize" You throughout our busy days, and especially when we take communion. Amen

April 22

I LOVE YOU, LORD

Jesus said to Simon Peter, "Simon son of John, do you love me more than these?" "Yes, Lord," he said, "you know that I love you." Jesus said, "Feed my lambs." John 21:5

One of my all-time favorite Christian songs is the 1996 release, "I Love You, Lord" by Laurie Klein. A sacred prayer to me, I sing the words aloud with a CD, or in my head in the shower. I feel the presence of God slow me to a pace worthy to call "unceasing prayer" (at least for a moment).

The lyrics are simple but profound): "I love you, Lord/And I lift my voice/To worship You/Oh, my soul rejoice/Take joy, my King/In what You hear/Let it be a sweet, sweet sound in Your ear." The composer is a gifted poet and writer, a real-live person who struggles with prayer just like I do. I expected her to be this totally together woman who manages life's disasters and triumphs with great grace, penning songs on the back of her electric bill while waiting in line to pick her kids up from school. Not so!

Klein describes herself as a "hummingbird," struggling to slow herself down enough to spend quality time with God. "I'm a Monk Wannabe" she says. Decelerating due to illness a few years ago, she learned to nurture herself in small ways, carrying around a basket she called her "portable cloister," which included scented hand lotion, a nail file, and other worldly trappings to calm her body, mind and spirit. During this humbling quiet season she had a revelation: "The one moment we can fully inhabit is the one we often sidestep: this one."

How freeing it is to think of "unceasing prayer" as a moment-to-moment experience, rather than a tedious, down-on-my-stiff-knees penance I must pay for my sinful nature! The sacred can truly be found in the small things we often overlook, if we stop overlooking them and see them as holy.

Yes, Lord, I love you! Help me in my failure to recognize You loving me back in the everyday moments of my life. Amen

April 23

HOW MUCH HIGHER, LORD

Those who hope in the Lord will renew their strength. They will soar on wings like eagles; they will run and not grow weary, they will walk and not be faint. Isaiah 40:31

On the rare occasion when other birds threaten them, eagles don't get their feathers ruffled. They just spread their wings and circle upward, until no other flying creature can reach them. High above all other forms of life on this planet, they stay there until the menace has passed.

Stillwater, Minnesota teen Zach Sobiech knew what it felt like to "Fly A Little Higher." His mother Laura chose this line from Zach's now-famous song, "Clouds," as the title for her memoir about Zach's battle with osteosarcoma, a rare bone cancer most prevalent in children and young adults, with one of the lowest survival rates for pediatric cancer. Zach and his family and friends lived out everyone's worst nightmare: three and a half years from diagnosis to their final goodbyes. He was only a senior in high school when he left this world, but this remarkable young man brought the light and love and grace of Christ to thousands of individuals around the globe with his music, courage and faith. His mother's seemingly insurmountable task of writing their story gives credit to the Master for His unfathomable faithfulness and guidance along the way. When her grief must have still been so raw, Laura wrapped the story of this tragic event in splendor that could only come from a heart wholly devoted to God and to her family. She captured Zach's spirit with her eloquent writing, interjecting real-life daily living and down-home family humor with much grace and good timing. After reading the book, I said, "If only I can live my last days with half the strength and faith Zach showed, I am certain I will hear my heavenly Father say to me as he surely did to Zach, 'Well done, thou good and faithful servant.'"

Eternal Father, in Zach's own words, You are "sitting there holding a rope" when we descend into our darkest hour. Help us remember "...someday, I'll see you again/we'll float up in the clouds/and we'll never see the end." Amen

April 24

SOLVITUR AMBULANDO

Blessed are those who have learned to acclaim you, who walk in the light of your presence, Lord. **Psalm 89:15**

Carefully, I began making my way through the labyrinth, a huge canvas circle on the floor of our church gymnasium. Lacking good balance, my first few steps were tentative, feeling my way in a new dimension. When I began to get the hang of walking between the "walls," my body relaxed and I felt a subtle tug on my spirit. Gradually, the experience shifted. I was less aware of my feet and more conscious of my breathing and thought processes. Before I made it to the "core" of the seven circuits, I began to softly sing Twila Paris' "Center of His Will": "I've been on the edge before, and I have felt the chill/But I could never live outside the center of Your will." I meditated on these words as I reached the "core," turned around and walked back to the "mouth," or opening, completing the exercise.

I had always been fascinated with the labyrinth at the cathedral in Chartes, France, built about 1200 AD. Parishioners often walked the path on their knees for repentance. Today, people walk the labyrinth for many reasons: to relax, meditate, or just for fun. The Latin term *solvitur ambulando*, "solved by walking," describes the labyrinth experience, which can help us resolve complex personal issues and reduce mental anguish.

Labyrinths are thought to enhance right brain activity, illusion and creative thought. For me, the event opened the floodgates of my soul. By the time it was over, I had sung the Paris lyrics several times. The labyrinth took on special meaning, as a symbol of being in the Holy of Holies, God's throne room. A profound sense of His presence washed over me, and I prayed Paris' lyrics: "Keep me in the center of Your will."

Holy God, Your presence is precious to me. Help me to remember my distress can always be "solved by walking" in Your paths. Amen

April 25

I NEEDED THE QUIET

He leads me beside quiet waters, he refreshes my soul. **Psalm 23:2-3**

I used to take my health for granted. Although I was born with a curved spine, I rode horses every day as a child, keeping my body more fit than most of my friends. When I *quit* riding horseback, I began to experience back problems, joint issues, inflammation, and a whole host of other physical symptoms which took more than a small bite out of my vitality. For years, I pushed myself beyond what was safe and healthy, raising two daughters, working days as a college counselor and nights playing drums in the band. During those years, the Lord seemed to be saying He would carry me through, but I couldn't imagine what was ahead.

During my first hospitalization, I was given the poem, "I Needed the Quiet" by Alice Hansche Mortenson, which has meant more to me than all the medical treatment and pharmaceutical wonders I've been given over the years. Mortenson's poem speaks of God's knowing exactly what we need and when we need it. Even illness or debilitation can be embraced as a gift from God when viewed from His perspective. Most likely written when she was ill herself, Mortenson's poem says, God "whispered so sweetly of spiritual things. Though weakened in body, my spirit took wings." It was in that first period of recovery I learned I could not expect to bear any spiritual fruit while living in the fast lane of life on earth. "No prison, my bed," Mortenson's poem continues, "but a beautiful valley of blessings instead." Left to ponder my situation alone, I began to feel the presence of Jesus more intensely. As a new Christian, it was necessary for me to have a period of "cloister" where I allowed Jesus to fully bear the cross of my dismal human condition in order to find true growth in Christ. And when at last I was released from the hospital, I found a new appreciation for my life, the beauty of God's world, and His gentle response to my illness.

Healing Lord, thank You for good things we sometimes don't appreciate, and for upholding us in our distress. Amen

April 26

STYROFOAM IS FROM HELL

He split the rocks in the wilderness and gave them water as abundant as the seas; He brought streams out of a rocky crag and made water flow down like rivers. **Psalm 78:15-16**

I recently read about life at Amundsen-Scott South Pole Research Station in Antarctica. Because of the ecological importance of using only biodegradable products, the man in charge of station supplies was berating residents for bringing in unacceptable items. "Remember," he said over the loudspeaker, "paper comes from trees; Styrofoam comes from hell."

As a mom I was relentless about making my kids understand that dropping even one gum wrapper was wrong. If we all did that every day, it would amount to a lot of trash. My daughters are in their forties now, with kids of their own. In just that space of time, the accumulation of litter in the world has grown exponentially. Americans each throw away about three pounds of garbage daily, amounting to well over 150 million tons per year. Only about a third of this would be recyclable, if people took the time to do so. The Great Pacific Ocean Patch is a soupy collection of marine debris—mostly plastic—extending from just off the coast of North America all the way to Japan. We are wrapping our planet in garbage, one soda can at a time.

It must break God's heart to see His beautiful creation lying in disarray. When He brought this planet into being, He said, "It is good," not "it's good, but man will ruin it." Littering is a sin against God's handiwork. We are murdering out planet. Satan just loves to see us wreck all God has created, whether it be our love for each other or for our earthly natural resources. As Christians, we can be responsible for ourselves, teach our children the importance recycling and not littering, and pray others will see the error of their ways.

God of Creation, forgive us for our complacency in caring for your planet. Amen

April 27

CONCERNED BYSTANDERS

Which of you, if your son asks for bread, will give him a stone? Or if he asks for a fish, will give him a snake? If you, then, though you are evil, know how to give good gifts to your children, how much more will your Father in heaven give good gifts to those who ask him! **Matthew 7:9-10**

I could hear the man from inside the women's restroom in the large medical building. He was in the men's room, shouting at his little boy, pushing and shoving too. The boy began to cry. I glanced at another woman drying her hands. She looked worried and afraid. "Will you find someone in this building to help, and I'll try to talk to the man when he comes out?" She agreed, and hurried out the door.

Out in the hallway, the child's face was red and swollen. He was holding one elbow with his other hand. "What's going on here?" I asked the man. "None of your business!" he shouted. "My kid just needed a talking to!" By now, several people had gathered, including a dentist. "Let's go back into my office and see if we can set up another appointment," the dentist said to the man. "I'm not bringing him back on another day!" the father yelled. "He needs to learn how to behave!" Everyone but the father seemed to understand the little boy was just frightened, first of the dentist, and then of his father. Eventually, a building administrator came and, with the dentist, escorted the man into a private room. Another employee took my name and number, and I actually got a call from the clinic a few days later telling me protective services had been called and were taking "appropriate action."

I was on auto pilot, and bravery wasn't an issue. I couldn't stand by and let this cruel father treat his child like that. As a "concerned bystander," I wanted to do all I could to help. How much impact could we have if we all spoke up when something didn't look right? I believe Jesus would want that.

Perfect Father, not all earthly parents live up to Your expectation to give children what they need. Help us to intervene when it is possible to do so, to keep children safe. Amen

April 28

ERIN'S LAW

Through the praise of children and infants you have established a stronghold against your enemies, to silence the foe and the avenger.
Psalm 8:2

"Growing up in Illinois public schools.., I was educated with my classmates on ...drills: fire...bus...stranger danger....I learned the eight ways to say 'NO' to drugs... I never had to take cover because of a real tornado...stop, drop, and roll or run out of a burning building...evacuate a school bus due to an emergency... Where was the drill on how to escape a child molester?...the lesson plan on sexual abuse, safe/unsafe touches, and safe/unsafe secrets....I was not educated on 'How to Tell Today or How to Get Away.' I was never educated on 'My Body Belongs to Me.'"

These are the words of Erin Merryn, a survivor of childhood sexual abuse, whose mission is to Erin's Law passed in all fifty states, to provide age-appropriate curriculum about child sexual assault for children pre-kindergarten through twelfth grade, and training and resources for teachers, school staff and parents. Nineteen states have passed the law as of 2014; eighteen more are currently reviewing the law.

How can we, as imperfect humans, turn a social issue as serious as this around ourselves? Why won't God intervene? It is well-known that pedophiles cannot successfully be rehabilitated, and yet our justice system continues to let them out of prison when they have "served their time." When have survivors finished "serving their time?" Some of them feel they themselves would be better off locked away when these perpetrators go free.

Jesus prayed to the Father, "You have hidden (God's truth) from the wise and learned, and revealed them to little children" (Luke 10:31). Do we expect those little children to survive into adulthood on their own, or do we work to transform society to give? Let's pass Erin's Law in every state.

Come Lord Jesus, save our children. **Amen**

April 29

WISDOM WORDS

Heaven and earth will pass away, but my words will never pass away.
Matthew 24:35

Thanks to my mother's tutelage (*n., teaching and guidance*), I have a pretty good vocabulary. So I was naturally chagrined (*n., frustrated, annoyed*) when I ran across a recent *Increase Your Word Power* article in Readers' Digest Magazine, including "examples of verbal misuse (and abuse!)." I thought I knew the meanings of all of these words, but was I amiss (*adv., mistaken*)!

Take *noisome*. A combination of *noise* and *bothersome?* No. How many correctly answered *stinky?* Or *allusion*. Thinking of your favorite magician? Wrong again. *Allusion* means *indirect reference*. Change the *a* to an *i* and you have a character pulling rabbits out of hats and dissecting his aide-de-campe (*n., assistant*). One more: *diffuse*. Thinking about bomb squads and terrorists? Unless they are both spreading things freely about, you missed it again! We *defuse* bombs, disagreements and ugly rumors. A photographer *diffuses* light.

For years, I didn't know "suffer" meant "to allow." Luke 18:16 says, "Let the little children come to me." The King James translation says "suffer" instead of "let," making one think Jesus didn't want to be bothered with the rowdy kids! Look at Psalm 2:11: "Serve the Lord with fear, and rejoice with trembling." Fear can be interpreted as "respect" and "awe." Because we know God is good all the time, we can dutifully honor and highly respect Him even while we are rejoicing..

The Word *is* God (John 1:1). God says His Word "shall not return to (Him) empty, but it shall accomplish that which (He) purpose(s)" (Isaiah 55:11). Each time we read the Bible, those "words" bring hope, healing and miracles. The more we infuse (*v., allow to be filled with*) ourselves with the Word of God, the more Christ-like our minds become. Describing God's love and power is the *only* way we should use the word *awesome (adj., causing feelings of fear and wonder)*!

Living Word, fill us with Your goodness and marvelous love. Amen

April 30

UNFRIENDLY

You are my friends. John 15:14

Mark Zuckerberg created a new land called Facebook. The citizens' identity "profile," includes photos, interesting facts about themselves, and a life they choose to show us. Usually, that life includes exciting highlights—happy vacations to faraway places, children and grandchildren doing adorable things, and cats—lots of cats. Maybe the citizen will include a special personal item in his or her cyber-resume, such as a new car or boat, or $300 shoes or expensive jewelry). Drama is important to many; shocking facts and photos sometimes appear with predictable regularity on certain people's pages. A Facebook resident's worth is measured by the number of "friends" he has. A "friend" is a person who can view the cyber-life of another person, only by permission. If disagreements ensue, a citizen may "unfriend" another citizen. The topography of this land is flat, but one can still get lost.

Facebook doesn't have very good law enforcement. Crimes of all sorts are committed that go largely unchecked. Cyber-bullying of teenagers sometimes results in the targeted person taking her own life. Everyone agrees this is heartbreaking, but the Facebook rulers don't do much about it. They just sit back and collect the money they make from ads citizens are forced to view.

God has a "facebook" too. It's called the Bible. He has a "presence" on every page; in fact, the words in the Bible *are* God. The Bible contains exciting places like the wilderness of Kadesh, not made-up locations like Farmville. God doesn't change the layout of the Bible without notice. No one tries to hack into the Bible. If they go there, it's to read the Word of Life and try to live a better one. There are no crazy cat videos in the Bible, although there is a great story about a lion and a guy named Daniel. God never "unfriends" those who believe in Him. Start your Bible account today!

Ever-Present Father, cause us to seek Your "face" in the one true "facebook," the Bible. Amen

May

May 1

GOD'S GROUPIES

Then Jesus told his disciples, "If anyone would come after me, let him deny himself and take up his cross and follow me. Matthew 16:24

I have played traveling Polynesian revue and a polka band. Small as they were, we did have our own "groupies," people who "followed" our band, adored our music, and hung on our every word. Some planned their vacations around where we would be playing, showed up at our house unannounced, and bought us a meal or expensive gifts. One loaned us a motorhome. These groupies must have thought our relative "fame" would rub off on them, making them a little famous too.

Jesus had groupies, just there for the glitz. Some weren't ready to give up all they had to follow Him. When Jesus told a wealthy young man to give all his money to the poor and then follow Him, the man "went away sorrowful, for he had great possessions" (Matthew 19:22). Jesus had preached many times that we can't "serve both God and money" (Luke 16:13). It's easier to stuff "a camel through the eye of a needle" (Luke 18:25) than take your money with you to heaven!

The ultimate "groupie" in Jesus' time was Judas. Jesus picked this guy as part of God's plan, but couldn't the other disciples tell Judas wasn't "all in" from the beginning? Judas was upset when Lazarus' sister Mary anointed Jesus with expensive oil (John 12:6), not because he thought the money should be given to the poor--he was a thief who regularly helped himself to the contents of the money bag (John 12:6)! I'm not so different from Judas, sometimes questioning others' motives in giving (or not giving). And each time I sin, I actually do "betray" Jesus. Humility goes a long way in keeping things in perspective. It's not Jesus' "glitz" I want. It's His character.

Precious Jesus, I want to follow You, not so Your fame will rub off on me. I want You to fill my mind with Your love and power. Amen

May 2

A GAUNTLET WITH A GIFT IN IT

For we do not know what to pray for as we ought, but the Spirit himself intercedes for us with sighs too deep for words. Romans 8:26

Victorian poet, Elizabeth Barrett Browning wrote these words: *God answers sharp and sudden on some prayers/And thrusts the thing we have prayed for in our face/A gauntlet with a gift in it.*

Many think Liz's "gauntlet with a gift" was her husband, Robert Browning. Born in England in 1806, Liz was the oldest child of a domineering pious father of twelve who wanted none of his children to marry, instead sending most of them to oversee the slaves on his Jamaica plantations. Opposed to slavery, Liz refused to go, staying home to write poetry. Fascinated by her volumes, rhymester Robert Browning wrote to her in 1844. Eventually they married on the sly, saving Liz from certain spinsterhood. Her father disinherited her, but she and Bob had a lifelong bond that is clearly expressed in Liz's poems: "How do I love thee? Let me count the ways."

Having been "raised" by an alcoholic mother and a codependent father, my problem-solving skills went largely undeveloped. College and grad school brought me out of my shell to some degree. But I still dragged my fears and insecurities with me, convinced I was destined to "settle" for what I could get. My first marriage was a tortured union which ended in a fiery divorce. Though I had chosen Christ as my personal Savior, sometimes it still seemed I was doomed to live an unhappy life.

Then God brought me Patrick, a man of integrity who loved the Lord and had triumphed over his own demons. He is my soul mate, a sharp and sudden answer to a prayer I hadn't dared utter. God truly does give us more than we can ever ask or imagine.

Giver of Life, help us in our lack of faith that You will always provide for us at just the time we need it. Amen

May 3

GREEK TO ME

(The Greeks) came to Philip, who was from Bethsaida in Galilee, and asked him, "Sir, we wish to see Jesus." John 12:21

In the 12th chapter of John, Jesus was busy fulfilling ancient Scripture by arriving in Jerusalem riding on a donkey. The people welcomed him with great fanfare. The word was out that Jesus had brought Lazarus up out of his tomb, topping everything else He had done. The people were excited.

Everybody was there for the Passover: Jews from near and far, the chief priests, scribes and Pharisees, and even some gentile Greeks, curious about all the activity. "The whole world has run off after Him!" the Pharisees cried (John 12:19). Some Bible commentaries said the Greeks were a discerning folk and wanted answers to all of their rhetorical questions, or they wanted to ask Jesus to come with them on a sort of "missionary trip." The Greeks approached Phillip—he had a Greek name, possibly making him more sympathetic to their cause. "We want to see Jesus," they said. Phillip didn't know what to think, so he grabbed Andrew, and they found Jesus.

Nobody except Jesus understood that there wasn't time to have a philosophical discussion about foreign evangelism. Jesus began speaking of His own death and "glorification," but everyone missed the point.

I am so much like these Greeks sometimes. I'll be studying the Bible, concentrating and cogitating—and bam! Suddenly I'm thinking more about what's important to me than what God might be trying to say to me. But God may want to speak to me in a "still, small voice," through whatever it is I'm reading or praying about. Getting sidetracked as we all do is like saying, "Just a minute, God. You aren't as important as *this*." When will I ever learn that God is patient with me? Why can't I be patient with Him?

Pull me back, Lord, from my human daydreaming and help me focus on Your Word and Your message. Amen

May 4

VOLUNTEERS ANONYMOUS

My son, do not lose sight of these—keep sound wisdom and discretion, and they will be life for your soul and adornment for your neck. **Proverbs 3:21-22**

I've found a new program called Volunteers Anonymous. Unlike other "self-help" programs, "Volunteers Anonymous" only has one step: Just Say No! Members practice this one word, NO, in front of a mirror until they can say it without laughing or crying or adding foolish words like "I'm really sorry." There are no meetings to attend because no one in Volunteers Anonymous will agree to be responsible for finding a place and setting a time to meet.

This is the answer to everything! Can you stay with the grandkids while their parents go on a six-week photo safari in Kenya? No. Will you chair next year's church picnic? No! (Actually, I'm pretty sure I have a funeral that day…) Please help with the Adopt-A-Highway cleanup in the city's worst neighborhood! NO!!! And I'm just getting going!

I recently heard it said you can believe alone, you can pray alone, you can worship alone, but you cannot live out your faith alone. Belief is private, but faith is public—something to be lived out in the presence of community. Jesus said to go make disciples (Matthew 28:19). He didn't say "Hide your head in the sand and let somebody else be the fall guy." The Holy Spirit was sent to help us understand and activate our own special gifts, whether we are to heal or help or be hospitable.

The key, then, is balance. Each of us needs to understand what we do best and then do it as often as we are able. If I'm not good at serving at funeral lunches, then I should avoid doing it. If I like drama and I can be in a skit at church to help others understand a parable, then I should be hamming it up on the pulpit. Make it yours and make it fun! God will love all you do!

Holy God, don't let us be ostriches but rather companion animals ready to do what we do best. Amen

May 5

CINCO DE MAYO

Your servant has killed both the lion and the bear; this uncircumcised Philistine will be like one of them, because he has defied the armies of the living God. **1 Samuel 17:36**

Cinco de Mayo is more than just a party in Mexico's history. In late 1861, a sizeable French naval fleet landed at Veracruz and drove the Mexican president and his government out of the city. The French advanced toward Mexico City, but met resistance near the town of Puebla. On May 5, 1862, the poorly equipped Mexican army of about 4500 defeated the 8000-strong French army, considered to be the strongest army in the world at the time. The battle at Puebla was a great symbolic victory for the Mexican government and bolstered the resistance movement. Time Magazine described the victory as "a Mexican David defeating a French Goliath."

Although France won the war, the United States began sending help to Mexico after our Civil War. The French withdrew, and in 1867, a new, legitimate Mexican government was finally established. Since the Battle of Puebla, no country in North or South America has been invaded by any other European military force.

The suggested imagery of David and Goliath is significant, because it helps us realize "underdog victories" did not only happen in Biblical times. Mexico is and has been a predominately Christian nation, with Roman Catholicism established during the Spanish colonial era (1519-1521. It is quite feasible the Puebla residents relied on the power of God when faced with an imminent invasion. The celebration of this successful battle from 1862 until the present is a reminder of the power of God revealed through human faith in action. The Mexican people and their descendants world-wide have preserved a national pride by remembering Cinco de Mayo. And you thought it was just about the tamales.

God of All Nations, mankind seems bent on having wars, but we know You are the path to peace for us all. Ameen

May 6

WALTER EGO

***Whoever brings ruin on their family will inherit only wind, and the fool will be servant to the wise.* Proverbs 11:29**

My grandparents were all gone before I came upon the scene. My mother described her father, Walter, as erratic and impulsive. Never having a set vocation, he would disappear for months at a time, leaving my grandmother Birdie Mae to fend for herself. While away, he would buy a defunct business or some worthless land, but nothing ever worked out for him. He got home long enough to get Birdie Mae pregnant eight times, the last effort producing my mother. Mother's oldest brother refused to talk to her until she was twenty-two, holding her responsible for her own procreation.

I believe Walter must have suffered from bipolar disorder. As the baby, it always fell to Mother to "see to" her dad as he lay alone in the back bedroom. Her mother would make her take him food or something to drink, but she was terrified to enter the room. Sometimes, he would bang his head against the wall, repeating the word "Stupid" over and over. My grandfather's dysfunction took its toll on my mother too: she bore her own demons of depression and alcoholism until her death at age ninety-six.

I refuse to allow my family's demons to dwell in me. If my grandfather had lived today, he might have had treatment for his issues. Unfortunately for him—and his immediate family—there was no help available then. But I know my life in Christ has kept me healthier than I might have been if I had lived by my family's rules, sweeping "mental" problems under the table. As a retired counselor, I believe in the help we can obtain from skilled and reputable mental health professionals. The combination of a "sound mind" in Christ and a healthy understanding of our own personalities and backgrounds can serve us well and give us many years of happiness.

Jesus, help us learn Your temperament and be transformed into the mentally, physically, spiritually and emotionally healthy people You want us to be. Amen

May 7

NEGATIVE ATTENTION

For I do not do the good I want to do, but the evil I do not want to do—this I keep on doing. **Romans 7:19**

If you are a parent, you may have observed your child "acting out" to get attention. You make a phone call and the child begins exploring the cupboards. When the mail carrier comes to the front door, suddenly the cat gets let out the back. You leave your "tween-ager" home alone for the first time, and she invites the neighbor kids in for a "party." You believe you are a good parent, but your child's behavior is challenging

Sometimes, this acting out behavior can turn negative and becomes more severe. Foster children may behave badly to "test" their foster parents, especially if the children have been moved more than once, or if they blame themselves for what is happening, even if, by adult standards, their biological parents have acted carelessly or abusively. This profound confusion on the part of the child may take years to unravel. If the foster family can outlast the child's attempts to push their buttons they cycle may be broken. Then the child will hopefully say to herself, "These people must really care about me because they have put up with my bad behavior and still stuck by me."

Sometimes, we as Christians act like children with abandonment issues. We do some surprising things in an effort to "reject" God's love because we feel we aren't worthy. We may react to life events in ways which shows we don't trust God. When we do this, we are repeating the actions of those who shouted "Crucify Him!" in that courtyard so many years ago. Jesus willingly went to cross for us then, and He would do it again. Jesus will not abandon us, even though we might dare Him to do so. Jesus is Emmanuel—God with us—and He isn't going anywhere. Let's crawl into His lap and thank Him for putting up with His children's "acting out" behavior.

Triune God, when we say we believe, You adopt us into Your family and You welcome us home. Amen

May 8

NO OTHER NAME

And there is salvation in no one else, for there is no other name under heaven given among men by which we must be saved. **Acts 4:12**

In the chapter previous to today's Scripture, Peter and John encounter "a man lame from birth" at the temple gate. Peter says to the man, "Look at me....In the name of Jesus Christ of Nazareth, rise up and walk!" The beggar gets up leaping and praising God (Acts 3:1-10). It was crystal clear to the lame man by what power he had been made whole again, and he wanted the world to know about it. He didn't set out to convince everyone to believe in this Jesus; he just told people what he knew to be true.

I speak to many different groups of people: church members, book clubs, civic organizations, law enforcement, mental health professionals, and healthcare practitioners to name just a few. Some of my talks are delivered in faith-based settings, some in secular. But my message is always the same: I believe that I was saved from almost certain death through the power of God, and being saved (both physically and spiritually) has given me a responsibility to help other victims of violence. As a believer in Jesus Christ as the Son of God, it is my wish that all those who hear me would believe as I do. But whether conversion to Christianity is the result of what I say to them is not important. That's God's work, not mine. My intent is never to tear down another's beliefs or to reject or exclude anyone by what I say. I give an eye witness account of what happened to me, and share the hope and peace which I have as a result of that transformation.

Today, we try to be "inclusive," sometimes afraid to speak up for what we believe for fear it will "offend" someone. As Christians, we are commanded by God to "bear witness" and proclaim the gospel "to all nations" (Mark 13:9-10). If we do this with great love, we will offend no one.

Author and Perfector of my Faith, ensure that I offend no one in proclaiming Your love and power. Amen

May 9

UNPLUGGED

Come to me, all who labor and are heavy laden, and I will give you rest. **Matthew 11:28**

I am not a "techie." My first laptop computer came with lots of bells and whistles, and a one-year service contract so I could call a True Techie at any time, night or day, and ask for help. Of course, I didn't need any help until the service contract expired. The very next day, the laptop quit working.

I called anyway. I begged, I pleaded. "It's probably something really simple," I wailed. "Can't you just extend the service contract one more day?" "I'm sorry," said the disembodied voice, with a thick foreign accent. "Our policy is very strict. If I provide you help, I will have to charge $45 to your account." I was desperate, so I gave her my credit card number.

"Okay, ma'am," came the distant voice. "Please turn off your computer and unplug any electrical cords or devices." I followed her instructions. "Now, remove the sliding plate on the back of the computer and remove the battery. Wait one minute and reinsert the battery." She paused dramatically and then said gleefully, "Your computer should operate perfectly now!"

Memoirist Ann Lamott said, "Almost everything will work again if you unplug it for a few minutes, including you." Paying $45 for a "no-brainer" solution to my problem was one of Life's Little Lessons. I want stuff to work with the minimum amount of effort on my part. Users' manuals are for other people; I want to turn a device on and GO! But that's not what God wants us to do in this life. I didn't count, but when I was looking for today's Scripture quote, I'm pretty sure the word "rest" appears in the Bible far more often than "rush." Over and over, Jesus says to us, "Come," and He will always be there to slow us down and give us a clearer perspective. No $45 fee for that.

Calming Spirit, fill me with the patience I lack and help me slow down and listen to Your voice. Amen

May 10

THE ROMAN ROAD

For all have sinned and fall short of the glory of God. **Romans 3:23**

The Roman Road to Salvation is eight verses in the Book of Romans which lay out the Gospel message. The "road" begins with the acceptance that we're sinners like everybody else (Romans 3:10 and 3:23). Adam and Eve started it, bless their hearts, and we've been mired in sin ever since. At first I said, "I'm not a sinner! I drive safely and I recycle my waste product, smile at strangers. As a counselor, I help people. But do I follow God's laws to the letter? Well…no (Romans 5:12 and 6:23).

So I do deserve God's chastising. But He had a plan: He sent His only Son, Jesus, to walk this earth as fully human *and* fully God And His same precious Son went to the cross and died for us—and then got raised up again to show us the meaning of eternal life (Romans 5:8). We only have to *believe* with our hearts and *ask* with our mouths (Romans 10:9). It's that simple! No hoop jumping, no "cosmic report card" of all our good deeds. God promises "to all who received him, to those who believed in His name, He gave the right to become children of God" (John 1:12). Just make the *decision* to believe and the fireworks begin. God shows Himself in mighty ways and quiet moments. Believe me, He *does* hear us (Romans 10:13).

What's next? Our faith makes us *want* to follow God! That desire is built into the deal. The rewards—in this life and in heaven—are so great, why would we turn God down? Three elements arise in front of us: spend time with God in prayer and studying His Word, seek out other believers for healthy fellowship, and tell others what has happened to us. If we do these three things faithfully, our lives will become more meaningful, our days more peaceful, and our faith stronger. Once you try God, you'll never go back!

Redeeming Father, move us to continue in Your walk and Your ways and stir us to share Your story with others. Amen

May 11

LOCATION, LOCATION, LOCATION

In my Father's house are many mansions: if it were not so, I would have told you. I go to prepare a place for you. John 14:2 (KJV)

Property No. 1: A handyman's dream! In the historic Left-Behind Neighborhood. Slightly rundown, Diablo Developers promising to revive area soon. Two small bedrooms, one closet-sized bath, no garage, outdated appliances, no air conditioning. Back yard includes five-foot rusted chain link fence and two Rottweilers. Neighbors friendly, firearms necessary.

Property No. 2: New home in gated Foreclosure Acres Neighborhood, five bedrooms ("en suite" bath in master bedroom), six additional baths, five car garage, in-ground swimming pool, tennis court. Plenty of closets for your earthly possessions you haven't used or needed in years. High solid fencing between properties to prevent neighbors from trying to have fellowship with you. Sophisticated security system will keep intruders at bay so all your hard-earned money is safe. Financing available but you probably won't qualify.

Property No. 3: Mansion in Heaven, located on Eternal Life Parkway with easy access in the twinkling of an eye. Designed and built especially for *you* by the Master Builder. Constructed to last for eternity. Number of bedrooms and baths flexible depending on need. Lush yard and gardens that maintain themselves, self-cleaning house. Friendly community. Visit with people you haven't seen in years! Pets allowed, especially all the ones you lost. Meals served communally with all the Saints. Well-planned leisure activities include sitting at the feet of the Master, rejoicing endlessly, singing and making music in your heart. Individual Eternal Life Insurance policies purchased for you at great expense. You pay nothing: the property is a gift bestowed upon all who believe Jesus Christ is the Son of God and He died on a cross to save us. Mortgage holder: Jesus Christ. Property value: priceless. God will decide when you move in. See John Chapter 14 and Revelation Chapter 21.

Master Builder, when life on earth gets tedious, help us remember that You have a wonderful place where we will spend eternity with You. Amen

May 12

NORMAL NORMAN

Be careful to obey so that it may go well with you and that you may increase greatly in a land flowing with milk and honey, just as the Lord, the God of your ancestors, promised you. **Deuteronomy 6:3**

The *Saturday Evening Post* magazine appeared in my parents' mailbox once a month, with Norman Rockwell's paintings on the covers. The people in his paintings looked like people I knew—over there. Not our family, not those close to me. The people in my life were dysfunctional and distant, tiptoeing around issues in our home. But the folks who inhabited Rockwell's works inspired me to believe that life could be—was—different someplace else.

Three hundred twenty one of Rockwell's painting appeared on the covers of the *Post* for forty-seven consecutive years. People called it the "greatest show window in America." Rockwell himself observed, "Without thinking too much about it.., I was showing the America I knew and observed to others who might not have noticed." My childhood self had noticed. I was mesmerized. But until I met Jesus Christ and laid down my life for Him, I only hoped that idyllic life could be mine.

Through the years, I have heard others speak of Rockwell's "cute" paintings as being an impossible portrayal of life. "It just isn't like that today," people say. I believe Rockwell's work, like Scripture, gives us something to strive for. Perfect family dinners in the paintings and the timeless wisdom in the Bible may not seem "normal" sometimes. We as humans will wander off the path and fail to get it right many times. But when I view the idyllic vignettes of life in the paintings, or when I read the wonderful counsel in God's Word, I get a clearer view of what He intended for this world, a glimpse of what eternal life will be like. The faces of Rockwell's characters glow with Christ's light, and I hope I glow that way too sometimes.

Perfect Lord, You promise us life eternal just for believing in You. Grant us daily hope. Amen

May 13

BUILDING UP SELF E-STEAM

Suddenly an angel of the Lord appeared and a light shone in the cell. He struck Peter on the side and woke him up. "Quick, get up!" he said, and the chains fell off Peter's wrists. **Acts 12:7**

Peter's liberation from prison has always fascinated me. Herod had just killed James "by the sword," which "pleased the Jews" (Acts 12:2-3). Now he had thrown Peter in jail, chained to the wall with "four squads of soldiers" (v. 4) keeping an eye on him. "An angel of the Lord" came and caused the chains to fall away (v. 7), escorting Peter right past the sleeping guards and out the prison door. Peter "went to the house of Mary" (v. 12) where some of the other Christians were staying. Because one of the major themes of the book of Acts is the apostles "following in Christ's footsteps," some Bible commentators liken Peter's escape as a sort of "resurrection," like Jesus' escape from the tomb.

I used to cry when I read the Bible, first because I was so moved by the life-giving words I found there, but also because I didn't think I was worthy to follow after these early Christians. I did not believe I could ever muster up the courage they exhibited in the face of persecution and almost certain death. (Most of the apostles were martyred in some way, including Peter, who asked to be crucified upside down because he also did not feel worthy to die the same way as his Christ.) "I could never say that about myself," I thought. "I'm too weak to think I could die for my beliefs." Then I began to realize, in the unlikely event I was ever put to death for being a Christian, I would not travel that road alone. God would be my strength, just as He has been my strength for all the earthly crises I've endured. Now, I can say boldly, I am holy and blameless, saved and free. If I am ever called on to die for my faith in Christ, I know He will be there to walk with me through that valley.

Holy King of Angels, save us from persecution for our faith in You, and walk with us through times of trial so we may endure all that comes our way. Amen

May 14

TRUTH OR CONSEQUENCES

Jesus said to him, "I am the way, and the truth, and the life. No one comes to the Father except through Me. John 14:6

In 1950, Ralph Edwards, the host of the radio quiz show *Truth or Consequences*, announced he would air the program from the first town that renamed itself after the show. Hot Springs, New Mexico responded, and the program was broadcast from there until it ended in 1988. The game show moved from radio to television, asking contestants to correctly answer a trivia question (the "truth") before "Beulah the Buzzer" sounded. If wrong, they were made to perform crazy but harmless tasks (the "consequence"). Edwards said, "Most Americans are darned good sports," many answering the questions wrong so they could act silly on national television.

It was simpler time, when *Truth or Consequences* was on the air. People only had to dress up like a sultan or be covered in bright yellow chicken feathers as their "consequence." Nothing like some "reality" shows today where folks eat living arachnids or scrub down a seven thousand pound elephant. In 1950, America was in love with television. Entertainment was straightforward, people were willing to laugh at themselves. The program always ended with, "Hoping all your consequences are happy ones!"

God longs for us to travel His road, to hold His hand, and to return to Him when we don't know the answers. "My burden is light," He tells us (Matthew 11:30). "I will give you rest" (Exodus 33:14, Deuteronomy 12:10, Matthew 11:28). There is no "Beulah the Buzzer" to tell us our time is up, that we haven't gotten it right. God welcomes us to come to Him, confess our shortcomings, and "purify us from all unrighteousness (1 John 1:9). There are "consequences" in this life, some we bring on ourselves and some, sadly that others deliver to us. But God is always there, even in the worst of times, to give us hope and help us on our way.

Thank You, God, that you make all our consequences good ones. Amen

May 15

GAMES PEOPLE PLAY

As far as the east is from the west, so far has He removed our transgressions from us. **Psalm 103:12**

In 1964, psychiatrist Eric Berne published a book called *Games People Play*, about his psychological theory of "transactional analysis" for studying interactions between individuals. Berne defined a number of "games," or predictable exchanges, between people in which habitual experiences are repeated, including the emotions accompanying those experiences. One of the most universally understood "games" Berne put forth was "Ain't It Awful?" Berne said this game "is common among certain types of middle-aged women with small independent incomes" (this was 1964). In this game, Player One says: "I heard Mrs. So-and-So got caught with her hand in the till…etc." The other Players either "buy in to" what the Player One is saying, continuing the game, or they refuse to participate, and the game ends. Other games have interesting names like, "Kick Me" (symbolically wearing a sign saying "Do Not Kick Me," and then wondering why one gets kicked) and "Why Don't You? Yes But" (Player One makes a sensible suggestion to Player Two who says the idea is impossible because…).

What kinds of games do we try to play with God? One is "God Pal," where our prayers become one-sided conversations in which we "cozy up" to God and tell Him all the passions of our hearts, completely omitting praise and worship and—oh yeah, what would God's will look like? Or how about "Gotcha God!" We conjure up specific prayers with exact specifications and even deadlines, and when we don't get the answer we want, we blame God for letting us down. Here's my favorite: "Go Fish." We confess our sins, God removes them "as far as the east is from the west," and He throws them into the bottom of the sea. We just have to go fishing… God's grace is not a game; it's a gift. Take it—and stop playing games!

Healing Father, we thank You that You welcome us into Your loving arms without playing games. Amen

May 16

GOD'S HAPPY MEAL

I gave you milk, not solid food, for you were not yet ready for it. Indeed, you are still not ready. **1 Corinthians 3:2**

The church in Corinth was divided, engaging in childish arguments over who was the most excellent Christian leader, like groupies fighting over their favorite rock stars. Paul's letter warned them not to allow the church to fall apart over these differences. Paul had taught them well, but now the people were acting like spoiled children, on a slippery slope to failure.

All new converts have to start with basic teachings ("milk") and progress to more advanced knowledge of the Word of God ("solid food"). The Greeks had long believed themselves to be great thinkers; perhaps they thought they knew all about the way of Christ. They didn't understand God works through humility and weakness, not through boasting and debate. Paul remembered his own conversion and the intense teaching, making him fit for evangelism (Acts 9). He was determined to show the Corinthians the importance of humility, faithfulness, and patience.

As a new Christian, I wanted to grasp "how wide and long and high and deep is the love of Christ" (Ephesians 3:18). But a genuine understanding of Christ needs time to "percolate," to sink in slowly. The process truly is like feeding a child, first pure mother's milk, then solid food, and eventually, the child can make "food choices" for herself. Spiritual "food choices" include continued time and energy invested in studying God's Word. Do we choose a physical diet that does not nourish our body, or do we choose wholesome, healthy and natural meals that make us grow strong, think clearly, and satisfy our bodily hunger? Meditating on God's ways will always result in a more satisfying spiritual "meal," and there is a prize in every bag!

Indwelling Spirit, help us remain faithful to Your teachings and keep us from rushing to "complete" our faith. Amen

May 17

DON'T WORRY, BE HAPPY

In the multitude of my anxieties within me, Your comforts delight my soul. **Psalm 94:19**

Bobby McFerrin's song, "Don't Worry, Be Happy," was number one on the U.S. pop charts in 1988. The tune is simple and upbeat, and the lyrics reminds us all we have a choice to be happy in all circumstances (1 Thessalonians 5:18). "Don't Worry, Be Happy" was written in the middle of McFerrin's sophisticated career. "Don't Worry, Be Happy" may be McFerrin's most well-known song, but his musical gifts are astounding.

I have joked for many years that worrying is my spiritual gift. But spiritual gifts are given to us by God to serve Him. Time spent worrying is pretty much a wasted effort, an opportunity for Satan to swoop in and convince us to follow him instead of God. There is no such thing as "fruitful fretting."

It took many years of concentrated effort and lots of prayer for me to learn to set aside my worrying and pray instead. When I do this, it brings me great comfort, keeps my blood pressure down, and generally makes my days (and nights) go much better. I revert to my old worrying habits occasionally, but if I ask Him, God will graciously guide me back on track and replace my anxious thoughts with "the peace that passes all understanding" (Philippians 4:7). Then I am ready to use my real spiritual gifts in the furthering of God's kingdom here on earth.

Jesus said that the Father values each one of us and promises to take care of us (Matthew 6:25-34). Worry causes physical ailments from heart attacks to strokes to preventable accidents and keeps a number of pharmaceutical companies in the black. Let's listen to Jesus (and Bobby McFerrin), and choose to be happy.

Jesus, help us to remember we are of more value than the sparrows, and our Heavenly Father will take care of us. Amen

May 18

SUCCESSFUL SURGERY

In God I trust and am not afraid. What can man do to me? **Psalm 56:11**

It was a shock to see Billy for the first time. I was glad his sister asked me to meet her at his house before he got home. Her brother had surgery for mouth cancer, and he needed a social worker. We discussed services the county could arrange: transportation to medical appointments, nurse visits, meals, and emotional support. Billy would need to sign paperwork.

Suddenly Billy was standing in the doorway looking frail and shy. His face was horribly distorted from the surgery, but his eyes told a greater story of despair. In his sister's words, "the surgeons went too far." In trying to save her brother's life, they had burdened him with a gross disfigurement, the inability to eat solid food, and a drastic personality change from a gregarious single farmer to a miserable recluse.

I learned to decipher his horribly garbled speech. He told me he wanted to take his own life. His circumstances were so deplorable he didn't want to go on. Even though his cancer had been the result of years of chewing tobacco, Billy still blamed the doctors. In his quiet hours, he could not get his head around why they hadn't just let him die.

I was only twenty-eight years old and interviewing for a different job. I talked him into going to a couple of cancer recovery support groups with me before I told him I was leaving. I think of Billy often. I've prayed the people in that support group met some of his needs, along with other county employees who came after me. Billy did not deserve to live without hope, and I felt inadequate to provide any real help for him. I regretted never asking him if he was a believer; county workers were not supposed to discuss religion with our clients. I learned an important lesson: never let the chance go by to offer the hope of Christ those who desperately need it.

Father, we look forward to a day when there will be no more disease or death. Amen

May 19

HARD HEADED

He guards the course of the just and protects the way of his faithful ones. **Proverbs 2:8**

The deck on our house is made of hard and resilient *ipe* wood, found in the forests of South America. *Ipe* lasts longer than redwood, and is resistant to insects. One day a woodpecker tried pecking at the surface of our deck.

Woodpeckers ought to have concussions, if not traumatic brain injuries from all the head-banging they do. My head hurts just thinking about this. But the bone structure of the woodpecker's head acts like a tiny "seat belt" for its skull, protecting the brain inside. Woodpeckers move their heads around constantly, no one area of the head gets pounded too badly. The lower portion of their beaks is made of a strong material to soften the blows.

I can be hard-headed, metaphorically beating my head against hard objects even though I know I will get no place. Whether I believe the end result will be good (sticking with hopeless relationships) or bad (eating chocolate several times a day and expecting to lose weight), I persevere in the futile behavior long past the point where I should have abandoned it and tried something different. Albert Einstein defined *insanity* as "doing something over and over and expecting different results," then I guess I am certifiably bonkers. I do this with God's teachings too. Scripture tells me God works all things for good (Romans 8:28) but I question His motives when I am suffering. Knowing God calls us to be thankful in all circumstances (1 Thessalonians 5:18), I still fly into a tizzy when I receive unwelcome news.

If we are supposed to "put on the mind of Christ" (1 Corinthians 2:16), why doesn't God provide little "seat belts" for our brains? The answer is, He does. Today's Scripture, Proverbs 2:8, says God "protects the ways of His faithful ones." That means the little woodpecker and us.

Faithful Father, help me feel Your loving arms around me today. Amen

May 20

A PERFECT WEDDING

The Spirit and the bride say, "Come!" And let the one who hears say, "Come!" Let the one who is thirsty come; and let the one who wishes take the free gift of the water of life. **Revelation 22:17**

When I was younger, I played drums in a band, and many of our "gigs" were wedding dances. I've seen all kinds of celebrations: lavish, simple, elegant and cheesy. One stands out among all others: the Wedding From Hell.

First, there was a snowstorm. The dance hall was not far from where we lived, so we blazed a trail on roads that should have been closed. The hall was almost empty; many of the guests had stayed home. The wedding party was in a funk. The groom and his pals were making good use of the open bar; the bridesmaids were helping the bride redo her make-up, already damaged from crying. We overheard the couple's parents arguing over who should pay for what, a decision best not left until the last minute. Liquor flowed and at night's end, the bride's mother was passed out on the floor. No one offered to help her. "Just let her sleep it off," the bride's father said. We loaded our equipment and headed out in the continuing blizzard. Later, we heard there had been an altercation in the honeymoon suite, and the bride left her new husband the following morning.

A wedding should be viewed as a sacrament, not a reality TV episode. God must have cried that night as this dysfunctional family played out the unfortunate scene. Scripture describes another wedding in the last chapter of the Bible, Revelations 22: the culmination of the entire Gospel story. The moment we've all been waiting for is here: we, the "bride," finally hear Jesus, the groom say, "Come!" We respond from our weary hearts, knowing that our "sun will never set again, and (our) moon will wane no more; the Lord will be (our) everlasting light, and (our) days of sorrow will end" (Isaiah 60:20).

Lord, help us keep Your sacraments holy until we see You face-to-face. Amen

May 21

ONE JOKE OVER THE LINE

The circumcised believers who had come with Peter were astonished that the gift of the Holy Spirit had been poured out even on Gentiles. Acts 10:45

Archie Bunker taught me about tolerance. The fictional, larger-than-life bigot from Queens, played by Carroll O'Connor, in the 1970s sit-com *All in the Family* brought me face-to-face with my own family's prejudice. I had vowed to break the cycle of dubious regard my family had for people "not like us." But as I watched Bunker and his supporting cast interact about every controversial topic under the sun, I realized we are all in some ways a little "misinformed" about how others view the world.

Bunker was an equal opportunity bigot. Whatever it was, he was against it. He was bad tempered, and unkind to his slightly dingy but universally endearing wife Edith (Jean Stapleton). Yet there was an absence of malice in Archie's attitude; he was a product of his time, his background, and his lack of exposure. He wasn't stupid; he was just "under-informed."

Archie redeemed himself somewhat over the years. When he "accidentally" joined the Ku Klux Klan, he later showed clear disdain for the group when he learned what they were about. He was asked to speak at his good friend's funeral, but mellowed when he realized the friend was Jewish. In all the episodes I watched, I felt my spirit responding with love for misinformed Archie.

When Peter preached the good news about Jesus in Acts, the Jewish Christians shocked the "gentiles" received the gift of the Holy Spirit right along with them. Peter said everyone who believes in Jesus is welcome in this new kingdom of God. Let's not be Archie Bunkers by putting man-made limitations on what God has deemed open to all.

Holy God, open our hearts to the ways of those who love You but are not exactly like us. Amen

May 22

THERE'S AN APP FOR THAT

May He be like rain falling on a mown field, like showers watering the earth. **Psalm 72:6**

I love rain! It has rained steadily for two days. I couldn't work in my gardens, but I enjoyed watching the sheets of water drench the parched earth. I drank in the fresh smell and marveled at the cloud formations as they rolled across the sky like gray taffy being pulled while it's still warm.

Then, I picked up my phone and viewed the whole storm on my weather app. In this age of instant information, I frequently fall prey to the "electronic" version of life instead of the real one. There is so much "stuff" at our fingertips today. People send me emails with photos of foreign waterfalls and exotic birds I will probably never see in my lifetime. Those images are nice, but what happened to walking out our back doors and inspecting our way across the yard? I may not encounter white tigers and green-winged macaws, but I can hear a cardinal's song or see a baby squirrel.

The Bible has a list of "apps." They're in the back of my NIV. I don't have to download or install them, and they are free. They came with the Bible. My Bibles' list is called "Perspectives From The Bible," and it gives me Scripture passages for whatever is on my heart. When I am afraid, I can go to 1 Timothy 1:7 (The Spirit God gave us does not make us timid, but gives us power, love and self-discipline.) Matthew 7:5 has advice when I have a disagreement with someone: "First take the plank out of your own eye, and then you will see clearly to remove the speck from your brother's eye." When worldly things tempt me, James 4:7-8 advises, "Resist the devil, and he will flee from you." Philippians 4:8 summarizes, "Whatever is true, whatever is noble, whatever is right, whatever is pure, whatever is lovely, whatever is admirable—if anything is excellent or praiseworthy—think about such things." And God said, "There's an app for that!"

Wise God, help us turn to Your Word for advice about our world. Amen

May 23

LORD OF LAUGHTER

Then our mouth was filled with laughter, and our tongue with singing. **Psalm 126:2**

God's Word has a message that begs to be taken seriously. But the discerning reader cannot help but see snippets of humor there too. The Bible is about people, and we *are* pretty laughable.

It's amusing to think Pharaoh would disregard Moses' warnings from God. Pharaoh said *he* didn't need this big God. Soon, the Egyptian ruler was up to his eyeballs in frogs, boils, and locusts. Then God struck down all the first-born Egyptian sons, including Pharaoh's own boy. Pharaoh finally told Moses to "get out of Egypt," but Moses' challenges were just beginning. Fickle Pharaoh changed his mind suddenly and sent his troops after the fleeing Israelites. Moses was in the doghouse when his people said, "Was it because there were no graves in Egypt you brought us to the desert to die?" (Exodus 14:11). Those ingrates! Smarting off to Moses instead of believing God would somehow save them! The Israelites got a big surprise. The joke was on Pharaoh's army when the Red Sea opened up and let God's people through, and then swallowed up all the soldiers. Years later, when the Israelites were happily worshiping idols, God said to them, "Go and cry to the gods which you have chosen; let *them* rescue you in the time of your torment" (Judges 10:14). If that doesn't sound like typical family squabble rhetoric, I don't know what does!

In the New Testament. Phillip tells his friend, Nathaniel, "We have found Him of Whom Moses...and...the prophets wrote, Jesus of Nazareth" (John 1:44). Nathaniel turned his nose up at Phillip and snorted, "Can anything good come out *Nazareth?*" (v. 46). "Come and see," Phillip told him. Nathaniel did, and the rest, as they say, is history.

Lord, You make all things beautiful, and You created humor too. Help us to laugh at life's absurdities, including ourselves. Amen

May 24

TAKE THE LID OFF YOUR LIFE

John replied in the words of Isaiah the prophet, "I am the voice of one calling in the wilderness, 'Make straight the way for the Lord.'" **John 1:23**

If God ever does a remake of The Earth, say on another planet in another galaxy, I want to play the part of John the Baptist. I'm not so crazy about wearing itchy camel's hair clothing, and I've never eaten a locust. But John has the very best part in the whole drama because he gets to be loud and get noticed! He's the one who comes around before anybody knows much about Jesus, shouting out to the world that things are about to change drastically. John has known Jesus his whole life—he even knew to "greet" Jesus when they were both still in their moms' tummies (Luke 1:41). I do wish there would be a script revision, though, because I don't really want to have my head chopped off and delivered to Herod on the palace china.

John knew what he was called to do, and he was just hanging around baptizing everyone else he could persuade to get wet. He made it clear from the beginning he was just the messenger, and the *real* Baptizer was about to show up with a whole different program. When Jesus did show up, John was not so much at a loss as to what to do as he was amazed the honor was being bestowed on him.

Maybe they will have a sort of "community theater" in heaven, and I'll get my chance to play John there. I can just imagine reenacting that pivotal moment with Christ, with me standing in the river in my size petite-small camel robe, and Jesus comes walking down the hill. I would have rehearsed my lines, and I'd be prepared to do my job. Then Jesus would take one look at me and say, "My child, you lived your life on earth shouting about Me from the rooftops. Let Me be the One to bestow sacraments on you now."

And I'd faint.

Lord, You have given me more than I could ever hope or imagine in this life. Let me declare Your mighty deeds to all I meet. Amen

May 25

JUNGLE TRIAGE

I called to the Lord, who is worthy of praise, and I have been saved from my enemies. **Psalm 18:3**

My husband Patrick describes serving as a helicopter medic in Viet Nam as being "like a bad acid trip." One particular incident stands out in his memory, when his helicopter team tried to rescue some downed infantry.

"We were terrified," he told me. "It was pitch black, and we were in the mountains…no radar…no relay stations nearby, and it was foggy." Aircraft often crashed into mountains or trees in Viet Nam., pilots frequently developing vertigo so they didn't know which way was up or down. Patrick continued, "The ground troops were reporting bad injuries, and they were firing flares to show us the way. We were all afraid a flare would hit our chopper and ignite our fuel. We never got the rescue accomplished, and we even had trouble finding our own way back." He was haunted because they were unable to save these soldiers.

Later, Patrick and I watched a historical documentary about military medics. Several veterans whose lives had been saved by medics were interviewed, among them many prominent U.S. citizens. Survivors expressed gratitude for the medics who saved their lives. They returned to the United States, married, had families, and lived full lives, often in spite of many serious injuries. Patrick was mesmerized by the stories. I asked him, "Did you ever stop to think about all the people walking around who wouldn't be here today if it wasn't for you?" He replied "I never looked at it that way."

Life is hard and war is hell. This Memorial Day, stop and remember all the brave men and women who have helped to ensure our daily freedom. Better yet, thank some in person.

Father of Peace, world peace seems impossible sometimes. We pray for a day when we will all live in peace, in this life or the next. Amen

May 26

THE JOY SET BEFORE ME

For the joy set before him he endured the cross, scorning its shame, and sat down at the right hand of the throne of God. **Hebrews 12:2**

When I was a teenager, my only source of joy in an otherwise out-of-control home life was riding my mare, Lito. Feeling her spine rise and fall as I gripped her bare back with my legs was pure heaven. Riding this wonderful, caramel-colored steed, I felt free of all my troubles. The Colorado mountain air was crisp as we wound through the trails in the mountains near our home. The sky was like a cobalt blue glass bottle shimmering in the sun.

Riding was life itself. My horse and I were bonded forever, protected by the whisper of the wind through the ponderosas. Riding was my only way to feel independent from my demented home life. I could make my own decisions, like riding in a thunderstorm with lightning crackling close enough to make my hair stand on end. I would sail my horse over log piles, past jagged granite slabs and swaying scrub oak that snapped to attention as we raced passed. I could spur my horse close enough to the edge of a mountain reservoir to see our reflection in the water. Then, WHOOSH! Off the ledge we jumped into the water, with Lito paddling as though she'd done it every day of her life. She swam all the way across the reservoir before she climbed out of the water on the sandy shoreline. During my troubled youth, the adrenalin rush of horseback riding was my greatest joy.

I now know that joy is one of God's abiding characteristics, one He shares with all who believe in Him. I have joy on a daily basis, even in the midst of my worst days. It is against God's nature to be sorrowful, because He is the creator of all that is good. The experience of happiness from anything other than God cannot compare to the unexplainable joy He brings, and joy is His abiding presence in our lives.

Son of God, thank You for enduring what we call sorrow to give us joy in You. Amen

May 27

THIS TIME YOU GAVE ME A MOUNTAIN

You will thresh the mountains and crush them, and reduce the hills to chaff. **Isaiah 41:15**

When I was in my twenties playing percussion in a road show, our lead singer performed "You Gave Me A Mountain." The powerful song brought tears to the eyes and a hefty round of applause, if not a standing ovation. The song *moved* people. I could not imagine the pain that went into composing the lyrics of the song.

"You Gave Me A Mountain" was written by Marty Robbins in the 1960s. The lyrics describe troubles the singer had overcome, from his mother's death to his father's bitterness over her loss, to his own wife leaving him and taking their baby boy. The singer is now facing something beyond what he thinks he can endure. "This time You gave me a mountain," he says to God, "a mountain that I may never climb." As I heard the song night after night, I wondered what his "mountain" could have been.

Today was a painful day for me, my arthritis taking its toll on my mind, body and spirit. As I lay quietly trying to will the pain to abate, I thought of this song once again. It suddenly became clear to me perhaps the singer wasn't anticipating a life-threatening event, or even an emotional trauma such as the ones he had already experienced. Perhaps the "mountain" was simply "the straw that broke the camel's back," that one-more-thing that made everything he had endured suddenly unendurable. Those of us who live with chronic pain—physical or emotional—have all been through times when we think our pain cannot get any worse. But when it does, it is a blessing to know God will hold us in our aloneness and our fear. He will say, "Do not fear, I will help you" (Isaiah 41:13). He promises us, "When the earth and all its people quake, it is I who hold its pillars firm" (Psalm 75:3). He walks with us through the valley. With God, we can face our mountains.

Healing Lord, be with us in the nighttime of our pain and also when joy comes in the morning. Amen

May 28

SUFFERING FOOLS GLADLY

Like snow in summer or rain in harvest, honor is not fitting for a fool.
Proverbs 26:1

One of the times I feel the most "un-Christian" is when I am assaulted by telemarketing calls, especially the electronically generated ones with a voice recording on the other end of the phone saying "Congratulations!" or "Don't hang up!" They call both my home and my cell phones at inopportune times. Now they use stolen or "burner" phones, so the area codes are often the same as mine, causing me to hope to hear a familiar voice on the other end. Then I'm stuck again. A radio spoof depicted telemarketers launching a phone campaign against the terrorists. After receiving several hundred annoying calls in a short period of time, the terrorists ran screaming from their bunkers and the group was disbanded.

How God would deal with telemarketers? He would probably answer every one. He knows everything so He could possibly help the caller improve his sales technique. But He doesn't need anything, so He wouldn't be interested in any products. If the caller had a quota, God would be sympathetic with the constraints of this world's business models, and He might be able to steer the telemarketer into the pursuit of more lucrative, less stressful employment. In the unlikely event God ever got annoyed by the calls, He could begin speaking in tongues in some ancient, long-dead language. That should slow them down. (Come to think of it, maybe I could try that…)

I should try to be more patient with telemarketers. They have to make a living, and maybe it's the only job they can find. God does want us to be productive while we are here on earth. It might always be hard for me to deal with these unwanted phone calls, but next time one comes through, I'll try to stop and say a prayer and ask God to bless the caller. I still won't answer, but maybe I'll feel better.

Patient God, help us remember not to sweat the small stuff (and it's all small stuff). Amen

May 29

MOTORCYCLE MAMA

***Consider it pure joy, my brothers and sisters, whenever you face trials of many kinds, because you know that the testing of your faith produces perseverance.* James 1:2-3**

"You'd better try on your cycle gear," my husband said. Wanting me to ride with him more, he bought me expensive, state-of-the-art safety gear. He added, half joking, "If you can't get yourself in and out of the suit, you can't go along." I glared at him, working the snaps on the pants liner, arthritic fingers curled in pain. *I want this*, I told myself. *He's doing everything on my bucket list with his buddies, without me there!* It was true, all his trips were "with the guys." I love my husband, and I wanted to go on this trip to Montana, a place I'd never visited. I wanted to see those mountains.

I almost had the twenty-plus pound suit on, looking like an aging cosmonaut, as he watched me over his newspaper. Finally, he got up and helped me finish. "We won't be on the road until noon every day if you make me do this all by myself," I wailed. "I want to go, but you have to help me a little bit." Some would think I am crazy, or he's stubborn, or maybe a little of both. But our marriage is a happy blend of give-and-take, especially since we came to it "later in life," with entrenched quirks and habits and dissimilarities. We have both stepped out of our comfort zones for the benefit of our relationship.

I think my relationship with the Lord is a little like this. God challenges me daily to do things I may not think I am able to do. I may complain and struggle to "git 'er done," but God is always patient with me. And when I don't think I can pull something off, He is there to give me strength and encouragement, and yes, an occasional small miracle to help me through.

Father, this life is full of joys and challenges. Ride with us as we travel our many varied paths. Amen

May 30

MINDFULNESS

For I have always been mindful of your unfailing love and have lived in reliance on your faithfulness. **Psalm 26:3**

"Mindfulness" is a busy buzz word these days. Definitions range from the Buddhist term anapanasati to Webster's definition, "maintaining a non-judgmental state of heightened…awareness of one's thoughts, emotions and sensations…in the present moment." My daughter teaches her four children "mindfulness" when she tells them to pay attention or risk injury. Certain psychiatrists believe they coined the term for its stress-reducing benefits. Most agree "mindfulness" is an attribute of consciousness that promotes well-being. If someone pushes a piano out of a third story window while you are walking by, "mindfulness" can prevent you from getting schmushed.

The Lord told Joshua to "keep (His Word) always on (his) lips; meditate on it (be mindful of it) day and night" (italics mine). God promised Joshua he would "be prosperous and successful," i.e., stress-free. The psalmist wrote about "mindfulness" in Psalm 26, when he petitioned the Lord to deliver him from his enemies because he had been a good and faithful man. "I lead a blameless life," he claimed, "deliver me and be merciful to me."

King Solomon wrote about mindfulness in Proverbs. Being in communion with God can reap untold benefits. If we pay attention to what God is telling us, we will "understand what is right and just," follow "every good path," allow wisdom to enter our hearts, and be guarded by understanding (Proverbs 9:2-9). Even Mary marveled at how God could be "mindful of the lowly estate of His servant" and chose her to bear His Son (Luke1:48).

Mindfulness is a practice God invented. He is mindful of us. Let's be "mindful" today and hear the voice of God.

Jesus, You say You will call us by name and lead us out of danger. Help us keep our minds and hearts focused on You. Amen

May 31

LITTLE MERCY

Surely goodness and mercy will follow me all the days of my life.
Psalm 23:6

Young Johnny was greeted by his friend Tommy as he entered the school yard. "Who's that?" Tommy asked, pointing to a little girl and her mother walking along behind Johnny. "That's little Mercy Goodness," he told his friend, "and her mom, Shirley." "Do you know them?" Tommy asked. "No, not really" came the reply. "But how do you know their names?" asked Tommy. Johnny said, "my mom prays every day when I leave, and she says, 'Shirley Goodness and Mercy will follow you all the days of your life.'"

Sometimes children have a hard time understanding the "grown-up" words they hear at home, church or school. There are many kids' bloopers, like the little girl who said the name of her favorite hymn was "Gladly the Cross-Eyed Bear." Or the little boy who was told the plaques in the narthex were in memory of people who had died in the service, and the child asked, "Which one? The early service or the late service?" A youngster reciting the Lord's Prayer: "Our Father Who art in heaven, how do you know my name?" Our pastor talked about God being everywhere, asking, "Where is God now?" One child blurted out, "I think He might be in Ohio!"

This past Sunday, the youth at our church conducted the entire service. I was honored to accompany them on the drums, playing with other adult musicians as those kids sang their hearts out leading the congregation in song and liturgy. It filled me with joy to see all these young people to whom the torch will soon be passed to continue the work of the church. Little ones amuse us, but they also amaze us in the way they embrace God's joy and the work He asks us to do. If you have any little ones in your life, remember to tell them you appreciate them, and remind them God does too.

Father of Young and Old, help our youth to embrace Your wonderful ways and to live out their lives in service to You. Amen

June

June 1

NO LONGER AVAILABLE

You make known to me the path of life; you will fill me with joy in your presence, with eternal pleasures at your right hand. **Psalm 16:11**

It's happened again. A product I have purchased and used for years has been discontinued. After all my years of loyalty, the company didn't consult me or send me a notice. They just stopped making the product without a care in the world for what I am going to do now. I even asked the store manager. She said the company couldn't get the ingredients they needed any more.

I search for my favorite brand of ice cream, which now declares, "New Package! Same Great Taste!" But, as any fool can tell, the quantity has been reduced. Who do they think they're kidding? My favorite pencils, always made of wood strong enough to sharpen repeatedly, are suddenly being made of…what? Scraps from old barns? They fall apart the first time I try to sharpen them! The fabulous seasoning I always bought at our meat market? I'm told the guy who made it is "off the grid." A Viet Nam vet, the fellow apparently concocted this stuff in his basement using a secret formula even his mother doesn't know. He just decided he was tired of making "Sammy's Salt," and the heck with the world's grillers. He even took down his website, sammyssalt.com. I haven't tasted a good hamburger since this happened.

Isn't it nice to know you can always open the Bible and find the same "ingredients?" Genesis is always right before Exodus, and Paul still got zapped on the road to Damascus, and the story of Jesus' ministry is the same yesterday, today and tomorrow. People have tried to "repackage" the Bible, but they can't change the message. Why? Because that message is God-designed and God-breathed. The Word is God. You can't mess with it. God never goes out of business or "off the grid" or takes down His website (does He even need one?). In this world of change, the one constant thing is God. It's comforting to know God is everlasting.

Eternal God, thank You for being the one constant in a world that isn't. Amen

June 2

GUERILLA WEED CONTROL

No one can serve two masters. Either you will hate the one and love the other, or you will be devoted to the one and despise the other. You cannot serve both God and money. **Matthew 6:24**

I tugged and I dug and I pulled, and finally the foot-long root of the thistle gave way. Its root was a foot long with little hairy tendrils on it just waiting to reproduce themselves. I wanted our front plantings to look just like Dick's yard next door: perfect, pristine, all in a neat row, behaving themselves like good little children in church. How did he keep his place looking so nice?

Just then, Dick came out of his garage carrying a huge plastic container with a spray nozzle. Was that…*weed killer?* He walked along his planting beds, squirting away. I could hardly contain myself. "What's that?" I asked. He looked up and said, "It's called 'Weed Bead.' I spray it around my plants about twice a month." "You *do?*" I said. "I thought your gardens just behaved themselves." Dick laughed. "Oh, no, I have to help them along."

I've always tried to be an organic gardener, pulling weeds until my hands and my back ached. Densely-planted flowers and veggies should fight off weeds, shouldn't they? All the worms and crawly critters in the soil were supposed to be there, right? What if I could just *spray* all my worries away? I dug out a huge dandelion. Suddenly, to my surprise, my garden fork unearthed a six-inch lizard who glared at me before he scurried indignantly away. Eventually, I compromised and began spraying only the weeds in front of our house, where the neighbors could see. I pull the others.

There is no compromising when it comes to following God. Jesus said we can't serve both God and money. I may be double-minded about my gardening, but placing Jesus at the center of my life is non-negotiable.

Lord of Flora and Fauna, help us make wise decisions about the earth You have placed in our care. Amen

June 3

FREE WILL OFFERINGS

You must present as the Lord's portion the best and holiest part of everything given to you. **Numbers 18:29**

I was asked to speak to a group of recovering alcoholics and drug addicts at their Friday night meeting at a small, charismatic church in northeast Missouri. Having spoken to groups of students for years, I was not particularly nervous, but I was still honing what I wished to say and trying to do the will of God. I spoke without notes, from the heart, for about forty-five minutes, and answered questions afterwards. When I was done, not only did I receive a standing ovation, the pastor of the church insisted on taking a free will offering. I was given more money than I would have asked as a speaker's fee. As if that wasn't enough, the pastor asked me to come back Sunday morning and preach!

This experience taught me several things. First, I learned I have something valuable to say. Apparently, my life experiences and the way I have "come through the fire," so to speak, resonates with many people. Maya Angelou once said "There is no greater agony than bearing an untold story inside you." We all have a story to tell, and if we tell it as a way to help others, God will bless the telling. The second thing I learned was God would truly guide my words and cause me to say what the hearers want to hear. After I speak, I am humbled to realize the words are not so much "mine" as they are God's voice of hope through me.

Last, I learned the "free will offering" given that night was not just a plate of money. My talk was my "free-will offering" to those present. Isaiah 50:4 says, "The Lord God has given me the tongue of a teacher that I may sustain the weary with a word." If I am willing to use my God-given talents as a "sacrifice" for Him, I will always reach the hearts of others.

Tender God, bless the telling of our stories that we may sustain each other with our words. Amen

June 4

STICKY SITUATION

Put away from you all bitterness and wrath and anger and wrangling and slander, together with all malice, and be kind to one another, tenderhearted, forgiving one another, as God in Christ has forgiven you. **Ephesians 4:31-32**

Christian singer/song writer Twila Paris wrote a song called "Bonded Together," about her relationship with Christ. Any separation would "tear out a heart," either God's or hers. Their relationship is "like a metal alloy" or an "amalgamation." (*Amalgamates* and *alloys* are created by melting and mixing two or more metals together.) God's bond is "a holy fusion."

Epoxy is a strong adhesive including two resins used for sticking items together to last, indoors or out in the elements. Many brands recommend putting the glue on both surfaces, allowing them to "set" for a few seconds and then sticking the two objects together. This last step ensures a stronger hold. I know this for a fact because I have tried to rush the process and the end result is usually failure. My garden angel remains single-winged because I did not hold the broken pieces together long enough following an unfortunate "fallen angel" incident.

Ephesians 4:31-32 says there are two steps to repairing damage done to human relationships. First we must get rid of all bitterness and anger towards another, and *only then* are we able to forgive. To banish all ill feelings towards another, we need to repent of our sin of having those feelings to begin with. If the first step is not undertaken seriously and completely, the idea of forgiving the other person is like a bitter pill stuck in our throats.

Peter said, "Repent and be baptized…in the name of Jesus Christ so your sins may be forgiven" (Acts 2:38). Turning away from our sins allows us to receive forgiveness from God, and it allows us to forgive other people so we can move forward in our relationships. Those are glues that stick!

Merciful God, thank You for Your overwhelming grace in helping us bond to You and to the people in our life. Amen

June 5

SPIRITUAL WELFARE OR WARFARE?

Therefore take up the whole armor of God, so that you may be able to withstand on that evil day, and having done everything, to stand firm. **Ephesians 6:13**

The last thing my father said to me the night he died was, "Promise me you will look after your mother's welfare." The job would not be easy. My mother suffered most of her adult life from alcoholism, never gaining victory. My dad tried to control her drinking for years, with no success. He enabled her habit, buying her alcohol and assuming all household duties, rendering her irrelevant. She deteriorated into a helpless, demanding woman, never dealing with her drinking problem or her profound depression.

Both my parents believed in God, but their isolated lifestyle five states away from me left them with no one to look in on them. When my new husband and I moved Mother near us, I felt more like I was engaged in "warfare" with her than seeing to her "welfare." My constant prayer was that I could renew her hope in God. I was never sure that happened before she died.

This same scenario existed with my teenaged girls. The older one is outgoing, capable and responsible.. Through the efforts of her best friend's family, she accepted Christ at age sixteen and never turned back. My younger daughter faced many challenges due to a traumatic brain injury sustained when she was a child. She has a heart as big as the sky, but little ability to make wise decisions. She walked away from the Christian life and today often seems like a boat without a dock. I pray differently for both my daughters, and I know God loves them more than I can ever imagine.

Paul told the Ephesians to "be strong in the Lord and in the strength of his power" because our enemies are "the spiritual forces of evil" (Ephesians 6:10, 12). Life can be a heartbreaker sometimes, but God is faithful. He will "work all things together for good for those who are called to His purpose."

All-Powerful God, we place our spiritual welfare and warfare in Your capable hands. Amen

June 6

THE GOSPEL ACCORDING TO ME

All who exalt themselves will be humbled, but all who humble themselves will be exalted. **Luke 18:14**

I forget I've been retired from my counseling career for several years, and occasionally I try to diagnose the problems of people I meet. I don't say anything to them of course, but now and then, in my head, I'm thinking, this person is this or that and should probably do this or that to be more effective in life. I tell myself I do this because I really *do* care about people and I want to *help* them. (All my friends who are reading this will now think I'm psychoanalyzing them every time we have coffee together.)

Hell-oooooooooooooooooo? Can you spell "Pharisee?" Jesus told the parable of the Pharisee and the tax collector, two guys who happened to be at the temple praying at the same time. The Pharisee "trusted in (himself) that he was righteous" (Luke 18:9), and he put on quite a show there in the church courtyard. Lifting his shining face to the heavens, the Pharisee began, "God, I thank you that I am not like other people…like this tax collector. I fast twice a week; I give a tenth of all my income" (Luke 18:11). *Look at me, everybody!* That's what he was really saying. *I'm such an expert at my Jewish faith* (feel free to substitute *Christian faith*, or anything else you like to brag about), *and God just loves every word coming out of my squeaky-clean mouth!*

But there's the old tax collector, a Jew who *collects money for the Roman government that occupies their nation!* His neighbors hate him, but he has to make a living somehow. So he takes his guilt and remorse about the state of his life, and he lays it all at God's feet. He's "beating his breast and saying, 'God, be merciful to me, a sinner!'" (Luke 18:13). The Lord says, "You guys just don't get it! The humble tax collector is more in God's favor than the boastful Pharisee!" Jesus says, "Keep it simple. Remember: you are a sinner."

Redeeming Lord, thank You for forgiving us our sins, including that of boasting. Amen

June 7

MOST LIKELY TO SUCCEED

Turn my life from looking at vanities; give me life in Your ways. **Psalm 119:37**

My high school graduating class chose the student "Most Likely to Succeed," whatever *that* meant! I can't remember who was chosen (not me. I was painfully shy.). But, I ran into the class nerd a few years later. Billy Berkowitz planned to study archaeology, which sounded like a typical nerdy career path to me. I ran into him when I was visiting a display of ancient architecture at the Denver Art Museum for my art history class. He was there for his archaeology studies at a different college. Suddenly, he wasn't so nerdy. He was nice looking and talked enthusiastically about collecting artifacts on a trip his class made to Egypt. He gave me all sorts of validation about my interior design major. Why had I never thought he was cool?

No, I didn't marry him! I never even went out with him. My point is success is not necessarily in the eyes of our stuck-up high school class mates. Webster's first definition of "success" is "the fact of getting or achieving wealth, respect, or fame." So is wealth the first thing we must acquire before being called successful? I expect it depends on who we rely on to make that judgement. The definition of "success" should be a personal thing, right? Does this make a gang lord who has the most notches in his homemade gun a success? What about the supreme underachiever who just wants to sit in his parents' basement and play video games until he's old and gray?

For Christians, there is another component to success: remembering. Moses told the disgruntled Israelites to "remember (they) were (slaves) in Egypt." Wandering the desert in relative discomfort *was* success in God's eyes. Have you traveled in the direction God wanted you to go? Have you honored God with your decisions? Have you remembered when you were struggling with life decisions? Do you use your talents to edify God's world and His children? If so, then you are one of God's "Most Likely to Succeed!"

Shepherd God, Your ways are successful ways. Lead us in right paths. Amen

June 8

FIRST DO NO HARM

"Love your neighbor as yourself." Love does no harm to a neighbor. Therefore love is the fulfillment of the law. **Romans 13:9-10**

Primum Non Nocere, or First Do No Harm, is a guiding principle for physicians. This creed means whatever the procedure, the patient's well-being is the primary consideration. Scholars disagree with about the idea's origin, but avoidance of maltreatment is a fundamental principle taught in healthcare throughout the world. Caution must be used when implementing a treatment where the risk of harm may outweigh the chance of benefit.

We Christians would do well to live by the principle, First Do No Harm. In Romans 13, Paul discusses the Christian's responsibilities in society. Public servants are seen as God's servants. Paul is correct that these officials should be acting in a godly manner; when they don't, God's kingdom is not being pursued here on earth. What if our government leaders followed the principle of *First Do No Harm*? The political landscape would look a lot different, and the judicial system would surely need an overhaul.

Paul goes on to say we should "let no debt remain outstanding, except the continuing debt to love one another" (Romans 13:8). I'm fonder of some of my neighbors than others, but hadn't thought much about loving my neighbor being a "debt." My love is *due* to my neighbor because God *first loved me*. Knowing God loves me energizes me to spread the love of Christ to all I see. When I view my neighbor through the lens of First Do No Harm, I am suddenly surprised to see the harm I sometimes do just standing still! I join the "casserole brigade" after a neighbor dies, carrying food to the family, but perhaps I've not been so "neighborly" the rest of the days of the year. I'm going to try to "first do no harm" every day!

Loving Father, You want no harm for Your children. Empower us to help You in this work. Amen

June 9

VOLUNTOLD

Go therefore and make disciples of all nations, baptizing them in the name of the Father and of the Son and of the Holy Spirit.
Matthew 28:19

In a small church like ours, we say we are being "voluntold." There are so few of us, we pretty much know if we're asked, we ought to say "yes," unless doing so would be a significant hardship on our lives. We all pull together to get things done and it seems to work well.

When Jesus said goodbye to His disciples just before he ascended into heaven, He did *not* say, "Listen, guys, if you think you'd like to help out and maybe do at least a small part of the Father's will, could you try to find a little time in your busy fishing and tax collecting lives to spread a little bit of the Gospel here and there, you know, if you can?" Good grief, no! What did He say? He said, "GO!" And they went. They didn't wait for a committee decision. They didn't try to delegate the responsibility to others with less standing in the New Christian Fellowship. They obeyed, which was also part of what they were asked to do. The rest of Matthew 28 says they were to be "teaching (others) to obey everything I have commanded you" (v.20). They knew the drill, and they knew, beyond a shadow of a doubt, that Jesus was counting on them.

Remember the old story about the rocks in the jar? You put big rocks in a jar and ask people if they think it's full. They say "yes," and then you put in small rocks, then pebbles, then sand. Now it's full. But you have to put the important stuff into your lives before the small rocks, pebbles and sand fill up your time. So let's not sit around and wait for the time to materialize for us to do God's work. Let's put that Rock in the jar first.

Jesus, You are our Commander In Chief. Send us, give us the words to say, and rejoice with us. Amen

June 10

ENERGIZER!

The steadfast love of the Lord is from everlasting to everlasting. **Psalm 103:17**

I love the Energizer Bunny! Because I'm a drummer, I have collected a number of these Pepto-Bismol® colored bunnies over the years. According to the Energizer Battery website, the Bunny was created in 1989 and he has been "delivering boundless energy, innovation and smiles for fans of all ages" ever since. In his iconic flip flops and sunglasses, he embodies enviable get-up-and-go. Even his tag line, "Keep Going," is trademarked. The Bunny has flown as the "Hot Hare Balloon," taller than the Statue of Liberty, held together with 84 miles of thread, with size 98 EEEE shoes. He has even faced "the dark side," but his foes were defeated because they used inferior batteries in their weapons. The Energizer Bunny was chosen one of the top ten advertising icons of the Twentieth Century.

The ultimate "energizer" in my life remains my Savior, Jesus Christ. Born more than 2000 years ago, he lived on earth only 33 years, and is technically "dead" to most people still living in this world. But He lives on in the hearts of all believers. I think He deserves the "Energizer" award for all time! We are human, and thus have limited energy. But God is immortal, and everything about Him is limitless: His energy, His love, His power, His patience… The list goes on indefinitely. Though we can't see Him with human eyes, He is everywhere, all the time, and His mercy is all around us.

Jesus never wore sunglasses and flip flops, and He never had green hair or won a marketing award. He walked everywhere here on earth, so he must have had boundless energy. He's certainly not pink, but He fills the skies all around us. He's able to vanquish any evil foe, physical or spiritual, with a single word. Best of all, He doesn't need batteries since He has an endless source of power that comes from His Father in heaven.

Energizer God, lend me Your steadfastness so I may reach those here on earth who do not know You. Amen

June 11

POLISHED ARROW

He made my mouth like a sharpened sword, in the shadow of His hand he hid me; He made me into a polished arrow and concealed me in His quiver. Isaiah 49:2

The first time I stood in front of an audience to tell my faith story, I was understandably nervous. My talk about being delivered from a near-death experience at the hands of a rapist was hosted by the two-year college where I had worked as a counselor until my retirement. Several dozen people—students, staff and community members—stared expectantly at me, wondering what I had to say. I knew I had to deliver my message of God's miraculous rescue in a secular manner. I clearly was not in a church, and I saw former students of different faiths (or no faith). None of my two decades as an entertainer did anything to quiet the butterflies in my stomach.

When I began to speak, the Holy Spirit guided my words. Through me, a message of hope and resilience following trauma unfolded smoothly. I knew by the questions at the end of my talk I had touched many of those present.

Who am I to have been given this remarkable opportunity to serve my Lord by speaking to total strangers about what His love means to me? And to be doing it in a secular setting with the perfect words delivered to my brain and out of my mouth was mind-boggling. I recalled the Casting Crowns song, "Who Am I?" about the wonder of knowing that the Lord of the universe "would look on me with love and watch me rise again." God spared Moses from his fear of public speaking by allowing Aaron to speak in his place. God did me one better: He allowed me to speak His timely message myself, but with words given to me by the Spirit.

Do you get the jitters when you are asked to explain your faith? Why not ask the Master Speech Coach for help? He will give you the right words at the right time. Remember, the world is waiting to hear your story!

Guiding Spirit, make my words like polished arrows that hit the target every time. Amen

June 12

PRUNED BRANCHES

I am the true vine, and my Father is the vine grower. He removes every branch in me that bears no fruit. Every branch that bears fruit He prunes to make it bear more fruit. John 15:1-2

"I have a blog idea," my friend Pat told me at church last Sunday. "Come over and I'll show you." The next afternoon, I drove to her home and she led me into her upstairs bedroom. She opened the window, pointing to the tree outside. "There," she said triumphantly. "See where it's been pruned? It's all healed up." She then showed me a recently trimmed tree in the back yard, raw and slashed up, as if it had just undergone surgery. Which it had.

Another friend, Gary, is a tree surgeon. He takes care of our diseased and damaged trees and shrubs, lopping off dead wood and generally trying to keep them healthy as long as possible. Our vegetation flourishes under Gary's care. He is like a "tree whisperer."

The fifteenth chapter of John is about God pruning us so we can bear more fruit, which was the point of my friend Pat's object lesson. Much of this chapter parallels Old Testament teachings, in which God deals with the "unfruitful" Israelites (Isaiah 5:1-7; 27:2-6). Jesus now describes Himself as "true vine," and His Father as "the vine dresser." "Just as the branch cannot bear fruit by itself unless it abides in the vine," Jesus continues, "neither can you, unless you abide in me." Vine dressing, or pruning, can be painful, but the end result is that we "bear much fruit" (verse 5), or bring benefit to the lives of others. "Apart from (Christ)," we can't build true Christian character in ourselves nor influence others to do so. Jesus' words about throwing unproductive branches into the fire (v. 6) make many think of hellfire and brimstone. But another view could be our bad habits can be pruned away and replaced with new growth. My friend Pat was right: pruning hurts, but God does it out of great love. We survive and thrive!

Father, remove all that is in me that does not glorify You. Amen

June 13

DEM DRY BONES

Prophesy to these bones, and say to them: O dry bones, hear the word of the LORD. Thus says the Lord GOD to these bones: I will cause breath to enter you, and you shall live. Ezekiel 37:4-5

I knew my body: there was something very wrong with my hip. I was three months post-surgery, but the pain in my leg following my total hip operation was too intense. Both the surgeon and my husband (who was his colleague) were saying it was all in my head. No, it was in my *hip*, and it *hurt!*

Then, a news report gave credence to my fears. My hip implant had been recalled. An MRI showed a huge bursitis, the largest one my husband had ever seen. Blood tests revealed worse news: my blood was full of chromium shavings. I underwent a second surgery, debriding of the entire hip joint of metal shavings, a good deal of blood loss and a two-unit transfusion. Almost five years passed from the original surgery until I could say I was "okay."

I trusted my surgeon. The implant company…not so much! But all through the ordeal, I was acutely aware it would be God Who would breathe new life into my bones (and the implant!). I suffered from a serious bout of depression during this time, because my first book was being published as I went in for the second surgery. Not to be defeated, I took several copies of the new book to the hospital with me. ("What is in this *bag?*" my husband asked.) I sold them all to hospital staff members and had some interesting conversations as a result.

God gave Ezekiel the power to prophesy to those bleached and long dead bones on an ancient battlefield and restore them to life. He could unquestionably heal my hip. Yes, I had my doubts about my situation, but God is faithful, and a little surprising!

Healing Father, thank You for caring for my body here on earth, and for your promise of a new one when I get to heaven. Amen

June 14

WHAT'S IN A NAME?

But Barnabas took (Saul), brought him to the apostles, and described for them how on the road he had seen the Lord, who had spoken to him, and how in Damascus he had spoken boldly in the name of Jesus. **Acts 9:27**

Names in the Bible often mean something special. Barnabas means "Son of Encouragement," because as a member of the early church, that's what he did best. One of Barnie's first and perhaps biggest assignments would be working with the new convert, Saul, or Paul as he became known. Saul was a zealous Jew who had been busy "breathing threats and murder against the disciples of the Lord," because he thought Jesus was a fake. Heading to Damascus to hunt down more of Christ's followers, Saul was struck down and blinded by Jesus. After tutoring under Ananias, Saul returned to Jerusalem hoping to hang out with the disciples. "No way!" they said. "Not that jerk!" Enter Barnabas, who *encouraged* the disciples to take a second look. Later, Saul began referring to himself as "chief among sinners." Saul's name got changed to Paul, which means "small." No small coincidence here.

Examples of meaningful names abound in the Bible. Isaac means "laughter" because his mother Sara thought it was hysterical God allowed her to bear a child at her advanced age. Isaac's dad was pretty proud though, because he would be living up to his name, which means "father of a great multitude."

I think my name means something like "One Who Makes Wise Cracks," or "She Who Never Finishes a Project." But God loves me more than I love myself. Why else would He forgive me for all the dumb things I've done? So maybe God would name me "Meditates While Gardening," or "Plays Drums for God." He might even call me "Tries Hard to Please." Whatever name God would give me would surely reflect that He loves me immeasurably and watches over me as one of His own. Now that's a name I can live with!

Abiding Father, whatever You choose to call each of us, help us live up to Your expectations. Amen

June 15

MUSCLE MEMORY

This is the covenant that I will make with them after those days, says the Lord: I will put my laws in their hearts, and I will write them on their minds. **Hebrews 10:16**

I learned in physical therapy that my muscles have memory. According to healthguidance.com, "muscle memory is the ability of our mind to capture a particular activity or movement." If you learned to ride a bike as a child, you will always be able to ride a bike. There might be a slight learning curve to get back into the old activity, but it's never as steep as the first time you learned. Our muscle memory registers certain muscle movements which can be performed flawlessly even after a break of many years.

Most theorists agree our muscles get accustomed to a particular sequence performed time and again, because of the neural pathway that develops from repetition. Following my left hip replacement, playing drums was hard. I could not make that leg keep time, or function as part of my team of limbs doing separate things at the same time. I also lacked proprioception, or the ability to make my limbs move independently of each other. Drummers use all four limbs and cross the "midline" of the drum set to create a "fill." With practice, I regained the ability to do all this.

The heart is a muscle too, and the Bible talks about the heart's muscle memory. In Hebrew 10:16, Paul quotes Jeremiah 31:31-32, in which God told the Israelites He would "put (His) laws in their hearts and…write them on their minds." In Scripture, the "heart" is the center for physical, emotional, intellectual, and moral activities. "Man looks at the outward appearance, "says Samuel, "but the Lord looks at the heart" (Samuel 16:7). Does your heart remember God's covenants and obey them, or do you need to renew your "muscle memory?"

Creator God, You made each muscle in our bodies. Teach us to use them for Your glory. Amen

June 16

JIGSAW PUZZLE

The earth is the Lord's, and everything in it, the world, and all who live in it. **Psalm 24:1**

Jane Goodall, the British-born anthropologist and animal activist, studied primate behavior in the wild, changing the understanding of animal behavior worldwide. Recently quoted in Reader's Digest Magazine, she said, "I like to envision the whole world as a jigsaw puzzle… overwhelming.., but if you work on your little part of the jigsaw and know people all over the world are working on (theirs), that's what will give you hope."

Jigsaw puzzles generally make my brain hurt. I know they sharpen the mind and reduce stress in most people. They take a lot of time and patience, kind of like Goodall's studies of primates. But I don't have an innate desire to "solve" the entire puzzle by myself. I prefer to think of myself as just one piece of the puzzle, connecting to a few others, who connect to a few more, and so on.

When we consider this huge world and how little space each person takes up on the planet, we can be exceedingly humbled. And yet the same God Who created everything we see and all we don't see knows each of our names and all of our thoughts and concerns. Luke 12:7 says even the very hairs on our heads are numbered and known by our Lord. We are indeed a very tiny puzzle piece, but God empowers each of us to do our part. God told the Israelites, "This day…I have set before you life and death, blessings and curses" (Deuteronomy 30:19). He challenges us to "choose life," and that life is the Lord's way (v.20). We may feel like tiny, insignificant puzzle pieces in the vastness of this life on earth, but we have an all-powerful God who tells us we are precious and honored in (His) sight" (Isaiah 43:4). We must work with the puzzle piece we have been given, for the good of the whole puzzle-earth.

Gracious Lord, embolden me to use my talents for the benefit of others. Amen

June 17

FRESH FROM HEAVEN

You created my inmost being; You knit me together in my mother's womb. **Psalm 139:13**

There are many accounts of small children telling their parents they remember the time before they were born. I read about a boy who said all the children made their own flowers in their favorite colors, and the flowers sang to them. When shown pictures of Jesus, a little girl said they were nice but the real thing was nicer. One child even said she chose her parents, and had trouble getting them together on earth so she could be their child!

The psalmist believed God knew him before his birth. Today's Scripture, Psalm 139, goes on to say, "My frame was not hidden from you when I was made in the secret place…woven together in the depths of the earth." If we believe God created us, does it make sense to be convinced He spoke to us and held us before we left His "workshop?" The apostle Paul said, "We are God's handiwork, created in Christ Jesus to do good works, which God prepared in advance for us to do" (Ephesians 2:10). Could there have been some "marching orders" given before we began life as we know it?

Why don't we remember being in heaven? Researchers have tried for years to identify the cause of "infantile amnesia." Even mice and monkeys forget their early childhood. A recent study suggests rapid neuron growth in children disrupts the brain circuitry, erasing early memories. Young children also have an undeveloped prefrontal cortex causing infant amnesia.

I like to think of the Triune God holding me, kissing me, and sending me to this life, complete with a mission and a purpose that I will only discover if I remember Who God is. I am comforted to think going back to heaven when I die will rekindle these memories and remind me I truly am "home."

I praise You, Lord, that I am "fearfully and wonderfully made," and loved immeasurably by You. Amen

June 18

TEN THOUSAND LAKES

You measured the waters in the palm of Your hand. **Isaiah 40:2**

My home state of Minnesota lays claim to the slogan, Land of Ten Thousand Lakes. In reality the state boasts 15,232 bodies of water larger than ten acres. From tiny Lake Itasca at the headwaters of the Mississippi River to the state's largest, Mil Lacs Lake, covering 132,516 acres, the beauty of our lakes is astounding. Many varieties of fish grace our waters, and surrounding shores and forests are filled with wildlife. Native vegetation lends a primeval quality to the lake banks. A heavenly sight!

Lake Minnetonka, in the heart of the Twin Cities, features 125 miles of shoreline. Beautiful homes line the shores, from hundred year old summer cottages to opulent mansions. On Sundays, it seems each person living there owns a speedboat, jet ski, or pontoon, all vying for the best space in which to enjoy fishing, water skiing, or generally tearing around the lake burning up fuel. Quiet summer afternoons seem to be a thing of the past.

Fishing enthusiasts were surprised this year when the Minnesota Department of Natural Resources declared a one-fish per day, specific length limit for the state's premier fish, the walleye, on Mil Lacs Lake. Previous years had seen the walleye population rapidly declining due to over-fishing. Unlimited fishing hasn't been seen in this state for many decades, all due to anglers keeping more than their share.

God created our lakes, rivers and oceans and gave mankind "dominion over the fish" (Genesis 1:26), among other things. Psalm 24:1 says, "The earth is the Lord's and all that is in it." If we are to be good stewards of this beautiful planet on which we are privileged to live, we must be mindful of others with whom we share God's bountiful resources.

Creator God, forgive us for not taking care of Your bountiful earth as we should. Help us share Your gifts with everyone. Amen

June 19

A HOUSE OF PRAYER

"It is written," He said to them, "'My house will be a house of prayer'; but you have made it 'a den of robbers.'" **Luke 19:46**

Another mass shooting happened, this time in a house of God, the Emanuel African Methodist Episcopal Church in Charleston, South Carolina. Nine people are dead, including the pastor. They were holding a Bible study, innocent believers, studying about God's peace. The gunman even sat with them and prayed before he began shooting. He said, "I have to do it," and then something else about blacks taking over "our" country. "*Our*" country?

My heart is heavy tonight, as it always is following one of these incidents. The President pointedly said the United States has more of these mass shootings than any other civilized nation. Why? Lack of reasonable gun control? Failure to identify potential shooters before the guns are purchased or fired? Hatred? We may never know the answers or be able to implement a solution. Only God knows why this is happening over and over and over.

Only God knows, the same God who tore up another sanctuary but for different reasons. He had just made His triumphant entry into Jerusalem, on a donkey instead of a nobler steed. We now call it Palm Sunday, when the people lay palm fronds across His path (Matthew 21:8). "Hosanna!" the people cried, "Blessed is He Who comes in the name of the Lord!" (v.9). When He entered the temple, He "overturned the tables of the money changers and the benches of those selling doves, and would not allow anyone to carry merchandise through the temple courts" (Mark 11:15-16). Jesus wanted the people to have the same reverence for His Father's house as He had. The same reverence the members of a quiet Bible study had for their historic church on a Wednesday night in June, 2015, in Charleston, South Carolina. The same reverence four young black girls had for their church, the 16th St. Baptist Church in Birmingham, Alabama in 1963.

God of Justice, hear our cry! End this violence and hatred; bring lasting peace. Amen

June 20

MYSTERY WRITER

***Listen, I will tell you a mystery: We will not all sleep, but we will all be changed— in a flash, in the twinkling of an eye, at the last trumpet.* 1 Corinthians 15:51**

Everyone loves a good mystery novel, keeping you on the edge of your seat at each twist and turn in the plot, never giving away "whodunit" until the very last minute. We all like the way we are pulled into the plot, biting our nails until we can turn the page to discover what's next. One person in a discussion said she liked the chaos-to-order of a mystery: chaos caused by the mystery (the villain), but then someone (the hero) comes and fixes it all. Our hearts pump and our adrenaline surges. We race to the end of the book. Most of us try to put the clues together and solve the thriller ourselves, but a really good mystery writer will fool us all until the very last page.

The Bible says part of God's plan must remain a mystery to us all. In 1 Corinthians 15:52, Paul says, "For the trumpet will sound, the dead will be raised imperishable, and we will be changed." I don't know about you, but those very words get the blood pounding in my ears! Paul also describes Christ's second coming in 1 Thessalonians 4:16: "For the Lord himself, with a cry of command…will descend from heaven, and the dead in Christ will rise first." As if that's not enough, Paul continues, "Then we who are alive, who are left, will be caught up in the clouds together with them to meet the Lord in the air; and so we will be with the Lord forever." That's us believers, folks! What a wild ride that will be!

Though the word "rapture" never appears in the Bible, the idea has given rise to many publications, lectures, books and movies. But it is good to remember what Jesus said in Matthew 24:36: "No one knows the day or the hour when these things will happen, not even the angels in heaven or the Son Himself. Only the Father knows." God as Mystery Writer is leaving the ending of His story for…the end!

Mysterious Lord, enable us to trust You until You return for us. Amen

June 21

COMPUTERS! WHAT A JOKE!

"I am the way, the truth and the life. No one comes to the Father except through Me." John 14:6

On a website called computerjokes.com, I learned "state-of-the-art" refers to any computer I can't afford. "Obsolete" means the computer I now own. And "microsecond" is the time it takes for a "state-of-the-art" computer to become "obsolete." I learned a "keyboard" is the standard way to generate computer errors, and a "mouse" is an advanced input device to make computer errors easier to generate. I should probably just sell my computer and start using paper and pencil again! But who would buy my computer anyway, if it's already obsolete and just generates computer errors?

I think Jesus is kind of like a computer Himself. Yes, this is true, and it can all be documented in Scripture. Jesus enters your life if you ask Him to. In Matthew 7:7, Jesus says, "Ask and it will be given to you; seek and you will find; knock and the door will be opened to you." Then, He scans your problems, whatever they may be. Jesus doesn't care what's happened in your life before. Once you are His child, you are a new creature (2 Corinthians 5:17). God's cosmic computer skills also include the ability to edit your stress away! When we begin to understand and accept God is God and we are not, our perspective of what causes us stress changes drastically. We begin to experience "the peace of God, which transcends all understanding" (Philippians 4:7). Jesus preached, "Do not worry about your life, what you will eat or drink; or about your body, what you will wear" (Matthew 6:25). He is faithful to download solutions to our problems if we follow Him and study His ways. Jesus deletes our worries completely and invites us to "Come to (Him), all you who are weary and burdened, and (He) will give you rest" (Matthew 11:28). Jesus saves us from a lifetime of being lost in cyberspace, and welcomes us into eternal life when we are finally deleted from this earth. I like Jesus' computer terminology!

Come Lord Jesus, be my Personal Computer! Amen

June 22

KINTSUKUROI

He will purify the Levites and refine them like gold and silver. Then the Lord will have men who will bring offerings in righteousness. **Malachi 3:3**

Kintsukuroi is the Japanese art of repairing broken pottery with gold or silver lacquer, making the pieces beautiful once again. The practice of *kintsukuroi* has been around for centuries. The Chinese glued pots together with ugly metal staples, but Japanese craftsmen soon created a "more aesthetic means of repair." *Kintsukuroi* was so popular some deliberately smashed their valuable pottery in order to repair it using gold lacquer. *Kintsukuroi* "treats breakage and repair as part of the history of an object, rather than something to disguise," more beautiful for having been broken.

How like these broken vessels we are! We spend our entire lives vacillating between good and evil. Children soak up what adults teach them, helpful or hurtful. Our personalities are shaped by our physical abilities and attributes, our family's economic standing, and opportunities afforded us in life. As adults, we put educational opportunities and job history (or the absence of) into that emotional blender, along with new relationships, marriage, children, physical and mental health or illness. Now there are cracks everywhere! Worldly voices offer "just what we need," not all legitimate or appropriate. They may shout so loud it's hard to hear anything else.

No wonder we need Jesus! He's more than the glue that holds us all together; He's the *gold* in the cracks of our lives! Belief in Christ makes the difference between using plain old school paste to patch up our problems and having the Master Craftsman bring His golden love and healing to make us all the more beautiful—and useful—for the brokenness we experience. "When He has tested me, I will come forth as gold," said Job in the middle of his trials (Job 23:10). Let's choose Jesus as our Sacred Artist Who repairs with gold.

Jesus, Refiner of our souls, come to us and heal our brokenness. Amen

June 23

PALIMPSEST

Though your sins are like scarlet, they shall be as white as snow; though they are red as crimson, they shall be like wool. **Isaiah 1:18**

Internist Victoria Sweet's memoir, *God's Hotel: A Doctor, A Hospital, And A Pilgrimage To The Heart Of Medicine* (Riverside/Penguin Books, 2012) describes her practice at Laguna Honda Hospital in California. In this place for hopeless cases unable to pay for their treatment, "slow medicine" was practiced, without the constraints of "managed care." Dr. Sweet also studied Medieval Latin, to learn to read the handwriting of the preprint Middle Ages. Parchment was expensive then. Scholars scraped the former text away, reusing the parchment when they could. *Palimpsest*, shadow texts, could sometimes be discerned beneath another text. I immediately thought of our modern term, "repurposing." Dr. Sweet had another epiphany.

"Underneath our scientific modern medicine," Dr. Sweet wrote, "was an earlier way of understanding the body—erased, to be sure, just a faint shadow on the consciousness but active in our thoughts and desires." In other words, we understand our own bodies far more than modern medicine gives us credit. Dr. Sweet's learned to look for the obvious and listen to the patient, instead of tests and lab results. Diagnosis and treatment becomes a partnership when doctors help patients see their "shadow selves."

We have a "partnership with God. Each believer has a "shadow self," a former life of sin that God has erased, cleaned up and thrown into the deep blue sea. But the "text" of our old lives may peek through the new life written over the old. We feel guilt, shame and remorse. We must then remember that God is our partner Who comes to us to remind us of the shadow. The meaningful text of God's scripture covers us, redeems us, and blots out all our old transgressions. Give God your shadow self today.

Cleanse me, Lord, and I will be clean. Wash me and I will be whiter than snow (Psalm 51:7). Amen

June 24

LET US SING!

At his sacred tent I will sacrifice with shouts of joy; I will sing and make music to the Lord. **Psalm 27:6**

My daughter, granddaughter and I had a chance to hear the Ugandan Children's Choir at a Christian music festival. These children, all orphans, were so happy and animated and *talented!* They sang and danced, and the boys played drums and hollowed-out logs. I emailed my friend and fellow writer, Betty Liedtke, who has started a fund to help young women in Uganda break free of the cycle of poverty and prostitution.

Betty said she had seen similar children performing in Uganda. In an article written for the Chanhassen, Minnesota, Villager paper in 2012, Betty said she and her companion were "invited to view a performance by (female) students…leaving…that afternoon to compete in the National Music Festival in Kampala." They were "mesmerized by the girls – by their clear, strong voices, their powerful and energetic dance moves, and the bright, engaging smiles that seemed wider than their faces." Having just seen a similar group, I heartily agreed with Betty that these kids were already champions.

Her article says she and her companion later came upon the bus carrying these same girls. The bus had a flat tire, just being fixed. Betty asked if she could take a picture of the bus. She was ushered *into* the bus, where each Ugandan girl posed and grinned as she snapped photos. Betty believed "their excitement about the music festival, their cheerful-by-nature personalities, and the positive attitude and upbringing they learned at school" was reason for the smiles, along with the fact they remembered Betty from when she was cheering for them at their school that morning.

Betty says, "Let us pray" in Uganda often means "Let us sing." The world is the Lord's and we are all worshiping together!

Lord of the Earth, let us sing! Amen

June 25

TOMATO TOES

(Those) whose delight is in the law of the Lord, and who (meditate) on his law day and night...(are) like a tree planted by streams of water, which yields its fruit in season and whose leaf does not wither—whatever they do prospers. **Psalm 1:2-3**

This year, I ordered my tomato plants from a catalog. I was unable to plant them until late May. By then, they were beginning to get "leggy," long stalks below spindly little leaves. I knew just the solution: I planted the tomato's "toes" deep into the soil, burying the stalk up to the first set of leaves. A tomato planted this way will quickly develop roots along the buried stalk, ensuring the tomato plant will flourish and become bushy. I anxiously await the appearance of those bright red orbs with salt shaker in hand.

As the true Master Gardener, God knows just how each of us must be "planted" to flourish and produce for His kingdom. Like my tomatoes, some of us may be "leggy," having somehow shot up on our own without much care from God. Some of us come to Him when our "stalks" are weak need to be buried up to our eyeballs in His Word so we can be "rooted and established in love" (Ephesians 3:16). He is faithful to us, helping us catch up on our new life as He sees us showing signs of growth.

Folks who come to Christ as babies have nurturing parents and a faith community. They are like seed that is planted, and "God gives (them) a body as he has determined" (1 Corinthians 15:38). Both the "early" and "late" bloomers are equally loved by Him as His precious children. As the Apostle Paul says, "If we are children, then we are heirs—heirs of God and co-heirs with Christ" (Romans 8:17). When God is the Gardener, we "will flourish.., bear fruit in old age.., stay fresh and green" (Psalm 92:13). If we want to be strong servants of the Lord, we must "humbly accept the word planted" in us, which can save us (James 1:21).

Nurture us and grant us growth in You, O Lord. Amen

June 26

PEACE, BE STILL

***Be still, and know that I am God; I will be exalted among the nations, I will be exalted in the earth.* Psalm 46:10**

"The more I get alone, the more I see I need to get alone more," begin the lyrics of "Still," a song written and recorded by Nathan and Christy Nockels. It is difficult for me to be still and alone in God's presence. I've always considered staying busy a virtue. I am hard-wired to be *doing* something. This need to be active is why I never seem to complete anything at all! I live a life of busy-ness, with unfinished "business" keeping me stressed out. I know God wants me to slow down—He doesn't have to draw me a picture! Why, then, why is it *so hard* to listen to His heeding and just *be still?*

Three Gospels record the Spirit driving the Lord into the wilderness to be alone after His baptism. Satan showed up, uninvited, but Jesus rebuked him. Later, Jesus got up "in the morning while it was still very dark…and went out to a deserted place to pray" (Mark 1:35), even though Simon and his companions went looking for Him (v.36). The Lord knew how important it was to get away from "the maddening crowd" and spend time with His Father, to be obedient to His calling.

When I am quiet—while I'm gardening or walking or meditating (which isn't often enough, apparently), I can see so clearly the benefits of this practice. Silence has its own cadence, if we listen, a rhythm all its own. My heart beats, my blood pulses, and my spirit rises to meet the Lord. I notice beauty all around me, in the miniscule things I would miss if I were involved in some seemingly important life activity. God cannot sing over me when I am roaring in my own ears about some earthly concern. Even prayer can be silent; the Holy Spirit groans within me if I just admit I don't know what to say (Romans 8:26). Perhaps *this* is the answer: to seek the quiet times with the Lord over all else, until even crazy times seem quiet.

Calming Lord, come to me in my quiet moments and make them grow into a lifestyle of peace. Amen

June 27

WILD KINGDOM IN MY LIVING ROOM

Then God said, "Let us make humankind in our image... and let them have dominion...over all the wild animals of the earth." **Genesis 1:26**

Our property is home to many kinds of wildlife: songbirds, frogs, snakes, gray squirrels, and one cute little red squirrel that lives under our deck. I've never seen another red squirrel around. Why doesn't he have any other little squirrel friends or a squirrel girlfriend? He torments our dogs and eats all my birdseed, but he's so cute, I've never had the heart to chase him away.

When my husband was out of town our dogs were restless all night long. Letting them out the next morning, I heard a strange noise in the living room. Imagine my surprise when I found the little red squirrel looking up at me. He registered surprise too, and he promptly bounded down the stairs into our basement. I scurried down right after him, not to try to catch him, but to shut the door, for heaven's sake! I didn't want the little rascal to come back up those stairs! It slowly dawned on me he must have gotten in through the dog door, and been in the house all night, upsetting the dogs.

Squirrels can be very destructive when they are someplace they'd rather not be. Like inside a house. I am blessed with wonderful neighbors, and here they came, like the Ghost Busters, three grown men toting live traps, ladders, work gloves and snacks. They set traps. They searched the basement. "Are you sure you saw him inside?" they asked repeatedly. When they left, they said, "He will make a ruckus in that the live trap." No ruckus. No squirrel. Later, we called an exterminator who was very helpful. "Open all the windows in the basement," he said, "and the squirrel will leave." Duh! We opened them, the squirrel got out and the adventure was over.

I guess that squirrel didn't know God gave humans dominion over him!

Maker of All Living Things, teach us to live peacefully with all Your creatures. Amen

June 28

FRIENDLY SKIES

We who are still alive and are left will be caught up together with them in the clouds to meet the Lord in the air. 1 Thessalonians 4:17

Airlines have changed. Gone are the days when flight attendants changed clothes three times during a three hour flight, served full meals to *everyone*, and still managed to stay unruffled throughout the journey. Getting there used to be half the fun! Getting there *now* seems to be *most of the problem*!

Nowadays, airlines seem to be more concerned with the almighty dollar than the lowly passenger. Fares have skyrocketed, probably due to the need for the CEO to live an outrageous lifestyle. Everything costs extra: baggage, meals, snacks. Last time I flew, safety information was no longer delivered by a live person. We now watched an amusing video: fasten your seat belts, emergency exits were located *here*, what to do "in the unlikely event." But now we got comic relief: a cliché of ducks sitting in a row; tiny men refusing to remain in the seats by the escape hatch because they could not open it "in the unlikely event;" and dad putting the oxygen mask on his little girl who then put a mask on her dolly. Clever, yes. Worth an inflated fare to get where we were going? Probably not.

Paul tells the Thessalonians "the Lord himself will come down from heaven, with a loud command, with the voice of the archangel and with the trumpet call of God." Now that's what I call Friendly Skies! Jesus will be our Pilot, our Flight Attendant and our Savior all in one. When Jesus comes, we won't need a reservation or a high-priced ticket. Everything will be provided for us at no cost. We won't need a life vest, and we certainly won't have to worry about food. A marvelous banquet awaits us where we are going. No flight delays, airsickness, stuffy cabins, fear of flying. Just Jesus accompanying us on the ride to our eternal home. Now that's a trip to die for!

Lord of the Universe, we await the day when You return for us and we fly the friendly skies at Your side. Amen

June 29

A BUSY DAY

The crowd that gathered around him was so large that he got into a boat and sat in it out on the lake, while all the people were along the shore at the water's edge. **Mark 4:1**

Jesus' ministry was no nine-to-five job with vacations, benefits and 401Ks. He was crazy-busy all the time. Early on, He began teaching the crowd of people, which grew so large He had to get into the boat offshore. He taught them about the wonders of God's kingdom. Later, He said to his disciples, "Let us go over to the other side" (Mark 4:35). They all piled into the boat and started across. Soon, Jesus was sleeping, but a ferocious storm blew up. The disciples were afraid, but Jesus just told the wind to stop and it stopped.

When they landed on the other side, they encountered a demon—well, many demons in one guy. The demons were so numerous, they called themselves "Legion." Jesus threw the demons into a herd of pigs, and all the animals jumped off a cliff (Mark 5:1-16). Then, Jesus and the boys *got back into the boat* and went across the lake again, *the way they came*. They just went across the lake to cast out one guy's demons? The disciples were probably thinking this was not a wise use of Jesus' time. But they didn't have a chance to say anything because here came Jairus, a synagogue leader, begging Jesus to come heal his dying daughter. Off they go again to Jairus' house, but a woman who had been hemorrhaging for twelve years decided if she could touch Jesus robe, she would be cured. With the crowd pressing in on Him, Jesus suddenly realized some of His power had been tapped. "Who touched me?" He asked. So He stopped to help this poor outcast of a woman which meant He didn't get to Jarius' house in time to heal the girl. People said she was already dead, but Jesus knew better. They all went there anyway, and Jesus woke the girl up and told her parents to get busy and fix her something to eat (Mark 5:21-43).

Whew! This was all in one day! And you thought *your* job was stressful!

Lord, thank You for Your boundless energy in caring for us! Amen

June 30

GARBOLOGY

For his sake I have suffered the loss of all things, and I regard them as rubbish, in order that I may gain Christ. **Philippians 3:8**

I am grateful for garbage collection. Living in a suburban neighborhood as we do, there isn't much we can do with our garbage except pay to have it picked up. One of our neighbors burns his—or most of it—and it stinks to high heaven. We compost what we can for use in the garden, and we recycle as much as possible, but we can't get away from the need to have some hauled away. Thank goodness *someone* is willing to remove it!

On an educational website, naturebridge.com, I learned the average American throws away about 4.4 pounds of trash each day. In 1973, a couple of students at the University of Arizona coined the name "garbology" for a class project, and the idea is now an academic discipline. You can go to college and major in "the nature and changing patterns in modern refuse, and thereby, human society." These "modern day archaeologists" can tell a whole lot about people by the things they choose to discard. Studying trash has led to public service campaigns, "creative repurposing" of items, and a general awareness of waste.

God has been studying "garbology" since he created the earth. Adam and Eve made quick work of getting rid of that apple core, and God dealt swiftly with them on that issue. But it was the "sin" of lying about it that broke God's heart. What God wanted from the first humans He created was a completely trusting and transparent life devoted to Him. Eventually, God sent His only Son to take all of the "junk" out of our lives—emotional, spiritual, mental, and yes, physical. Psalm 103:12 says God removes our transgressions "as far as the east is from the west." Aren't you glad He's is in the garbage removal business?

Blessed Redeemer, save us from ourselves and distill our lives to be lives lived only for You. Amen

July

July 1

LIFT OFF!

***The heavens are telling the glory of God; and the firmament proclaims his handiwork.* Psalm 19:1**

Once when my husband Patrick and I visited my parents' home, my father asked me to find the Bible passage about "my Father's house." The only Bible my parents had was a condensed version with no chapters or verses. I began searching the Gospels: Matthew, Mark and Luke, stopping at the end of John 13. It was getting late and Patrick and I returned to our hotel room. The next morning, the devotional Patrick and I read was John 14:2, "In my Father's house are many mansions; if it were not so, I would have told you. I am going there to prepare a place for you...I will come back and take you to be with Me that you also may be where I am." Later, I found the passage in my parents' Bible, read it and marked it for my father.

When my father died in 2002, I delivered a short eulogy at his funeral. I spoke of my father's love of aviation, how he had trained on "bi-planes" (two-winged craft that preceded modern airplanes), graduating from Army Air Corps Flight Training in 1931. His life had spanned the first flights of crude flying machines all the way to the space age. "My father watched with great interest as aviation 'grew up,'" I said, "all the way to men and women in outer space. Like those astronauts who wear a 'space suit' so they can survive in an unfamiliar environment, we wear 'earth suits' while we are in this world. We are seeing my father in his 'earth suit' for the last time today, but he has actually gotten a new 'suit,' a new body because he is with our God in heaven."

I know I will see my parents again one day when I join them in heaven. The Bible says it is God's will that "all who see the Son and believe in Him may have eternal life, and I will raise them up on the last day" (John 6:40). I rejoice when I think of my father taking that last flight. What a ride!

Eternal Father, I await the day when I will rejoice with You in heaven! Amen

July 2

LIONS AND TIGERS AND BEARS!

Be alert and of sober mind. Your enemy the devil prowls around like a roaring lion looking for someone to devour. **1 Peter 5:8**

When I was small, I had recurring nightmares about zoo animals running around loose in our neighborhood. Recently, my nightmare became a reality for the people of the ex-Soviet republic of Georgia. In the capitol city of Tbilisi, surging waters during a massive flood allowed many zoo animals to escape their enclosures. Rescue workers labored to help the people, keeping an eye out for hundreds of lions, tigers, jaguars, primates, and many other wild beasts. One news clip showed zoo employees carefully approaching a huge hippopotamus as he lumbered back and forth under a freeway overpass. People were told to stay in their houses and keep a close eye on children. At least a dozen people and a number of animals were confirmed dead. Zoo officials were devastated at the loss of these rare and expensive animals. I had flashbacks all week.

Escaped zoo animals are a rare occurrence, but there is another treacherous predator in our midst. Peter's first letter tells his readers that Satan is "like a roaring lion." Christians need to be vigilant spiritually, watching for Satan to try to attack. Peter says to "be sober-minded; be watchful" (1 Peter 5:8), and to "resist him" (v. 9). But Christians needn't fear Satan because we have the assurance of protection "by God's power...through faith..." (1 Peter 1:5). We can take courage that we are not alone in our battles with the Evil One.

Just as it is hard to see zoo escapees running around your neighborhood, we sometimes get complacent and think we have Satan on the run. John 8:44 reminds us that "When (Satan) lies, he speaks his native language, for he is a liar and the father of lies." Remember that Jesus used Holy Scripture to ward off Satan's temptations (Matthew 4:1-11), and we can use that same Scripture any time we need to.

Watchful Father, help us to stand firm and not be tempted by Satan's tricks. Amen

July 3

IS IT ANY WONDER?

And they were calling to one another: "Holy, holy, holy is the Lord Almighty; the whole earth is full of his glory." Isaiah 6:3

When I was a child, we learned about The Seven Wonders of the World, now called The Seven Wonders of the *Ancient* World. Apparently, there are now a number of *modern* lists of the wonders of the world. This makes sense, since mankind has come a long way since the original list was compiled. The only one of the *ancient* list I remembered without looking them up was the Hanging Gardens of Babylon. If you remember any of them, you are probably over fifty years old. If you can list them all, you should be on trivia quiz show. But it made me question just who is putting these lists together.

Things get more interesting when we look at the *new* Seven Wonders of the World announced at a declaration ceremony on July 7, 2007 (07.07.07). In a popularity poll led by Canadian-Swiss researcher Bernard Weber, more than 100 million votes were said to have been cast via the Internet and by telephone. The new list includes the Great Wall of China and the ninety-eight foot tall Christ the Redeemer statue in Rio de Janeiro, Brazil.

Every one of the wonders on both these lists was built by mankind. I was reminded of the story of the Tower of Babel in Genesis 11. All the people on earth at that time spoke one language and they decided to build "a tower with its top in the heavens and make a name for (themselves)" (v. 4). God didn't think that was such a great idea, so He decided to "confuse their language there, so that they (would) not understand one another's speech" (v. 7). God wanted the people to worship only Him and not themselves or other people. The Lord gives us our talents and abilities and He wants us to make use of them. But the real glory on this planet we call home is in the wonderful works of God.

Oh Lord, thank You for Your beautiful creations and for those made by Your people. Amen

July 4

UNDER GOD

The wicked shall depart to Sheol, all the nations that forget God.
Psalm 9:17

Our nation is under attack. Not from foreign armies or homegrown terrorists, but from those who don't seek the wisdom of the Lord in all that is done on earth. Though the United States was first founded to honor God, we have collectively lost that premise. Our first president, George Washington said, "It is impossible to rightly govern a nation without God and the Bible." President Ronald Reagan (1981 to 1989) said, "If we ever forget that we are a nation under God, then we will be a nation gone under." If we as Christians believe this, it is our duty to preserve this principle.

I'm not suggesting that we all head for our armed bunkers to fight to the death to defend our beliefs. But if these are indeed our beliefs, we need to stand up for them in our daily lives. Faith begins within the family, and the Bible says we are to "teach (God's words) to (our) children, talking about them when (we) are at home and when (we) are away, when (we) lie down and when (we) rise" (Deuteronomy 11:19-20). From the leaders of our families to the leaders of our government, we must constantly remind ourselves that we have no authority except that which is granted to us by God. Isaiah prophesied that all "authority rests upon (Jesus') shoulders," and "His authority shall grow continually" (Isaiah 9:6-7). How dare we think anything else about who we are and what power we ourselves have!

Our nation was founded on the sound principles of religious freedom and separation of church and state, but we are vulnerable to forgetting that Christ's love is for everyone, even those who do not believe in Him. This Fourth of July, remember our nation's founding principles and thank God for the freedoms we enjoy in this country.

God of All Authority, we pray that the United States will always be "one nation, under God." Amen

July 5

THE TRUE WIZARD

To the only wise God, through Jesus Christ, to whom be the glory forever! Amen. **Romans 16:27**

The Wonderful Wizard of Oz was originally a children's novel written by L. Frank Baum and illustrated by W.W. Denslow. First published in 1899, the story was made into the motion picture we know so well in 1939.

After a tornado hits the family's Midwest home, Dorothy discovers she and her little dog Toto are not in Kansas anymore. The Good Witch gives Dorothy a pair of ruby slippers belonging to her suddenly departed sister, the Bad Witch, who succumbed to Dorothy's house falling on her. The Good Witch tells Dorothy the only way to get back home is with help from the great and powerful Wizard of Oz. On her way to find the Wizard, Dorothy and Toto befriend a Scarecrow, a Lion and a Tin Man. Together they set off to find the Wizard, amid flying monkeys, melting witches and other distractions. When they eventually locate the Wizard, they discover he is not so great and powerful and is, in fact, an ordinary man from Omaha behind a partition that Toto knocks over. The "wizard" finds a heart for the Tin Man, courage for the Lion, and a brain for the Scarecrow. After another encounter with the Good Witch, Dorothy clicks her ruby slippers together and repeats, "There's no place like home" several times with her eyes closed. Suddenly, she and Toto are back in Kansas and learn the entire adventure was a only a dream caused when the tornado rendered her unconscious.

The real truth is, all the human "wizards" put together are not as wise as God! The Lord isn't from Omaha (although He spends a lot of time there, I'm sure). He doesn't hide behind a wall and try to scare people (but we need to be in awe of Him and respect Who He is). He is more powerful than all the evil people in this world and He loves us more than we can imagine. Tall tales are entertaining, but let's remember Who the True Wizard is!

God of All Wisdom, keep us safe from harm until we are home with You. Amen

July 6

ARTISTRY

O LORD, how manifold are your works! In wisdom you have made them all; the earth is full of your creatures. **Psalm 104:24**

I love art! I marvel not only at the old masters, but at friends and acquaintances who render their subjects with much more raw talent and creative interpretation than I can imagine. Michelangelo is a perfect example of a human being who possessed an extraordinary gift for artistic expression. Painter, sculptor, architect and poet, he completed two now-famous sculptures at the age of sixteen, and was recognized as a Renaissance master during his own lifetime. Perhaps his best-known works are the paintings in the Sistine Chapel in Rome created between 1508 and 1512. The chapel's ceiling paintings are rendered in such detail it's impossible to imagine they were painted upside down!

Most people can barely draw a stick figure right side up! But even today, artists continue to try to create works that look like or at least represent the things we encounter on this earth. Whether worldly art is created out of joy or anguish, whether it represents good or evil, the fact is, a human being still created it. Human art can never come close to resembling the creations of our Lord. It seems baffling that artists spend a lifetime trying to capture and interpret what God can do instantly!

When God speaks to ever-faithful Job, He reminds him that mankind can never know or do all that God can. Human artists can never truly understand how God "laid the foundations of the earth" (Job 38:4), or how He caused the dawn to "take hold of the skirts of the earth and the wicked be shaken out of it" (v. 13). A paint brush can never correctly render "the way to the dwelling of light" (v. 19) or depict the true "way for the thunderbolt." We praise God for the talents of mankind and the joy works of art give us in this life. But only God has created this world as we know it.

Great Artist-God, grant us appreciation for Your mighty works. Amen

July 7

ALL WE NEED

Again I tell you, it is easier for a camel to go through the eye of a needle than for someone who is rich to enter the kingdom of God. **Matthew 19:24**

Navin R. Johnson is a jerk! The iconic character, played by Steve Martin in the 1979 comedy movie, "The Jerk," is so dense he doesn't realize he is a white man adopted by a black family. Navin leaves home, suffering a number of misadventures before inventing the popular Opti-Grab for slippery glasses. Together with his new wife, Marie (Bernadette Peters), the Johnsons live in wealth and splendor ...until a motion picture director (Rob Reiner) sues Navan, claiming that the Opti-Grab diminished his eyesight, resulting in the unfortunate death of a stunt driver. A touching scene ensues in their soon-to-be foreclosed mansion, where Navan tells Marie they can get along okay as long as they have each other...and then he begins picking up favorite items one at a time to add to what will make them truly happy. "You're all I need," he tells Marie, "you and this ashtray..."

Marie and Navin's black adoptive family search relentlessly until they find him homeless and broken. The whole family rejoices and Navan even begins to dance with perfect rhythm—something he never could do before

This story reminds us of many truths. Wealth and fame can be fleeting. Families are what we make them. Prejudice is learned. Goodness prevails in the end. Jesus spoke of the difficulty for the rich to find true happiness if they value their possessions too highly (Matthew 19:21 and 24). When asked where his mother and his brothers were, Jesus pointed to his disciples and said, "Here are my mother and my brothers" (Matthew 12:49). Though Jews during Biblical times did not associate with Samaritans, Jesus had a life-changing conversation with a Samaritan woman at Jacob's well (John 4:4-26). And Jesus also told His followers that evil will be defeated (John 12:31). Thanks be to God for the truth of His Word!

Praise You, Great God, for happy endings! Amen

July 8

DEAR DEPARTED

For it is by grace you have been saved, through faith—and this is not from yourselves, it is the gift of God— not by works, so that no one can boast. **Ephesians 2:8-9**

Why do we give eulogies at funerals? Do we try to list every good thing a person did in the hopes that he will be viewed favorably? Sort of a final Face Book post, saying, "This person's life was full of accomplishments and she made a difference in this world." If we are asked to speak on behalf of a loved one, we necessarily make nice comments. Even if the deceased was a complete louse, at the last farewell, everybody wants to be kind.

I often think about when homeless people die and no one comes to claim the body. How sad. The person might have been the greatest friend, parent, child, or lover in his or her life, but now there is nobody to say so. Maybe there were (or still are) people who knew the dear departed, and would be sad to learn that the death had occurred. But no one except maybe an undertaker is there when a loner is buried.

Christians believe that at least One Person shows up at every funeral, be it a lavish affair with an expensive casket, or a quiet burial in a pine box. That Person is Jesus. He's always there to deliver His own personal eulogy for us, and it's His voice we actually hear from our caskets. If we have been devoted Christians, Jesus first says, "Well done, good and faithful servant" (Matthew 25:23). He might say the words of today's Scripture passage, "It is by grace you have been saved, through faith" (Ephesians 2:8), to let us know that we didn't need to do anything but believe in Him to spend eternity in paradise. And He will probably add, "Take heart, son (or daughter); your sins are forgiven" (Matthew 9:2), to assure us that nothing we have ever done or even thought of doing will separate us from His love. And each of us will "see the Son of Man sitting at the right hand of the Mighty One and coming on the clouds of heaven" (Mark 14:62).

Lord of Life and Conqueror of Death, come for me at my time. Amen

July 9

GOD'S NOT A BOARD GAME!

But when he, the Spirit of truth, comes, He will guide you into all the truth. John 16:13

One of my favorite board games growing up was Clue, where players compete to be the first to figure out who murdered the game's victim (Mr. Boddy), in what part of the Tudor Mansion , and with what weapon. Was it Miss Scarlett in the Conservatory using a Lead Pipe? Or Colonel Mustard with a Revolver in the Billiard Room? The answers are drawn from three piles and put into an envelope which no one is allowed to see. These are the "facts" in the case. Players roll the dice and move along the mansion's corridors or into the various rooms. With six characters, six murder weapons and nine rooms, the players have 324 possibilities. While a player has his piece in a particular room, he may make "suggestions" about the case, allowing others to disprove him. Thereby, the choices are narrowed, and players may make notes, recording who and what has already been suggested, and therefore eliminated. If a player believes she has solved the case, she can make an accusation, which she checks by looking in the envelope. If she is wrong, she's out of the game, and on it goes.

Thank goodness we don't have to keep guessing what's in God's envelope! The Lord doesn't want us to be uncertain about the future; in fact, He tells us, "I know the plans I have for you.., plans to prosper you and not to harm you, plans to give you hope and a future" (Jeremiah 29:11). Jesus wants us to know the truth right up front. He says, "I am the way, the truth and the life" (John 14:6), and He promises us that He is "full of grace and truth" (John 1:14). Jesus received "living words (from the Father) to pass on to us" (Acts 7:38). We don't have to be in a certain room or place to know the answers to life's questions; Jesus is with us wherever we are. We don't have to worry about who to trust, since the Lord "will keep the needy safe and will protect us forever from the wicked" (Psalm 12:7). And we can rest assured that receiving God's love isn't a board game; it's a gift.

Abiding Father, thank you for Your blessed assurance. Amen

July 10

CONFIDENCE IN THE FLESH

For it is we…who serve God by his Spirit, who boast in Christ Jesus, and who put no confidence in the flesh. **Philippians 3:3**

Every week, there is some news item about a famous person getting into trouble in his or her personal life. Compromising photos of starlets suddenly appear on the Internet; high-profile athletes get jailed for drinking and driving; well-known politicians admit to accepting bribes. When I see stories like this, I think, "I'm just an ordinary citizen, and I don't get into *that* kind of trouble!" What makes it so hard for people in the public eye to be good? It seems to me that we have continued to lower the bar on what is acceptable behavior in our society. One reason for this is our own tolerance for people of many different persuasions—indeed, our nation was founded on the very freedom to be who we are without hassle from the government or courts to behave in a certain way! If people want to believe they are something special, or they think their way of life is right, we as a society get out of their way and let them be. When they sometimes cross the line and break the laws of our country, they are always surprised that they get busted.

Billy Graham once said, "True freedom consists not in the freedom to sin, but in the freedom *not* to sin" (italics mine). Knowing Christ as our personal Savior causes us to *desire* to be a good person, even though we frequently miss the mark. Psalm 42:1 says, "As the deer pants for the water, so my soul longs after You." Christ's amazing act of salvation stirs in us a desire to live as He did. 1 John 1:7 says, "If we walk in the light as He Himself is in the light, we have fellowship with one another, and the blood of Jesus his Son cleanses us from all sin." And when we do slip up, we know that we can run right back to our Father, confess our sin, and be made whole again. Ephesians 1:7 says, "In him we have redemption through his blood, the forgiveness of our trespasses, according to the riches of his grace." That's the way to build confidence!

Redeeming Father, lead us in paths of righteousness for Your Namesake. Amen

July 11

DELAYED GRATIFICATION

Forgetting what lies behind and straining forward to what lies ahead, I press on toward the goal for the prize of the heavenly call of God in Christ Jesus. **Philippians 3:13-14**

"Delayed gratification" means the ability to discipline yourself in the short term in order to enjoy greater rewards in the long term. The term was first "coined" in the 1960s by a psychologist named Walter Mischel. In his research, Mischel designed the "marshmallow test." The experimenter would give four-year-old children a marshmallow and tell them they could either eat the marshmallow now, or wait fifteen minutes and have two marshmallows. The children had to sit in a room with the marshmallow sitting right in front of them. Some could not resist, but other children displayed delayed gratification and waited to get two marshmallows.

Mischel followed these children and learned that their test performance was an indicator of how they would behave years later. Children who resisted the marshmallow grew up to be "more likely to resist temptation, have better social responsibility, exhibit better ways to cope with frustration and stress, and strive for higher levels of achievement in many areas of life." Now, any mother worth her salt probably could have come to the same conclusion without thousands of dollars and countless hours of work! And were the "marshmallow eaters" treated differently than the "marshmallow abstainers" in subsequent years, so it became a matter of self-fulfilling prophesies?

"Delayed gratification" is a value for most of us, and is in fact very Biblical. Paul tells the Philippians to resist the easy way and continue to live for Jesus, because the reward of eternal salvation is greater than any "prize" in this life (Philippians 3:13-15). Isaiah insisted that "Those who wait for the Lord shall renew their strength, they shall mount up with wings like eagles, they shall run and not be weary, they shall walk and not faint" (Isaiah 40:3). Are you one of God's "marshmallow abstainers?" His rewards are eternal, you know!

Lord, help me seek what is right and good! Amen

July 12

ENTER INTO SUFFERING

The soldiers planned to kill the prisoners to prevent any of them from swimming away and escaping. **Acts 27:42**

Guarded by a Roman Centurian, the apostle Paul was being brought to Rome on a ship to stand trial for following Jesus. But the weather was rough and it appeared the ship would be destroyed (Acts 27:20). Everything that could be spared was thrown overboard. Paul had a visit from an angel of the Lord, who told him, "Do not be afraid, Paul. You must stand trial before Caesar; and God has graciously given you the lives of all who sail with you" (v. 24). Paul encouraged the two hundred seventy-six men on board to eat and keep up their strength, promising that no one would be lost (V. 31).

Many of the ship's crew believed Paul's presence was the cause of the bad weather. They plotted to kill him and the other prisoners, but the Centurian thwarted their plan. As a high-ranking Roman officer, he was under no obligation to save Paul's life. He must have seen many prisoners perish under his watch. What was Paul to him? He must have believed that Paul was truly a man of God. After all, he had angels visit him! The Centurian saw something in Paul that resonated with him, something that changed the way he viewed this one prisoner. That something may have been Paul's willingness to enter into the suffering of each and every person on that ship.

When I speak to groups of people about God's miraculous rescue of me from the hands of a gun-wielding rapist, I invariably have someone come to me afterwards to tell me her (almost always it's a woman) story of survival. I talk with every one of them, either right there on the spot if possible, or we meet for coffee another day, or we at least have a telephone conversation. I have never turned anyone down. I owe it to other survivors to share my reason for hope for a life after trauma. It's such a small thing to do, to spend time with another one who is seeking relief from unspeakable pain.

Healing Lord, kindle a willingness in me to reach out to those who need Your love. Amen

July 13

RED LETTER LIFE

After he was raised from the dead, his disciples recalled what he had said. Then they believed the scripture and the words that Jesus had spoken. John 2:22

The term "red letter day" originated in ancient Rome when important days appeared on the calendar in red ink. In Medieval manuscripts, special text also appeared in red. Another use of the term was in the English High Court, when presiding judges wore scarlet robes. Many countries refer to public holidays as "red days." The term now refers to private occasions (graduations, weddings, births, return from combat, etc.) or special days and holidays (Christmas, national holidays, paydays). "Red Letter Day" might even describe a sale at an auto dealership or an offer of discounts at a mall.

In red letter edition Bibles words spoken by Jesus are printed in red ink. The inspiration for printing the words of Jesus in red comes from Luke 22:20, *This cup is the new testament in My blood, which I shed for you.* In 1899, Louis Klopsch, then editor of *The Christian Herald* magazine, conceived the idea of printing a New Testament with the words of Jesus printed in red. Klopsch asked his mentor, Rev T. De Witt Talmage, what he thought. Talmage replied, "It could do no harm and it most certainly could do much good."

My first Bible, a "red letter" King James, was given to me by my sister, Barbara, when I was young. I didn't read much of it or understand it until I accepted Jesus as my Lord and Savior at age twenty-eight. Then, to my surprise, I plowed through much of the New Testament in short order, devouring the text—especially that in red—like a child's primer. I even had a dream I was *eating* my Bible, long before I learned that God told Ezekiel to "eat this (scripture), and go, speak to the house of Israel" (Ezekiel 3:1-3). Since that time, the words of Christ have shaped my daily attitude, provided me with comfort and courage in distress, and afforded me daily joy and peace. Jesus' "red letter words" have given me a "red letter life!"

Living Word, fill my mind with red letter thoughts! Amen

July 14

THEN I AM STRONG

Therefore I am content with weaknesses, insults, hardships, persecutions, and calamities for the sake of Christ; for whenever I am weak, then I am strong. 2 Corinthians 12:10

"You never know how strong you are until being strong is the only choice you have." This anonymous quote describes how my life has evolved from a dysfunctional train-wreck to peace, serenity and courage. Born prematurely to a mother who was told by insensitive male doctors to get pregnant to save her marriage, it seemed I was burdened with huge responsibility before I was even out of my crib. My earliest memory is sitting at the top of the stairs listening to my parents arguing over my mother's drinking while singing a childish song in my head about being the "Peace Maker" in our family. My self-esteem plummeted every time my military father had to uproot his family and move to another Air Force base. Another new house, new neighborhood, new friends—if I was lucky enough to make any. My older sister was my only saving grace, trying to "parent" me in the absence of both my career-minded father and my drunken mother.

At twenty-five, suffering at the hands of a gun-wielding rapist seemed like the absolute end of the line for me—until I cried out to God and watched the rapist flee instead of chaining me to a tree. Thus began my slow but steady faith walk, with the help of a trustworthy and ever-present God. With Him as my guide, everything about me changed. I grew into myself, into the person God wanted me to be. I still fail Him every day of my life, but I know He forgives and He is faithful to me no matter what.

When I wrote my memoir, I quoted 2 Corinthians 12:10 in the title: *Then I Am Strong: Moving From My Mother's Daughter to God's Child.* The Apostle Paul recognized the source of his power: God and God alone. Paul—and I—know that we are totally dependent on God for all that we accomplish in His name.

All-Powerful God, grant me Your strength to survive life's trials. Amen

July 15

BIBELETS

***The Lord's Word is flawless.* Psalm 18:30**

Comedian Rich Hall coined the term "sniglet" on his 1980s HBO television series *Not Necessarily the News*. A sniglet, according to Hall, is "any word that doesn't appear in the dictionary, but should." Hall eventually published several books containing his own siglets and those submitted by fans. The books' entries are arranged alphabetically as in a dictionary, including phonetic pronunciation cues and definitions. A few examples of sniglets appear below:

Hawaska (huh-WA-skuh) (proper name) In an atlas, the rectangular box just off the coast of California which contains Hawaii and Alaska.

Disconfect (dis –kon-FECT) (verb) To sterilize the piece of candy you dropped on the floor by blowing on it, assuming this "removes" the germs.

I believe the Bible should get equal time. Below are some "Biblets!"

Frauduaevangalist (fra-ja-ee-VAN-je-list) (noun) Any person who preaches the Word of God for personal gain and not to further His kingdom.

Ramapredicament (ra-ma-pri-DIK-a-ment) (noun) Abraham's situation when the Lord asked him to sacrifice his own son, Isaac, before a male sheep arrived to take Isaac's place.

Unfiend (uhn-feend) (verb) Activity performed by Jesus and later by disciples and apostles, to rid a person of a demon or demons.

Perhaps God doesn't need our help to define His miraculous works, but I'm pretty sure one of His endearing qualities is a sense of humor!

God of the Holy Word, laugh with us over life's little conundrums! Amen

July 16

BUSINESS ON THE WATERS

Some went out on the sea in ships; they were merchants on the mighty waters. **Psalm 107:23**

The Discovery Channel's "Deadliest Catch" is a popular reality series following Alaskan crab fishermen on the Bering Sea. Wikipedia gives a chilling recap of the dangers of commercial fishing: "In 2006, the Bureau of Labor Statistics ranked (the occupation as having) the highest fatality rate.., almost seventy-five per cent higher than….for pilots, flight engineers and loggers." Because of the conditions in the Bering Sea, the death rate is about one fisherman per week. Almost every crew members on these boats will be injured at least once due to "the severe weather conditions…and the danger of…heavy machinery on a…boat deck." Watching "Deadliest Catch" seems to mesmerize most of us. Whether they are courageous or just plain nuts, crew members perform this because of the incredible profits.

God created the waters of the Bering Sea. In the words of the Psalmist, "He spoke and stirred up a tempest that lifted high the waves" (Psalm 107:25). He can cause the waters to mount "up to the heavens and…down to the depths" (v. 26), and "in their peril (the crew's) courage melted" (v.26). This Psalm could be describing the disciples' experience in Mark 4. The Sea of Galilee is 696 feet below sea level, thus being subject to violent downdrafts and sudden storms. When these conditions occurred, the disciples could not understand how Jesus could be "in the stern, asleep on a cushion" (Mark 4:38), a detail included only in Mark. Jesus was after all fully human, and he was probably exhausted after preaching the parables to a massive crowd. He wasn't afraid because…well, because He was also fully divine! Storms did not ruin His day, as He demonstrated so clearly when He "rebuked the wind and said to the sea, 'Peace, Be still!'" (v. 39). I don't know if the Deadliest Catch crew has prayed to God, but I'm guessing they all have!

Lord, we thank You for Your unfailing love and wonderful deeds for mankind. Amen

July 17

OUR LAST WALK

But ask the animals, and they will teach you... In His hand is the life of every living thing. Job 12:7, 10

When our Bassett Hound, Bayfield, was diagnosed with lymphoma, my husband and I were devastated. His sister Beulah, the runt of the litter, was overweight and she aged faster than her brother. Nearly blind, she depended greatly on Bayfield. Both at the end of their expected life span. Confused and sad, I wrote a letter, as I imagined Bayfield would write to us:

"Come with me on this walk—you know I love to walk! I'm a bit slower than before. You can see in my liquid brown eyes that I don't feel well. I will bring my integrity, that quality in all dogs that prevents us from being insincere, and you bring your caring, your love and devotion to me. Be sure my leash is on; I won't need it much longer. I don't want you to get lost.

"'Pick three to five things, your pet loves,' my doctor said. 'When he stops wanting to do those things, it's time.' When I can't enjoy my favorite activities any more, let me go. The choice is really mine, and I don't want you to feel bad (although I know you will)."

Soon, the ear infection that had started it all was out of control. He could fight no longer. Lab reports showed he was toxic. That morning, we couldn't find him. Beulah was frantic, searching, unable to see. In the garage? Not there. The back yard? No. We found him in the master bathroom, hiding from all of us. We made the decision to let them both go together. We couldn't watch him suffer any more, and his sister would have died of a broken heart. Those who don't think our pets have souls have never looked into the eyes of a beloved animal. If heaven is a place of perfect happiness, then I am sure our Bassetts will be there.

Lord, You know when a sparrow falls. Bless and keep our beloved animals with You. Amen

July 18

IT'S IN THE CONTRACT!

Rejoice greatly, O daughter Zion! Shout aloud, O daughter Jerusalem! Lo, your King comes to you; triumphant and victorious is He, humble and riding on a donkey, on a colt, the foal of a donkey. **Zechariah 9:9**

Madonna wants twenty international phone lines. Beyonce's dressing room has to be 78 degrees. Justin Bieber won't perform unless he gets a full-size ironing board and an iron (who irons his shirts?). Katie Perry draws the line at carnations—none of those for her! Twenty white kittens and a hundred doves demands Mariah Carey, and animal rights activist Sir Paul McCartney bans fur, leather and meat from the premises of his performances. Some say these outlandish requests are just to ensure the venue managers are really reading the contracts. Really? I thought it was because these celebs think they are really something special. Like my father used to say, these people put their pants on one leg at a time just like the rest of us.

The greatest Celebrity of all time did not act like this. The words humble and humility appear ninety-six times in the Bible. Jesus did not insist that people recognize Him as the great and mighty person He was. He "did not regard equality with God as something to be exploited," states Philippians 2:6, "but emptied Himself, taking the form of a slave, being born in human likeness" (v. 7). Christ forgave divinely that we might learn to forgive others (Ephesians 4:32). He calls us to be holy in all our conduct because He is our holy example (1 Peter 1:15-16). And when He knew His hour was near, and "that he had come from God and was going to God," He poured water into a basin and washed the disciples' feet (John 13:4-5). Peter, shocked at Christ's servant-like actions, cried, "You will never wash my feet!" (v. 8). But Jesus said, "Unless I wash you, you have no share with Me." Peter allowed himself to be served by his unpretentious Lord, this Servant King who knew no pretense, no conceit. This is God's daily covenant—contract—with us.

Lord, when I begin to think I'm someone special, remind me that I am! I'm a child of God! Amen

July 19

SURVIVING

And I said, "This is my anguish; but I will remember the years of the right hand of the Most High." I will remember the works of the Lord; surely I will remember Your wonders of old. Psalm 77:10-11

Surviving. We use the word in many ways. Obituaries list survivors. We tell dramatic youngsters they will survive without the latest and greatest gadget. When asked how we are, we say, "I'm surviving." People get lucky and survive deadly diseases; soldiers survive roadside bombs; law enforcement officers survive a shootout. A recent car ad shows smashed-up automobiles and people exchanging glances. One says, "They survived." The word is used often, but only those who have survived a truly life-changing, gut-wrenching personal disaster know how deep the word "surviving" can cut.

Country singer Emmylou Harris recorded a soulful song called "Boulder to Birmingham" about a lost love in which she laments, "the hardest part is knowing I'll survive." Going on with life after a great loss is grueling.. Sometimes we wish we had been taken instead. But Christa Wells' tune, "Held," recorded by Natalie Grant, suggests a different approach. The lyrics "When the sacred is torn from your life and you survive" are countered with a description of what we can expect from the God of the Universe. We will simply be held, while we cry, while we grieve, while we come to grips with what's left and realize we still have much to be thankful for. Psalm 27:5 says, "He will hide me in His shelter in the day of trouble; He will conceal me under the cover of his tent; He will set me high on a rock." Jesus says, "Come to me, all you that are weary and are heavy laden, and I will give you rest" (Matthew 11:28).

Though our feet feel less tethered to the earth, we rejoice that we are citizens of heaven, even now. This is not the end. It's the beginning of a "new normal" here on earth. We look forward to life eternal when this life is done.

Everlasting Father, hold me through the storms of this life. Amen

July 20

PACKING THE BARBIE BAG

He charged them to take nothing for their journey except a staff—no bread, no bag, no money in their belts—but to wear sandals and not put on two tunics. **Mark 6:8**

"How much room do I have?" I asked my husband as I packed for my first long distance motorcycle trip from Minnesota to the BMW Motorcycle Owners' rally in Billings, Montana. He produced a little cloth bag. "This is *it*?" I cried. "I can't make it with this small a bag for a whole week!" He rolled his eyes and said, "You have to, Honey. That's all the room you get."

My husband's idea of packing for a week's trip on his cycle includes (besides what he is wearing): a pair of zip off pants, two tee shirts, an extra pair of socks, his itsy-bitsy shaving kit, and two pairs of underwear which he plans to wash out in a roadside stream and hang from the back of the moving bike to dry. For me, a few more item are needed: several changes of clothing in varying weights and coordinating colors (for fair or inclimate weather); several pairs of socks; short and long pajamas; enough underwear to change twice a day (in case I fall into said roadside stream); sandals for walking; sandals to wear in the campground shower; three hats; fourteen pounds of make-up, hair products, sun screen and beauty utensils; my Kindle, IPhone, chargers, power packs and three flashlights. All this had to fit into this Barbie-sized bag that is constructed to go into one of the bike's two saddlebags. My husband drew the line at my can of bear mace.

When Jesus sent forth His disciples on their first Healing and Delivering Mission, He told them to take nothing with them. Isn't that just like a man? No clothing except what they had on, just one pair of sandals (none for the shower!) and one tunic. The reason was, of course, that Jesus knew people—some people at least—would welcome the disciples coming in His name, and their needs would be met. He will meet my needs too, me with my little Barbie Bag.

Grant us traveling mercies, Lord! Amen

July 21

FLOW CHART

Without any doubt, the mystery of our religion is great. 1 Timothy 3:16

Flow charts are probably very useful if they are done correctly, but I stumbled onto a collection of interesting ones on the website mentalfloss.com. Take, for example, the valuable chart that helps young people decide if they should "friend" their parents on Face Book. The questions include: "Do you live at home?" and if so, "Do you talk to your parents?" Another valuable diagram asks the important question, "Should I Work For Free?" Points to help you decide: "Is it for your mom?" and "Is the business 'non-profit' or just not making a profit?" How To Write Song Lyrics begins with the words "na na na" repeated about fifty times. I think the idea is that, if you can't think of any lyrics, you probably should stop trying to write songs. And my favorite: Are You Happy? suggests that if you are, "keep doing what you're doing," and if you're not, "change something."

Well, that's a revelation! And probably good material for struggling evangelists and mental health counselors. God doesn't need flow charts since He made everything and knows how it all works (even us!). But He does pose some thought-provoking questions. "What do you think about the Messiah?" He asks in Matthew 22:42. "Whose Son is He?" The Pharisees answered, "The son of David." But Jesus pointed out that David called Him "Lord," which he would not have done if the Messiah was his offspring. Thus ended that flow chart; the Pharisees were stymied. Jesus admonished his followers not to judge others: "Why do you see the speck that is in your brother's eye, but do not notice the log that is in your own eye?" All the hypocrites in the crowd were quickly put to shame (Matthew 7:3). And John 5:6 reveals that He asked a man crippled for life, "Do you want to be made well?" Jesus wasn't playing games; He wanted to know if the man's faith in Him was sincere. How each of us answers the questions Jesus asks will determine the flow of our lives and the way we chart our course.

Holy God, challenge me to follow You and only You. Amen

July 22

SHIFTING SAND

For it is by grace you have been saved, through faith—and this is not from yourselves, it is the gift of God. **Ephesians 2:8-9**

Ruth Bachman is an author, inspiring presenter, cancer survivor and advocate, and my friend. In her book, *Growing Through the Narrow Spots*, Ruth says, "In 2003, I was a left-handed woman…a wife, a mother, in apparent good health." She was diagnosed with sarcoma of the left hand, wrist and forearm. The only option to save her life was amputation. Her sister died of melanoma twelve years before. Ruth had one word for cancer: "evil."

Ruth says, "Spending time in solitude, prayer and meditation—moving from my head to my heart—helped me to say 'Yes'…I would move forward and grow through this experience." She says, "cancer was the narrow spot in an hourglass and (I) was the sand." Sand is abrasive, uncomfortable when we find it someplace unexpected. But that irritation can also move us to change our attitudes about life, healing, change and even cancer. "We all know what happens to the oyster when sand gets into it," she says. "It grows a pearl." Ruth's challenge is, "Don't just go through the narrow spots. Grow through them." In spite of her amputation, Ruth insists, "I am whole because I have come to understand that wholeness resides inside. It requires being patient with myself and present with God." Ruth's "sand"—her being— is the same after passing through the narrow spots; it's just rearranged.

Jesus "cured" the ten lepers. Only one, a Samaritan, came back to thank Him (Luke 17:11-19). Jesus said, "Your faith has made you well" (v.19). Ruth believes "there is a significant difference between being cured (the absence of disease) and being well." She continues, "The word "health" comes from *halen*, meaning whole. That tenth leper was restored to wholeness of mind, body and spirit. His faith made it so."

Lord, heal our wounds and calm our spirits as we pass through the hourglasses of life. Amen

July 23

BESIDE MYSELF

I do not understand my own actions. For I do not do what I want, but I do the very thing I hate. **Romans 7:15**

Sometimes I feel there are two of me: the believing one and the doubting one. It can be a perfectly good Christian day, and whammo! I crash plunk into a very carnal brick wall and start acting like I'm possessed by demons. My speech suddenly spirals down to less-than-edifying, and I can feel the chill of being out of sync with God. Other times, I am so in love with Him, I have no cares in this world. Everything around me seems sacred; nothing or no one can push my buttons. I'm soaring on the wings of the Holy One Who has placed my feet in high places.

Why do we as humans have these spiritual mood swings? Why, once we have declared our love for Christ, do we backpedal and behave like our old selves? It's because of Adam and Eve—let's blame them! But when I'm on that mountain top of spiritual joy, how do I get from there to the dismal valley of discontent? God always loves me, but it's hard to remember that.

The apostle Paul must have been an intense man. A zealous "Christ hater" in his former life, Paul gets a complete instant overhaul on the road to Damascus (Acts 9). He morphs from hate to love and becomes one of the most revered promotors of our Lord. But even Paul struggles with the "split personality" thing. He still does the things he knows he shouldn't (Romans 7:15) and he even struggles with how to share his faith. "For if we are beside ourselves (i.e., a little crazy), it is for God," he tells the Corinthians, "if we are in our right mind, it is for you" (i.e., preaching the good news without too many theatrics) (2 Corinthians 5:13). I have to remind myself of Paul's very words, "Pray without ceasing," which came in the middle of "rejoice always," and "give thanks in all circumstances" (1 Thessalonians 5:16-18). This formula can keep us all from torturing ourselves when we fail.

Forgiving Father, You have to grace to forgive; let me have the humility to accept. Amen

July 24

NANCY MEANS GRACE

For God hath not given us the spirit of fear; but of power, and of love, and of a sound mind. **2 Timothy 1:7**

"I was only eight years old when Nancy began to change," says Cathy Plantenberg. "It could have been the wind for the little I understood. That wind took "hold of our home and locked us all out in a ferocious snowstorm." Cathy's childhood memories of her beautiful older sister diagnosed with schizophrenia are sad. Cathy felt Nancy "was thrown across the room, all the warmth…sucked from her heart," taking away "her compassion, patience and intelligence," leaving her "brittle, frightened and enraged." That was in the late 1950s.

Today, Cathy is Nancy's caretaker, visiting her in the long term care facility where she resides after years in a state hospital, group homes and other placements. Shock treatments left Nancy with the mind of a child, but her sister now describes her as "one of the most cheerful people I know." When Cathy comes, Nancy claps her hands in glee. They make art projects, sing songs and enjoy each other's company. When Nancy is especially happy, she grins at her sister and declares it "a six candy bar day." Nancy's joy has returned, even though the path of her life did not go the way it might have.

Many people fear those suffering from mental illness. It is important for us to remember Christ's commandment: "Go into all the world and preach the gospel to all creation" (Mark 16:15). How we go carry the Good News to others may change, especially for those who have limited understanding. Cathy cannot discuss deep theological matters with her sister, but she can enjoy her company as it is, be a much-needed advocate for her sister, and ensure she gets her needs met from care center staff, medical personnel and others. Most of all, Cathy can bring to her sister her own love of Christ and the unspeakable peace and joy that the Lord has given her.

Lord, grant us compassion and understanding for those with mental illness. Amen

July 25

EXPENSIVE WILL

For God so loved the world that He gave His one and only Son, that whoever believes in Him shall not perish but have eternal life. John 3:16

Do you believe God only wants good things for us? I do. Why, then, do terrible things still happen in this life? The theological answer lies in part in our own free will. Not that we, ourselves, wish for unfortunate occurrences. But God allows us to have free will because He wants us to choose. What kind of marriage results from one person demanding, or even forcing the partner to do certain things? We call that domestic abuse. Why would God want to control us in that way, when He loves us with a perfect love?

But God didn't leave us alone in this world to battle the forces of evil on our own with our dollar store super power capes. Life's perils fall into three categories: messes we get ourselves into, messes that just happen to us, and messes that other people inflict on us. God cares about all of them. He knows how everything will turn out, even the choices we make with our free will. A math genius can give me an equation and ask me to solve it. The whiz already knowing the answer doesn't change the choices I make to solve it. The answer doesn't change because the numbers are constant. God neither compels evil to occur nor forces us to be good. But He does have the final say in what happens to each of us at the end our lives.

In his book, *He Chose the Nails*, Max Lucado says, "Any injustice in this life is offset by the honor of choosing our destiny in the next." In today's scripture, John says that "whoever believes" in Christ "shall not perish but have eternal life." It looks so simple, but we have a choice here: to believe or not to believe. Free will allows us to make that choice; it's not automatic. So "free will" is actually very expensive, when you think about it. Choosing not to believe can cost us peace and joy in this life and the assurance of everlasting life in heaven.

Lord, I choose You! Amen

July 26

BABBLE STUDY

Come, let us go down, and confuse their language there, so that they will not understand one another's speech. Genesis 11:7

"This Bible study is boring!" she said. "It just ask us to repeat exactly what's in the reading!" As the facilitator of the group, I had to agree with her. I had chosen the study from an internet source and had not reviewed the material carefully enough. Everyone in the group wanted something more than just regurgitating the words from the Bible. We wanted thought-provoking questions that asked us to dig deep into our spiritual beings and grow as Christians. I promised to be more discerning in the materials I ordered.

Our Lord wants us to dig deep too. First Thessalonians 1:5 reminds us the "message of the gospel came to us not in word only, but also in power and in the Holy Spirit and with full conviction." This is no child's first reader we're dealing with here. The Word of the Lord "has the power to save your souls" (James 1:21), and God "sustains all things by His powerful Word" (Hebrews 1:3). Psalm 119 speaks of God's Word as "a lamp to my feet and a light to my path" (v. 105); a "hiding place," a "shield," and a place of "hope" (v. 114). We are to stand in awe of God's Word (v. 161) and "seek understanding" of it (v. 169). Isaiah 55:11 declares that God's Word "shall not return to (Him) empty, but it shall accomplish that which I purpose." Paul told the new converts to think of God's Word as spiritual food. They were "not ready for solid food" to begin with, but "solid food is for the mature" Christian who has learned the building blocks to understanding.

When the people of Babel tried to build "a tower with its top in the heavens," God scattered them and confused their language so they would return to Him (Genesis 11:4,8). The term "babble" now means nonsense or gibberish. Let's take the sacred Word of God seriously and not conduct "babble studies!"

O God, You Word is precious to me. Let me meditate on it always. Amen

July 27

SMOKE AND MIRRORS

I will ponder the way that is blameless. Oh when will You come to me? I will walk with integrity of heart within my house. **Psalm 101:2**

Pathological liars fascinate me. Maybe I feel this way because the concept of integrity is so very important to me. As a child, I could not trust my alcoholic mother to tell me the truth or to do what she promised. As an adult, I seem to hold myself and others to a higher standard because I have seen first-hand how lying is so hurtful to the liar and the recipient.

Pathological lying is defined as "a long history of frequent and repeated lying for which no apparent psychological motive or external benefit can be discerned" (source: Psychological Times). "Normal" liars feel remorseful; but guilt, shame, regret, or even possible consequences do not affect the behavior of the pathological liar. Treatment is difficult if not impossible because the liar doesn't want the therapist to know the truth (if indeed the liar gets as far as the therapist's office in the first place). I can still see Bernie Madoff looking shocked when he was arrested for bilking hundreds of senior citizens out of their life savings through his Ponzi schemes.

Obviously, God doesn't condone lying, since He Himself is Truth personified. Proverbs 12:22 says, "The Lord detests lying lips." Paul says the ungodly (including liars) "are without excuse...For although they knew God, they did not honor him as God or give thanks to him, but they became futile in their thinking, and their foolish hearts were darkened" (Romans 1:21).

Evangelist Rick Warren says, "Integrity is built by defeating the temptation to be dishonest; humility grows when we refuse to be prideful; and endurance develops every time you reject the temptation to give up." God is not smoke and mirrors; He's honesty and transparency.

Lord, guard my heart and mind against those who use lies to hurt others. Amen

July 28

THE DEVIL IS IN THE DETAILS

Watch out for false prophets. They come to you in sheep's clothing, but inwardly they are ferocious wolves. **Matthew 7:15**

I once read that Billy Graham's wife, Ruth, was seated next to an FBI agent at a dinner. He told her he worked in the department that tracked the making of counterfeit money. Mrs. Graham said, "You must study a lot of phony bills." "No," he replied, "we study the real ones, so that when we see a fake one, we will know the difference."

I have watched the news aghast to see that ordinary human beings can be persuaded to drink the Kool Aid with men like Jim Jones, or barricade themselves inside a bunker at Waco, Texas with David Koresh. I have plowed through Jon Krakauer's *Under the Banner of Heaven*, the story of the polygamous, fundamentalist, spiritually abusive Mormons. I've studied Hal Lindsey's *Satan Is Alive And Well On Planet Earth* with one eye closed because I couldn't bear to read Satan's abuse of ordinary people. How does ISIS convince kids to join their hateful group? How do people get so far off track that they might find the words of these false prophets compelling?

Third Millennium Ministries posted an article entitled "The Distinguishing Marks of False Teachers," written by Thomas Brooks in the early 1600s. Brooks warned us to keep an eye out for spiritualists who are "men pleasers" (Jeremiah 23:16-17); cast "scorn and reproach upon…Christ's…faithful" (2 Corinthians 10:10); "spew out the devices and visions of their own heads and hearts" (Jeremiah 14:14); dwell upon "things…of the least importance…to the souls of men" (1 Timothy 1:5-7); "disguise…dangerous principles and soul-deceiving notions with very attractive speeches" (Numbers 24:17); try harder to "win men over to their opinions than to improve their behavior" (Matthew 23:15); and "exploit their followers" (2 Peter 2:1-3). We must always be alert to Satan's treachery!

Protect us, O Lord, from the enemy and his warriors. Amen

July 29

WHEN THE GOOD GUYS LOSE

Render service with enthusiasm, as to the Lord and not to men and women. **Ephesians 6:7**

Shortly after my husband and I were married, a series of events made my work life, as I had known it, a thing of the past. To put it bluntly, the good guys lost—and the bad guys won.

There is no "good" time to lose one's job, but at the time, I was also dealing with my father's declining health in another state, and my own health was precarious. In the middle of the hostility at work, a bunch of crazy men flew planes into the World Trade Center and the Pentagon and the nation pulled together to face 911. The workers at the college didn't pull together to do anything. We all felt defeated at the hands of some incompetent and power-hungry administrators. It was one of the worst times in my life.

Occupations are important. "What do you do?" is often the first question asked of us. The first answer usually isn't that we worship the Lord Jesus Christ (although it should be), or even that we are a wife/husband, mother/daughter, volunteer, blood donor, amateur gardener or avid recycler. We answer with what we do for a living. When our livelihood is taken from us, we feel devalued and useless. We grieve for the loss of our productive self. I was able to "claim" a position at another college, but not before my father's death, mother's relocation, and many anxious moments.

Throughout this time, I never lost my faith. Just as Joseph had done when he was sold to the Egyptians by his own brother (Genesis 39), I did my best to maintain my integrity, serving students and applicants with a smile on my face and carrying out my job duties responsibly. Praying diligently every day and night, I stood on the promise that God would see me through. And He did.

Lord, see us through the storms of life with integrity. Amen

July 30

PROVE IT!

***All things came into being through Him, and without Him not one thing came into being.* John 1:3**

I know that God exists! How do I know? Because of the "before and after affect." When I was schlepping around the earth as a young twenty-something and thought I was smarter than everybody (including God) I was a different person. I was profoundly sad, with an attitude that nothing in life would ever turn out right for me. I was scared of everything: sickness, being alone, death, nightmares. I endured years of insomnia because of all the things that worried me. Once I accepted Christ, my fears went away for the most part. I began sleeping like a rock, my attitude improved, my choice of friends improved, and I found that "peace that passes all understanding."

But don't take my word for it! I went right to the source: Google! On the site, http://www.everystudent.com/features/isthere.html , Marilyn Adamson lists six reasons why God exists:

1. Our planet's complexity points to a deliberate Designer who not only created our universe, but keeps it going. (The human brain holds and processes your emotions, thoughts and memories.)
2. The universe flashed into being, and scientists cannot find out what caused that to happen. (If not by God, how was it created?)
3. The universe operates by uniform laws of nature, not by chance.
4. The DNA code informs and programs a cell's behavior. (Every cell contains a detailed instruction code, a mini-computer program.)
5. God exists because He pursues us. (He has surrounded us with evidence of himself every day.)
6. Jesus Christ is the most specific picture of God revealing himself to us. (No other religion claims that.)

Almighty God, thank You for creating and sharing this amazing world with us! Amen

July 31

A "MASSAGE" FROM GOD

I am bringing you good news of great joy for all the people. Luke 2:10

The 1963 production of "The Pink Panther" starred Peter Sellers as the bumbling Inspector Jaques Clouseau. The "Pink Panther" is the world's largest rose-colored diamond, bearing a tiny flaw resembling a panther. The plot centers on the attempted theft of the gem by the Phantom, whose accomplice is Clouseau's wife. The poor inspector is so inept, he is constantly looking in the wrong place at the wrong time to foil the theft. The jewel is actually planted on Clouseau at one point, making him appear to be the real thief. The inspector speaks Speaking English with a heavy French accent, Clouseau asks the hotel desk clerk conspiratorially if there is a "message" for him, but pronounces it "massage." A hilarious exchange ensues where the clerk believes Clouseau wants a back rub, when all he is looking for is a private communication regarding the jewel theft.

"The Pink Panther" makes me think of the message of the Good News. Some people just can't understand what that "message" is all about. They believe its meaning is one of guilt and shame. They just don't realize that God sent His only Son to live among men and die on a cross to save us all. It took a mighty miracle on God's part to bring me into His everlasting arms. Only then did I begin to see the life-giving magnitude of Christ's story.

Like the humorous scene in The Pink Panther, "the message about the cross is foolishness to those who are perishing, but to us who are being saved it is the power of God" (1 Corinthians 1:18). What the world calls "God's foolishness is wiser than human wisdom." "God's weakness is stronger than human strength" (1 Corinthians 1:25). Those who do not heed the call of God are like Inspector Clouseau, missing message altogether. The kingdom of God is the precious gem, the "pearl of great price" (Matthew 13:45-46), and Satan is the thief who tries to keep us from seeking Him.

Holy God, open everyone's ears and eyes so that all may believe. Amen

August

August 1

GOD ON THE CEILING

Whenever you pray, go into your room and shut the door and pray to your Father who is in secret; and your Father who sees in secret will reward you. **Matthew 6:6**

Ever notice when some people pray, they look up at the ceiling? Is God floating up there like some renegade helium balloon? Other people look at the floor, which of course is a sign of humility, but why do we do that? I know there is no "right" way to pray, and I am not the authority on that subject anyway. I struggle to make time to pray, often flinging out "drive by" prayers as I go about my daily activities. Like an old west gunslinger, I shoot off little requests and concerns with both barrels blazing. Pow! Pow! I have to pray when the ideas come to my mind because I'm getting forgetful as I grow older.

I have tried over the years to have a more disciplined prayer life, to "pray unceasingly" as Paul suggested (1 Thessalonians 5:17). I've made lists and tried to follow guidelines I've read or heard about, but I can't seem to stick to it. I've prayed out loud in a big booming voice like I imagine God would use, and I've prayed silently in the middle of the night. Many years ago I was immensely relieved to read that God doesn't really care if our prayers are in a certain format or even how long or how often we pray. It's what's on our hearts that He wants to know, in whatever way we can communicate it.

One thing I do know: prayer is not bargaining with God. Prayer is not a tactic to beguile or force God to do something for us. Prayer is serious, an admission that we are NOT God, and we are nothing without Him. We need His divine help all the time, every day. He's more than willing to listen to whatever we bring to him: our happiness and our sorrow, our praises and our passions. It's important to listen too, and be patient for an answer. And don't forget, the Holy Spirit is always there to pray in holy sighs if you can't find the words (John 14:26).

Holy Spirit, help me remember what I've learned from You about prayer. Amen

August 2

ANTHONY DO NOT!

My little children, I am writing these things to you so that you may not sin. But if anyone does sin, we have an advocate with the Father, Jesus Christ the righteous. **1 John 2:1**

When in college, my daughter worked as a respite care giver for a family with a mentally challenged child whom I will call Anthony. The boy's favorite activity was to listen to a recording of the song "Macho Duck." Over and over and over again. He was not allowed to touch the turntable so his parents instructed my daughter to play the record for him as many times as he wanted. When the song ended, Anthony would say, "Macho Duck please!" and clap his hands. Sometimes he would also say, "Anthony DO NOT!" presumably because he had heard the phrase more than once. This simple request from Anthony nearly drove my daughter up the wall—which is probably why Anthony's parents wanted respite care once in a while.

Sometimes people feel God is always telling us "DO NOT!" Biblegateway.com says those two words appear 1838 times in the Old and New Testaments combined! The Lord has been commanding us *not* to do things ever since He told Adam and Eve they were allowed to eat from every tree except…well, you know the story! (Genesis 2:15-17) God's Ten Commandments have both "dos" and "do nots" (Exodus 20). Proverbs is full of ways we should "keep God's commandments." In Matthew 14:28, Peter asks Jesus to "command" him to walk across the water to Him. Jesus threw demons out (Matthew 4) and raised the dead (Luke 8, John 11).

But the best and most amazing commandment Jesus ever issued is the one He called The Greatest Commandment: "You shall love the Lord your God with all your heart and with all your soul and with all your mind and with all your strength" (Mark 12:30). Then He said, "The second is this: 'You shall love your neighbor as yourself.' There is no other commandment greater than these" (Mark 12:31). Let's play that over and over!

Lord, I want to do Your will. Help me to follow all Your commandments. Amen

August 3

WOBBLY WEEBLES

We are afflicted in every way, but not crushed; perplexed, but not driven to despair; persecuted, but not forsaken; struck down, but not destroyed. **2 Corinthians 4:8-9**

"Weebles wobble but they don't fall down" was the slogan for the adorable Little People introduced by Fischer-Price Toy Company in 1969. I was charmed by the design of this tiny family: dad, mom, brother, sister, baby and even a little dog. Their egg-shaped bodies had a weighted bottom—a feature I share with them! They never tipped over and seemed to be in constant movement as little fingers grasped at them or tried to arrange them in family activities. Fisher-Price claimed Weebles had an attention-grabbing effect on children, and their popularity soared for a couple of decades.

God made people to be like Weebles. If we trust in our Divine Guide, we may be battered about by life's swells and sloshes, but we can rest assured that our loving Father will carry us through any storm. Christ is like the weights in the bottom of the Weebles. He is the "ballast" for not only our bodies but our emotions, our minds, and most importantly, our souls.

The apostle Paul suffered first when he met the Lord on the road to Damascus and was stricken blind; then from shunning and misinterpretation from his fellow Christians who did not trust him at first. He endured imprisonment, shipwreck, hunger, fatigue, and a "thorn in the flesh" (2 Corinthians 12:7) that is never identified. Some say his "thorn" may have been Paul's guilt for formerly being "a blasphemer, persecutor, and insolent opponent" of Christ (1 Timothy 1:13). Paul "received mercy because (he) had acted ignorantly in unbelief, and the grace of our Lord overflowed" for him (v. 14). The Lord made it clear to Paul His grace was all Paul needed to come out on top (2 Corinthians 12:9). Paul's suffering and endurance serve as an example Christians are promised not only eternal life, but abundant life here in the world, life full of indescribable joy and comforting peace.

Faithful Lord, center my soul as I weather the storms of life. Amen

August 4

JESUS INTERRUPTED

But now even more the report about Him went abroad, and great crowds gathered to hear Him and to be healed of their infirmities. Luke 5:15

In my professional life, I greatly appreciated the service of administrative assistants. A good assistant can make the difference between a smoothly-run system and one that bogs down and frustrates both workers and those we serve. Office assistants directly affect the quality and quantity of the work accomplished. Many become so good at their jobs, they instinctively know what is needed. In the workplace, interruptions are the real job: how we view them and how we handle them. The assistants make us look great. The work they do, often in the background and without much fanfare humbles me.

Jesus didn't have an administrative assistant, an electronic calendar, email, IPod, smart phone, a policy and procedure manual, or weekly updates on who needed His healing services and how services would be scheduled and delivered. He wasn't told how long He should meet with any one person, yet He never seemed to be rushed to get to His next appointment or meeting. But strangely, Christ's ministry was one of constant interruptions.

Consider a typical Day in the Life of Jesus. Our Lord had just heard about the death of John the Baptist (Mark 4:29). No time to hang around and mourn. His disciples returned from their Adventures with New Powers, all abuzz with things they had done and taught in His name. He tells them to join Him for a relaxing boat ride (v.30). Suddenly, here came the Multitudes, running around the lake and beating Jesus and the boys to the other side (v.35). Jesus taught them for a while, then realized they must be hungry too. He arranged a meal for five thousand Close Personal Followers (vs. 35-43). Then, He tells the disciples to hop back into the boat and head for the other side. After prayer time, Jesus treks right across the lake to overtake the boat, giving Peter a lesson in water walking on the way. Could you have kept up?

God of Boundless Energy, energize me! Amen

August 5

BAGGAGE CLAIM

Come to me, all you that are weary and are carrying heavy burdens, and I will give you rest. Matthew 11:28

Have you ever had luggage hassles while on a trip? First, I always pack about six times the stuff I'll need. Who knows? Maybe we'll run into the Prince of Sweden while visiting the rellies in Missouri, and I'll need that sequined maxi dress and $300 pumps. What if they have a tsunami in northern California and I'm caught without my rain slicker and Wellies? At the airport I'm praying my bag doesn't weigh over fifty pounds, because then I'd have to pay extra above and beyond the outrageous price of the ticket. I've gotten creative about carry-ons, but how much can you wear under your regular outfit and still be able to fit into those tiny airplane seats?

Losing your luggage is awful. Watching that conveyor belt go around and around and not seeing your old familiar bag come down the chute is scarier than watching a horror movie. Once, traveling with a girlfriend, her bag was the first one out, but mine never showed up. We looked and looked and finally filed a report with a disinterested airport employee wearing a button saying, "I can help!" She didn't. As we made our way out of the baggage section, I spotted my bag in a far corner under a poster stating, "Don't touch that bag until you're sure it's yours!" Apparently, someone hadn't read the poster and tossed mine away when it was clear it wasn't the right one.

God makes the term "baggage claim" a no-brainer: we collect the baggage, He claims it and disposes of it. End of story. No lectures, no extra fees, no inspections or pat downs without our shoes on. No matter what we've been dragging around or for how long we've been dealing with it, we can deposit it at the cross and walk away. Ephesians 1:7 says, "In him we have redemption through His blood, the forgiveness of our trespasses, according to the riches of His grace." Thanks be to Him for His enduring grace!

Compassionate Lord, take our burdens from us and grant us peace. Amen

August 6

THE WEST WAS ONE

O God, you are my God; earnestly I seek you; my soul thirsts for you; my flesh faints for you, as in a dry and weary land where there is no water. **Psalm 63:1**

Along the Lewis and Clark Trail, I was a modern Sacagawea, not on foot but "two up" on my husband's motorcycle. Cows in one group and horses in another, and the antelope grazing a respectable distance away, not wanting to mingle with the domesticated beasts. At least the cows and horses knew enough to stay in the shade. Both would need water, of course. Plenty of that: creeks and rivers in such a desolate land. "Fences?" the antelopes seemed to scoff. "Just jump them, silly cows."

Houses with holes in them, shells you could look right through, once home to a family. Babies born, birthdays celebrated, baking powder biscuits cooling on the kitchen sideboard. Sadly, before this, a different people who were almost annihilated. Man's inhumanity to man. What did God think? All that hatred, when all He wanted was peace.

He was there, of course, and He's been there all along. He caressed the antelopes' eyelashes and calmed the babies' tears and fears. Pioneers and Paiutes, sodbusters and Sioux: God was with them all. The Great Spirit, He was called by some, and that He was. Many tears were shed, many dreams dashed, and still the land survived: dry, windy, barren. Today, this same land is home to farmers and ranchers, and towns and cities have sprung up all around. Progress, it's called. Unfortunately, we rarely stop to think of the brave men and women of many colors, shapes and sizes who fought for their own kind of dream, who looked to God the Great Sprit to sustain them through victory and loss.

Our Lord's young mother sang, "His mercy is for those who fear him from generation to generation" (Luke 1:50). The sun will rise all of our days because of His great love for us. "Let us then with confidence draw near to the throne of grace," Hebrews 4:16 says, "that we may receive mercy and find grace to help in time of need." If not for those who were brave enough to persevere, none of us would have survived.

Everlasting God, hide us in the shadow of Your wings till life's storms pass by. Amen

August 7

MOUNTAIN SOUNDTRACK

Who has measured the waters in the hollow of His hand and marked off the heavens with a span, enclosed the dust of the earth in a measure, and weighed the mountains in scales and the hills in a balance? Isaiah 40:12

First the roadside stream, sparkling crystal tears rolling over cheeks of colored rock. Next the perfume of the pines, bending to gentle breezes. More aromas curled up from the wildflowers hugging the ground around the trees and streams. As our motorcycle climbed the road to Bear Tooth Pass in Montana, the canyon walls surrounded us with rugged stones, tiny rivulets of water tumbling down from pillows of melting snow clinging to the outcroppings. Our passing scared the grouse from the brush, and hawks wheeled slowly overhead. A symphony of sights, sounds, and smells caressed the air around us.

My soul had come home, for it was in the Rocky Mountains I first felt the gentle touch of God's hand on my trembling shoulder. Too much time had passed since I last visited these higher elevations, and I sensed immediately I should come here more often. Can a place alone evoke a closeness to God? I asked myself. Yes, came the clear and decisive answer, because God is in the things that bring you peace.

Where do you find peace? Is it in the mountains, as it is for me? Do you relish the sounds of the ocean surf pounding on the sand and the beach rocks? Hiking woodland trails? Looking into the eyes of the ones you love: a partner, a child, a pet? In a sanctuary made for quiet reflection? Some even relish being in a loud and rowdy place with thumping Christian music resonating in one's bones. God prepared them all, so those of us who have different temperaments might find solace in the places that speak to us so perfectly.

"The mighty one, God the Lord, speaks and summons the earth from the rising of the sun to its setting" (Psalm 50:1). How comforting are these words! He will give "heed to the words of (our) prayer" (Psalm 66:19. He will sanctify us continually and keep us on right pathways. Let's seek Him in those special places that speak to the soul!

Father, sanctify me in the places I love most. Amen

August 8

IMMORTAL, INVISIBLE

Now to the King eternal, immortal, invisible, the only God, be honor and glory for ever and ever. Amen. **1 Timothy 1:17**

First Timothy 1:17 was the basis for the classic hymn, "Immortal, Invisible, God Only Wise." The composer, Walter Chalmers Smith (1824-1908), was a hymnist, poet and minister of the Free Church of Scotland. His poetic side flows freely throughout this beautiful song, describing the Christian experience in words as timely today as they were at the hymn's creation.

Smith invites us to approach this "God only wise" with sure footing and childlike trust. God is swathed "in light inaccessible." We're unable to see Him with our human eyes. Angels even "veil their sight" in His presence. Yet this seemingly unapproachable God is the source of "all life...both great and small." God, Smith writes, is "the true life of all." God is "invisible" to us on earth, but we "know" Him through the eyes of faith and His words. "Whoever has seen me has seen the Father," Jesus says in John 14:9.

"We blossom, we flourish," Smith continues. The Lord knows "the plans (He has for us), plans for (our) welfare and not for harm, to give (us)a future with hope" (Jeremiah 29:11). Smith describes the clouds as "fountains of goodness and mercy," and the mountains as God's "justice...soaring above" us. His absolute power is everlasting: He is the Ancient of Days.

Smith's writes, as we "quickly grow frail...wither and perish," our God will "never fail." He counts the hairs on our head and concerns Himself with our daily discontents as long as we live. Then, we will see the "Father of grace...in splendor," no longer veiled but fully visible "face to face."

Next time you hear or have a chance to sing this fine old hymn, meditate deeply on its words and meaning.

Ancient of Days, thank You for the words of these wonderful old hymns! Amen

August 9

BLANK CARTOON SQUARES

The upright give thought to their ways. **Proverbs 12:29**

One of my favorite comic strips is Mutts by Patrick McDonnell, whose characters are a dog, Earl and a cat, Mooch. The strip portrays Earl and Mooch as would-be animal super-heroes trying to make life better for their fellow earthlings. My favorite episode is one in which Mooch finds Earl in bed one morning with the covers over his head. Mooch tries several approaches to get Earl to join him for a day of adventure, but Earl is having no part of it. Exasperated, Mooch finally says, "Who is going to save the world today?" Thus follows a blank cartoon square with no dialog, in which the reader can almost see Earl's little brain spinning. In the last square, Earl then rises from his bed with the covers still completely engulfing his head and body and starts out the door, saying to Mooch, "Okay, let's go."

We are so like Earl! We grow complacent or bored or tired or afraid of doing the Lord's work sometimes, and we just want everyone (including God) to leave us alone! We've done the bake sales, vacation Bible school, served on church council and attended the pastor's special Bible studies. We've even ventured out of our comfort zones and done our best to help some wayward soul. Wash, rinse, repeat. We want a little time off from all of this! We're not even sure we're doing it right…

So we find ourselves in one of those "blank cartoon squares" of our lives. Thinking it over. Vacillating between wanting to do our part for the Lord and being human enough to think we've done enough already. Sending sideways prayers up to God, because we're afraid if we meet Him head on, He'll want us to do even more! He is there in our hour of indecision. He is the blanket over our heads. Courage is fear that has said its prayers. Step out of that "blank" place in your life and move forward! God will lead you there!

Great God, You know our fears and foibles. Meet us and guide us in the next square. Amen

August 10

IT'S NOT EASY BEING SHORT

When Jesus came to the place, he looked up and said to him, "Zacchaeus, hurry and come down; for I must stay at your house today." Luke 19:5

I've been short all my life, since I was born (I weighed in slightly prematurely at 5 pounds 6 ounces), right on through adulthood. Now I'm getting shorter as I age, and because I have two spinal curves, I'm getting shorter in an unbalanced way. It's not fair. I can never find people in a crowd, and forget seeing the musicians in a large concert hall. Modern kitchens are made for statuesque people, so I need a step stool to reach anything on the upper shelves in my cupboards. The seat in my car must be moved way forward for me to reach the pedals—and then I can barely see over the steering wheel. Someplace I read short people should wear solid colors to make them look taller. I wore a yellow jumpsuit once and some other short people shouted "taxi!" at me and tried to climb into my pockets.

Jesus encountered a short person one day, and He knew just how to handle him. Zacchaeus was a Jewish "publican," or overseer of tax collectors. Because he was "vertically challenged," Zacchaeus wasn't able to push through all the folks on the ground. He ran ahead of the throng as fast as his little legs would carry him and climbed up into a sycamore tree to see Jesus (Luke 19:34). Zacchaeus was not entirely consumed by his possession of material wealth because he was so interested in seeing this Man many thought was a heretic. But his name means "pure," and although he was part of the establishment, Zacchaeus believed Jesus had something to offer.

Imagine the little man's surprise when Jesus not only noticed him, but spoke directly to him and said He was coming to his house for a little visit (v.5). Zacchaeus tells Jesus he will give half of his possessions to the poor and repay anyone he has defrauded fourfold. "Today salvation has come to this house," the Lord said to him. I'll bet Zacchaeus felt ten feet tall.

Atoning Christ, thank You for looking at us with eyes that see only our best selves.

August 11

COURAGE

I can do everything through Him who strengthens me.
Philippians 4:13

I first met Kathi Holmes as she walked into our writers' group luncheon, cane in hand. During the introductions I learned she was on the final round of editing her book entitled *I Stand With Courage: One Woman's Journey to Conquer Paralysis*. In 2008 her doctors told her she would be paralyzed for the rest of her life. She was now standing, walking, and driving. I later found out there was more to her story than her recovery.

Kathi has been a Christian all her life. She refers to herself during the time prior to her paralysis as an "inactive Christian." As she lay in a hospital bed paralyzed from the waist down, unable to roll over or sit up by herself, she began talking to God. All she asked was for Him to give her the strength to carry on in whatever condition He chose. "Thy will be done," she repeated over and over.

During the many months ahead she struggled with strenuous and exhausting physical therapy, never believing she would walk again, but striving to do the best she could. What she didn't know was God had a plan for her.

God blessed her more than she could have ever imagined. God sent her first grandchild, Olivia, into her life. Olivia became the motivation for Kathi to strive for more mobility. She wanted to be a proper grandmother. Olivia and Kathi learned to walk together at the same time. Kathi is now the grandmother of Olivia and Isabella. Isabella never knew her paralyzed grandmother.

God also led her back to church. While still paralyzed she began wheeling up to her local church in her power chair. Now she is active in church activities, Bible studies, teaches Sunday school and volunteers serving meals to the homeless. She walks her dog twice a day and works out at a therapy pool twice a week.

Jesus asked a man who had been paralyzed for thirty-eight years if he wanted to be healed (John 5:6). We must have faith and trust God before He can make us well. God gave Kathi more than she asked for, and for this she is eternally thankful to our all-powerful God who showed her that miracles do happen.

Healing Lord, give us the courage to ask for what we need. Amen

August 12

THE PINNOCHIO TRINITY

So if anyone is in Christ, there is a new creation: everything old has passed away; see, everything has become new! **2 Corinthians 5:17**

Disney's animated motion picture, Pinocchio, is based on the Italian children's novel by Carl Collodi. Geppetto, a kindly old woodworker, creates a wooden marionette which he names Pinnochio. Geppetto makes a wish that his creation would become a real boy. A Blue Fairy comes in the night and brings Pinocchio to life, telling him he must prove himself "brave, truthful, and unselfish" before becoming a real boy. Geppetto is happy to see his puppet alive, but soon sees Pinocchio making many poor decisions.

Disney morphed the original Pinocchio from an uncooperative brat to an adorable, loving child easily led astray. Jiminy Cricket is added by Disney, assigned by the Blue Fairy to serve as Pinocchio's conscience. Pinocchio seems to be a simple tale teaching kids the benefits of hard work, honesty and getting along with others. There more to the story than meets the eye.

Upon closer inspection, much of this story is Biblical. Geppetto is God and we are Pinocchio—a puppet in the Father's loving hands until He breathes life into us through the Blue Fairy, Who is the Holy Spirit. We're off to school—the school of life—but we need another guide to walk alongside us and aid our "humanness" with its joys and pitfalls, tears and triumphs. Who will teach us how to conduct ourselves in this life? Enter the Christ, disguised as none other than Jiminy Cricket!

If this is a stretch for you, dear reader, you may need to find a five-year-old to hang out with for a day or two! A simple fairy tale can remind us about our relationship with the Triune God: we can follow in Christ's footsteps, or we can be a lump of wood and watch our noses grow when we mess up.

Creator God, You fashioned me in Your image and breathed life into me. Keep me always in Your loving care. Amen

August 13

HERE COME DA JUDGE!

Judge not that you would not be judged. **Matthew 7:1**

Laugh-In, an American sketch comedy television program, was hosted by comedians Dan Rowan and Dick Martin from 1968 to 1973 on the NBC television network. The program was a showcase of comedic talent. One of the most popular sketches was "Here Come De Judge" introduced by black comedian Flip Wilson playing a stuffy magistrate with black robe and powdered wig. Each segment featured a hapless defendant coming before the judge. Hilarious courtroom scenes made audiences double up with mirth. Several celebrities played The Judge, including nightclub comedian Pigmeat Markham, who originated the term in his song, "Here Comes The Judge." One of the last to appear as The Judge was entertainer Sammy Davis Jr., who milked the part for all it was worth, even including his well-known dance routines accompanied by his own singing voice.

I have friend who always says, "We are not to judge others, but we can be fruit inspectors." While her statement is amusing to me, it points out an interesting dilemma for Christians. Can we look upon the lives of others and assess the "fruits" they bear? And is that different than plain old judgment?

Scripture tells us to "resolve…never to put a stumbling-block or hindrance in the way of another" (Romans 14:13). Passing judgement on others can indeed be a stumbling block. When we choose to stress what is different about us and others, instead of how God's love brings us together, we make others feel defensive. If we can frame our differences in love, we can then say, "You do things this way, which is one approach. What do you think about my approach?" This opens a dialog that is non-threatening and positive. Wouldn't God want us to express ourselves this way? As James 5:9 says, "Beloved, do not grumble against one another, so you may not be judged. See, the Judge is standing at the doors!"

Judging God, You are the Only One qualified to judge us, and You do so in love. Amen

August 14

HELP YOURSELF!

And He said to me, "Son of man, eat whatever you find here. Eat this scroll, and go, speak to the house of Israel." So I opened my mouth, and He gave me this scroll to eat. Ezekiel 3:1-2

In 1977, within twenty-four hours after I made a decision to follow Christ, I began to have strange dreams. One of the most puzzling was when I dreamed I was eating my Bible. A new Christian friend told me the story of the prophet Ezekiel. The Lord told him to literally eat the scroll containing God's laws and precepts, "fill (his) stomach with it." Ezekiel found it to be "as sweet as honey" (v. 3.). He was to go "speak to the house of Israel" (v.1).

Speaking to the house of Israel during that time was not exactly like preaching to the choir! As a nation and a people, Israel was discouraged because they were in captivity in Babylon, and they did not have much hope for a good outcome. They needed to understand the exile was God's way of disciplining them for not being faithful to Him. God told Ezekiel not to expect much because "all the house of Israel (had) a hard forehead and a stubborn heart" (v. 7). But God had also made Ezekiel's head hard and his spirit stubborn so he would not falter in his task of steering his fellow Israelites back towards their Lord (v. 9). God promised the prophet He would make the words Ezekiel said to the people powerful (v. 10). God said, "Go to the exiles, to your people, and speak to them. Say to them, 'Thus says the Lord God'; whether they hear or refuse to hear" (v. 11).

Has God called you to speak out in love to someone you know and care about? Is it difficult to find the words so you can make your concerns understood without ruining your relationship with that person? Remember the same Spirit Who comes to us when we don't know how to pray (Romans 8:26) will also help you say the right words at the right time. If that doesn't work, I'll eat my Bible.

Father, guide me in sharing Your message of hope and healing. Amen

August 15

DON'T OVERTHINK THIS!

At that time Jesus said, "I thank You, Father, Lord of heaven and earth, because You have hidden these things from the wise and the intelligent and have revealed them to infants." Matthew 11:25

Sometimes I get way too involved writing these daily devotions! I come up with an idea (God gives me some every day), and I look for Scriptures quotes that fit. Then I do research (which can take hours, depending on how deeply I get into the subject and how lost I get on the internet). By the time I get around to writing, I'm ready for a nap! I believe I'll go take one now…

Well, that was refreshing! Now I'm ready to write again… So my point is that there is one simple message that I'm trying to get across, and that is the Good News about Jesus Christ. Today, I'm looking at Scripture to find "simple" ways to tell the Good News. God's my "Guest Writer" today!

Jesus knew how to tell His own story in uncomplicated words, which he did to Nicodemus, an educated Pharisee, when He said, "God so loved the world that He gave His only begotten Son that whoever believes in Him should not perish but have everlasting life" (John 3:16). This verse has been called "the Gospel in a nutshell" for good reason. In the very next verse, Jesus went on to say "God did not send the Son into the world to condemn the world, but in order that the world might be saved through him." Our position without God is made clear in Romans 3:23: "For all have sinned, and come short of the glory of God." But Romans 10:9 gives us hope because if we "confess with (our) mouth Jesus as Lord, and believe in (our) heart that God raised Him from the dead, (we) will be saved." Jesus said, "I am the way, the truth, and the life" (John 14:6) and it can't get much clearer than that! See how easy it was to write this entry with God's help? This isn't rocket science; it's God's Good News!

We thank You, Lord, for Your Good Word and our modern translations to help us keep it simple. Amen

August 16

THE DOG ATE MY BIBLE STUDY

But they all alike began to make excuses. The first said to him, "I have bought a piece of land, and I must go out and see it; please accept my apologies." Luke 14:18

I have a friend who shared a list she had made to help combat her own problem with procrastination. The list went like this: "I will not do any of the following things until I have completed my daily Bible study: read email, look at Face Book, do Sudoku puzzles, garden…" I need a list like hers, and I need to follow it! I'm better in the winter, when I can't go outside and sit on my deck first thing in the morning. When there is snow up to my knobby kneecaps, it's easier to sit in front of the fire with my first cup of coffee and get the Bible study done. If it's sunny and warm outside, I can easily be distracted by the flowers that need deadheading or the empty bird feeders. Not that those things are all bad, but it doesn't help me finish my Bible study.

Today's Scripture comes from a passage in which Jesus talks about a "great dinner" given by "someone" who invited many guests. But everyone invited began to make excuses, saying they had other things they needed to do and could not find time to join the host (Luke 14:18-20). The host got very angry, first ordering his slave to "Go out at once into the streets and lanes of the town and bring in the poor, the crippled, the blind, and the lame" (v. 21). When those people did not fill all the spots at the host's table, he sent the slave again to "compel people to come in, so that (his) house may be filled" (v. 23). Then the host said, "None of those who were invited will taste my dinner" (v. 24). God loves us so much that He longs for us to seek Him and spend time with Him. If we don't show enough interest to do as He wishes, He will find others to take our place. Let's don't be late to dinner—and get that Bible study done!

Father, You live in us and You want us to live in You. Fill us with the desire to seek You always. Amen

August 17

INVISIBLE

***Then suddenly a woman who had been suffering from hemorrhages for twelve years came up behind him and touched the fringe of his cloak.* Matthew 9:20**

I would never make my flight connection! A man with a cane requested a motorized cart. I asked if I could ride along. But when the cart came to pick him up, the driver looked me up and down and said, "He rides; you walk!"

I have dealt with "invisible" health concerns for most of adult life: profound osteoarthritis, and the accompanying depression. I don't "look" disabled because I get out of bed every morning, dress, and prepare for my day. That takes tons of energy. I am blessed to walk on my own, but my pain is real. I nap almost every day to quiet my central nervous system. I refuse to let strangers dictate to me how I should care for myself or feel about myself.

Amy Zellmer is trying to make a difference in this world for people with invisible disabilities. In 2014, Amy sustained a traumatic brain injury (TBI) in a car accident. Her brain no longer works the same, and she must and does try harder to pay attention and remember things. Her debilitating fatigue takes a toll on her body and her brain. A professional photographer, Amy also writes articles about TBI for Huffington Post. Her first book is called *Life With a Traumatic Brain Injury: Finding the Road Back to Normal.* Amy and I, like many others, are making the best of what we have to work with. We aren't going to let our health issues steal our lives from us.

The woman described in Matthew 9 wanted a better life too. "If I only touch (Jesus') cloak, I will be made well," she said (v. 21). An outcast with a chronic, invisible disease, her faith was strong enough to brave the crush of people to feel the healing power of His robe. Amy and I may not experience the total cure that Jesus gave, but His presence heals the broken places in our souls.

Healing Lord, thank You for touching me and making my spirit whole. Amen

August 18

FALSE PROPHETS

At noon Elijah mocked them, saying, "Cry aloud! Surely he is a god; either he is meditating, or he has wandered away, or he is on a journey, or perhaps he is asleep and must be awakened." 1 Kings 18:27

A TV news story told about young boys kidnapped and coerced into service with ISIS, and how they were rescued and reunited with their loved ones. It was gut-wrenching to see these reunions: thankful parents who thought they'd never see their little boys again, and traumatized youngsters, not so sure what was real or true anymore. I prayed instantly for all the children affected by this hateful ragtag band of hoodlums who profess to know all about the God of the universe and insist all "infidels" must be annihilated.

This is not a new story. In the ninth century B.C., Jezebel was the wife of Ahab the king of Israel. She worshiped a false god named Baal (1 Kings 16:31), but the Israelites knew Baal was just a stupid graven image. Jezebel commissioned hundreds of priests and prophets to enforce her beliefs. She persecuted the Israelite's priests and prophets, putting many to death.

The prophet Elijah took care of Jezebel's program in short order by assembling the priests and prophets of both the Lord and of Baal, on Mount Caramel (vs. 2—25). Each group cut up a bull to sacrifice. Elijah said the One True God would provide the fire. The Baal-ites huffed and puffed and prayed to their graven image, but alas, no fire. Elijah told the Israelites to build the altar and put a trench of water around it. He stepped forward and asked God to accept the sacrifice of the Israelites. And boy, did God deliver! "The fire of the Lord...consumed the burnt-offering, the wood, the stones, and the dust, and even licked up the water that was in the trench" (v. 38). Finally, Jezebel was thrown out of her high palace window and mauled to death by some angry dogs. Isn't it comforting to know God's going to prevail, no matter how sick or twisted the false prophets get?

One True God, Your justice will prevail on earth and in heaven. Amen

August 19

CHECKLISTS

So if anyone is in Christ, there is a new creation: everything old has passed away; see, everything has become new! **2 Corinthians 5:17**

I have lists and reminders all over the house, in my car, on my cell phone, and in my foggy little brain. I could never get anything done if it weren't for my little lists calling out to me. Most of the things on those lists get done; some have a permanent presence at the bottom of a mostly checked-off checklist. Those must not be priorities, or I would have done them by now!

Before I accepted Jesus Christ as my Lord and Savior at age twenty-nine, I had some different lists. Items on those lists included things like: buy wine, try to be less selfish, replace false eyelashes, force yourself to call your parents. My agenda looked very different in those days. I've stopped drinking, my parents are gone (and I miss them both, as dysfunctional as they were). I can't wear false eyelashes because I have chronic dry eyes. I'm still working on "be less selfish.." I'm human, and I'm a work in progress!

The cool thing is my "list" of the things I have accomplished since I started following Jesus is pretty long and getting longer all the time. I've stopped believing I'm the center of the universe because Ephesians 4:5-6 says we have "one Lord, one faith, one baptism, one God and Father of all, who is above all and through all and in all." Apparently, that's not me! I've forgiven lots of folks, including the man who assaulted me at gunpoint over forty years ago. Luke 6:37 says we aren't to judge or condemn others or we will ourselves will be subject to condemnation. It doesn't mean the assault didn't happen. I just don't want to assault the guy back any more. I also daily experience the "peace that passes all understanding" talked about in Philippians 4:7. This peace guards my heart and my mind and keeps me close to Jesus, which has totally changed my life. That's just the short list; you'd have to talk to Christ for all the details. But I know I'm on His list.

Transforming Christ, mold me and change me! Amen

August 20

YESTERDAYS AND TOMORROWS

Can any of you by worrying add a single hour to your span of life? Matthew 6:27

In my father's belongings, I found the essay below, hand printed, unsigned, entitled "One Day At A Time:"

"There are two days in every week about which we should not worry: two days which should be kept free from fear and apprehension. One of these days is Yesterday, with its mistakes and cares, its faults and blunders, its aches and pains. Yesterday has passed forever beyond our control. All the money in the world cannot bring back yesterday. We cannot undo a single act we performed; we cannot erase a single word said…Yesterday Is Gone!

The other day we should not worry about is Tomorrow, with its possible burdens, its large promise and poor performance. Tomorrow is also beyond our immediate control. Tomorrow's sun will rise, either in splendor or behind a mask of clouds…but it will rise. Until it does, we have no stake in tomorrow, for it is yet unborn.

This leaves only one day…Today! Any(one) can fight the battle of just one day. It is only when you and I have the burdens of those two awful eternities, Yesterday and Tomorrow, that we break down. It is not the experience of Today that drives (people) mad; it is the remorse or bitterness for something which happened yesterday and the dread of what tomorrow may bring. Let us, therefore, live but one day at a time!"

Why did he keep this? Did he get it from Alcoholics Anonymous or Alanon? I will never know the answer to these questions, but it connected me to my dad in a special way. The wise words could have been written by Jesus—in fact, they appear in a little different form in the 6th chapter of Matthew.

Precious Lord, You take care of the yesterdays and the tomorrows, and together we'll get through today. Amen

August 21

KINGS OF THE EARTH

***All the kings of the earth shall praise you, O Lord, for they have heard the words of your mouth.* Psalm 138:4**

Do you ever wonder if the people in power—the kings of the earth—have any idea what they are doing? I'm not speaking only about "third world" countries; I'm talking about supposedly civilized, advanced, "with-it" nations. I wonder a lot about what goes through the minds of people who make decisions that affect the masses. It especially bothers me when I think about the children, who are the future generations of "kings of the earth."

St. Paul resident and Christian songwriter/recording artist Sara Groves wonders that too. In the lyrics of her haunting song, "Esther," she tells about a young widow with no children. Esther went to Africa and fell in love with the children there. She worked tirelessly the rest of her life to bring justice, peace and food to those innocent kids. Groves tells about Esther going before "the kings of the earth" and asking them to help these children.

The United Nations Food and Agriculture Organization estimates about one in nine people in the world suffered from chronic hunger from 2012 to 2014. Most, 791 million out of 805 million, live in developing countries. One out of six children there are underweight. Poor nutrition causes nearly half of all deaths in children under five (3.1 million a year). About 11 million hungry people live in what are considered to be "developed" countries.

How can we help or know if our efforts are making any headway? We can help, even if it's only giving a can of soup to the local food shelf. But we know one thing for sure: the corrupt, selfish and cruel leaders of this world, like everyone else, will one day know Who God is. As Romans 14:11 says, "Every knee shall bow to (Him) and every tongue shall give praise to God."

Father of All Nations, we beseech You to turn leaders' hearts towards the starving children. Amen

August 22

A HORSE NAMED DIABLO

Do not hide your face from your servant, for I am in distress—make haste to answer me. **Psalm 69:17**

I rode my own horse daily as a youngster, but marriage, kids and a career led me on different paths. After retirement, a man offered to lease me his horse. I said, "I can do this!" I was going to be a senior seasoned cowgirl, confident in my equine skills and instincts, ready to climb onto a thousand pounds of raw energy, muscle and precision, and glide through the countryside.

The horse's name was Diablo—Spanish for "devil"—a certain clue. His owner introduced us with a five minute rundown of various horse-related (but not specifically Diablo-related) facts, and left me alone at the boarding stable. Another boarder offered to ride with me. "I'm leaving the gate open," she said as we left the paddock. "The owner said to let the other horses into the bigger pasture." Another clue (not to mention the thundering of my heart). I naively thought she knew what she was doing. Imagine my surprise when twenty of Diablo's close personal friends came charging through that gate. Things got ugly. I thought we were going on a trail ride. Diablo decided we were having a rodeo. His raw energy, muscle and precision erupted instantly as he raised all thousand pounds of his naughty self up on his back legs. Once. Twice. And the third time, the saddle twisted to the side with me still seated in it. My instincts told me to use all my strength to "right" that saddle, but the magic was pretty much gone. My legs and arms trembling, I dismounted Diablo to tighten the cinch, at which point he asserted himself yet again and bolted off with the rest of the herd.

Later, I mounted and rode Diablo around in the paddock to prove who was boss. Driving home, I considered why I was still alive and not spread over the rocky pasture in quivering chunks. I decided God is good. I promised Him I would try to make wiser decisions from now on.

Protector God, You came to my rescue with "that horse." Thank You! Amen

August 23

DEAD GIRL WALKING

But God, who is rich in mercy, out of the great love with which he loved us even when we were dead through our trespasses, made us alive together with Christ. **Ephesians 10:4-5**

What I valued before I knew Jesus Christ as my personal Savior looks good…by earthly standards. I was born into an upper middle class family, the second of two kids. My parents made a handsome couple. Mother was a real "looker" in her day, always dressing to the nines. My dad appeared especially important in his US Air Force officer's uniform. Our family lived in nice houses, we had a "nanny," and we enjoyed what Daddy called the "creature comforts." We never went a day without food, shelter, and nice clothing. Both my sister and I earned college degrees and worked in respected fields. By worldly standards, we were "good."

What our family did lack was a visible faith in God and a life rooted and grounded in the Bible. My parents were both raised in Christian homes, but neither attended church nor taught us girls about the God Who created us. When my mother's drinking was at its worst and she was perhaps in the throes of some self-examination, she sent my father and me to a Methodist church to be baptized (Mother was baptized at an old fashioned tent revival at age twelve). Away at college, my sister escaped this little ritual. Not much happened after this sacred event. Life went on pretty much the same.

When I was in my late twenties, ironically at another "tent revival" (this one held in a high school gymnasium), I went forward for the altar call and never looked back. All of a sudden I fully understood that I had been a "dead girl walking," and my life was garbage compared to what was promised if I followed Jesus. I have never regretted that decision, although I'm sure it took God divine patience (which He has!) to bring me along His path a few times. Jesus is not only my Savior but a Living Presence in my life to this day. And that's really "good!"

Praise to You, O Christ, for making Your home inside my heart! Amen

August 24

OBVIOUSLY AN ALCOHOLIC

God...will not let you be tested beyond your strength, but...will also provide the way out so that you may be able to endure it.
1 Corinthians 10:13

As a youngster, I didn't talk about my mother's drinking. I was ashamed of her, and I knew I'd be in serious trouble with both my parents if they ever found out I had shared our family's "dirty little secret." My sister and I—and my dad on occasion—used humor to soften the blow of a very ugly home life. When Mother woke up after being out cold for days, we referred to it as "Hurricane Mother making landfall." While intoxicated, she would refer to herself as a "gracious lady," which became fodder for lots of jokes. We girls were "gracious ladies in training" (a truly horrifying thought!). In my memoir, I wrote a whole page parody called "The Vodka Wars," with my parents battling it out over my father placing a rubber band around the vodka bottle and Mother moving it so he would think she was drinking less.

It was sad that we used humor in such a dark way to cope! When I finally decided I was an adult and could maybe tell my story to help others, I spoke on a panel of adult children of alcoholics at the college where I worked. I told the audience my mother often said, "I know I'm an alcoholic! That's why I drink so much!" To my great surprise, the comment brought the house down. I was delighted that they were listening, but shocked they were laughing at my mother's "disease." I had no idea what power humor could have to grab an audience's attention. They all got the point: Mother was in total denial that she needed help.

We as Christians may be doing the same thing my mother did. Sometimes we may say, "I know I'm a Christian. That's why I sin so much." But if you're like me, we sometimes continue to commit the same sins—minor as they may be—over and over again without seeking the help that is already right in front of us. God said He would provide an escape, so ask Him.

Let me walk close to You, Jesus. Amen

August 25

HUMAN HUMILITY

Humble yourselves before the Lord, and he will exalt you. **James 4:10**

"Humility is our bread, obedience our wine," says Dr. Calvin Miller in his book *Into the Depths of God*. "We gain true humility not by putting ourselves down but by standing next to Christ." Seeing how great the true Christ is, we are secure in our place of humility before Him. Miller should know: he accepted Christ with joy at the tender age of nine years and has dedicated his entire life and work to Christ. An author review on Christianbook.com, describes him as having "borne the indelible mark of the Holy Spirit."

How can we, as mere human beings, be expected to demonstrate humility as Christ did? Actually, Christ is the very best example of how to be humble. He gave up His heavenly home in glory and all of its rank and privilege to come into this broken world (Philippians 2:6-7). Jesus "emptied Himself, taking the form of a slave, being born in human likeness" (v. 7). Then, because it was His Father's great plan for the salvation of all mankind, Jesus "humbled himself and became obedient to the point of death—even death on a cross" (v. 8). Why? Nothing Jesus could have done in His human form—not His love, kindness nor healing of the sick—could have convinced mankind He was really God except His defeating death and rising from that grave.

When I was in the entertainment business and not yet in "God's business," I would become jealous of another performer until I realized I would never in my lifetime attain what she possessed in raw talent. It's like that with Christ: we must finally give over our egos entirely to Him to see that we are *not* Him. When we are full of ourselves, God can't fill us. The answer that satisfies my soul is, "No, I can't do what Christ did and does, and I never will be able to." The second part of the answer is, "Christ did it all for me." If that doesn't make us humble and obedient, nothing will!

Humble me, Lord, that I may be exalted in Your eyes. Amen

August 26

SHAGGY GOD STORY

Let the wise...understand a proverb...the words of the wise and their riddles. **Proverbs 1:5-6**

No, it's not a typo. You thought I wrote "Shaggy Dog Story," which is a long-winded story possibly including irrelevant information, ending in disappointment or a pun (which is often the same thing). Shaggy dog stories keep listeners interested because they want to know the outcome. Much of the "humor" involves the ability of the story teller to mesmerize his audience until the bitter end. My mother used to tell Shaggy Dog Stories. I can't remember any of them, but the punchlines have played in my mind as a loop tape for years. "It's of no consequence except to another hippopotamus." "On the other hand, she had a wart." I wish I could remember the stories...

So Jesus called the disciples together in heaven and said He had an assignment for them on earth. "My children have wandered away from My Word," said Jesus. Peter asked, "Are you sending us to Israel?" "No, Simon," He replied, "I'm sending you to Los Angeles. When you get there, you will need to purchase a vehicle." The disciples looked aghast. "The distances now are too far to walk, and Los Angeles is covered in asphalt, so your sandals will burn up." "What kind of vehicle should we purchase, Lord?" asked Thomas. "You will know the right one," Jesus said, smiling. And suddenly the disciples found themselves on Redondo Boulevard. They looked at Chevrolets, Fords, Dodges, Mitsubishis and Toyotas, trying all the miraculous features. "Nothing is big enough to hold all twelve of us," said Matthias. He was the newest disciple and he needed to be close to the others. "We cannot be separated," agreed Mark, "but Jesus said we would know which vehicle is right." Just then, a Toyota salesman approached the group and said, "Gentlemen, Toyota has just introduced a new vehicle the size of a limousine and seats twelve." "That's it!" Peter cried. "Jesus said we should all be in one Accord!" Now that's a Shaggy God Story!"

We praise You for humor, Lord. It keeps us going! Amen

August 27

A RIVER RUNS THROUGH IT

There is a river whose streams make glad the city of God, the holy habitation of the Most High. **Psalms 46:4**

In summer, 2015, the Animas River in western Colorado ran yellow-orange. The Environmental Protection Agency was examining an abandoned gold mine when a levee was unintentionally breached by heavy equipment, releasing nearly three million gallons of pollutants into the water: arsenic, lead, copper, aluminum and cadmium. By conservative estimates, there are over 500,000 abandoned and inactive hardrock mines strewn across the country. Clean-up would cost $50 billion. Some say the metals sank to the bottom of the river, posing no threat. Others weren't buying it. Drinking water was tested throughout the area, and farmers and ranchers worry about crops and livestock dependent on the river and the water tables below.

I picture God holding His beautiful gem, the Earth, in His hands and weeping over what mankind is doing to this planet. Those who rushed to the gold mines of the west in the 1800s were only concerned with getting rich, but the Bible says "the love of money is a root of all kinds of evil" and those who pursued wealth without scruples "pierced themselves with many pains" (1 Timothy 6:10). The treasure which the Lord created in the beginning was perfect because He made it so. He created humans in His image and gave them charge over the things on earth. But He also gave us free will, so we do not always display God-like qualities. Isaiah prophesied that if we could "pay attention" to God's commands, our "peace would become like a river" (Isaiah 48:18). Instead, another river has been contaminated.

God will have the final word. When this life is over, we will see "the river of the water of life, bright as crystal, flowing from the throne of God and of the Lamb" (Revelation 22:1)

Lord, we praise You for our beautiful earthly home. Stir us to take care of what You have created. Amen

August 28

PRIMARY COLORS

I have set my bow in the clouds, and it shall be a sign of the covenant between me and the earth. **Genesis 9:13**

Every single color you see on a computer screen is made from the three primary colors, red, yellow and blue! It seems impossible but it's true. If you want to get technical, there is "additive" color mixing, used in television and computers (a "pixel" is simply a juxtaposition of the three primary colors). "Subtractive" color mixing is the term used for pigments and dyes, an example of which is printing.

The amazing thing is God created all the shades and hues and brightness from a very small number of "colors." So if you have your Big Box of Crayons, you can choose Bright Red or Permanent Geranium Lake, Cosmic Cobalt or Wintergreen Dream, Unmellow Yellow or Blizzard Blue—and God knows all about every one of them. When He made the water in the lake behind your home or the grass in your lawn or the pink in your grandson's cheeks, He knew the names of all the shades and nuances of how those things would appear to the human eye.

Color means more to God than just what we as humans perceive on a daily basis. God felt color was so important He used it as a sign of His covenant with His people long before any of us were around. When Noah, his family and the animals-two-by-two finally found themselves on dry land, God told them to "be fruitful and multiply, abound on the earth and multiply in it" (Genesis 9:7). Then He told them He was making them a promise: "never again shall all flesh be cut off by the waters...and never again shall there be a flood to destroy the earth" (v. 12). As the storm clouds cleared and the flood waters receded, God gave the people a sign by placing a rainbow—raindrops and sun crossing paths—in the sky, displaying a full range of all the colors of light reflected off drops of water (v. 13). What a sign!

A rainbow of color was the sign of Your promise, O God! Amen

August 29

SYMBIOTIC RELATIONSHIPS

Submit yourselves therefore to God. Resist the devil, and he will flee from you. James 4:7

A symbiotic relationship is a close, prolonged association between two or more different organisms that may, but not necessarily, benefit each member. "Symbiosis" comes from two Greek words meaning "with" and "living." One mutually beneficial symbiosis is a cattle egret eating the insects disturbed when cattle rustle the grass as they eat. Barnacles attaching to whales are not harmful, just annoying to the whale. If you've ever tried to enjoy a Midwestern summer evening outdoors, you know about a type of symbiosis that is harmful to humans: mosquitos feasting on your arm while you try to eat your bratwurst. You are the "host" and the mosquito is the "parasite."

Symbiotic relationships occur in the spiritual realm as well. The indwelling Christ is beneficial to those of us who seek His face and welcome His full direction on our lives. In Romans 8:9 Paul says "the Spirit of God dwells in you." Paul even says we are "God's temple" created by Him so He may "dwell" in us (1 Corinthians 3:16). And we are to "let the word of Christ dwell in (us) richly," teaching us "wisdom" and making us want to show gratitude with "psalms, hymns and spiritual songs to God" (Colossians 3:16).

There are also spiritual parasites. In Mark's version of the Parable of the Sower, God's Word is like seed dropped on a path. But "Satan immediately comes and takes away the Word that is sown" (Mark 4:15). Satan is hungrier than those backyard mosquitoes, prowling around "like a roaring lion...looking for someone to devour" (1 Peter 5:8). How can we rid ourselves of these unwelcome parasites? Jesus gives us that authority! Luke 10:19-20 quotes Jesus saying to the seventy appointees, "See, I have given you authority...over all the power of the enemy; and nothing will hurt you." Satan can do nothing to hurt us. God has already won the battle.

Father, we want to be close to You. Help us to banish spirits in Your name. Amen

August 30

STRONG WILL, STRONG WON'T

Your will be done, on earth as it is in heaven. **Matthew 6:10**

Do you ever feel like God's will is written in invisible ink that fades from the page while you are trying to discern it? It often feels like a game of hide and seek when I try to imagine God's will for my life or even my moments. Such an elusive thing, to be following the will of a God I can't see with my very naked eye, One Who does not converse with me audibly on a daily basis, with my humanness and ego blocking the way much of the time anyway. I still don't feel I have a grasp on that mysterious thing called God's will.

I know that God's will is strong, but many times my won't seems to be stronger! Frequently, I come back to my theory that the only way to stay really close to God and follow Him all the time is to move to a cloistered monastery where the only thing to do is worship God. Even that's ridiculous because people who live in monasteries have to do stuff every day too. They have to cook and wash dishes and do laundry and fix the place up and take care of the animals if they have them. Even in a silent monastery, there has to be some kind of communication. Otherwise, how would they decide what to have for dinner on Tuesday night or call the paramedics if one of them falls and breaks a bone?

Maybe when the apostle Paul says, "Pray without ceasing" (1 Thessalonians 5:17), he is really talking about learning to multitask for Him: develop that "attitude of prayer" so well that you can do it while you are answering the phone or walking to the bus or getting gum out of your child's hair. Perhaps the key is developing and maintaining a relationship with God where our entire being is focused on communicating even when we think we're not. If we can "do" God all the time, while we "do" life, His will becomes ever more apparent to us.

Lord, I want to do Your will. Help me with my "won'ts." Amen

August 31

A DAY IN THE LIFE

I believe that I shall look upon the goodness of the Lord in the land of the living!
Psalm 27:13

I've decided to be more intentional about recognizing my blessings. and today was a good day to start. Our air conditioned home is a rambler, with everything we need on one floor. It's easy for me to maintain and not wear myself out. Our yard is large and full of flowers and trees. Even though I can no longer take very good care of the gardens, I love seeing the vegetation, the birds, and yes, even the squirrels from my deck. I ate a perfect peach for breakfast and went to a meeting of nice people.

I came home in time for an appointment with a decorator—we need a new paint job. But she was running late and called. That was okay because I rescheduled and then took a nice long nap. My husband went to a picnic without me, so I could stay home and write, which I did. I took a break and went for a long walk in our suburban neighborhood which borders two parks. A half block from home, I was met by a young fawn that still had her spots. She watched me walking toward her, so I stopped, afraid that I would frighten her. I spoke softly to her and to my great surprise, she began walking toward me! I told her she was a silly fawn, that she didn't know me very well and her mother would probably not be happy if we struck up a friendship. She twitched her ears, and then reluctantly, it seemed, she bounded off into the woods.

My husband was home when my walk was over and we chatted a while. Then I sat down to write this page. Without even thinking about it, I had spent the entire day praising God in the things I saw and did, the highlight of which was God sending the adorable little fawn to visit with me.

Praise You, God of all the universe, for caring enough for me to bless me each and every day! Amen

September

September 1

POSTCARDS FROM THE LEDGE

The demons begged Jesus, "If you drive us out, send us into the herd of pigs." He said to them, "Go!" So they came out and went into the pigs, and the whole herd rushed down the steep bank into the lake and died in the water. **Matthew 8:31-32**

Suicide is *not* demon possession. It has been called "a permanent solution to a temporary problem." The tenth largest cause of death in the United States, suicide accounts for more fatalities than murder. Suicide attempts impact an even greater number of people than completed suicide. More survive suicide attempts than die, needing long-term mental health services.

In my counseling career, I have talked more suicidal people off the ledge than I care to remember. I *vividly* remember those who did not survive. It is a horrible, helpless feeling to have a person's life in your hands and not know how things will turn out. One situation is engraved in my memory as I was the last person to speak to a man who took his own life. A destitute drug addict, he lived alone in a tiny apartment. I had taken him a hotplate and some food because his stove didn't work. The next morning he was found dead, and not from an overdose. He hanged himself with a belt.

Mental health professionals know we cannot blame ourselves when suicide occurs. But the next time I spoke to a despondent person (who happened to be my superior), I realized he was crying for help. I immediately called his home. His wife answered and said he had gone bowling. A positive sign, but I wasn't leaving things to chance. I asked her to tell him I had enjoyed our conversation earlier and was looking forward to talking some more. The next morning he was in the mental health unit. I don't know if my words had encouraged him, but I knew I had tried. We are to "Bear one another's burdens, and in this way (we) will fulfill the law of Christ" (Galatians 6:2). Walking away from a suicidal person is not suicide prevention.

Holy God, heal Your children's wounds and set us in a place to be of help to those we know. Amen

September 2

DO YOU DO VOODO?

Then it goes and brings along seven other spirits more evil than itself, and they enter and live there; and the last state of person is worse than the first. **Matthew 12:45**

I visited Cap Haitien, Haiti in the late 1970s, soon after benevolent dictator Jean-Claude "Baby Doc" Duvalier reopened the island for tourism. From the safety and opulence of our cruise liner, we Americans ventured into town and got the culture shock of our lives. Signs of profound poverty were everywhere. Catholic mass was just letting out, and we watched many of the native "parishioners" walk across the street to a row of voodoo parlors, where we were told, people had curses placed on each other. Our group then boarded a tour bus and went on a guided excursion, the last stop being a cultural "show." We watched beautiful and talented native dancers and singers and ate Haitian cuisine until the final act appeared with a flourish. A wild-eyed voodoo priest, dressed in a frightening costume with his hair in dreadlocks, thrilled the audience by walking on broken glass and hot coals, swallowing a stick of fire, and lying on a bed of nails, apparently having placed himself in a trance so he would feel no pain. For his grand finale, Voodoo Man gyrated and made ghastly noises before setting himself completely on fire. An assistant put the fire out immediately and the crowd went wild. Except me. I was, to put it bluntly, creeped out. I felt an evil presence during the entire "voodoo show." I just wanted to leave.

My visit to Haiti made a profound impression on me, because of the poverty but also because of the occult practiced there. I do not believe in "courting" evil, and it has haunted me since then to realize this impoverished nation seemingly accepted the practice of voodoo. Many Haitians do not practice voodoo and believe in Jesus as the Son of God, and I now have a greater admiration for Christian missionaries who have willingly offered their time and talents to minister to the Haitian people.

Father of all nations, I am thankful for those who are able to do Your work in foreign lands with people who need to hear Your Good News. Amen

September 3

JUST LIKE MARY

May your friends be like the sun as it rises in its might. **Judges 5:31**

My friend Mary McFarlane has enjoyed reading my daily devotions. Mary is an excellent writer and I've often told her she should pen a book. So I asked her if she'd like to be a "guest writer." Here is what she sent me:

Meg Corrigan is a longtime friend. Years ago Meg inspired me to get up early in the morning with a desire to begin my day by searching God's Word. Jesus chose Meg and called her to follow Him, and in obedience she took His hand and never let go. Now with her quick wit and uncanny talent Meg shares God's truth and forgiveness. It is evident Meg sits at the feet of Jesus and depends upon the Spirit of God to assist her to share her daily perception of Scripture. God divvies up a large piece of her writing skills and daily insights for her readers.

This is so like Mary! I had wanted—and expected—her to write something about herself. But instead she wrote about me. Now I want to tell you why Mary is my very special friend! We met in a Bible study and I learned quickly she is a soldier for Christ. Mary's heartfelt, well-thought-out and pertinent comments encouraged all in the group. When a member was having a tough time, Mary would speak peace over that person, thereby blessing the entire room. I learned Mary dealt with health issues while also shepherding her husband Mel through his own medical crises. Before she and Mel retired, Mary would often tell of times she witnessed to customers at the storage locker facility they managed—people who had lost homes and jobs and needed to store belongings until a better time. She cared about them all.

Do you have a friend like Mary? Today, thank God for that person's friendship and then call or go see that friend and say how much you care about him or her.

Lord, You have made each one of us "blessed to be a blessing." Stir us to tell others how much they mean to us. Amen

September 4

DEFINITELY BETTER

***We are…struck down, but not destroyed; always carrying in the body the death of Jesus, so…the life of Jesus may also be made visible in our bodies.* 2 Corinthians 4:8-10**

Self-absorbed parents. Breast cancer. Loss of spouse at a young age. Child with Autism. Another with a rare blood disease. All these happened to Caryn Sullivan—by page 38! In her memoir, *Bitter or Better,* this award-winning journalist tells of a life fraught with tragedy but lived with hope.

I had seen Caryn many times at our mutual writers' group, Women of Words. She always dressed and acted professionally, with a gentleness about her that belied all she had been through. When she appeared at my summer backyard luau dressed in Boho Island style, I was delighted to see she knew how to have fun. (She came in second in the hula contest.) I had read some of her poignant and inspiring columns in the St. Paul Pioneer Press newspaper. But until I read her long-awaited memoir, I had no idea how strong, compassionate and caring this woman was. I had found a soul mate.

Throughout her life, Caryn, like me, had been quietly secreting away her pain and sorrow while deftly honing her survival skills. Yet she has remained courageous during each crisis and has emerged stronger for every sorrow. Maybe she is just a faster learner than I am, but I admire her steady resolve.

Caryn says people who live well "make choices, consciously or not…(placing) a high value on being students of life…they count humor among the essentials in their toolkits…they are crafting their legacies." She credits writing with "preparing (her) for, and helping (her) grow from, adversity." As a journalist, she found her stories to be "a recipe for navigating life." Caryn says she is not perfect, but her faith has allowed her to "live with a peaceful heart." She goes on to say, "Action rarely engenders regret, but inaction almost always breeds…guilt and remorse."

Father of Hope and Healing, teach us to have faith You will walk with us through the dark valleys. Amen

September 5

THE SHADOW OF THE ALMIGHTY
Guest Writer Gloria VanDemmeltraadt

He who dwells in the shelter of the Most High, who abides in the shadow of the Almighty, will say to the Lord, "My refuge and my fortress, my God, in Whom I trust." Psalm 91:1-2

Promises are easily made and just as easily broken. All of us have memories of promises made we desperately wanted kept. Sadly, we have many memories of those same promises and hopes being dashed, sometimes by circumstances we couldn't control, but mainly by human failings.

The religious song, "On Eagle's Wings," was written from the words of Psalm 91, which is considered a promise of protection. Onno VanDemmeltraadt, in his youth in war-torn Indonesia during WWII, cherished the words of Psalm 91, and held fast to this promise of God's protection. It has been a life-long source of comfort and peace in times of trouble.

As Psalm 91 is a prayer of protection, verse 1 could be called the verse of protection. Isn"t it odd 91: 1 or 911, reminds us all of that fateful day in 2001 of American history, when we realized how much we needed God's protection? It is believed David wrote Psalm 91, and he speaks of God's work in his life thousands of years ago. Today, God's promises are still there – still to be counted on – still protecting those he loves: "Because he cleaves to Me in love, I will deliver him; I will protect him, because he knows My name" (Psalm 91:14).

Psalm 91 reaffirms how the grace of God protects us throughout our lives, "With long life I will satisfy him, and show him My salvation" (Psalm 91:16). Above all, it confirms how God sticks to His promises – always.

Dearest Lord of promises kept, we are grateful for your presence and for your shelter in which we dwell. Amen

September 6

CATCH AND RELEASE

***And they may come to their senses and escape from the snare of the devil, after being captured by him to do his will.* 2 Timothy 2:26**

My husband left yesterday for the Minnesota State Bass Fishing Tournament, which he fishes every year. The lake is off limits one day before the two day tournament. The guys go a week early to "pre-fish," practicing "catch and release." After all your hard work getting the fish to take the bait, negotiating it past weeds, rocks, dock pilings, and sunken junk, and getting it into the boat, you have to let it go. During the tournament, fish are kept in a "live well," a tank in the boat with recirculating lake water to keep the fish alive. Then, the fish are weighed to determine who wins. After this, the bass are carried carefully back to the lake and sent on their way. The bass anglers pride themselves in losing very few fish during these tournaments.

In my mind, "catch and release" fishing is a little like an alien invasion, at least from the fish's point of view. So Bubba Bass is swimming peacefully along the shore when he gets hoodwinked by a plastic worm that looks real and smells real, thanks to some wicked technology to permeate the plastic with stinky stuff. Bubba thinks, "What's this?" Before he knows what hit him, he's pulled out of the water with a ripped lip, and a very large, strange being is looking him over, touching him, pulling something out of his sore lip, and in some cases kissing him (yes, it's true!). Then he swims around in a little tank with some other fish for what seems like forever until he gets handled some more before he's returned to the lake. The other fish don't believe the tall tale he tells! "Must be the fermented milfoil," they hoot.

Aren't you glad God doesn't treat us like this? The Lord doesn't use some sort of bait to win us over. He just offers us the best deal in the universe, to have all our sins forgiven and live forever.

Lord of land and sea, praise You for offering us salvation with no fishing line attached. Amen

September 7

HERE'S LOOKIN' ATCHA!

(Christ) is the image of the invisible God, the Firstborn over all creation.
Colossians 1:15

My first experience with a pastor was at age twelve in Colorado Springs when my mom "made" my dad and me get baptized. The pastor was a large man with a kindly but authoritative manner. When he preached, I thought I must be hearing God Himself, and his image stuck with me for a long time.

I now know Jesus in the flesh was the perfect image of God. Christ came in human form to live among us so we might know both Him and the Father. Jesus was, as we say, "the spitting image" of His Dad. The words *image* and *icon* come from the Greek term *eikon*, a representation of something else. God is Spirit (John 4:24); we can't see him. Jesus in the flesh became a *representative* of God so we would know what the Father looks like and acts like. When we look at Christ, we are looking at God too (John 14:9).

In the same way, those who profess to believe in Jesus Christ as the Son of God also "represent" both God and Jesus. It is our job to share Jesus with everyone we meet (Matthew 28:19). In the words of Teresa of Avila:

"Christ has no body now but yours. No hands, no feet on earth but yours. Yours are the eyes through which He looks with compassion on this world. Yours are the feet with which He walks to do good. Yours are the hands through which He blesses all the world. Yours are the hands, yours are the feet, yours are the eyes, you are His body. Christ has no body now on earth but yours."

So when you speak to someone about the faith that has set you free, know you represent Jesus. You can say to your listener, "Here's Jesus, lookin' atcha!"

Jesus God incarnate, embolden us to be Your hands and feet and eyes and body in this world. Amen

September 8

A METAPHOR FOR LIFE

For if God did not spare the angels when they sinned, but cast them into hell...then the Lord knows how to rescue the godly from trial, and to keep the unrighteous under punishment until the day of judgement.
2 Peter 2:4, 9

Comedian Maripat Donovon in her "Late Night Catechism" series uses the children's board game Chutes and Ladders to explain the concept of heaven and hell. "Good" believers climb the ladders and gain rewards; "bad" believers slide down the chutes and are punished. A funny sketch!

Chutes and Ladders has long been considered to be a metaphor for life itself, with two schools of thought. The "morality" supporters believe "the "ups" and "downs" represent moral choices and their consequences." The "emotional" camp contends a game of chance can't be moral choice. The "emotional" followers believe "the highs and lows of Chutes and Ladders (represents) various emotional highs and lows...an individual's emotions are more susceptible to whim and...chance than their moral decisions."

Are Christians really in a game of Chutes and Ladders? Is this all being a believer amounts to? No! First of all, the concept of life being like the board game is flawed from the outset. God's grace isn't in the mix. If grace was part of the game, there would be no need to roll the dice to find out if we were rewarded or punished. Christ came down from heaven to preach the Good News, and He died on a cross to pay for our sins. When we ask, sins are simply forgiven. For the very reason we believe in the healing power of Christ's redemptive act, we are in another "board game" in which we are to share our joy and newfound hope with others we meet. Each person must make his or her own decisions between moral chutes and ladders in life. But God has called us to walk with our fellow human beings and be helpmates for them in their journey, just as others have helped us in ours.

Your promises are no roll of the dice, Lord. Thank You for Your steadfast love. Amen

September 9

ANGLER MANAGEMENT

Follow me, and I will make you fish for people. **Matthew 4:19**

My husband Patrick and his bass fishing club are just winding up another season of tournaments. The club belongs to a national association of bass anglers, and the members compete each year to send some of their members to fish in a statewide tournament held in early September. Until I married my husband, I never realized what it takes to manage a club like this. Patrick has, from time to time, served in just about every office in the local club and several at the state level. Membership dues are collected and sent in, records kept of the weight of each angler's catch at each tournament and for the season. And that's just the local club! Patrick can tell you on which lake he's caught every fish he's ever caught, how much it weighed and what kind of artificial bait he used (all competitive bass fishing is "catch-and-release"). Although I only fish with him occasionally for fun, he even remembers every fish I've ever caught.

Jesus had a fishing club too, and the men in His club kept Him busy. From the moment He walked by the Sea of Galilee and called Peter, Andrew, James and John to join His ministry, He had his hands full. These first disciples of Christ knew about fishing, but they were clueless what they were getting into with the Lord. I've often thought how charismatic Jesus must have been to get these men to drop everything they had ever known, leave their boats, their families, and their life styles, and follow a Man they'd never met. But in spite of the Christ giving the boys clues about Who He was and what was to come, they seemed clueless until the very end. "Destroy this temple and I will raise it again in three days" (John 2:18-19). "The Son of Man will be delivered over to the chief priests and the teachers of the law. They will condemn Him to death" (Matthew 16:21). Even though they did not fully understand, Jesus did not give up on the disciples, and He won't give up on us. And we know the happy ending of the story!

Patient Lord, open my eyes to see all You do in my life. Let me not be clueless! Amen

September 10

WE ARE REFUGEES

Some wandered in desert wastes, finding no way to an inhabited town; hungry and thirsty, their souls fainted within them. Then they cried to the Lord in their trouble, and He delivered them from their distress; He led them by a straight way, until they reached an inhabited town.
Psalm 107:4-7

Topping news reports in the fall of 2015 was the picture of the dead body of a Syrian boy being pulled from the water on a Turkish beach. The three-year-old child, Aylan Kurdi and his family had been trying to flee from a town near the Turkish border plagued by heavy fighting between Islamic State and Syrian Kurdish forces. Aylan, his mother and five-year-old brother were also among the dead when a fifteen-foot boat capsized en route to a Greek island. His father Abdullah was the only family member to survive. In 2014, 3,500 people drowned trying to reach European shores.

The photograph of Aylan's tiny body shook the world and spurred many into action to help with one of the greatest human catastrophes in modern times. More than four million Syrians have been forced to leave their home country since fighting began there in 2011. More refugees from Iraq and Afghanistan have risked their lives to find safer places to live. The world is in shock at how they have been treated. Inhumane decisions by government leaders have led the refugees to ask, "Why are we being treated this way?"

Why *are* they being treated this way? It seems an impossible situation for all concerned. Terrorist thugs are taking over areas where people have lived and worked and raised families for generations. The refugees are not bums and drug addicts begging for their next meal. They have skills and want to work. The world needs to respond. God demands they respond. People of faith around the world are praying world leaders will quickly develop a plan to meet all the issues: relocation of the refugees, ending terrorism in these war-torn countries, and opening the hearts of those who can help.

Great God of all nations, move Your mighty hand and make peace reign. Amen

September 11

WE STILL REMEMBER

Our message of the Gospel came to you not in word only, but also in power and in the Holy Spirit and with full conviction.
1 Thessalonians 1:5

I was riding a train to see my new granddaughter shortly after the September eleventh terrorist attacks. I was going by train, not because I was afraid to fly, but because I was too tired to drive the five hours to see my daughter's family.

I went to the dome car to do some reading. A woman about my age was sitting by herself. I was certain she had been crying. When the opportunity presented itself, I began a conversation with her. She soon told me she was a United Airlines flight attendant who had been on a flight to Seattle when the attacks occurred. She revealed that she had known every single one of the crew members on Flights 11 and 93, which crashed into the North Tower and a field near Shanksville, Pennsylvania, respectively. Vowing never to fly in an aircraft again, she was making the very long train ride from Seattle to Boston, where she would begin attending the memorial services for her friends. She had recently lost her husband to cancer and had no children. Her coworkers had been her family.

Suddenly my five hour ride and personal exhaustion seemed trivial. As I listened to her, I prayed silently for God to give me the words and the *courage* to bless this women's journey somehow. Except for my new friend's frequent periods of weeping, we talked for almost the entire trip from Minneapolis to Milwaukee, where I got off to meet my daughter. Although we exchanged first names, I did not get her full name and contact information. I had the strong sense I was there for a reason, for a season—however short—and my purpose was to be with her on a portion of her long ride home. I prayed someone else would take my place. We hugged and I said I would pray for her. She said, "I'd like that." And we parted.

Gracious Lord, empower us to share the Gospel with power and conviction when You provide us with a chance. Amen

September 12

NATIONAL CONFESSION

If My people who are called by My name humble themselves, pray, seek My face, and turn from their wicked ways, then I will hear from heaven, and will forgive their sin and heal their land. **2 Chronicles 7:14**

What if our entire nation held a "national confession day?" Sounds outrageous, doesn't it? To get everybody on the same page, all believing that confession of sins is not only good for the soul, but also a way to show Almighty God we love Him and want Him to be the center of our lives? Now that would be a day for the media to go wild!

In the Old Testament, a Jewish man named Nehemiah was an important servant of the king of Persia (Nehemiah 1:11), where the Israelites were captives. The Persian king allowed Jews to return to their homes in Judah, but some, like Nehemiah, stayed in Persia. Nehemiah had a deep love for the Jewish people, so when his brother reported back from Judah that the people were miserable and Jerusalem was in shambles, Nehemiah wept (Nehemiah 1:1-4). The Persian king allowed him to go to the homeland (Nehemiah 2:8) where he directed the people of Israel in rebuilding the temple, the city, and the government of God's people (Nehemiah 7:1-4).

Nehemiah wasn't done yet. He then assembled all of the people and led them in a national confession, addressing their sins and God's mighty works. The people were reminded how God had created them, sustained, chosen and provided for them, delivered and multiplied them, and defeated their enemies (Nehemiah 9:6-15). By the time Nehemiah got done with them, the people were on their knees begging for God's mercy (vs. 26-31).

I wish we had a man like Nehemiah who would run for president and lead our nation in taking a searching, honest look at our sins as individuals and as a nation.

Lord, guide our nation in wisdom and strength and let no sin go without full confession and repentance. To You be the glory. Amen

September 13

ABANDONED EXPECTATIONS
Katie Sluss, Guest Writer

May the Lord now show you kindness and faithfulness, and I too will show you the same favor because you have done this. 2 Samuel 2:6

This August, I had the pleasure of accompanying my church on a mission trip to Denver, Colorado. Our goal was to provide services to the homeless, helping with meals, handing out baked goods and burritos, and playing bingo with the residents at a retirement home. If someone were to ask me where I saw God the most, I, without a doubt, say in the people we served.

The theme of our mission was 'abandon expectations,' and our expectations certainly did not come true. Most of us are used to seeing the common stereotype of homeless people in television and film— hostile, aggressive, sitting on the side of the street with a cup for money. This was not true in the slightest. We had the pleasure of talking to many people we were serving, and getting to know them. These were some of the sweetest conversations I have ever had. These people were the kindest, most down to earth people I have ever met. They made me so happy, and made me laugh and smile so much. It was kind of ironic that the people in the bleakest situation can be the happiest.

The humor and brightness in these people's eyes wasn't the only thing that surprised me. You'd think that they would have lost all hope and faith in God by now. Again, this wasn't true in the slightest. Not a single person objected when we asked if we could pray for them. Many people told us that God was very close in their hearts, and that being in their situation had actually strengthened their faith. Everyone was so respectful and thankful, responding to our help with "thank you"s and "God bless you"s.

Dear God, please continue to share Your kindness with the people that need it the most. Please let Your love radiate through them and let them inspire others just as they did me. Don't let them lose hope. Help them keep going. Amen

September 14

LEAVING CORPORATE

Elijah passed by (Elisha) and threw his mantle over him. He left the oxen, ran after Elijah, and said, "Let me kiss my father and my mother, and then I will follow you."
1 Kings 19:19-21

I have friends who say they "left corporate" because of the stressful pace of the work environment in a large company. They made a conscious decision and took a huge risk to depart from what was familiar, highly revered in our society, and financially lucrative for them, to pursue a less taxing type of work. Each was elated with the outcome, calmer, happier, more fulfilled and self-assured. They never seem to miss the fancy lifestyle they may have enjoyed, and they all say they wish they had done it years earlier.

Elisha, a poor plough boy, "left corporate" to follow Elijah. Although his name means "My God Is Salvation," Elisha expected to spend his lifetime ploughing fields behind his oxen, which is what he was doing when the prophet Elijah came by and casually threw his cloak over Elisha's shoulders. When a prophet placed his mantle over another man's shoulders, this was a formal call for that man to follow in the prophet's footsteps. This was a job offer no man would turn down: the passing of Elijah's calling on to Elisha. Elisha slaughtered his oxen and served the cooked meat to all of his friends. He couldn't go back to "corporate," he had made his decision and he stuck to it. Elisha performed more miracles than other Bible figure except Jesus?

When we make a decision to follow Christ, we are also "leaving corporate." The world measures success in many ways which are directly contrary to the Way Christ wants us to live our lives. Jesus asks us to rise up, make a decision, and leave our previous lives to follow Him. I don't know about you, but I've never been sorry. I still have to live *in* this world, but I am no longer *of* this world, and that is quite a calling!

Jesus, thank You for throwing Your mantle on me and making me one of Your own. Amen

September 15

MINE!

***You ask and do not receive, because you ask wrongly, in order to spend what you get on your pleasures.* James 4:3**

I don't know the original author, but I've seen several versions of Toddler Property Rights. A few of these are: If I like it, it's mine; If it's in my hand, it's mine; If I can take it from you, it's mine; If I had it a little while ago, it's mine; If it's mine, it must never appear to be yours in any way. You get the idea. They are called "the terrible twos" for a reason: children at this age are totally egocentric and convinced the entire universe only revolves around them. There have been many books written about how to survive Toddler Temper Tantrums and all their ramifications, but sometimes, it just takes time and maturity for the child to move into a more agreeable place.

How like these toddlers we sometimes are! Everything on this entire planet was created by God and is on loan to us while we live here. It's not the other way around. This is the real Law of the Universe, but we miss the point continually. If I like something, I may buy it and call it "mine," but it is still from God. He provided the path to my purchase, including my ability to earn or save the money to buy the item. If I pick up a rock or a stick on a walk in the park, not only does it probably "belong" to the park, but God placed it there in nature so many people could enjoy it, not just me. If I steal something from another person, it's not "mine;" it may have been placed in the care of the person from whom I stole it, but it's still God's. And if I think someone is "mine," as in a relationship, I'm violating one of God's most important laws: each person is a child of His and is not a "possession."

In praying to the Father, Jesus said, "All Mine are Yours, and Yours are Mine; and I have been glorified in them" (John 17:10). Those are God's laws and they are the best laws of all.

Lord, make us ever mindful of what being "Yours" entails. We thank You that You count us as part of Your family. Amen

September 16

THE ASTONISHING THING

***Here is an astonishing thing! You do not know where He comes from, and yet He opened my eyes. We know that God does not listen to sinners, but He does listen to one who worships Him and obeys His will.* John 9:30**

I love the story of the blind man in John 9! He doesn't have a name, so let's call him "Guy." The disciples are once again clueless about the connection between sin and suffering, asking Jesus if Guy or his parents sinned. Jesus' answer speaks volumes about why He came to live among people here on earth: "Neither this man nor his parents sinned; he was born blind so that God's works might be revealed in him" (v. 3). The Lord proceeded to restore Guy's sight with some of His own spit and some mud and some instructions to wash in the pool of Siloam. When Guy returned, his sight was fully restored and he was jubilant. The people couldn't believe it, so they took him to the Pharisees, and then of course, the real circus began.

The Pharisees didn't believe Guy's story either because, he was, after all, a commoner and might have been lying. His parents were summoned and they testified that their son had indeed been born blind. They told the Pharisees to ask the son himself what happened because he was "of age," which just tickles me. Nobody probably talked to the Pharisees like that back then! It must have been where Guy got his spunk, because he challenged the Pharisees too. If it all happened today, he would have said, "Bug off! Can't you see I'm healed? You all want to trash Jesus because you say you don't know where He came from, but DUH!!! What does it really matter? Here is the astonishing thing: I was blind and now I see. What more proof do you need?" Guy also let the Pharisees know he himself prayed to God, and all the Jews believed miracles happened because of devout and fervent prayer. So there.

Let's all be Guy and believe so completely! What a world this would be!

Caring Father, we thank You for all the types of healing You do in this world. Amen

September 17

STEP BY STEP

No one can serve two masters, for either he will hate the one and love the other, or he will be devoted to the one and despise the other. **Matthew 6:24**

In all my years of counseling and social work, I have never found a better model for making positive changes in one's life than the Twelve Step Program of Alcoholics Anonymous (AA). Bill W. and Dr. Bob, as they are known today, began the organization in 1935. Dr. Bob got sober first, using a model he developed. AA was born when Dr. Bob helped the first person, Bill W. The principles developed by Dr. Bob apply to almost any situation in which a person is trying to achieve a more healthful lifestyle.

The Twelve Steps have been adapted to reach people from many countries, cultures, and religions. After admitting in Step One that the member is "powerless over alcohol" and one's life has become "unmanageable," Step Two necessitates believing that a "Higher Power" can restore one's sanity. "Higher Power" has come to mean many things. In his book, *Dry*, Augusten Burroughs describes a friend whose "higher power" is a cup of Starbuck's coffee. The beauty of the Twelve Step program is that it works for many.

Today's Scripture comes after the Sermon on the Mount. Jesus is setting forth the principles for a spiritual lifestyle in everyday activities. It is in Chapter 6 He introduces the Lord's Prayer. Throughout these passages, He is really listing some "steps" for living a Christ-like life. In verse 24, He is actually talking about the dangers of people being slaves to money, but we can substitute any unhealthy practice here. The Twelve Steps follow Jesus' principles: we are to *choose* to turn our lives over to God (Step 3), search ourselves diligently (Step 4), admit our shortcomings (Step 5), and be humble in asking God for help (Steps 6 and 7). The rest of the steps follow in line with the same idea of walking with God every day—every minute! Are you working God's program?

Lord of health and wellness, quicken us to see Your plan for our lives. Amen

September 18

SEX AND THE CHURCH

Or do you not know your body is a temple of the Holy Spirit within you, which you have from God, and you are not your own?
Corinthians 6: 19

Al Vernacchio teaches sex to kids in a religious school. His curriculum gets youngsters thinking about the responsibilities they have to themselves and others regarding sexuality. Vernacchio is the Upper School Sexuality Educator at Friends' Central School in Wynnewood, Pennsylvania. He also organizes sexuality-themed programs, provides parent education on sexuality, and is one of the faculty advisers for the Gay-Straight Alliance.

A human sexuality educator and consultant for over twenty years, Al has lectured, published articles, and offered workshops throughout the country on sexuality. His work has been featured in "Teaching Good Sex," a November 20, 2011 cover story in The New York Times Magazine. In addition Al has given three TED Talks, and his blog, "For Goodness Sex," is found on the Psychology Today website. He wrote *For Goodness Sex: Changing the Way We Talk to Young People About Sexuality, Values, and Health*.

I heard Vernacchio speak to an audience of sexual assault victims' advocates and prevention specialists at the Minnesota Coalition Against Sexual Assault 2015 annual conference. He told the group, "To end a rape culture, we must talk about a consent culture." Vernacchio likens our society's sex culture to a baseball game: competitive, with an emphasis on "scoring." He prefers to think of human interaction, sexual or otherwise, more like ordering a pizza, giving individuals a choice (ability to consent or not) in the process.

God created physical intimacy as a beautiful gift to be shared with another, a selfless gift of wholeness. Until we begin sharing that message with young people *before* they are misinformed by movies, television, advertising, and their clueless peers, we can't expect see the culture change.

We thank You, Lord, for Your precious gift of our bodies. They house our souls and they are sacred to You. Amen

September 19

IF YOU'RE GONNA PLAY WITH JESUS…

***When the Son of Man is seated on the throne of His glory, you who have followed Me will also sit on twelve thrones, judging the twelve tribes of Israel.* Matthew 19:28**

Country music group Alabama had a hit song called "If You're Gonna Play in Texas, You Gotta Have a Fiddle in the Band." The words describe a performance in Houston when someone requested "Cotton-Eyed Joe," usually including a fiddle solo. The heckler said, "We love what you're doin', boys don't get us wrong/There's just somethin' missin' in your song." Alabama member Jeff Cook opened up his fiddle case and the crowd went wild. If Cook hadn't fired up his fiddle, the boys might have been tossed out on their ears!

Is there something missing in the song you are singing to Jesus? Is the Lord just a background singer in your band? Do you play your "gig" the way Jesus would have you play it, or do you just do your own thing and don't care who's watching? The Savior was pretty specific about how to follow Him. We are to "carry our cross" (Matthew 10:38, John 12:26, Luke 14:27), a shocking metaphor for discipleship! Christ is asking us to die to our self-will and embrace God's will, whatever the cost may be. In Matthew 10:38, Jesus even says "whoever does not take up the cross and follow Me is not worthy of Me." That sounds harsh! He must be serious about this! Earlier in His ministry, He told commercial anglers Simon and Andrew, "Follow Me and I will make you fishers of men" (Mark 1:17). Bringing others into the Kingdom of God is still our responsibility today. Jesus said we are to set aside any commitment hindering devotion to Him (Matthew 8:22). And He told a wealthy man not to let his financial assets become his god" (Matthew 19:21).

In today's Scripture Jesus promised the disciples abundant rewards in the next world. Our rewards will be there too, and no one will be heckling us.

Great High Priest, You ask so much from us, but You gave so much for us. Thank You! Amen

September 20

WHERE ARE YOU, PEGGY SUGARS?

I will delight in Your statutes; I will not forget Your word. **Psalm 119:16**

When I was young and full of myself, I worked with a young woman named Peggy Sugars. That's her real name—or was, since she was single at the time and had a nice boyfriend. So maybe she's married now to the nice boyfriend and has some grown-up nice kids and nice grandkids too. Anyway, Peggy was a secretary and I was a counselor at a "sheltered workshop," a place where people with disabilities worked because they couldn't work anyplace else, or until they were able to get a different job. Peggy always sat alone at lunchtime and read her Bible, and several of us thought she was really dumb. We never bothered her, but we whispered among ourselves about how "good" Peggy probably thought she was, and what a different life she led than those of us who were "cool."

I was such a different person then. It was while I worked with Peggy that I was sexually assaulted at gunpoint one Sunday afternoon and very nearly lost my life. I didn't come back to work right away, but when I did, I had to walk right by Peggy's desk to the director's office to speak with him about what had happened. He was a Christian too, and I'm sure he read his Bible a lot. He was very kind to me and told me to take as much time as I needed to get back into my job. When I left his office, I walked right back by Peggy's desk.

I always wondered if Peggy had prayed for me after the assault (and maybe before as well). Soon, I left that job and city and moved far away. Later, as a result of having survived the assault, I became a Christian myself. One of the first people I thought of was Peggy. Was I ever clueless when I knew her! She was actually one of the kindest, most wholesome people I had ever met, but I never even thought having Christ in her life made her that way. I'm not proud of how I acted around Peggy, but I sure wish I could talk to her now!

Father, forgive us for old sins we can do nothing about. Amen

September 21

FACING THE INEVITABLE

For God so loved the world that He gave His only Son, so that everyone who believes in Him may not perish but may have eternal life. John 3:16

Author, actor and humorist Will Rogers once said, "The difference between death and taxes is that death does not get worse every time Congress meets." Rogers died in 1935 and people are still fussing about taxes. We are destined to be taxed in some fashion in this world, whether it is by monetary government taxes or emotional and physical taxes placed on us by the rigors of this life on earth. Jesus said, "In the world you face persecution" (John 16:33). It's a given that our earthly existence will not be easy.

Will Rogers' comment notwithstanding, death gets *better* for the practicing Christian. In John 16:33, Jesus continues by saying, "But take courage; I have conquered the world!" How comforting it is to know He has won the battle against death and human suffering. Satan keeps trying, but he might as well not even leave his bunker because he has already lost the entire war. And we do not need to be "taxed"—bear the burden—regarding our future because it is resting firmly in God's hands. The psalmist knew this when he wrote, "Trust in him at all times, O people; pour out your heart before Him; God is a refuge for us." (Psalm 62:8). This verse ends with the word, *Selah*, which many Bible scholars say means to pause and think about the passage. If we take time to meditate on Psalm 62:8, the words assure us of God's unfailing character, His abiding willingness to listen to all we have to bring before Him, and His strength to provide us with a place to hide and be safe until the storms of life have passed. All of this, coupled with His promise of a new heaven and a new earth (Revelation 21:1-2), means we can live without fear of what congress—or any other earthly entity—might do to harm us.

Great God of all that is, we thank You for being our refuge and strength, our protector and friend. We worship You and adore You because of the depth of Your love for us. Amen

September 22

CROSSING THE BORDER

Hear now, you rebels! Must we bring water for you out of this rock?
Numbers 20:10

After his mother set him adrift in a basket and he was found by Pharaoh's daughter, Moses spent his first forty years living large in an Egyptian palace. Moses eventually decided his place was among his own people. He then served God faithfully, leading the Israelites to freedom from Pharaoh and acting as a go-between for God and the people for forty more years in the wilderness. Moses had an exemplary career as a faithful follower of God.

But once, Moses and his brother Aaron tried to take credit for God's work. The people were complaining about the absence of water. "Why did you bring us out of Egypt into this miserable place?" they said. So Moses and Aaron rounded up the people and Moses said, "Listen, you rebels, shall *we* bring water for you out of this rock?" (Numbers 20:10) Moses gave the rock two good whacks and out came water "abundantly." God was displeased that Moses and Aaron didn't give *Him* credit for the miraculous act. "Therefore," the Almighty said, "you shall not bring this assembly into the land that I have given them." (Numbers 20:10-12) God even let Moses *see* the beautiful land from the top of Mount Nebo. But He didn't let Moses set foot over the line.

Well. That seems harsh! Moses and his brother were, after all, *human*, and God knows humans make mistakes. So what happened to Moses? He died there in the wilderness, but Moses shows up again in the Bible, and there is a happy ending. Matthew 17 tells of Jesus' transfiguration on a high mountain where "His face shone like the sun, and His clothes became dazzling white." (v. 2) Peter and James were there, and suddenly, so were Moses and Elijah. Moses was wrapped in glorious light just like Jesus. God had a big surprise for Moses, even after it seemed He had given up on His faithful servant.

God of Perfect Timing, grant that we may trust You, even when it seems Your ways are harsh. Amen

September 23

MILK AND COOKIES

Man did eat the bread of angels; He sent them food in abundance.
Psalm 78:25

When my mother-in-law, Ellie Corrigan, passed away at age eighty, those of us gathered were sad to see her go. But we were also relieved she was no longer in pain. Someone had brought homemade cookies, and another person found milk in the hospital refrigerator. There beside this beloved wife, mother, grandmother and sister, we all shared the milk and cookies. "It's what she would have wanted us to do," someone said. "If she could, she'd be up serving us!" What might have seemed irreverent to some was a beautiful shared ritual in honor of Ellie's passing.

Why do we eat when people die? Since my family moved often, I had never been to a funeral until I was in my twenties. Even then, I remember thinking, "How can people eat or sleep after a death?" Those things were the furthest from my mind at the time. I spent several wakeful nights and lost a couple of pounds before my body gave in to hunger and fatigue.

Dr. Holly Prigerson, a bereavement specialist, was quoted in the Sun Sentinel as saying, "Grief triggers the fight-or-flight mechanism....When grieving people say they don't feel like eating, That's because the body is prioritizing for survival." But we must eat to live. Food brought to the home by friends and relatives and meals served after funerals provide emotional support as well as encouragement for the bereaved to rejoin the living. They are exhausted from caregiving and worry, and the provision of food by others helps them move forward. James 1:27 says, "Religion that is pure and undefiled before God, the Father, is this: to care for orphans and widows in their distress." So break out the casseroles ("hot dishes, as they are called in the Midwest) and the milk and cookies and help someone through this most difficult of times.

Lord, You take the sting out of death, but when those left are hurting, help us be a healing balm to them. Amen

September 24

METAPHORS BE WITH YOU

For who is God except the Lord? And who is a rock besides our God?
Psalm 18:31

The Bible proves that God is a Wordsmith. He invented words and their meanings, and He can certainly fling them around better than any of us.

Webster defines metaphor as "a word or phrase naming one thing that is used to refer to another thing to suggest that they are similar." One purpose of Scripture is to paint a word picture of God, His character, and His will. Metaphors do this. There is so much rich, powerful language used to tell us Who God is, one is almost overwhelmed by the images. Today's Scripture likens God to a rock, signifying that His people can rely on him for absolute protection and salvation. He is unique too; there is no other being like Him. Who else has three distinct Beings in one package? The rock metaphor is used to show that the Lord is worthy to be praised. Psalm 19:1 says, "Let us make a joyful noise to the Rock of our salvation!" And Deuteronomy declares, "The Rock, His work is perfect, and all his ways are just. A faithful God, without deceit, just and upright is He" (Deuteronomy 32:4). Isaiah says He is "an everlasting Rock" (Isaiah 26:4), and both Joel and Jeremiah call Him "my strength and my stronghold, my refuge on the day of trouble" (Joel 3:16 and Jeremiah 16:19).

Scripture makes it clear that Jesus is a Rock too. The Messiah's kingdom is eternal and immovable just like a big boulder. Daniel prophesied, "The God of heaven will set up a kingdom that shall never be destroyed, nor shall this kingdom be left to another people" (Daniel 2:44). And Jesus referred to Himself as "the stone the builders rejected" (Matthew 21:42; also prophesied in Psalm 118:22). Next time you see a beautiful boulder in a natural setting, say a little prayer of thanks that our God is the Rock we can count on for strength, shelter, salvation and eternal life.

My Rock and My Redeemer, I thank You from the bottom of my heart for keeping me safe and secure in the cleft of Your great Rock. Amen

September 25

I SURRENDER SOME

Where your treasure is, there your heart will be also. Matthew 6:21

What if Judson Van De Venter and Winfield Weeden had named their famous hymn "I Surrender Some" instead of the title they gave it? The real title is "I Surrender All," and that's exactly what it means. We are to strive to surrender everything in our lives to Christ because He did the same for us. We are human, but with God's help, we can give Christ everything.

What if Jesus went through the lyrics to this song and studied them with us? The first verse talks about freely giving Christ all we have. Most of us probably don't just hand everything over to God; we want to place conditions on what we will give. "Sure, Lord, I'll work at the food shelf, but I can only do it when I have nothing else going on." Or in the song when it says "I will ever love and trust Him," do we really? All the time? Until the end of our lives? Sometimes in the darkness of my fear, I think, "I'm all alone in this, and I'll probably fail!" Instead, I should be thinking, "I know God's got my back, even though it doesn't feel that way right now." And what about the line, "In His presence daily live?" What does it look like, when I'm racing around in traffic screaming inside my brain for all the other drivers to make way for me?

Am I sure I bow "humbly at His feet?" Maybe I didn't yesterday because I was overtaken with pride of self or righteous indignation. Are my "worldly pleasures all forsaken" for my God, or do I own some great "prize" I can't take with me when it's my time to meet my Maker?

In today's Scripture, Jesus said our hearts aren't with God if they are focused on earthly "treasures." Our song's lyrics continue: "Let me feel the Holy Spirit…Now I feel the sacred flame." It is only by surrendering all to the Lord that we truly know "the joy of full salvation."

Holy God, take all of me now. Amen

September 26

I SEE YOU

***O LORD, who shall sojourn in Your tent? Who shall dwell on Your holy hill?* Psalm 15:1**

Integrity is doing the right thing whether anyone is watching or not. To please God, I need to demonstrate integrity all the time. Psalm 15 lists traits needed for integrity. First we must "walk blamelessly" and uprightly (v. 2). Are we only out to please ourselves, or are we doing our best to honor God? Are we promoting good things, or do we sometimes dabble in the not-so-good stuff? Next we must treat others with respect, "speak the truth" about others, and not "take up a reproach," or unduly place the blame on others (v. 3). Verse 4 says: "In whose eyes a vile person is despised." Whoa! Are we supposed to despise others? We can avoid people whose attitude toward God differs greatly from ours. Unless, of course, we are moved to tell this "vile" person about the hope that is in us....

Also in verse 4, we see that a person of integrity "swears to his own hurt." This means if we make a promise, we take God as our witness, and we don't try to get out of what we say we'll do, even if it costs us something to carry through. Verse 5 says we should "not put our money out at interest," or "take a bribe against the innocent." In Biblical times, Israelites were forbidden to charge interest to one of their own. The ideal person deals generously and fairly with all people, allowing others to gain the resources they need to live.

And the Psalm ends with this: "He who does these things will never be moved." Being intentional about integrity grows into a habit, and the habit grows into a way of life. The Holy Spirit helps us to toe the line, so to speak, by reminding us when we get off track. God sees everything we do anyway. But we are always welcome in His tent on His holy hill, where we can sit at His feet and learn His ways.

Father, guide me until integrity is my way of life. Amen

September 27

IT'S FOR YOU

Restore to me the joy of Your salvation, and uphold me with a willing spirit. **Psalm 51:12**

What if God called you right here, right now, on your ever-present cell phone? What would you say? I'd ask Him how I seem to drift away from His presence so easily, getting caught up in the cares of this world and forgetting what it feels like to be "on fire" for Jesus.

Thirty-eight years ago, when I made a decision to place Christ first in my life, I literally lived and breathed Him. Each day, I took hour-long prayer walks near my home, sat on a lake bank and prayed until I was almost dizzy. Christian music was always on in my car, and I sang my lungs out praising my Lord. I used to describe the feeling I had as being like a golden cord attached to the top of my head, stretching all the way up to heaven. God seemed to be sending spiritual energy through that cord night and day.

That's how it is when we fall in love: we are "all consumed." Nowadays, I do not love my Lord any less. I've just "settled in" to a lifelong relationship with Him. He has become my constant and true Companion, as comfortable as an old pair of shoes. That's good—but I miss the old days when I could not wait to get alone with Him, to burn inside with the power and majesty I had only just discovered. How do I recoup that "on fire" feeling, diligently purifying and distilling all my daily thoughts and actions into a "spiritual soup," rich and thick and satisfying?

Perhaps the lesson here is like making soup: we bring it to a boil, and then we let it simmer until it is done. God hasn't allowed me out of His marvelous sight. He's only letting my life "cook down" until I am exactly the person He wants me to be. Pass the salt, please.

Loving Father, You know what is best for me. The joy of Your salvation is ever before me. Amen

September 28

O LOVE THAT WILT NOT LET ME GO

I trusted in your steadfast love; my heart shall rejoice in your salvation.
Psalm 13:5

I wish I could write these devotions as easily as George Matheson wrote the lyrics to "O Love That Wilt Not Let Me Go." The nineteenth century Scottish minister was home alone one evening when he was overcome by the urge to pen the words. Matheson said, "Something happened to me…which caused me the most severe mental suffering. The hymn was the fruit of that suffering…the quickest bit of work I ever did in my life. I had the impression of having it dictated to me by some inward voice…the whole work was completed in five minutes…it never received at my hands any retouching or correction" (hymntime.com). In one night,, Matheson wrote: "O Love, wilt not let me go/I rest my weary soul in Thee/I give Thee back the life I owe/that in Thine ocean depths its flow/May richer, fuller be."

Whiteestate.org reports Matheson was born with poor vision, his eyesight gradually worsening until he was almost totally blind. He was academically gifted, and his sisters learned Latin, Greek, and Hebrew to help him study. Matheson became a minister of the Church of Scotland. He was able to memorize sermons and sections of the Bible; listeners were often unaware he was blind. Later in life, he devoted himself to spiritual writing.

Perhaps Matheson's lack of physical vision gave him the ability to "see" in other ways. He said of himself, "I have no natural gift of rhythm. All the other verses I have ever written are manufactured articles; this (hymn) came like a dayspring from on high." A deeply spiritual man, Matheson undoubtedly identified with those around him who suffered either mentally or physically in some way. I often sing the third verse to myself when I am having an uncomfortable day: "O Joy, that seekest me through pain/I cannot close my heart to Thee/I trace the rainbow through the rain/And feel the promise is not vain/ morn shall tearless be."

You are the Composer of my life, Lord. Bless me in times of anguish. Amen

September 29

WHERE WAS GOD WHEN I GOT CANCER?
Guest Writer Diana Merkl

For I was hungry and You gave me food. I was thirsty and You gave me drink. I was sick and You visited me. Matthew 25:35

On the day the doctor told me I had cancer I came home and called the church office asking to be included in prayer. My pastor came to my house and prayed for my understanding, acceptance and healing. How could a single parent with two teenagers and no nearby relatives gain any understanding, acceptance and especially healing. I had a lot to learn.

Getting chemo became a part of my life. A friend would drive me to the hospital, another would sit with me during the day long drip and others took turns spending the night to keep me safe. Medication caused memory loss.

I have saved boxes of cards and notes from all the people who sent them. Some put meaningful bookmarks and kitchen magnets in them. I clung tightly to the message which read: "Do not be afraid on the days you forget to pray because your friends are lifting your name." One Sunday when I was sitting in the back row of church, the choir sang. As they were filing down the aisle to the back every choir member either hugged me or squeezed my hand or touched me. I was moved to tears at the outpouring of love.

I received flowers and plants and laughed at the helium balloons and stuffed animals. I loved the pretty scarves for my bald head. I insisted on wearing frilly nightgowns in the hospital and not unattractive hospital gowns.

Where was God when I fought cancer? Right where God is today in healing smiles, hundreds of messages of love, in the good thoughts of friends, in hugs and tender squeezes of a hand, in gifts of food and rides, in the listening ears and especially all the prayers. Right where God is today and every day working through each one of us.

Father God, keep us always mindful of those suffering around us. Guide us to be a healing presence in their lives. Amen

September 30

A SIMPLE TRAIN RIDE

Deliver me from those who work evil; from the bloodthirsty save me.
Psalm 59:2

On August 21, 2015, Americans and lifelong friends Anthony Sadler, Spencer Stone and Alek Skarlatos, and British passenger Chris Norman, boarded a train bound from Amsterdam to Paris together. Suddenly, a shirtless man emerged from the train car's bathroom carrying a loaded rifle. The four young men sprang into action and overtook the gunman, Ayoub el-Khazzani. The gunman carried with him an AKM assault rifle with 270 rounds of ammunition, a Luger M80 automatic pistol with a full cartridge, a box-cutter and a water-bottle-sized container full of gasoline. French Prosecutor Francois Molins said the man "wouldn't have hesitated to use all the arms in his possession—assault rifle, pistol and box-cutter—if it wasn't for the remarkable intervention of the passengers." The three Americans and the Brit were given medals of valor and other recognition from France, Britain and the United States for heroism in the face of certain disaster.

Why did these four young men act without a moment's hesitation, risking their own lives to save those innocent people from the gunman? Skarlatas and Stone were members of the US National Guard and US Air Force respectively, with military training in battle and survival skills. But Sadler and Norman were ordinary citizens. Would we have done the same? Accounts of everyday heroes bolster my faith in humanity and help me realize that God is working through average people every day to protect those in harm's way. As news broadcasts are quick to tell us, not all violence is foiled. But when attacks of this nature are quelled, we all have a sense that good has prevailed.

Jesus considered asking the Father to save Him from the suffering ahead, but He knew it was all part of God's plan (John 12:27). For the Christian, our Lord's death and resurrection were the ultimate "rescue mission." God has already vanquished the enemy.

Save us from the time of trial and deliver us from evil, Lord. Amen

October

October 1, 2015

MAYBE I'LL JUST GO AWAY

Husbands, love your wives and never treat them harshly. **Colossians 3:19**

October is Domestic Violence Awareness Month. Demonstrations and marches are held to help people understand the scope of this problem. The National Coalition Against Domestic Assault reports twenty people per minute are physically abused by an intimate partner in our country—more than ten million men and women every minute. One in three women and one in four men have been battered by an intimate partner.

In 1981, country singer Roseanne Cash wrote and recorded "Blue Moon with Heartache" about a woman in an abusive relationship. The haunting chorus says, "Maybe I'll just go away today." At that time, I was eleven years in to an emotionally abusive marriage. A well-meaning Christian had told me, "Divorce is not an option for a Christian." I repeated that mantra through another nine years in the relationship before deciding I could take no more. The basis for her stern statement was the verse prior to today's Scripture, "Wives, be subject to your husbands, as is fitting in the Lord" (Colossians 3:18). I have since learned that the Bible says many other things about marriage, comparing it to God's love for and relationship with Israel. Isaiah 62:1-5 paraphrased says, God protects and purifies "her" (Israel), honors and values her, and identifies Himself with her by giving her a new name. Later, Paul described the "marriage" between Christ and the church (Ephesians 5:21-33). The Bridegroom (Christ) shows his love by protecting and purifying His bride, honoring her and valuing her.

Treatment for batterers is only marginally successful. Batterers often switch to non-violent, less trackable control measures. Fear and lack of funds keep abused partners in abusive situations. Nightly news broadcasts report more tragic outcomes in families living with violence. No woman or man should get beat up in her/his own home. Christ would not sanction these unions.

Father, we pray for an end to all domestic violence. Amen

October 2

GOD'S PEDICURE

How beautiful on the mountains are the feet of those who bring good news, who proclaim peace, who bring good tidings, who proclaim salvation, who say to Zion, "Your God reigns!" Isaiah 52:7

My feet are ugly! My toes are bent in every direction from arthritis, my heels are rough no matter how much I sandpaper them, and they are both flatter than a pancake. I'm on more than the legal limit of anti-inflammatory medication. But it's not how my feet *look* so much as what they *do* that the Lord cares about. Even if I can't comfortably walk long distances, I can carry God's message of peace and salvation the short distances I'm able to go. I can also praise Him that I am still able to walk at all.

Here are a few of my other limitations, and what God does through me even with them: My memory is getting a little fuzzy now that I'm—ahem—*maturing*, but not to worry. God invented the Internet (well, He created the people who invented it and gave them the brains to do it), so I can look stuff up anytime. My eyes aren't so hot any more either, but now have an electronic reader (also invented by the people God created) and I can blow the font size up until I can read it from across the room. I have a phone that is *way* smarter than I am which gives me a sense of safety and security when I'm out and about. My new car is also very smart, with things that ding every time I am about to make a mistake. (I now realize what the little toy car images in the side mirrors are for: there's a *real* car there when they are showing.)

The Lord can take all of our limitations and spiff them up until our individual gifts shine like diamonds. He says our bodies are His "temples" of the Holy Spirit because He lives in us. And God has a whole committee of angels who keep your temple and mine shining like the very jewel it is.

Redeeming Lord, Thank You for fixing our feet and our hands and our minds to serve You in the best way we can. Amen

October 3

GARGLING GRANDPARENTS

He has told you, O mortal, what is good; and what does the Lord require of you but to do justice, and to love kindness, and to walk humbly with your God? **Micah 6:8**

Every time I watch television, I find out something I didn't know. Apparently, I'm driving the wrong car, wearing outdated clothes, and not keeping my hair as shiny as it should be. My shoes need insets, I can buy two pair of glasses for the price I just paid for one, and several advertisements are telling me I need to ask my doctor about new medicines for conditions I didn't even know I might have. Recently, I saw a very disturbing ad. An elderly gentleman got dressed up and left his residence in what looked like an assisted living facility. His face lit up in the lobby, where he encountered some family members, two of whom appeared to be new parents. The couple offered the old man the baby, and as he took the child in his arms and started to hold it close to his face—we were interrupted and this question blazed across the television screen: DO YOU HAVE GRANDPARENT BREATH? Well. I never thought of that. My husband and I have ten adorable grandchildren and I've held every single one of them as babies. I must have been off my rocker not to realize I could be knocking the poor child dead in his little booties when I breathed on him!

These companies don't give us much credit for figuring most things out on our own. I've suspected for a long time—although I really don't want to believe it—these companies are only in it for the money. God doesn't want us to worry about all these worldly things. Micah got it right when he said God really doesn't require much from us. We are to "do justice, and to love kindness, and to walk humbly with (our) God." It doesn't matter what brand of deodorant we use, or whether we wear designer clothing or belong to a particular country club. We can all sing in God's choir (but I'll be sure to use some mouthwash so I won't offend my fellow choir members).

Gracious Father, we want to please You and follow Your ways. Amen

October 4

NEIGHBORLY LOVE
Guest Writer Kathi Holmes

"When the Pharisees heard that He had silenced the Sadducees, they gathered together, and one of them, a lawyer, asked Him a question to test Him. 'Teacher, which commandment in the law is the greatest?' He said to them, "You shall love the Lord your God with all your heart, and with all your soul, and with all your mind. This is the greatest and first commandment. And a second is like it: You shall love your neighbor as yourself. On these two commandments hang all the law and the prophets." Matthew 22:34-40

Some of my empty nester friends have downsized to community living. There, people of different ethnicities, religions, political persuasions and values live close to each other and share common space. There are usually rules to follow, but some people don't like being constrained by rules and there could never be enough rules to cover every disagreement. Some want to have a dog or a cat in their unit. Others do not want dogs or cats. Some want to post ornaments on their doors. Others feel this is inappropriate. Some vehemently argue their religious or political views. These concerns are not earthshaking, but they can cause friction between neighbors.

Everyone is part of God's creation. He made each of us unique. We don't all agree, but yet he asks us to "love our neighbor." Only God knows who is right and who is wrong. It is not for us to judge, but to desire the best for all of God's creations. We are asked to reach out to our neighbor and offer help and support when needed. We are asked to cleanse our hearts. At the very least we are asked to calm our tongues, which is not always easy when we get angry. As the 19th Century Russian philosopher, Nikolai Berdyaev, said "Bread for myself is a material question. Bread for my neighbor is a spiritual one."

God of Love, calm our anger with our neighbor, ease our frustrations and help us to learn to love our neighbors as You love us. Amen

October 5

OUR QUIET HOME

If you return to Me and obey my commands, then even if your exiled people are at the farthest horizon, I will gather them from there and bring them to the place I have chosen as a dwelling for My Name.
Nehemiah 1:9

When I was divorced and living alone, I sat on a lake bank one day praying. I was lonely and a little bit frightened, because even an electronic security system had not banished all my nightmares of getting assaulted again. I asked God if I would ever find a life partner who was on the same page spiritually as I was, a man with whom I could share my wildest dreams and darkest secrets and still feel safe. I wasn't accustomed to getting immediate answers from God, but that day, I felt a strong sensation in my chest. Then in my mind's ear, at least, I clearly heard God say this: "Marriage is not a contract, Meg. It's a sacrament."

Besides freaking me out a bit, I had to digest that statement and figure out what God meant. I thought I had married for love the first time, but I discovered control and love cannot occupy the same space at the same time. I had not had success meeting anyone who seemed suitable since my divorce, and I wondered what that guy would look like. After more prayer and contemplation, I decided God was telling me not to "settle" for just anybody just because I was alone. And did He deliver! I met and married the love of my life, Patrick, a Christian man with insight and common sense and devotion to following God. Our marriage truly is a sacrament, a union under God's watchful eye. The most amazing thing to me is our home is a Christian home, the first one I've ever lived in. The constant dysfunction I grew up with and lived with during my former life is just plain absent. Yes, we squabble, and I'm the first to admit my old habits of blowing up on occasion have been hard to break. But we both love the Lord and place Him first in our lives, and this makes for a calm and quiet home.

Jesus, You are our Great High Priest, and You make this union work. Amen

October 6

BABIES, BABIES, BABIES!

He took him outside and said, "Look up at the sky and count the stars—if indeed you can count them." Then He said to him, "So shall your offspring be." **Genesis 15:5**

Midwife, mother, grandmother, doula, world traveler and author of *Ma Doula: A Story of Birth*, Stephanie Sorensen lives and breathes birth. A "Doula" is a woman experienced in childbirth who provides advice, information, emotional support, and physical comfort to a mother before, during and just after childbirth. Stephanie is that in spades.

"My books are about the courageous men and women…who have fled war, torture, famine and genocide, coming to the U.S. with hope (that) they can once more live in peace," she says. "They dare to fall in love again…have babies again….provide a better life for their families. They come from every country and background imaginable; from Africa, Laos, Vietnam, China, Thailand, the South Pacific, Mongolia, Burma, Europe and South America. Against all odds they….(bring) absolutely nothing with them… but hope. My books are…are about these amazing survivors starting over, from scratch."

Birth is timeless, cross-cultural, a universal experience, and God-breathed. When God told Abram his offspring would outnumber the stars, a miracle was happened. Abram's wife Sarai was barren, but Isaac was born. Abram, or Abraham, as God later named him, had multiple offspring. Each was a unique individual and a tiny miracle in God's eyes. Babies give us hope. Those who devote themselves to helping birth babies are doing God's work in its purest and most basic form. Sorensen has now given birth to a book celebrating the first tiny breath of each of God's human creations, made in His image. Get your scrubs on. It's time to push!

Creator God, we praise You for the hope that new babies give us, and we pray for Your blessing on each special person who assists these little ones in entering this world. Amen

October 7

THE STEWARDS OF GOD'S MYSTERIES

Think of us in this way, as servants of Christ and stewards of God's mysteries. **1 Corinthians 4:1-2**

Sherlock Holmes is a fictional detective created by Scottish author and physician Sir Arthur Conan Doyle. This sleuthhound has almost magical ability to solve even the most puzzling crimes. He uses judicious reasoning, outlandish disguises and forensic science to solve crimes.

Those who spend their lives following Christ and wish to know Him in an ever-deepening way are also "super sleuths." God's "mystery" is Jesus Christ. Paul tells the Colossians, "My purpose is that (mankind) may be encouraged in heart and united in love, so they may have the full riches of complete understanding, (to) know the mystery of God, namely, Christ, in whom are hidden all the treasures of wisdom and knowledge" (Colossians 2:2-3). A "mystery, "in the New Testament, is something that was hidden to those living in Old Testament times, but is now revealed. In Mark 4:11 Jesus explains to those closest to Him "the secret of the kingdom of God, but for those outside, everything is in parables." Now that Jesus has conquered death and ascended to heaven, God's mysteries are for all of us who believe.

Imagine how excited Isaiah must have been when God revealed to him, "The people who walked in darkness have seen a great light" (Isaiah 9:2). That light is Jesus Christ, the Son of God, Emmanuel (God With Us). Paul used the word *mystery* twenty-one times in his Epistles. Every time, the "mystery" involved a wonderful declaration of spiritual truth God revealed to mankind (Ephesians 3:5).

So get out your spy glass, trench coat and deerstalker cap and read a thriller inspired by God and solved by our personal Super Sleuth, Jesus Christ.

God of Mystery, thank You for revealing Your truths to us through Your Son Jesus. Amen

October 8

ATHEISM BY PROXY

In Him we have redemption through his blood, the forgiveness of our trespasses, according to the riches of His grace. Ephesians 1:7

Here's a poisonous parent: Madalyn Murray O'Hair, the woman who gave herself full credit for getting prayer booted out of all U.S. public schools. I would even call Murray O'Hair a perpetrator of emotional "Munchausen by Proxy." This strange disorder is a rare form of child abuse involving the fabrication of illnesses or symptoms by a primary caretaker ("by proxy"). Murray O'Hair's son Bill was caught in the middle of his mother's penchant for atheism, communism, and several other "isms." Without Bill, Murray O'Hair would never have thought to pursue legal action against Bill's school—and ultimately the entire country—to have prayer removed from public educational institutions. In the process, she turned Bill, his younger brother, and Bill's own daughter into staunch atheists and hate-filled people.

In his book, *My Life Without God*, Bill Murray describes his mother as evil. This is a sad story, but a story of redemption with a happy ending for Bill, at least. He was sucked into his mother's hate-filled world for so many years, but was finally able to break away and become healthy and whole himself. He gives credit for this miracle to the very Person his mother hated most: Jesus Christ. Once Bill realized the falseness of his mother's beliefs, it was a quick trip to the other side, where he accepted Jesus as his Lord and Savior. He even followed his mother around on her poisonous speaking circuit, standing outside the stadiums and theaters, handing out Christian literature and speaking to anyone who would listen about the Gospel.

Sin and evil are alive and well throughout the world. Though Murray O'Hair was one of the more blatant prophets of malevolence, many families still create dysfunction of unbelievable proportions for their innocent children. The spider's webs spin until no escape seems possible. But there is a way out, through the Son, Jesus Christ. Do you know someone who needs Jesus?

Deliver us from evil, Lord. Amen

October 9

HOLY PARAKEETS!

The Advocate, the Holy Spirit, whom the Father will send in My name, will teach you everything, and remind you of all that I have said to you. **John 14: 26**

When I was in seventh grade, my only sister went off to nursing school and left me to care for her beloved blue parakeet, Petie. The bird lived in a cage in our family room, just off my bedroom. I passed by him several times a day. "Pretty bird!" he would say. He was a nice little bird, and my sister loved him very much. But I had a more exciting animal to occupy my time, my horse that I rode daily. I wasn't interested in that little parakeet, and all I ever did was feed it and change the paper in the bottom of the cage.

One day, Petie didn't call out to me. I slowly approached his cage, hoping beyond hope that he wasn't…dead. But he was, crumpled on the bottom of his cage in a little blue heap. I was overcome with guilt. My sister was actually quite forgiving, making me feel better. But I carried that guilt with me for many years, even dreaming I was locked in a pet store alone overnight with cages of budgies chirping at me. I realized I could have easily cared more for that tiny bird. A lesson learned and remembered.

Sometime later, I came across the word, parakletos, the Greek work used in the Book of John to describe the Holy Spirit promised by Jesus. Parakletos is defined as "one who consoles or comforts, one who encourages or uplifts; hence refreshes, and/or one who intercedes on our behalf as an advocate in court." Suddenly the similar word, parakeet, no longer gripped me when I heard it! As far as I know, the two words are not related in any way, and maybe I'm stretching the point. But it helps me to think of the word parakletos and how it describes the Holy Spirit. He never forgets me when I call out to Him and He teaches me how to pray when I can't think straight.

Parakletos, come into my life each day and dwell in my heart. Amen

October 10

LAYERS OF UNDERSTANDING

I pray that you, being rooted and established in love, may have power...to grasp how wide and long and high and deep is the love of Christ, and...that you may be filled to the measure of all the fullness of God. **Ephesians 3:17-19**

A sandstone rock formation near the Arizona-Utah border is known as The Wave. The rock is popular for its colorful, undulating stripes eroded into the Navajo sandstone of the Jurassic geological era. The striations were first formed by slow water runoff. Troughs were formed, and the runoff slowed more. Then the wind took over, creating more patterns. Continued erosion of the rock is dependent upon the speed and direction of today's winds.

We can develop layers of understanding of the Bible. As we study the Word of God and become more and more familiar with Bible times, the Holy Spirit opens our hearts and minds so we are able to more fully understand what God is telling us through His Word. Someone completely unfamiliar with the Bible, as I was before I became a Christian, may feel the Word is impenetrable, like a rock formation. But like a rock formation, the stories in the Bible have grown deeper over time as God's people have seen the threads that carry through the great and mighty work of our Lord.

Sunday school students at our church learn a very basic way of describing the themes of the Bible: the Old Testament means "Jesus is coming," and the New Testament means "Jesus is here." This is pretty simplistic for most adults studying God's Word, but Christ's coming was predicted by Old Testament prophets and comes true by the time we get to the Gospels. Intertwined with this theme is the problem of sin and the solution of Christ dying as a once-for-all sacrifice for all the sins of humankind. God's Word is not an impenetrable rock formation. It is living and breathing and moving inside of us every day in the form of the Holy Spirit.

You are our immovable Rock, Dear Lord, but You are also moving and flowing in us every day. Amen

October 11

BETTER LATE THAN NEVER
Guest Blogger: Nadia Giordana

For God so loved the world, that He gave his only Son, that whoever believes in Him should not perish but have eternal life. John 3:16

How many times had I heard this verse, spoken it, repeated it, and never understood the full meaning. Why did it take me so long? Perhaps because I didn't go to church regularly as a child or young adult. Somehow I didn't get the true message until I was about fifty years old. It came by example.

During a deeply dark time in my husband's life, he woke up early one Sunday morning, turned on the television, and saw Dr. Charles Stanley. Something Dr. Stanley said caught his attention and before he knew it, somehow everything clicked. His explanation: although he had a good Christian upbringing, the program brought him back to the fold.

Soon, my husband began reading the Bible. He bought additional bibles and read them too. He began going to church every Sunday, always asking if I wanted to go along. I always declined. Coming home excited and rejuvenated, he would tell me how happy it made him feel, what he had learned. He never missed a Sunday for more than a year. I noticed the change in him, and finally one day I thought, *I have formed my opinions about the Bible from things I have heard from other people and/or read in dubious books.*

Then it occurred to me, *I've never read the Bible myself, start to finish, cover to cover—ever!* Soon I was genuinely interested. I picked up two, then three other Bibles and read them simultaneously, verse by verse, comparing versions, absorbing it all. There were things I still didn't understand, and some questions were raised, but the hunger to know and learn more was insatiable. I had crossed the threshold from unbelief to being a child of God. *Better late than never* should be my motto. When I think about how few people ever make this transition even later in life, I realize how lucky I am.

Loving Father, thank You for giving me the chance to know You, even now. Amen

October 12

A NEW NORMAL

The boundary lines have fallen for me in pleasant places; I have a goodly heritage. **Psalm 16:6**

As a college counselor, I conducted workshops for single moms to help them make positive changes in their lives. During that time, I was newly divorced with two adult daughters. I could relate to these women trying to improve their lives and provide for their children without much outside support. I always discussed how to establish a "new normal," "rituals," and "boundaries" for the single moms and their families.

Rituals have been around forever. Early rituals were determined by basic human needs: food, water and shelter. People hunted, gathered, and grew all their own food, built their own shelters located near a source of clean water. Today's basic needs are the same, but are fulfilled in different ways. Inflation in most countries has made it difficult to keep up with rising costs. Education and training are even more important. How we help our children feel secure can depend a great deal on how we embrace new rituals and set down new boundaries during change. One woman had trouble explaining to her kids where all the money went with none left for extras. One payday, she had her entire check cashed in one dollar bills. She placed the money on the kitchen table, gathered the kids around, and together, they divided the money into piles for each of the bills due. There wasn't much left over, and the kids learned about budgeting. They wanted to do the exercise every month so they could "help" mom pay the bills. A new ritual was born.

The psalmist talks about "boundary lines" being "pleasant places." Boundaries can help us feel secure, and they can also teach us about God's goodness and provision. If we truly believe that God is in control and will take care of us, then we can be content with our lives through good times and times of change.

Grant us bread, O Lord, and help us trust in You to provide it. See us through the inevitable changes in life. Amen

October 13

HITLER'S NANNY

And the great dragon was thrown down, that ancient serpent, who is called the devil and Satan, the deceiver of the whole world—he was thrown down to the earth, and his angels were thrown down with him. **Revelation 12:9**

Did it ever occur to you that even people we deem to be the most evil started out as innocent babies? Ira Levin's book and movie, "Rosemary's Baby," cause us to wonder if evil people spring fully wicked from the womb. But most of us think of babies as being innocent and wholly incapable of evil. I once saw a television drama about Adolf Hitler's nanny. She had a dream that this child would be totally evil and would be responsible for the cruel death of millions of innocent people. I don't know the ending. I turned the channel when the nanny was contemplating her next step. Scary as this image is, somebody held that baby and fed him, changed his diapers, and cuddled him, not knowing the horrible things he would do later in his life.

Why does God allow evil people to exist at all? Doubters would say a good and loving God would not permit this. How do we as Christians answer these suspicions? One basic premise we must accept is that God knows better than we do how to run the world (Isaiah 55:9). We know from the Book of Revelation that God wins the battle with Satan and his evil minions in the end. I found the most comfort for this issue of evil in a little book called *Soul Weavings: A Gathering of Women's Prayers* edited by Lynn Klug (Augsburg Press, 1996). Included was a prayer written on a piece of paper near the body of a dead child in Ravensbruck, Germany, where 92,000 women and children died in 1945. The prayer said, in part, "O Lord…remember those of ill will…and when they come to judgement, let all the fruits that we (the prisoners) have borne be their forgiveness. Amen…" God will judge all of us, the "evil" and the "good." Our part is to live for Him.

God of All People, infuse us with forgiveness if not understanding. Amen

October 14

BIG GOD THEORY

***In the beginning…God created the heavens and the earth.* Genesis 1:1**

On Abilene Christian University's website, Gerald Hall writes about the age-old discussion between "creationists" (those "who cling to a literal interpretation of their own religious story of creation") and "cold, hard science," which "appears to paint humankind as a 'chance of evolution.'" Hall cites Saint Augustine, a fourth century theologian and philosopher, who said, "God did not wish to teach humankind things not relevant to their salvation." Augustine pointed out that the Bible "does *not* instruct us on things such as the form and shape of the heavens." In Hall's article, he concludes that both a religious explanation and a scientific account of creation can be held at the same time. "Science tells us *how* things occur," Hall writes, "and religion is concerned with the question of *why*!"

Maybe the "Big Bang" happened when God started moving stuff around to create the universe. Unless you are a Neanderthal, you know when objects move around the atmosphere, things happen. If you knock your best cooking vessel off the rock shelf in your cave, it's probably going to break. So why can't people just accept the fact a Superior Being decided at an opportune time to begin playing with the elements *He created* and shaped them into the water, the sky, the earth, the animals, Adam and his little friend Eve? There had to be a "bang" going on when all that happened, so maybe creationists and the scientists are talking about the same event.

Hall says scientists could be more "aware that religion and science are concerned with different questions." And Christians would get less worked up if they could be a little more metaphorical in their approach to the Bible. We can still declare our dependence on God, respond to His creation with awe, view the world as simultaneously orderly and beautiful, and accept our human responsibility to care for God's creation. End of argument.

O Lord, You are the Architect of the universe, whether You bang around or not. Amen

October 15

STUDENT OF LIFE

I have filled him with the Spirit of God, with ability and intelligence, with knowledge and all craftsmanship, to devise artistic designs, to work in gold, silver, and bronze, in cutting stones for setting, and in carving wood, to work in every craft. **Exodus 31:3**

My father was a student of life, spending every waking hour trying to learn something new. I'm certain he already had an inquisitive mind at an early age on his parent's farm. While my father was still in high school, Lee Briggs came to the county fair in his Pheasant biplane, produced right in my dad's hometown of Memphis, Missouri. Briggs was giving rides for two dollars. My dad pestered my grandfather for extra chores. When he had earned enough, he went up with Briggs in that airplane and had a thrill that lasted a lifetime. My dad graduated from flight school in 1931 and worked as a pilot until he retired in the late 1960s. He was good at math and mechanics and if he couldn't fix something, he'd build a new one. He read voraciously. He spent part of his career as "legislative liaison" from the Department of the Air Force to the U.S. House of Representatives and counted many legislators as his friends. The day before he died, he was still watching C-Span, a cable channel airing the proceedings of the federal government. You needed be prepared if you wanted to have a political discussion with my dad.

I seem to have inherited at least some of my father's desire to learn. I love to meet new people and find out about their lives, their beliefs and their insight. Besides studying the Bible, I read many types of books and magazines, and I try to find some kernel of wisdom in everything in print. I constantly look for concepts and ideas and quotations help me in my walk with Christ, and I am seldom disappointed. God provides so many ways for us to enrich ourselves in His world that none of us has an excuse for saying we don't know our Lord.

God of all Wisdom, thank You for providing us with things in this life to make us smarter, happier and more at peace than we were a day ago. Amen

October 16

MEMOIRS OF A COLLECTION PLATE

Honor the Lord with your substance and with the first fruits of all your produce; then your barns will be filled with plenty, and your vats will be bursting with wine. **Proverbs 3:9-10**

When the collection plate is passed your way on Sunday morning, you think it's as an inert object, right? What if that plate, like God's Word, was a living, breathing being that could talk? What would the Plate say to you? Encourage you to give *something* to the Lord, even if your income is small and your expenses large? Today's Scripture passage says we are to honor God with our possessions. Is the Plate saying, "Ten per cent is what the Bible says?" But ten per cent, or *tithing*, was an Old Testament commandment (Deuteronomy 14:22-19), not intended for today, right? Jesus told the rich young man, "Go, sell your possessions, and give the money to the poor, and you will have treasure in heaven" (Matthew 19:21). Who said anything about being perfect? None of us is perfect! And who can give all his money away? We have to live on *something*. The Plate must be wrong.

Today's Scripture also says we will prosper if we donate our "first fruits" (our best stuff) to God. But Jesus says the "prospering" part doesn't happen until we get to heaven, and only farmers have actual "fruits," as in crops, to donate these days. This is all very confusing! I think the Plate would tell us modern day Christians don't have the same covenantal relationship with God that the Israelites had. In fact, Jesus cautioned His disciples about expecting God to reward them with material things for doing His work (Matthew 10:8). Doesn't God own everything anyway? So maybe the Plate is telling us to examine how we handle *all* of God's blessings in our lives, not just our money. We can donate time, talent, knowledge and brain-power, and an infinite array of "blessings" which may be unique only to us. God created us, so let's get creative for Him! You can't put your whole self in the Plate, but the Plate can remind you to give more than just money.

Lord, You gave us what we don't deserve. Let us give You what You do deserve. Amen

October 17

NOTHING

***When Jesus saw the crowds, He went up the mountain...Then He began to speak, and taught them.* Matthew 5:1**

"I got *nothing* out of that church service today!" Have you ever said this to yourself? What does that even mean? Was I tired and completely unable to listen? Did I maybe even doze off? Was it some distraction, like the kids with their parents in the pews reserved for "The Least of These?" All the other pews are taken, so "those" people have to sit down in front, where they probably drive the pastor crazy. And the guy behind me sang so enthusiastically, but completely off-key. The sanctuary was freezing when we got there, but then it got really hot. Why can't the building staff get *that* right, at least! And the *same woman* is singing a solo again. She always gets asked. Why not somebody else? Please, God, fix all this!

If I get *nothing* out of a worship service, then God gets *nothing* out of me either. If we listen patiently, even the most boring sermon has some kernel of truth. Each song has uplifting words, even if someone sings them off key. How about praying for the family with the kid trying to swing from the banner pole? We can pray God will equip the parents to manage the child's idiosyncrasies in the best way possible. Also, if I have a headache or some personal problem I'm wrestling with, a worship service can provide me with a temporary respite from whatever ails me or fails me. If absolutely nothing else works out, I can at least visit with my friends over coffee afterwards.

In her book, *Give God a Year, Change Your Life Forever*, Christian author and speaker Carole Lewis talks about her frustrations in trying to change some unhealthy habits. She prayed, "Lord, I'm not willing, but I'm willing to be *made* willing." If something about a worship service doesn't fit my mood, I'm going to try Carole's prayer.

O Lord, sometimes my humanness keeps me from appreciating Your good gifts. When I'm not willing to see the good in things, help me to be willing. Amen

October 18

CAPTIVATED OR ENCAPSULATED?

For on my holy mountain, says the Lord God...there I will require your contributions and the choicest of your gifts... **Ezekiel 20:40**

Someone once said, "If you're all wrapped up in yourself, you're overdressed." If the only person your "package" is addressed to is you, you won't be getting much for Christmas. God is counting on each of us to be part of His team. Spending our time and energy only on ourselves will not be very satisfying. We will be like farm silos, each storing our own crops but not sharing with others. Like computer chips that disclose no information. All wrapped up and no place to go.

Sin is not only committing an offense against God. Sin can also be defined as shutting oneself off completely from God and His creation, including other people. I'm an extrovert and being around people energizes me. But both outgoing and in-looking folks have something to offer the Kingdom of God. If I could still my brain long enough, I could learn volumes from introspective Christians about prayer and meditation. Activities which often require long periods of stillness and concentration to be effective are the most difficult for me to tolerate. But it's when our own pursuits leave us *devoid* of God's goodness when we can be on a slippery slope.

Getting wrapped up in ourselves is an equal opportunity shortcoming. Everyone experiences it from times to time. Authentic spirituality in one's life cannot occur unless there is balance. God knows we can get tangled up in worldly pursuits. When folks are asked, "What do you do?" most answer with their occupations, but our livelihoods, by themselves, fall short of describing who we are. If we become so involved in our "doing" that we lose all other significance before God, we will soon find ourselves feeling farther from God than we want to be. Being *encapsulated* within ourselves leaves us little time to be *captivated* by all the things God is doing around us.

Call us, Father, in small ways or large, to become captivated by Your Word and Your people. Amen

October 19

THE WANNABEES AND THE SHOULDABEENS

Then I heard the voice of the Lord saying, "Whom shall I send, and who will go for us?" And I said, "Here am I; send me!" Isaiah 6:8

There once was a church with two families, the Wannabees and the Shouldabeens. Both families were quite set in their ways, and had no desire to change. For generations, no major variations occurred in the way each family conducted themselves. Of course, their daughters intermarried and changed their names to Mightbee and Oughtabee, but the children were all raised the same way. Once a Wannabee always a Wannabee, and the same went for a Shouldabeen. It was very hard to break out of the mold.

The Wannabees ruminated about all the things they would like to do but couldn't. One wanted to be council president, but he didn't know very many people, so he didn't get enough votes. Another thought being a Bible study leader would be nice, but no one ever asked her to do it, and it never occurred to her just do it. All the Wannabee children wanted to get involved in the youth group, but their parents never suggested it, so they figured those things were for someone else's kids. The Shouldabeens blamed everyone else instead of thinking it might be their own doing. If a Shouldabeen child did not get picked for the part of Mary in the Christmas play, the parents blamed the child who got the part. When Shouldabeen couples got older, they sat around in their rocking chairs and had heated discussions about all the things the church should have allowed them to do but didn't.

Are you a Wannabee or a Shouldabeen? Or are you a Here-I-Am, who stands up in the middle of the whole congregation and says, "*I'd* like a chance to do that! Let *me* try!" God loves every single Wannabee and Shouldabeen and all their offspring, but He can't work very well with them. Like Isaiah, we need to jump to our feet when opportunity presents itself to do something for the Lord.

Gentle Father, make me a Here-I-Am! I want to do something for You! Amen

October 20

DESTROYING THE MASTERPIECE

The earth is the Lord's and all that is in it, the world, and those who live in it.
Psalm 24:1

A $1.5 million masterpiece was damaged when a twelve-year-old Taiwanese boy tripped and fell, punching a hole in the canvas. "Flowers" by seventeenth century Italian master Paola Porpora was part of a Taipei exhibit showcasing artwork painted by or influenced by Leonardo da Vinci. The boy was listening to the guide and wasn't looking where he was going. He tripped and smashed a hole in the artwork. A security camera caught the whole incident, including the stunned looks of others around the boy.

Late night talk show hosts had a field day and jokes abounded. Since the average family income for the Republic of China is slightly over $26,000 American dollars annually, Museum Boy's family might be paying for that painting for several generations. The boy was on a required public school field trip. Could the Ministry of Education have coughed up the dough? Luckily, display organizer David Sun said the boy and his family expressed sincere regret and won't face punishment. "An Italian appraiser on hand immediately contacted the collector," Sun said after the incident. "We (repaired) the painting immediately on site and (it's) back on display."

Wouldn't it be nice if we had God's equivalent of "an Italian appraiser onsite" when people damage the earth? Every time a natural treasure is vandalized, or people pollute our waters and streams, or "progress" doesn't deal with environmental waste, our planet is left with scars. God's creation is "good" (Genesis 1:10, 12, 18, 21, 25, 31). We are given dominion over the earth and all that is in it, to develop its potential. We are to care for the earth, not destroy it, which makes us God's co-workers. If a Taiwanese pre-teen can feel remorse about accidentally damaging a great work of art, why do some people feel not a twinge of guilt when destroying God's earth?

Father, help us to preserve this earth as You would wish us to do. Amen

October 21

BEAUTIFUL THINGS
Guest Writer Nikki Abramson

He has made everything beautiful in its time. He has also set eternity in the human heart; yet no one can fathom what God has done from beginning to end. Ecclesiastes 3:11

In 2010, the worship band Gungor recorded the song "Beautiful Things," which immediately drew me in and challenged me. The lyrics say that God makes beautiful things out of us. That same year, I was in a car accident, totaling my car. Bedridden for seven months with a permanent neurological condition called dystonia, I thought, *How could God make this horrible situation something beautiful?* I was twenty-four, with my life and career ahead of me.

We all have our challenges in life. Some of us are single and lonely. Others experience the loss of a job or a relationship, are in a financial crisis or physically, mentally, or emotionally ill. I didn't think God could take physically ill Nikki with such a loss of dreams and make something beautiful out of that. He did for me and He will for you, if you trust Him to show you the opportunities that lie ahead. When I was able to fully surrender myself to Him, trust in His plan, and believe that God has a purpose in my suffering, He was able to shine brightly through my life. After all, this is not my life or my story, but His alone. God is the ultimate provider for us. So whatever trials you face, God can and will use it for His glory. He will make beautiful things out of us. It takes time. But remember that God's timing is perfect.

What is your challenge? Pray that God will take your messy situation and turn it into a beautiful thing. Accept the uncomfortable places in our lives. Ask God what to do about them. Trust in His plan. Watch His plan unfold and turn something ugly into a beautiful thing for His glory. Allow God to take your crisis and turn it into His beautiful canvas.

God, help us to trust and surrender to Your will and Your plan. Help us to trust that despite our circumstances, You will turn us into something beautiful that will allow others to see You more fully. Amen.

October 22

FRUITS BORNE OF SORROW

The spirit of the Lord God is upon me, because the LORD has anointed me...to provide for those who mourn in Zion—to give them a garland instead of ashes; the oil of gladness instead of mourning, the mantle of praise instead of a faint spirit. **Isaiah 61:1,3**

"I decided when he took my son, not to let him take anything else from me," she said, "so I put him in a box." These were the words of Patty Wetterling to a group of dinner companions at a sexual violence prevention conference. On this date in 1989, Patty and her husband Jerry's son Jacob was abducted at age eleven by a stranger on a country road near the family's home. His whereabouts are unknown. Her statement hit me like a ton of bricks. As a survivor of sexual violence, I allowed the man who assaulted me and was never caught to chew up a lot of my life, energy, and sensibility for many years. I suddenly realized that's why I have admired Patty so much and cheered for this woman as she has helped to change the landscape for missing and abducted children since that fateful day on a road by her house.

Where can we go when we bear unspeakable pain? How can we escape the clutching hands of an event which can never *not* have happened? For Patty Wetterling, she took her pain and used it as a springboard for good. Four months after Jacob's abduction, the Wetterlings founded the Jacob Wetterling Foundation (now the Jacob Wetterling Resource Center), a non-profit organization dedicated to child safety education. Patty chairs the National Center for Missing and Exploited Children and serves on many boards working to end violence against children. Patty's courage, generosity, steadfastness, and belief in a future world free of violence have borne fruit out of sorrow and goodness out of suffering.

Lord, thank You for these oaks of righteousness who carry Your love to a hurting and sin-ridden world. Amen

October 23

MAGNIFICENT OBSESSION

I pray that, according to the riches of His glory, He may grant that you may be strengthened in your inner being with power through His Spirit, and that Christ may dwell in your hearts through faith, as you are being rooted and grounded in love. I pray that you may have the power to comprehend, with all the saints, what is the breadth and length and height and depth, and to know the love of Christ that surpasses knowledge, so that you may be filled with all the fullness of God. **Ephesians 3:16-19**

Ann Graham Lotz once said, "If you and I ever truly know God, it will not be an accident. It will happen when…we abandon every other goal, every other priority, and embrace the God-filled life until He becomes our magnificent obsession." I want to be like that! I keep trying, but it is in the trying that I miss the mark. Maybe I just need to accept whatever God has in store for me, no questions asked. I know the times I have come to the end of myself, God was waiting there with what seemed like a new beginning, but which was really just a continuum of God's plan for me, ever unfolding. I can't really go to God "broken," because He doesn't see me that way. He sees me as His holy and blameless child, perfect in His eyes. He is just always glad I've taken the time to seek Him out and say, "Hey."

I've thought a lot about "praying without ceasing," which Paul writes to the Thessalonian church (1 Thessalonians 5:17). In that same passage, Paul says, "rejoice always" (v. 16), "give thanks in all circumstances" (v. 18), and "do not quench the Spirit" (v. 19). There is so much in this one passage, how is a person supposed to do all of it? Graham Lotz' answer is simple: make it our number one goal in this life. And the only way to do that is with God's power, not our own. Today's Scripture passage says that God is ready to grant us the power to do everything He wills us to do, "according to the riches of His glory" (Ephesians 3:16). The obsession is His with us as well as ours with Him.

Come, Lord Jesus, fill my empty places with Your radiant power. Amen

October 24

I'VE GOT SOUL

To you, O Lord, I lift up my soul. **Psalm 25:1**

"I've got soul" is an expression we hear in conjunction with certain music performed by the likes of BB King, Aretha Franklin, and Ray Charles. Soul music is a combination of Rhythm and Blues (R&B) and gospel, sometimes combining spiritual and secular music. Some say soul songs makes you *feel* the music as well as *hear* it.

British author C.S. Lewis once said, "You don't *have* a soul. You *are* a Soul. You *have* a body" (italics mine). My "personhood," what makes me *me*, is apparently different than what I've been led to believe. Lewis's point is that we (people) are eternal beings who just happen to store our souls in a temporary physical body while we reside on earth. Often, "soul" and "spirit" are used interchangeably, so what is the difference?

According to the website, gotquestions.org, "the spirit gives us the ability to have an intimate relationship with God" (John 4:24). As C.S. Lewis said, we *are* souls, but we *have* a body, and also a spirit. The word "soul" means "life," referring to spiritual and emotional experiences (Psalm 43:5).

Simply put, the *soul* is the essence of humanity's being; it is who we are. The *spirit* is the aspect of humanity that connects with God. The body is a convenient, self-contained package, home to the soul in this realm we call life.

O Lord, You have designed us intricately and well. We may not understand how You did it, but we thank You! Amen

October 25

THE SIXTH SENSE

If you confess with your lips that Jesus is Lord and believe in your heart that God raised Him from the dead, you will be saved.
Romans 10:9

Every school kid knows we have five natural senses: hearing, seeing, smelling, tasting and feeling. Evangelist Billy Graham says we have a sixth sense: the ability to *believe*. What does "believing" mean to you? Webster defines the word as "trusting in," or "accepting as true." I know I trust God, but why is that so? Part of the mystery of faith is we don't really know why we believe; we just do. Unlike me, some people are raised in a church family where it was an accepted thing to love the Lord throughout life. There are lots of stories about young people who don't follow Christ after their parents can no longer make them go to church. I heard about a pastor who found a deer inside the church one Sunday morning. When he told the parishioners about it, they all asked, "How did you get it out of the building?" His reply: "I confirmed it and it left on its own."

I, on the other hand, didn't get "into" church until I was almost thirty, and I haven't had any desire to leave. That doesn't mean I have any more or less faith than a person raised in the church. Faith is a very personal thing, which is part of the mystery. I can use my natural senses to *see* a person attending Sunday morning services, placing something in the collection plate, and taking communion. I can *hear* her singing with the congregation, and I can even *feel* a certain warmth about the person that would lead me to believe she is sincere. (The *smelling* and *tasting* parts might come in at a church supper.) But I don't *know* that person is a believer unless I spend time with her or him, and even then, I could be mistaken. But the important thing is that God knows, and it's nobody else's business except God's and the individual's. Like today's Scripture says, believing is a "heart thing." We know that we know that we know we believe, and God knows it too. Tell someone else today about your sixth sense: believing!

Holy God, we believe Your Word and we believe in You. Amen

October 26

VENOM OF VIPERS

Their throats are opened graves; they use their tongues to deceive. The venom of vipers is under their lips. Their mouths are full of cursing and bitterness. **Romans 3:13-14**

I know a couple who have been married many years, yet it is impossible to be around them for more than a few minutes before they are in an argument. Not just a small tiff; these people are ready to go for each other's throats and sometimes it seems they would, even with others around them. People's reactions vary, but most of us try to ignore them, make light of the situation, or just plain leave the room. Even though I know these people well, I do not understand, nor can I fathom how they've gotten to this place. What makes anybody—Christian or not—get so out of control in front of others? And if it's that bad with an audience, what is it like when they are alone? Nothing gets in the way of their antagonism towards each other.

When I was a college counselor and thought I was pretty smart, I used to have a saying: A healthy relationship is one in which two people who are totally capable of taking care of themselves *choose* to care for one another. Not "take care of" one another, but "care for" one another. Well, I've had to back off of that somewhat idealistic description of a "healthy" union in recent years. What about things like substance abuse and addiction? Profound physical illness or disability? Mental illness? Unforeseen events which leave one or both persons severely traumatized? The simple fact is, long-term relationships, especially marriage, are difficult for many of us. One thing is certain: without Christ as the head of the household, things can and do get dicey. If God is truly at the helm of our lives, our relationship with Him cannot help but affect our dealings with people. The first four commandments speak of loving God (Deuteronomy 5:6-15). The last six tell us how to love other people (Deuteronomy 5:16-21). Loving God and loving others are *interdependent* and require our total *dependence* on Him.

Loving Lord, You created marriage as a sacred bond. Grant us Your wisdom and patience in our unions. Amen

October 27

EXPRESS YOURSELF

May you produce children...and, through the children that the LORD will give you by this young woman, may your house be like the house of (an ancestor of David). **Ruth 4:11-12**

Do you ever wonder where expressions or *idioms* come from? An *idiom* is defined as an expression with a special meaning. The website grammarly.com lists a number of fun idioms with surprising origins. "Go the whole nine yards," for example has nothing to do with football. During World War II, the fighter pilots were equipped with nine yards of ammunition. When they ran out, it meant they had tried their best at fighting off the target. Hence, the expression came to mean "try your best." "Giving a cold shoulder" means being unwelcoming toward another person. In medieval England, people gave a cold piece of meat from the shoulder of the animal when the host felt it was time for a guest to leave. The message was, "You've overstayed your welcome." How about "don't throw the baby out with the bathwater?" We use it to mean don't get rid of something valuable while you are cleaning out things you don't need. Many years ago, people bathed very seldom, and those living in each household used the same water. Adult men bathed first, then the women, then the older kids and finally the babies—in water that was by now filthy. Moms had to take care not to miss a small child when emptying the murky mix!

My friend Bob Albers and I were emailing back and forth about the origin of the term "spitting image." I searched the Internet and found many different accounts as to how the expression came about. Some had to do with a child looking so much like his parent that he could have been "spat" from the mother or father's mouth. But the one Bob and I agreed we liked the most and thought was true declared the original saying was "spirit and image." If a youngster appeared similar to his parents, it was said he had both the "spirit" and the "image" of them. The words became slurred together, but this meaning seems the most flattering.

Lord, make us the "spirit and image" of You! Amen

October 28

VACUUM CLEANERS

So if you think you are standing, watch out that you do not fall.
1 Corinthians 10:12

Our daughter and her husband were arriving in one hour with their three year old son and a brand new baby. Three nights prior a huge storm had moved through packing straight line winds in excess of seventy miles per hour. When everyone emerged from the safety of our basements, we saw what looked like a war zone. Although no houses were badly damaged, thirty year-old trees blocked the streets. Power was out and debris was everywhere. Fallen trees had to be cleared. But I had company coming! Sweeping our house with a broom and dustpan, I desperately missed having electricity to run the vacuum cleaner, a simple appliance I had always taken for granted.

Seventeenth century French philosopher Blaise Pascal said, "There is a God shaped vacuum in the heart of every man which cannot be filled by any created thing, but only by God, the Creator, made known through Jesus." Many people come to Christ trying to fill that void. When I had completely run out of answers, options, and excuses, I came to Him. My life was on a downhill spiral and I believed I was destined to be unhappy and dissatisfied with myself for the rest of my days. But the indwelling Christ changed all of that, and now I feel my heart bursting with love for my Savior.

People have tried since time began to fill the "God shaped vacuum" with other things. Money, sex, drugs and alcohol, and any number of "philosophies" have been used in an attempt to satisfy the yearning people have to feel "whole." This world is filled with "vacuum cleaners" that try to suck out of people what could be a natural and gratifying relationship with the King of the universe. First Timothy 6:9 says, "Those who want to be rich fall into temptation and are trapped by many senseless and harmful desires that plunge people into ruin and destruction." Are you filling your "God shaped vacuum" with what is supposed to fit there perfectly?

Fill us, Lord, with Your perfect love.

October 29

YOU'RE GETTING WARMER

Fight the good fight of the faith; take hold of the eternal life, to which you were called and for which you made the good confession in the presence of many witnesses. **1Timothy 6:12**

"There are strange things done in the midnight sun," begins Robert Service's famous poem, "The Cremation of Sam McGee," published in 1907. The poem is about the cremation of a Yukon "sourdough" prospector named Sam McGee, originally from the fictitious town of Plumtree, Tennessee. McGee begs the narrator of the poem "to swear that, foul or fair, you'll cremate my last remains." The promise is made, and McGee freezes to death the very next day. A shipwreck becomes a crematorium. The poem ends when the narrator sees McGee sitting up, saying, "Please close that door. It's fine in here, but I greatly fear you'll let in the cold and storm— Since I left Plumtree, down in Tennessee, it's the first time I've been warm."

This gruesome story was one of my mother's favorites. She also had an almost maudlin attitude towards death, which made her interest in the poem all the more bizarre. Once, when she and I visited an old west museum in Colorado Springs, Colorado, we were viewing a horse-drawn hearse. I was studying how the whole thing fit together, how the horses would be harnessed up to pull it. Mother suddenly took a deep sigh and said, "Death is so sad." Because our family moved frequently, we rarely went to funerals. The few times we had an opportunity to attend a burial, my mother would make us kids stay home, probably because of her own attitude about death. Perhaps the poem resonated with her on some level I never understood.

With the Christian, death is something we can face knowing the outcome. I know I will go to heaven because the Bible says I will. I believe I will see my mother there too, because she believed in Jesus Christ. God's promises are true and faithful and I can count on them without fear or worry.

Heavenly Father, thank You for taking the sting out of death and giving us a crown of glory. Amen

October 30

SIGNS? I WONDER…

Others, to test him, kept demanding from him a sign from heaven. **Luke 11:16**

Does God ever give you signs? We've all met people who think *everything* is a sign, from a gum wrapper on the ground to something the clerk at Walmart says. I don't think I'd like to go through life that way, watching every second for a signal from God. On the other hand, isn't God speaking to us in some fashion all the time?

I had a sign shortly before I left my dysfunctional first marriage. I dreamed I had a huge glass shard in my arm that was bleeding profusely. I distinctly heard God say, "This glass is like your marriage. If you leave it in place, you will bleed to death. If you take it out, it will hurt but it will heal." Now I was pretty sure *that* was a sign, and it helped me make the decision to change my life. I've never regretted my decision, and I truly believe the dream was a profound message from God.

I've thought long and hard about my dream and what made me certain it *was* from God. I remember how it gave me the *conviction*, or certainty, ending my marriage was the right thing to do. It puzzled me that I could find no specific passage of Scripture to support that decision, but I knew God loved me and I knew He had great plans for me which I would never have achieved in my previous situation. From a human standpoint, at least, things were not going to change for me unless I made a new life for myself. I had spent my childhood in a dysfunctional family and, unfortunately I had chosen what was familiar to me rather than what was best for me. The *circumstantial evidence* was clear. Once the decision was made, I felt *God's peace* like I had not felt in many years, and I knew I could trust Him to *provide* for me, which He did, abundantly. It didn't matter to God how the *first* part of my life had gone; He was interested in the *last chapter*.

Heavenly Father, let me hear You clearly, whether You speak in a shout or a whisper. Amen

October 31

BOO-YA: RECLAIMING THE SACRED IN HALLOWEEN
Guest Writer Diane Keyes

Our Father which art in heaven, Hallowed be Thy name. Thy kingdom come, Thy will be done in earth, as it is in heaven... deliver us from evil: For Thine is the kingdom, the power, and the glory, forever. Amen. Matthew 6:9-13

Halloween has always been my least favorite holiday, until now. It seems there is more to the tradition than you'll find at the bib box stores. As leaves fall and chill winds and gray skies beckon us to hearth and home, we recognize autumn as a slowing down and moving inward, physically and spiritually. For millennia, Halloween was considered the 1st day of the autumn triduum with All Saints day and All Souls Day, coming between the fall equinox and the winter solstice; a time when the veil between this world and the next is thin. Celebrated to usher us into this quieter, more contemplative space, the autumn triduum honored our ancestors' lives, contributions, and passings, with a glimpse into the scary, yet compelling mystery of death.

Unfortunately Western culture kept only the traditions rooted in superstition: costumes worn to prevent ghosts from recognizing us, jack o' lanterns imitating skulls lit with candles to frighten spirits, and begging for wood to light a bonfire to keep away evil entities devolved into begging for candy.
Originally the word halloween meant "to make holy," *een* being the shortened form of evening. Viewed from this perspective, Halloween becomes significant to our lives as Christians.

To restore this sacred time, herald its coming with a short meditation. In a prayerful posture, call to mind all the saintly people, past and present, public and private, who have made your life possible. Pray for them. Thank them and God for their presence in your life. Acknowledge those who rise to your awareness, knowing God sends them with love and healing. Then allow Jesus to come, the One who is the Source of our good. Thank Him for your many blessings, including the challenges which help us grow into our best selves. Thank Him for transforming the shadow of death into the light of the resurrection. We have nothing to fear from darkness—we have Jesus. This Hallowed Evening take time to remember the true Spirit of the season.

Deliver us from evil: For Thine is the kingdom, the power, and the glory, forever. Amen.

November

November 1

I'M A SEENAGER AND A SEASONED SAINT

In old age they still produce fruit; they are always green and full of sap, showing that the LORD is upright. **Psalm 92:13-15**

On Face Book was an anonymous posting entitled, "I Am A Seenager (Senior Teenager)." Nowadays, you never know if some famous person wrote something you see on the Internet, because people are using other people's stuff and not even trying to give them credit. I hope someone famous like Donald Trump didn't write the "Seenager" piece, because if I use it, and he sues me, I'll pretty much be wiped out.

Here is why I'm a "Seenager:" I have everything I wanted as a teenager, only sixty years later; I don't have to go to school or work; I get an allowance every month (for doing nothing); I have my own pad; I don't have a curfew; I have a driver's license and my own car; the people I hang around with don't belong to gangs or use drugs; and I don't have acne. Life is great!

So what does it mean to be a "mature Christian?" We'll call it being a "Seasoned Saint." Here is what this means to me: I finally "get" why I go to church; my daily walk with Christ has profound meaning and has changed my life completely; I never get jealous of my girlfriends; now that I am happily married to a wonderful Christian man, dating is SO overrated; I'm not afraid to die; I'm not afraid to live either; I'm grateful for what I have and I don't wish for things like being a rich and wildly popular rock star; I love Jesus more every day.

Isaiah 46:4 says God will carry me even in my old age. Psalm 71:18 recommends praising God and proclaiming His word as long as we have breath. I hope to do this, while I'm living the rest of my life to the fullest.

Father of All Ages, grant me the ability to bring praise and honor to You throughout all of my days. Amen

November 2

DOUBT IS A DENT IN MY ARMOUR

He said to them, "Why are you frightened, and why do doubts arise in your hearts? Luke 24:38**

Lately I seem to be plagued with doubt. Just yesterday I wrote about being an "old sage" with a "mature" faith. Satan may be targeting me, because recently I've been posed with questions like, "Is God a man or a woman or both?" and "If we're all sinners, is there anything to be hopeful about?"

Like a child runs to her earthly parents when she is frightened or hurt, I decided to run to my Father in heaven to see what He would say about doubting. We all know the story of Jesus' disciple with the hapless nickname of "Doubting" Thomas. He was probably a good disciple or Jesus wouldn't have kept him on the job. So he didn't see Jesus the first time He appeared, and I'm not sure you or I would be convinced either, if our Christian friends came running to tell us they'd seen the Messiah. We might want a little proof too. But the point of the story is that *Christ responded*. He came back and proved to Thomas it was indeed He and He wasn't dead any more.

Thomas wasn't the only one who didn't believe it was Jesus in the flesh. The rest of today's Scripture passage has the other ten disciples quivering in their boots. They thought Jesus was a ghost. You'd think they might have even trusted that image alone, having spent so much time with Him. However, they had just been totally traumatized by the murder of their Friend and Teacher, so they probably weren't thinking too clearly. Jesus said, "Touch me and see; for a ghost does not have flesh and bones as you see I have" (Luke 24:39).

Sometimes by writing them out, I can answer my own questions. Though I may feel "targeted" or my doubts may surface from time to time, Christ still gives me strength. A little doubt is just a dent in my armour.

Jesus, thank You that we're in this together. Amen

November 3

THIS IS MY SONG

I will give thanks to you, O Lord, among the peoples; I will sing praises to you among the nations. **Psalm 57:9**

At church recently, we sang a hymn with which I was unfamiliar, but the words and melody touched me. It was written about a place I dearly love, the Hawaiian Islands. The lyrics of "This Is My Song," sometimes called "A Song of Peace," were written by American Lloyd Stone in 1934. Stone hailed from California, but ended up in Hawaii quite by accident and never left. He wrote prophetic words about the "God of all nations" at a time when Hawaii was a US territory. In 1893, a dozen or so non-native businessmen, who were reaping huge profits in Hawaii, overthrew Queen Liluokalani, declaring themselves the Provisional Government of Hawaii. The USS Boston stood at the ready at the time of the takeover. Hawaii became a state in 1959, but not without the loss of much of its heritage. Corrupt and powerful people want the best for themselves regardless of harm done.

The lyrics continue: "This is my song, O God of all the nations/a song of peace for lands afar and mine/here are my hopes, my dreams, my holy shrine/but other hearts in other lands are beating/with hopes and dreams as true and high as mine." I would like to think that Stone would only have written these words if he had been compassionate about the native Hawaiians and others whose land, heritage, culture and livelihood have been usurped by some greater power. The Hawaiians were truly refugees in their own land. An example of a native practice replaced with "modern" methods was the Hawaiian model for community-based native habitat management. After the Islands' waters and land became polluted, the state returned to the original methods, which now protect the bond between Hawaii and her people. I believe Mr. Stone would approve.

O God, "may truth and freedom come to every nation/may peace abound where strife has raged so long/that each may seek to love and build together/a world united, righting every wrong/a world united in its love for freedom/proclaiming peace together in one song." Amen

November 4

STARTER KIT CHRISTIANS

I fed you with milk, not solid food, for you were not ready for solid food. **1 Corinthians 3:2**

When I first laid down my life at Jesus' feet, I was in a word *clueless*. The only thing I knew was something profound happened at the moment I said "yes" to Him. I was not the same person. Within days—hours—of making that life-changing decision, I dreamed a dove descended onto my head, not knowing the dove is the symbol for the Holy Spirit. I read a King James like a first-grade primer. My life was a pile of newness about being a child of God, and I marveled each time I had a new feeling or experience.

I got to thinking, what would go into a "Starter Kit" for new Christians? On the website startingwithGod.com (who knew there was a website like that?), Barbara Francis says, "Getting to know God is like getting to know another person." In a new relationship with God, Step One is to *listen* to Him by getting into His Word, preferably with some direction from a more seasoned believer. Step Two is to talk to God, or pray. Anybody can pour out one's feelings, concerns and joys to the Almighty without much practice. In fact, the more casual one's prayers are the better. God doesn't want us to be professional orators. He is having a "come as you are" party.

Step Three is to talk to others about this new Person in your life. It's okay to tell everybody you know you have made a decision to follow Christ. We are "Christ's ambassadors" (2 Corinthians 5:20), and even as new believers, we can share our profound and life-changing experience with those we meet. Step Four is to talk to others who also know your new Friend. They can help new believers learn how to grow in Christ's love and produce fruit for God (Jeremiah 12:2). So that's the "Starter Kit." If you are a new Christian, try it out. If you have been a believer for a while, go find yourself a "baby" Christian and use this method to get to know her!

Jesus, You were new to all of us once. Enchant us with Your marvelous ways. Amen

November 5

PRESENT SUFFERINGS

I consider that the sufferings of this present time are not worth comparing with the glory about to be revealed to us. **Romans 8:18**

For the last few days, I have felt an arthritis "flare" coming on. Nothing I can do, no pill I can take, and no place I can hide will send the pain away. These episodes pop up when I least expect them. They can totally derail me.

Pain changes people, demands to be felt. It is impossible *not* to know you are in pain, and whoever says they never feel pain must not have felt what some of us live with on a regular basis. Not saying you're in pain is not strength. It takes strength to face any kind of pain, embrace it and move forward. Sometimes, it makes us act differently, but many times we just have to keep "acting" the same because we have things to do, responsibilities, deadlines. We can't let the pain stop us until…it just stops us. Then we rest because there is nothing else to do.

My best defense against pain is my faith in God. It takes deliberate, thought-out, decisive acts of faith to keep this old boat in the water. I give my pain to God because He knows what pain feels like: both the emotional pain of simply going through pain alone, and the physical pain of unbearable proportions that held Him to the cross for you and me. The apostle Paul knew about both kinds of pain. He told the Philippians, "I want to know Christ…by becoming like Him in His death" (Philippians 3:10). I don't want to "become like Him in His death." I don't want to die nailed to a cross, and the likelihood of that is remote (I think). But the next verse says, "if somehow I may attain the resurrection from the dead" (v.11). I know there will be pain in this life, but I will not let pain take my faith away, nor let it make me someone I am not. I am a child of God, and no physician in this world can treat my pain as well as He.

Gentle Healer, hold me in my worst hours of pain and do not let it rob me of my enduring faith in You. Amen

November 6

SHOW ME YOUR FRIENDS, I'LL SHOW YOU YOUR FUTURE

I regard everything as loss because of the surpassing value of knowing Christ Jesus my Lord. For His sake I have suffered the loss of all things, and I regard them as rubbish, in order that I may gain Christ and be found in Him, not having a righteousness of my own that comes from the law, but one that comes through faith in Christ, the righteousness from God based on faith. **Philippians 3:8-9**

The Germans have a saying, *Zu früh alt, zu spät Smart*, which translates, *Too soon old, too late smart*. This reminds me of my "experimental days," when I did not necessarily choose the best company to hang around with. Unfortunately, these "days" lasted until well into adulthood, of which I am not proud. Let's just say it took me a long time to discover the influence certain people had on my life. Although the lesson was learned later than I would have preferred (and after certain pain and suffering), I now know there is a difference between being friends *with* certain people and loving those same people *as Christ would have me love them*.

The Bible is specific about people we should trust. First Corinthians 15:33 says, "Do not be deceived: Bad company ruins good morals." You can't get clearer than that. Scripture says everything necessary for people to be like Christ is directly related to character. Not just any character, but God's character. The Old Testament tell us God commands us to "sanctify (ourselves)…and be holy, for (God) is holy" (Leviticus 11:44). The verse continues, "You shall not defile yourselves with any swarming creature that moves on the earth." Now I'm not sure God would have called the people I used to hang out with as "swarming creatures." But even in the midst of those relationships, I knew they were not good for me. Why did I stay friends with those people? Perhaps God had lessens for me about the importance of leaving those friendships. God can make a "teachable moment" out of any dumb ideas we come up with. Isn't it nice to know He always bails us out if we ask Him?

Lord, help me discern between those I can trust and those who need my trust to help them find You. Amen

November 7

MAKE YOUR BED!

I came that they may have life, and have it abundantly. John 10:10

A study by the National Sleep Foundation found bed makers were 19 per cent more likely to report a good night's sleep than people who leave their blankets messy. Who thinks these studies up, and how much do the researchers get paid to conduct them? The study cited "a connection between feeling good about your bed and your tendency to sleep through the night."

What if we surveyed practicing Christians? STUDIES SHOW THAT CHRISTIANS ARE MORE LIKELY TO BELIEVE IN JESUS AS GOD'S SON. Scientists at the Institute for Research of Obvious Things recently revealed of 10,000 Christians surveyed, on hundred per cent said they believed that Jesus Christ is God's Son and came into the world to seek and save the lost. Scholars throughout the world are stumped by these results. A book called the Bible states this belief is founded. Researchers question the origin of the data and think further study is warranted.

PEOPLE WHO BELIVE IN GOD SAID TO HAVE 'SPECIAL PEACE. A study conducted in a remote part of northern Europe has made the astonishing discovery in a survey of 30,000 adults and children who believe in God, every single one of them claim to have a "peace that passes all understanding." The study has been declared invalid.

MAN CLAIMING TO BE 'THE WAY, THE TRUTH AND THE LIFE' DEBUNKS RECENT STUDY. At the University of Superfluous Knowledge, a Man wearing sandals and a tunic recently conducted an individual peaceful demonstration against the Department of Redundancy Department. The Man was protesting the DRD's conclusion that the words "way, truth, and life" have no meaning in today's society.

Lord, we don't need surveys to know You are the way, the truth and the life. Your Word is all we need to know. Amen

November 8

THE GREAT I AM

God said to Moses, I Am Who I Am. And He said, "Say this to the people of Israel, I Am has sent me to you." **Exodus 3:14**

Who is this King of Glory Who calls Himself "I AM," as if nothing else *is*? Jesus used the "I AM" statement many times in His ministry. Here are a few:

Jesus said, "I AM the bread of life" (John 6:48). He is our supporter; He gives us all we need to sustain ourselves in this life. "I AM the light of the world" (John 8:18). Jesus lights our way and brings His healing into this dark world. John 10:9 says, "I AM the door." Christ is the way for us to enter the Father's presence, and we are full heirs of God's kingdom with Christ. In John 10:11, Jesus says, "I AM the good shepherd." He is our caretaker.

Jesus says, "I AM the resurrection and the life" in John 11:25. He lit the flame of our passion and made us alive in Himself. He promises us passage from this life through death into eternal life with Him. John 14:6 states, "I AM the way, and the truth, and the life." Christ is not only our leader and guide; He walks with us through the most troublesome events that occur in this earthly life. He is all truth; there is nothing false in Him. And John 15:1 says, "I AM the true vine." Jesus is the vine connected to God's mighty trunk. We cannot help but be sustained in our efforts when we are abiding in Him and He in us.

I AM is the God Who still listens, still answers, still heals, still forgives, still leads, directs, cares and loves us beyond measure. There is no power on earth or in hell which can withstand I AM's might. And He is as accessible to us at any moment as our own breath. We need only to whisper a prayer and that prayer rises like incense up to the heavens where God breathes it in and responds.

O Great I AM, I praise You for loving me, a tiny speck of sand in Your great universe. Amen

November 9

BORED AGAIN CHRISTIANS

And let us consider how to provoke one another to love and good deeds, not neglecting to meet together, as is the habit of some, but encouraging one another, and all the more as you see the Day approaching. Hebrews 10:24-25

What causes people to be bored in church? This is an age-old question, and congregations have struggled with it—or ignored it—for years. I've been to many different churches, and I can tell you what leaves me cold. First of all, it's not being made to feel welcome. I don't want people pouncing on me with a pitch for life-long membership. But it is nice to have someone tell me they're glad I came. Secondly, I like to know what to expect. Some churches don't hand out bulletins, and give no explanation of what the service will be like. Members apparently know, but visitors are clueless. I don't mind the big screens with the words for songs and the daily Scripture reading on them. At least they could let me know if there will be communion, special music, or a baptism. A church my parents attended for a while had immersion baptism at the end of each service. I wanted to stay and observe, but my father had one foot in the car before the first person arrived in her white robe. Unlike me, he'd "been there and done that" as a kid, and he apparently saw no benefit in seeing new people brought to the Lord.

Another one for me is a sermon with no emotion in it. I've heard sermons read. I wasn't allowed to do this in high school speech class, and I think seminary students might have already learned to speak without reading an entire text verbatim. I've heard sermons delivered in a monotone, and that worries me. How am I supposed to get excited about Jesus if the leader of the pack isn't excited? Hebrews 10:24 cautions us to "consider how to provoke" each other into doing good deeds. I've been provoked in church a few times, but it had more to do with not being inspired. Church is a package deal, and we are all responsible for making our church home a good one. As members or leaders or clergy, let's show some excitement for Jesus.

Lord, fill us with enthusiasm for You! Amen

November 10

ALL OF THE FLOWERS

"Truly I tell you, if you have faith the size of a mustard seed, you will say to this mountain, 'Move from here to there,' and it will move; and nothing will be impossible for you." Matthew 17:20-21

In my garden shed, I have a little sign bearing an anonymous quote, "All of the flowers of all the tomorrows are in the seeds of today." I see all of the beautiful flowers, shrubs, trees and vegetables I have planted. When we bought this house, the yard was a blank slate with very little landscaping. It did not appear dismal to me. I didn't see a yard void of plants, but a blank slate on which I could create endless beauty and produce healthy food to eat. I felt like an old-time "sodbuster," itching to get my hands in that soil.

The "soil" turned out to be mostly clay, liberally peppered with rocks. Our first summer here, I tore out my right rotator cuff shoveling, which required shoulder surgery plus a lengthy rehab period. Then I tore the same shoulder again, and sometime later, the other shoulder succumbed to my efforts to tame that dirt. I hired a neighbor with a back hoe to do some of the work, and he brought in "black dirt." *That* dirt was full of rocks too, and by now I had quite a geological collection. With weak shoulders *and* a "train wreck" for a spine, I learned to pace myself and ask for help when I needed it. But every spring, when I place tiny seeds in the now improved soil and I watch flowers and vegetables literally burst from the ground, I thank God for His part in my efforts. As Paul said in 1 Corinthians 3:6, he planted, another follower watered, but "God gave the increase."

I've never grown mustard, but lettuce and carrot and many flower seeds are so tiny they are hard to handle. How does God get all that "good stuff" into each tiny seed? I'll just chalk it up to another of His many miracles and watch my gardens come to life.

God, You are the Master Gardener of the earth. We praise You for the beauty all around us. Amen

November 11

THE ANGELS OF BATAAN

When you hear of wars and rumors of wars, do not be alarmed; this must take place, but the end is still to come. **Mark 13:7**

My father's sister, Ethel "Sally" Blaine, admired her military brothers. She became an Army nurse and was stationed in Manila during WWII when the Japanese bombed Pearl Harbor. Manila was the next target. Sally was among eighty-eight American Army and twelve Navy nurses who, along with a handful of physicians, moved 75,000 Filipino and American troops from a Manila hospital to the inhospitable jungles of the Bataan peninsula. "Hospital 1" on Bataan consisted of twenty-nine bamboo and grass sheds. "Hospital 2" was open air. Mosquitos, flies, contaminated food and water malaria, dengue fever and dysentery were rampant. The "Angels of Bataan," were the first U.S. military women to wear fatigues and combat boots.

Having succumbed to malaria, Sally lay on a cot in the middle of the open air "ward," giving orders to other nurses. Early in 1942, my aunt and a few other ill nurses were evacuated. They stopped for fuel but the sea plane bottomed out, damaging the fuel tank. The nurses hid, but were captured by the Japanese and transported to Manila. They avoided the "Death March" (April 9, 1942, when hospital patients and staff were forced to march sixty miles back to Manila, losing nearly 20,000 wounded and ill soldiers along the way), Sally and some other nurses were sent to an internment camp. For over three years, the nurses cared for their patients in deplorable conditions.

On February 3, 1945, American troops liberated the internees in Manila. In Sally's own words, "It was so exhilarating when…'Skinny' (Lieutenant General Jonathan M.) Wainright's old cavalry division liberated us…that we were intoxicated with joy for three days!" Aunt Sally's positive attitude, courage and faith kept her alive through an unspeakable ordeal.

Loving Father, war seems to be with us always. We pray for our military personnel and world peace. Amen

November 12

TRUST IN GOD, HOPE THROUGH JESUS

For God did not give us a spirit of cowardice, but rather a spirit of power and of love and of self-discipline. **2 Timothy 1:7**

Dutch Christian and holocaust survivor Corrie ten Boom once said, "Never be afraid to trust an unknown future to a known God." Ten Boom's family had hidden Jewish friends and neighbors until the Nazis took them all to concentration camps. Corrie was the only one of her family to survive. Even when we as humans cannot fathom what God has planned, we can rest assured that He *does* have a plan. God never said He'd keep us within what we believe to be our "comfort zone." It is when we get to the edge of that comfort zone that we begin to understand what trusting Him is like.

My life was a perfect example of this after I was sexually assaulted at gunpoint and was able to escape the attacker before he left me for dead. During the weeks and months after the assault, I was like a ship with no anchor, whipped about in the waves of my emotions and fear. I did not know Christ, but I saw God's power when I cried out to Him during the attack and the man fled from me as if Christ Himself had sent him packing. I didn't know what to do with that kind of power. I somehow knew invoking God's name was the ticket that freed me. I had no personal knowledge of His power until that day. Unlike Corrie, I didn't "know God" and therefore had no reason to trust Him. I was bound by my fear of being attacked again, which restricted my activity for years. The cold, hard fear did not begin to leave me until I laid my life down at the feet of Jesus.

God's Word contains a promise for every need we have and every problem we need to solve. Jesus came that we might know God in a personal way. The Spirit reminds us daily of the grace which heals us from all of our earthly woes.

Triune God, remind me often of the purity of Your Word and the incorruptibility of Your promises. Amen

November 13

THE VODKA WARS

And do not get drunk with wine, for that is debauchery, but be filled with the Spirit. Ephesians 5:18

As a method of survival, my sister and I used humor to deflect our anger and frustration about Mother's alcoholism. My father was an Air Force officer and we were used to "Military Speak." My mother was never victorious over alcohol, but sadly, the humor helped us cope.

We are reporting from a war-torn region known as the Living Room, where the fighting has intensified in the last few hours. The political issue at hand appears to be a deep-seated and long-running disagreement over a Smirnoff bottle divided at the Vodka Parallel into two regions known as Above and Below. Fighting erupted quickly between the Father Field Forces and the Mobile Mother Militia over the unauthorized relocation of the Rubber Band, which is believed to have been placed in a strategic location by the Father Faction to indicate an acceptable level of consumption of the contents therein. Sources here say the Father was on a routine reconnaissance mission undertaken to obtain, by visual observation or other detection methods, information about the activities of the Mother, to secure data concerning the geographic characteristics of said Rubber Band upon the surface of the Smirnoff Vodka Bottle. Visual observation led the Father to the realization that the Rubber Band had presumably been moved by the Mother, casting doubt as to whether or not the Mother had consumed more than the amount of the Smirnoff Vodka agreed upon, thereby violating the terms of the last of several Sober Treaties. The Father, clearly the more rational and conservative of the two factions, is demanding reforms. The question then becomes, "Was this simply human error or is it truly the unauthorized action of a subordinate?" The Mother, on the other hand, is quite obviously attempting to launch an organized movement aimed at the overthrow of the household through the use of subversion and possibly armed conflict.

Holy God, Thank You that Your power is greater than any addiction that can befall humans. Amen

November 14

A LETTER FROM YOU

And you show that you are a letter from Christ delivered by us, written not with ink but with the Spirit of the living God, not on tablets of stone but on tablets of human hearts. **2 Corinthians 3:3**

When I speak to groups about my amazing faith story, I like to end my talk with a "call to action." I will explain to my audience the importance of "concerned bystanders" in ending violence in our society. Whether we witness bullying, harassment, abuse, assault or human trafficking, we can all be informed observers and *do something*. Safe intervention may be impossible, but we can report what we saw or heard immediately. If we are the victims, we must ask for help from a trained advocate, agency or trusted friend or relative. Time is of utmost importance in solving crimes of any kind. If we care about ending violence, we must speak up for those who are victimized.

There is another reason we must take action, and that is for Christ. As Paul tells the Corinthians in today's Scripture verse, each of us is a "walking testimony" for Jesus, a testimony written "on tablets of human hearts." How I wish I had the luxury of having caring Christians at my disposal when I was assaulted! I am certain my experience would have been totally different if I had encountered some of Christ's followers at that difficult time in my life. As it was, I waited years to find what could have begun following the trauma I went through.

Whatever pain we see in the world, we can deliver compassion and action together. Paul points to the Holy Spirit's work in changing lives. We don't have to act on our own. The Spirit will direct us and give us courage to leave the mark of Jesus wherever we go. Paul wrote many letters to the new Christians in his day. We can be a "living, loving letter" from Christ with all the power of heaven behind us. Won't you write your letter today?

Galvanize our strength in You, O God. Do not let us walk through this world of pain without an outreached hand. Amen

November 15

BOLDLY GO

Let us therefore approach the throne of grace with boldness, so that we may receive mercy and find grace to help in time of need. Hebrews 4:16

Star Trek is an American science fiction entertainment franchise created by Gene Roddenberry, which debuted in 1966, with several spin-offs, both television and movie productions. A thirteenth theatrical feature will be released in July 2016 in time for the 50th anniversary of the franchise. *Star Trek* has become a "cult phenomenon" with fans, or "Trekkies," holding conventions worldwide. The series has its own "constructed language," Klingon. The series is also noted as an inspiration for many technological advances and for its progressive portrayal of multiracial and multispecies space ship crews working together in harmony. Both humans and aliens serve in "Starfleet," the space-borne humanitarian and peace-keeping armada of the "United Federation of Planets." Relationships among the Star Fleet crew are productive and peaceful. William Shatner, who played Captain Kirk, commented, "(Star Trek is) people looking for answers—and science fiction offers to explain the inexplicable, the same as religion tends to do…"

Star Trek characters go into space not knowing what—or whom—they might encounter. Their original "mantra" was "To boldly go where no man has ever gone" (later changed to "no person"). With God, we are encouraged to "boldly go" as well, into the throne room of His mighty power and grace. There, we can receive forgiveness for our sins, being washed clean. The Holy Spirit provides us with a special "language" when words fail us to express our human miseries and acclamations. Jesus came to earth on a humanitarian mission far greater than that of Starfleet: He came to seek and to save the lost, single-handedly, with no great fanfare. His "cast of characters" included Jews and gentiles, men, women, children, the marginalized, castoffs and infirm. Praise God that His following has lasted for over two thousand years! Just wait for the sequel.

Praise You, Mighty God, that we may come to You boldly and You will hear us. Amen

November 16

JABERWOCKY

Discipline yourselves, keep alert. Like a roaring lion your adversary the devil prowls around, looking for someone to devour. **1 Peter 5:8**

If you recognize the name *Jaberwocky*, you probably know of Lewis Carroll's infamous work, *Alice in Wonderland*. Carroll's original book was published in England in 1871 as *Through the Looking Glass and What Alice Found There*. In most versions of the story, the wily Cheshire Cat recites this nonsensical poem to a very confused Alice. The first verse goes: "'Twas brillig, and the slithy toves/Did gyre and gimble in the wabe/All mimsy were the borogoves/And the mome raths outgrabe." Nonsense? That's exactly what Carroll intended. But Disney left the best part out. The poem continues…

Shmoop.com says Carroll's works appeals to children, who "are entertained by the whimsy and fantasy." Adults "see these layers of complexity emerge." The site describes Carroll's creations as "funny and whimsical….dark, and bitter." The rest of the poem tells the tale of a battle between good and evil. The Jaberwock is a creepy creature who eats Jubjub birds and Bandersnatches for snacks. The hero (left to one's imagination) takes up her "vorpal sword" and waits near the Tumtum tree. With an "uffish" sound, the Jabberwock stands up "with eyes of flame" and "burbles" (*burbles?*). Our hero's vorpal blade goes "snicker-snack" and fells the mighty Jabberwock. (Actually, it's a boy in the poem, but we gals have to have equal time here.)

Don't each of us have Jabberwocks in our lives, figuratively or literally? Whether it's the monster under your three year old's bed, or the mortgage you are having trouble paying, or your tendency to overindulge in chocolate from time to time, we all want a hero to vanquish our foe when we just can't manage it ourselves. We have that Hero in Jesus Christ Who holds us in His warm embrace until the storm passes. Sometimes, too, Jesus makes us the hero in our own stories by giving us the power to send demons packing.

Faithful Savior, thank You for being our Hero. Amen

November 17

I WISH MY LORD KNEW...

Hear my prayer, O Lord; let my cry come to You! Psalm 102:1

Third grade teacher Kyle Schwartz of Denver, Colorado, asked her students to write an answer to a simple question, "I wish my teacher knew..." She planned to use the task as a way to get to know the children better. Many answers were straightforward: "I wish my teacher knew how to play video games," or "I wish my teacher knew more about soccer." But Schwartz got some shocking answers from her kids, many from underprivileged homes. One said, "I wish my teacher knew how much I miss my dad. He was deported to Mexico when I was three years old." Another: "I wish my teacher knew I got bullied on the bus." Schwartz posted some answers on Twitter in March, 2015. Many teachers tweeted they had started using the same assignment with incredible results.

Schwartz's idea jumped out of the schools and into other professionals' laps. One U.S. Coast Guard Admiral held an "I wish my admiral knew..." session. A therapist working with adolescents used "I wish my counselor knew..." People with debilitating diseases posted "I wish people knew that this disease..." A simple act the part of a single teacher began a movement in a nation where we've gotten lost in too much technology and too little face-to-face time.

God already knows all about our concerns, whether we write them down, pray, or just think them. The very act of praying releases God's wonderful grace, pouring down on us like a warm rain. He wraps us in His spectacular love and breathes new life into us each time we approach Him. We can call Him *Abba*, which means "Daddy," an endearment we've been given the right to use as joint heirs of God's kingdom with Christ.

We praise You, Holy God, that You are always available to listen to what we want You to know. Amen

November 18

ENGRAVED INVITATIONS

***Behold, I have engraved you on the palms of my hands; your walls are continually before me.* Isaiah 49:16**

When I was a little girl, my father was assigned to serve as Air Attaché to the American Embassy in Ottawa, Canada. He must have had official duties, but he always said all he did was take Mother to parties. We lived in a fancy part of the city in a home owned by the American Embassy. The parties which my parents attended were given by other dignitaries from all over the world. In turn, my parents held parties and invited these people to our house. I would sneak to a special vantage point at the top of our stairs and watch couples arriving at our opulent home dressed in the finest fashions. The women had perfectly coiffed hair, wore beautiful jewelry and lovely perfume.

Later, going through my parents' things, I found a box of engraved invitations to these Ottawa parties. I saw names of dignitaries from England, France, Spain, Portugal, Mexico, and many other nations. My parents were invited to a dinner in honor of the one-year anniversary of the death of their beloved first lady. Eva Peron died of cancer in 1952, and the invitation was dated 1953. Since my mother had given her dining room set to my niece Virginia (the same set she used to entertain in Canada), I made the decision to frame some of the invitations for Virginia to display in her home.

We are invited to the best banquet ever, and the invitation is engraved right on the palms of our hands. In heaven, there will be a lavish celebration just for us, with hosts of angels singing God's praises. We will be ushered into the throne room where the light of God's countenance will shine like the sun. The train of God's robe will spread out over the entire room. Jesus will sit at the Father's right hand, and we will be the guest of honor.

Almighty God, we look forward to our special banquet with You in our heavenly home. Amen

November 19

THE END OF THE BOOK

Therefore, my beloved brothers, be steadfast, immovable, always abounding in the work of the Lord, knowing that in the Lord your labor is not in vain. 1 Corinthians **15:58**

Any woman is welcome at our book club, and some come for the fellowship even if they haven't read the book. One member sometimes doesn't get to the end before the meeting date. She doesn't want us to tell her the ending, which makes discussing the book a little challenging. She will put her fingers in her ears and say, "La la la la" if we talk about the book's conclusion.

Some people are a little afraid of the Book of Revelation because of the descriptions of things to come. From Martin Luther to John Wesley to John Calvin, even the greatest of theologians have struggled with the last book of the Bible. There are several things we need to remember lest we fall off the edge of our consciousness and become, as Wesley described it, "utterly despairing" of ever trying to make sense of it.

First, remember Jesus is the central figure in Revelation. He *is the Revelation* (v.1:1). He himself tells us, "Do not be afraid" (v. 2:19). The book is about praising Jesus, so we can't get all bungled up in the rich and vivid word pictures. Also remember this is "apocalyptic literature," popular a long time ago and designed to give hope to oppressed people. The entire book, if read with a focus on Jesus Christ, tells us God is still in control right until the end, and He will free us from the enemy. Biblical scholar Bruce Metzger said, "The descriptions don't mean what they say; they mean what they mean." The frightening images are just that: images, meant to portray something, not to be taken literally. If you are still concerned, it might be best to read *this* book with a trusted friend or your local Bible scholar. Don't miss the last, rich Bible story of the All-Powerful Christ vanquishing our foe once and for all. And don't stick your fingers in your ears.

Jesus, we thank You that Your Word does exactly what it is intended to do. Amen

November 20

BLESSED TO BE A BLESSING

The LORD said to Abram, "Go from your country and your kindred and your father's house to the land that I will show you. And I will make of you a great nation, and I will bless you and make your name great, so that you will be a blessing. **Genesis 12:1-2**

God told Abram, or Abraham as he was eventually known, to leave everything familiar to him and set out on a journey with no known destination. Abraham was seventy-five years old when he finally reached the land of Canaan, the place promised by God. By today's standards, Abraham should have been receiving Social Security checks for several years, and sipping lemonade from his rocking chair on the porch. Instead, God sent him on a journey of importance for the human race. What would you have thought if, in your dotage, God told you He was going to make you "blessed to be a blessing" for the rest of the world? Abraham was not perfect. But perfection is not what God wants. He wants obedience.

Abraham's obedience to God is a unifying theme we see throughout the rest of the Bible. God chooses us; it's not the other way around. Our response as a person or a nation can have a profound effect on what happens next. Abraham had a heart for God, never questioning God's grand plan.

Do we as modern Christians have this kind of "trusting expectation" that everything will turn out for the best? Do we really believe Romans 8:28, "And we know that for those who love God all things work together for good, for those who are called according to his purpose?" Each of us is "blessed to be a blessing." That is our calling when we accept Christ as our Lord and Savior. What it means for each of us is in God's hands, not ours. Our part is to follow God's lead willingly. We can do that by studying His Word and learning His will.

O Lord, I am not perfect either, but I want to be "blessed to be a blessing" for You. Amen

November 21

TEXTS FROM JESUS

***Ask, and it will be given you; search, and you will find; knock, and the door will be opened for you.* Matthew 7:7**

What if the Lord started sending us signs via text messaging? What would those look like? I'm not very "text savvy," but I've learned a fair amount from my grandkids. I thought BTW meant "bring the wheelchair," but it turns out, it stands for "by the way." And TTYL means "talk to you later," not "louder." If I can figure this out, I'm sure Jesus would be a whiz at it.

So your smart phone makes the little sound that signals a text message coming in. You don't have Jesus in your address book, but He has more power than the cell companies, so His name appears clearly at the top of the message. The message says, IMU, which means "I miss you." *Please do not text back* OMG. That would most certainly offend your Lord and Savior. If you text back, BBZL ("been busy lately"), He might say, HT? ("how's that?"). You say, LIAB&U? ("life is a bear, and you?"). He says, IKICI ("I know, I created it"). Then He adds, STBU, which the kids think means "sucks to be you." But Jesus actually means "so try better understanding." Next, you text HOW? ("how?"), and Jesus fires back RYBIFU ("read your Bible, it's for you"). WDIS? from you ("where do I start?"). PG1 He says (page 1). OIC, you text ("oh, I see"). Then you add, CLESS ("clueless"), to which Jesus responds, IWSU ("I will show you"). You go get your Bible and open it to Genesis 1:1, and suddenly you are flooded with an intense understanding of the words printed therein. It's like they are A&W ("alive and well") and M&B ("moving and breathing"). You reply, IGIN! ("I get it now!"). Jesus says, TTYLF, which the kids think means "talk to you later, friend," but He really means, "the thing you longed for."

Jesus doesn't really need to text with us because He can actually talk to us without a phone. All we have to do is listen.

Deliver us from technology, Lord, and talk to us Your way. Amen

November 22

LORD OF LORDS, WORD OF WORDS

In the beginning was the Word, and the Word was with God, and the Word was God. John 1:1

Once when I was visiting my parents out of state, my father took me to the public library to print off my boarding pass for the trip home. My parents never owned a computer, but my father was fascinated with how easily I navigated my way around the airline's website and how I could type something, but if I made a mistake, I could simply delete it and type in the correct words. My dad was very organized and spent a good deal of time typing out lists and instructions and personal letters, all on an old Smith Corona typewriter. I too learned to type long before computers. Young people today don't realize the frustration of complete an entire document on a typewriter and finding an error. The entire piece would have to be redone.

Think of the dedication of people long ago who wrote longhand translations of the Bible in various languages. Then came the printing press and all the necessary type setting. What if no one had ever taken the time to make the words of the Bible available to others? Such perfect words would have been lost forever. But that was not God's plan. He set those people in the right places at the right time with the right technology to complete the job of passing His Word down through the ages. Isaiah 55:11 quotes God as saying, "So shall My word be that goes out from My mouth; it shall not return to Me empty, but it shall accomplish that which I purpose, and succeed in the thing for which I sent it." God's Word is His very essence coming to us for His purposes. How we receive it and what we do with it is of utmost importance.

Even though we may struggle to comprehend every nuance in the Bible, God's Word is critical to our journey here on earth as well.

You are the Word, Lord, and Your Word is life to us. Amen

November 23

OUTFOXING THE IMPOSSIBLE

We are hard pressed on every side, but not crushed; perplexed, but not in despair; persecuted, but not abandoned; struck down, but not destroyed. **2 Corinthians 4:8-9**

Canadian born actor Michael J. Fox was at the peak of his career when, at age twenty-nine, he was diagnosed with Parkinson's disease. This condition is a degenerative disorder of the central nervous system mainly affecting the body's motor coordination. Caused by the death of dopamine-generating cells in the brain, the disease has no known cure. Symptoms include shaking and difficulty walking and thinking, behavior problems, and dementia in later stages. Depression is also common among people with this diagnosis.

Fox waited several years before disclosing his condition to the public. Semi-retired from acting, he has become a strong advocate for research. He created the Michael J. Fox Foundation, and he has been given many awards for his tireless work for those afflicted with Parkinson's. In his first book, aptly named *Lucky Man*, Fox speaks of his initial denial of the disease, drinking to excess, and generally giving up. Fox is now sober, embracing his disease, and concentrating on being an advocate for others. His second book, *Always Looking Up: The Adventures of an Incurable Optimist* describes how Fox began campaigning for stem-cell research. A prime-time special, which aired in 2009, showed the actor's condition, his family, and his work.

Michael J. Fox is a prime example of an individual who turned a devastating diagnosis into a positive, life-giving message for others with debilitating diseases and disabilities. Life could have spiraled downward for Fox, leaving him bitter and depressed. But instead, he has used the gifts he had—notoriety and the public's ear—to transform his life into a living sacrifice for his fellow sufferers. Though his life may not have turned out the way he expected, his legacy will be far greater than that of a Hollywood superstar.

Lord, bless those who live with life-changing conditions and bless those who give so much back for their sake. Amen

November 24

WHICH PAIN IS BETTER?

My soul also is struck with terror, while you, O Lord—how long?
Psalm 6:3

She was about my age and close to my height and weight. We both had blonde hair. Depression had been an issue for each of us in the past. But there was one difference between us: when she hurt inside, she took a sharp object and carved up the skin on her wrists, her legs, whatever she could reach. She had been hospitalized for mental illness and then sent to the sheltered workshop where I worked as a counselor. It was 1972 and her program was called "work readiness:" preparing her for a job she would never be able to hold down because of her profound, untreated clinical depression. She had been placed in the laundry area, where she had easy access to wire coat hangers. Everyone was clueless. Nobody was cutting themselves back then, and I was the first person she had shown.

"Why?" I asked. I was naïve, just out of graduate school myself. Her answer: "Because I can control hurting myself. I can't control when other people hurt me." Cutting is a distraction, a brief respite from the emotional pain a person feels. "Self-harm typically starts at about age fourteen," says Karen Conterio, a former cutter and author of the book, *Bodily Harm*. "As more kids become aware of the practice, more are trying it," as young as eleven or twelve. The cutter may have serious emotional problems, a history of sexual abuse, or an unhappy home life. Some are just "regular kids going through the…struggle for self-identity," says Wendy Lader, PhD, clinical director for SAFE Alternatives, a program in Naperville, Illinois.

The cutting today's young people engage in is a psychiatric condition which needs treatment from mental health professionals trained in dealing with this condition. If Jesus were to encounter a cutter today, He would be in the healing business, not the business of exorcism.

Healing Lord, we beseech You to make Yourself known to these good children who feel the need to harm themselves. May they know that You provide light in their darkest hours. Amen

November 25

BEARING GIFTS AND TALENTS

Now there are varieties of gifts, but the same Spirit. **1 Corinthians 12:4**

Bill Elliston is a professional cyclist who happens to be married to my niece, Virginia. Our whole family knows that Bill is very dedicated to his sport. When he is not racing in events all over the globe, he coaches and trains in and around their home town of Easton, Pennsylvania, putting on hundreds of miles a week even in the off-season. Bill even rides his bicycle to his aunt's house, ninety miles from home, every year on Thanksgiving Day, no matter what the weather. He sets out on his cycle before Virginia leaves the house in the car with the food she brings to share at the family meal.

Virginia says they frequently arrive at the same time, but Bill gets far more attention. All the cousins storm out of the house, bringing Bill hot apple cider and holiday treats to replenish him after his arduous trip. Virginia jokes that she often stands quietly by in a snow bank, holding her casserole dishes and waiting for someone to notice her instead of her husband.

Our family all love Bill and we are very proud of him. However, this annual scenario reminds me how we often pay attention to those people in life who "make a splash" by having some outstanding talent, some highly observable trait we admire or envy. The quiet casserole-bearers often go through life overlooked and underappreciated. Both are loved by God; some just get more human attention than others.

The Bible says we all have talents, big or small, and each person's talent is equally important to God. Let's remember to notice—and express our appreciation—for those who perform small, quiet tasks that keep the world going. It's not all about the most visible, but also about those who perform in the background.

Let us be ever mindful, Dear Lord, of the talents of all Your beautiful children. May we show appreciation for the smallest gift brought in Your name. Amen

November 26

THE HOLY TRIANGLE

In the beginning when God created the heavens and the earth, the earth was a formless void and darkness covered the face of the deep, while a wind from God swept over the face of the waters. Genesis 1:1-2

My father was an Air Force pilot and he didn't believe in it. Not one branch of the United States military acknowledges its existence, but the Bermuda Triangle has been rumored for many years to have mysteriously swallowed up a number of aircraft and ships. The region forms a triangle from Florida to Bermuda to Puerto Rico, and many credit the mysterious happenings there to paranormal activity or extraterrestrial beings. Although the legends still abound, there has never been any significant proof the area is any more dangerous than other shipping channels used daily.

God, Jesus and the Holy Spirit form a different kind of triangle, one we can get lost in without fear. According to Wikipedia.com, "a *vortex* is a region in a fluid medium in which the flow is mostly rotating around an axis line." Examples of a *vortex* are smoke rings created by moving air; tornados and cyclones; and whirlpools made by circulating water. Once formed, a vortex acts strangely. I can imagine much swirling, twisting, and interacting in the power of the Living God, the *vortex* of love and grace surrounding Him. He walks with me, leads me, shelters me and most definitely *moves* both my soul and spirit—and sometimes even my body. John the Baptist described a coming *vortex* of Jesus' power when he said, "I baptize you with water for repentance, but One Who is more powerful than I is coming after me...He will baptize you with the Holy Spirit and fire" (Matthew 3:11). On the day of Pentecost, "suddenly from heaven there came a sound like the rush of a violent wind... Divided tongues, as of fire, appeared among them, and ...they began to speak in other languages..." (Acts 2:1-2). It is easy to get caught up in the *vortex* of God's power!

Blessed Lord, catch me up in Your power and love and send me far and wide in Your holy Name. Amen

November 27

TRANSPARENCY

But whatever anyone dares to boast of...I also dare to boast of that. Are they Hebrews? So am I. Are they Israelites? So am I. Are they descendants of Abraham? So am I. Are they ministers of Christ? I am a better one: with far greater labors, far more imprisonments, with countless floggings, and often near death. **2 Corinthians 11:21-23**

I am an open book. I meet someone new, and within ten minutes, they know more about me than they probably want to know. I never used to be that way. Growing up with my alcoholic mom and my very private dad, I was loathe to tell anybody about my family. Would my mother be in a drunken rage? Would my father be embarrassed for someone new to come to our home and see our dirty little secrets? Don't open *that* Pandora's box.

When I became a Christian, I discovered that we are *all* broken. Sharing our imperfect stories might just help other people through their struggles too. At first glance, Paul's words in today's Scripture might seem like "story topping." Is he saying, "Woe is me. I'm the most persecuted person on the planet, and nobody has had it worse off than I have"? Actually, he's saying the exact opposite. Paul wants people to know what he's endured in the name of Christ so others will identify with him and listen more closely because they've been through some challenging times themselves.

When I wrote my memoir, *Then I Am Strong: Moving From My Mother's Daughter to God's Child*, several titles were considered before this one was chosen. The final choice was another passage of Paul's words, 2 Corinthians 12:10, "Therefore I am content with weaknesses, insults, hardships, persecutions, and calamities for the sake of Christ; for whenever I am weak, *then I am strong*" (italics mine). The book reveals my days "BC" (before accepting Christ as my Lord and Savior), God's miraculous intervention, and my growth in Christ since that time. I believe it is through the transparent sharing of my experiences that I can best serve my Lord.

Stir us to tell our stories for Your glory, Lord. Amen

November 28

SOMETIMES PARENTS

The fear of the LORD is the beginning of knowledge; fools despise wisdom and instruction. **Proverbs 1:7**

My friend's granddaughter is very young and already has two little children and a "sometimes man" who seems ill prepared to raise these children with their mother. This young mother was recently diagnosed with a debilitating disease that will sap her energy and require medical monitoring for the rest of her life. She posted on Face Book that she is so tired she doesn't know if she can get through another day. My friend's daughter, the mother of this girl and grandmother of the two babies, also has health challenges. My friend is concerned for the future of her family members.

Many young children are not given the attention they so desperately require from those charged by blood and society to be their caretakers. Many parents, particularly those in low income brackets, are overwhelmed by parenting duties. Public assistance may seem the only logical sustenance for one with no role models, no job skills, no gainful employment. Babies happen with alarming regularity, and each child deserves a secure future with food, shelter, education and love every day. I saw the void in homes I visited in the 1970s. It had been there before I came, and it is still there today.

Families involved in a faith community have a better opportunity to connect with others struggling to balance home, family, and work. The visibility of families in need within the church community can lead to earlier intervention. Pastors and church elders provide a crucial service in helping people get help. Yet many times churches turn a blind eye to those who appear "different" or "too needy." God clearly states the poor in spirit will "inherit the kingdom of God" (Matthew 5:3). Is there someone in your church or community you have passed by? Let them know about God's amazing love.

Father of orphans and Protector of widows, lead us to peace and fairness for all. Amen

November 29

HOW LOW CAN YOU GO?

Then Abram fell on his face; and God said to him, "As for Me, this is My covenant with you: You shall be the ancestor of a multitude of nations. No longer shall your name be Abram, but your name shall be Abraham. **Genesis 17:3-5**

The *Limbo* dance originated on the island of Trinidad. A horizontal bar, known as the limbo bar, is placed atop two vertical bars. Participants must attempt to go under the bar backwards, looking up. A person is eliminated from the game when he knocks the bar off the side poles or falls down. Each round, the limbo bar is lowered slightly. The game is won when the last person is able to pass under the bar without touching it or falling.

Originally, the Limbo took place at wakes in Trinidad and Tobago, with people beginning low and gradually getting higher, to signify the dearly departed rising from this life to heaven. When the order was reversed, and accompanied by Afro-Caribbean drums, the Limbo became widely popular with tourists. Recording artist Chubby Checker's song "Limbo Rock" rose to number two on Billboard Top 100. Checker said, "How low can you go?"

The Limbo reminds me of another position important to our worship of God. Abraham fell *face first* on the ground when God addressed him individually and made a covenant with him. This was no tourist game: God was telling Abraham he wanted him to become the "ancestor of a multitude of nations." He even got a name change, from Abram to Abraham, a frequent occurrence when God had a special task for one of His chosen.

How low can *you* go to show your humility toward the Almighty? My pride often keeps me from admitting my total dependence on God, and I use my stiff joints as an excuse for not physically bowing before my Lord. But humility is a heart attitude we must practice if we are to realize God's greatness and our desperate need for Him in our lives.

Lord, help me bow low and humble myself in Your mighty presence. Amen

November 30

IN THE FULLNESS OF TIME

Joseph also went from the town of Nazareth in Galilee to Judea, to the city of David called Bethlehem...to be registered with Mary, to whom he was engaged and who was expecting a child. Luke 2:4-5

Many years ago, I studied the Bethel Series, a 1961 Bible study developed by the Adult Christian Education Foundation in Madison, Wisconsin. We reviewed all the events that came together just prior to the birth of Jesus, each with specific meaning. Christ came into the world at the perfect time.

Alexander the Great studied under Aristotle in their native country of Greece. As King of the Macedonian Empire in the fourth century B.C., Alexander brought the Greek language and culture to all of the nations he conquered, unifying the people in a new way. Within the next two centuries, the Roman Empire had expanded throughout Europe and beyond, leading to a long period of peace under Roman rule. The Romans built many roads, making trade possible among a wide variety of nations and peoples. The Romans rulers ensured there were no wars between rival tribes, nations, or factions. And every Hebrew man, woman and child knew about the old time prophets' predictions of a coming Messiah. Though many Jews were living beyond their native land of Israel, the dream of the Savior was still alive.

This period in history is referred to in Galatians 4:4-5: "when the fullness of time had come, God sent his Son, born of a woman, born under the law, in order to redeem those who were under the law, so we might receive adoption as children." The stage was set, the players were in place, and a star broke forth from its moorings in space and sped across the night sky. A man and his very pregnant wife found a stable when no room was left at the inn, and a Child was born. He came in the fullness of the world's time and yours and mine.

Thank You, Jesus, for being our "Wonderful Counselor, Mighty God, Everlasting Father, Prince of Peace." Amen

December

December 1

CHRISTMAS IS COMING!

For to us a child is born, to us a son is given, and the government will be on his shoulders. And he will be called Wonderful Counselor, Mighty God, Everlasting Father, Prince of Peace. Isaiah 9:6

I read a while back about a mother who cleverly engaged her children in the story of Advent. She purchased a nativity set, with all the usual characters: Jesus, Mary and Joseph, the shepherds, the wise men, a couple of sheep, a donkey and a cow. She set up the little stable in a prominent place in her house, and then hid all the characters. She gave her children clues where the pieces might be, with each appropriately far away from the stable to seem as if they were making a journey. Joseph and Mary arrived first, the shepherds were nearby, but the wise men had the biggest distance to travel. Of course, Jesus did not take His place until Christmas Eve, when the family read the Christmas Story from the second chapter of Luke.

I thought this sounded like a delightful way to get kids to look forward to Christmas for reasons other than the gifts they hoped to receive. Because I read this when I already had ten grandchildren, I worried that at this point in my life, I'd forget where I hid the little figurines. But God reminds us every Christmas of His unspeakable gift of His only Son, Jesus, Who entered this world as a human baby, lived among us, and went willingly to a horrible death to fulfill God's promise of redemption, once for all, for our sins. Although He did all of this in only thirty-three short years, His love lives on in the grace and compassion we as Christians still know today. Now *that's* an engaging story!

Lord Jesus, as we see You as a tiny baby at the celebration of Your birth, help us to remember that You are more than just a figurine in a manger scene. You are our Lord and Savior, Wonderful Counselor, Mighty God, Everlasting Father and Prince of Peace. Come, Lord Jesus!

December 2

CHRISTMAS JOY

Then the angel said to them, "Do not be afraid, for behold, I bring you good tidings of great joy which will be to all people. Luke 2:10

Recently, I saw an ad on television for a big box store's Black Friday deals. Listeners were assured that "more ways to Christmas joy" awaited them if they would rise before dawn and rush to the nearest location of this establishment for the best deals on toys, electronics, clothing and anything else that would bring them "joy."

I don't have to rise before dawn to know our nation has largely lost the true meaning of Christmas. When Jesus was born, an angel told the frightened shepherds not to be afraid, the news he brought was of "great joy which will be to all people." In today's Scripture, the angel didn't tell the shepherds to get their shekels ready to spend on worldly items. He didn't tell them joy was to be found in the marketplace. The message was about a Baby, the Prince of Peace, born of a teenage girl, who came to bring salvation to the world. A heavenly multitude of singers appeared and began to sing praises to God. The shepherds' lives were changed forever, and ours have been too. No gift receipt needed, no standing in line for hours waiting for a door to open, no battling crazy crowds to be the first to get a new item. Christ's love is given freely to those of us who believe. That's what Christmas is about, and we don't need a thirty-second commercial, a coupon, or a special code number to get in on the deal.

Great God of the Universe, assist us in resisting the worldly pull of material things which has tried to dominate the celebration of Your birth. Give us the words, especially during this holy season, to help others understand why You came and what an unspeakable gift You brought to us. Amen

December 3

SAVE US ALL FROM SATAN'S POWER

I am sending you to (your own people) to open their eyes and turn them from darkness to light, and from the power of Satan to God, so that they may receive forgiveness of sins and a place among those who are sanctified by faith in Me. **Acts 26:17-18**

I first accepted Jesus Christ as my personal Savior in October, 1977. So many things were new to me, since I had not been raised in a Christian home. I truly felt like a child again, taking in all the wonder of my new relationship with the King of the universe.

That December, the lyrics to my "favorite" Christmas carols suddenly had new meaning. The one I was most astounded by was "God Rest Ye Merry Gentlemen," which I had sung all my life at holiday parties and school events (yes, we were allowed to sing Christian songs in school back then). The line, "to save us all from Satan's power, when we were gone astray," suddenly had real meaning. Satan issn't just some cartoon character in a red suit brandishing a spear; he is a real being who delights in making people's lives miserable in a variety of ways. I now knew Satan had fallen from grace when he and his buddies tried to overthrow the kingdom of heaven, and he's had an ax to grind with God ever since. The Bible says even Satan's buddies the demons, believe in Jesus and shudder at the mention of His name (James 2:19) and Satan will one day be hurled down in defeat (Revelation 12:9). Thanks be to God we have a Protector in Jesus Christ, Who will always be with us to ward off Satan's lies and attacks!

Lord Jesus, in the season of Your miraculous birth, build in us an abiding trust and reliance on Your power to defeat our old enemy Satan, whenever we have gone astray. Thank You for having already won the victory over sin and evil. Amen

December 4

AND HOLY IS YOUR NAME

From now on all generations will call me blessed, for the Mighty One has done great things for me, and holy is His name. **Luke 1:48b-49**

I play drums and sing in the contemporary Christian worship group at our church. One of my favorite Advent songs is "Holy Is Your Name" by David Haas, based on Mary's "Magnificat" (Luke 1:46-55). This is a song of praise to Mary's God while she is visiting her cousin Elizabeth, who is also expecting a child who will become John the Baptist. I admit I have read this passage in Luke many times, and I sometimes "skim" the verses because I am so familiar with it. But, when this song shows up in our list for an Advent Sunday, singing and playing the tune takes me to a holy place.

Written in the first person, the song lyrics recount how Mary pours out her heart and soul to God for His astounding choice to involve her in His plan to save the world. Mary describes how God is now fulfilling what He had promised through the prophets: to send a Savior to this world to be "mindful of the people (He has) chosen." Yet this same God will "scatter the proud-hearted and destroy the might of princes." Each verse of the song ends with Mary singing, "And holy is Your name."

During this Advent season, everything around us seems to scream, "Buy me! I'm just what you need!" Let's remember the *real* reason for the season is about God's free gift to all who have sinned (which is everybody). Jesus is just what we *really* need. And Holy is His Name.

God of Everlasting Mercy, take us to a holy place during this Advent season so we may share with Mary, Joseph and the other players in marveling at the birth of Your Son. And Holy is His name! Amen

December 5

THE LITTLE DRUMMER BOY

And going into the house they saw the Child with Mary His mother, and they fell down and worshiped Him. Then, opening their treasures, they offered Him gifts, gold and frankincense and myrrh.
Matthew 2:11

The classic American Christmas song we know today as "The Little Drummer Boy" was originally named "Carol of the Drum." Composer and teacher Katherine Kennicott Davis wrote the song in 1941. The lyrics tell how a poor boy was summoned by the Magi to where Jesus lay. With no suitable gift to bring, the boy played his drum for the Christ. The boy recalls, "I played my best for Him," and "He smiled at me."

As a drummer myself, I was so moved by this song one Christmas, I took several pairs of old drumsticks, had holes drilled in them, and spray painted them gold. I put them together in the form of a cross, and then glued a decoupage picture of the drummer boy to the sticks, added a Christmas ribbon, placed a hook on the back for hanging, and gave them as gifts to family members. I take my own "drummer cross" to our church each December and hang it above the church's drum set.

I have often thought what it would have felt like to play a drum for the infant Jesus. It seems an odd thing to do, playing a drum for a baby. Drums can be loud, but they can also be played very softly. If I had a chance to bring something to the Baby Jesus, I'm not sure it would be my drum, but what should it be instead? In my mind, it wouldn't have mattered what I brought on that magic night two thousand years ago, and it doesn't matter what I bring today. Just so I bring myself, because that is all He wants. Just me, no worldly trappings or "stuff" to prove we can "do" something. It was a nice gesture of the little drummer boy, but Jesus would have smiled at him anyway. After all, Jesus loved that boy, whether he played the drum or not.

Come, they told me, bring myself to Jesus. He is my Rock and my Redeemer. Amen

December 6

A STRANGE WAY TO SAVE THE WORLD

***An angel of the Lord appeared to him in a dream and said, "Joseph son of David, do not be afraid to take Mary home as your wife, because what is conceived in her is from the Holy Spirit."* Matthew 1:20**

The Christian contemporary group 4Him recorded a song called "A Strange Way to Save the World" (written by Mark Harris, David Allen Clark and Donald Koch), which tells the story of Jesus' birth from the point of view of His step-father Joseph. The song has special meaning to me, since I am stepmother of three and adoptive mother of one, and I've always been fascinated by the special relationship that develops between children and non-biological parents.

Joseph must have had some very anxious moments when his fiancée, Mary, told him she was pregnant, especially when she shared the outlandish circumstances by which she got that way. We read in Matthew 1:19 that, after the angel came and told him Mary's story was true, Joseph "was faithful to the law, and yet did not want to expose (Mary) to public disgrace." Joseph took Mary as his wife, and wonder of wonders, God entrusted to Joseph the responsibility of raising His son while He lived on this earth. Let's hear it for step-parents!

The most amazing thing is that Joseph was human enough to wonder what on earth God was thinking. In the lyrics of the 4Him song, Joseph ponders the following: Why Mary? Why Joseph? Why at that time in history? Why a human-yet-God baby, born in a *manger* no less? The song goes on to say, when Joseph saw "the message from the angel come to life," all he knew was God's immense love for the world. Joseph shouldered his God-given responsibility to love Jesus and care for Him while He lived in the flesh among us. How can we do any less when He lives in our hearts?

God of Strange Ways, open our minds to see Your purpose in the world when it is clearly visible, and grant us faith to trust You when we cannot understand Your ways. Amen

December 7

THE DAY PARADISE WEPT

When the oppressor is no more, and destruction has ceased, and marauders have vanished from the land, then a throne shall be established in steadfast love in the tent of David, and on it shall sit in faithfulness a Ruler who seeks justice and is swift to do what is right. **Isaiah 16:4-5**

In 1941, on a Sunday morning at Howard Air Force Base in Panama City, my parents had just played a round of golf. Returning to the officer's club, they heard devastating news: the Japanese had just bombed the entire U.S. Pacific Fleet at Pearl Harbor. The tropical landscape was split into shards by 353 Japanese fighter planes, bombers, and torpedo planes, launched from six aircraft carriers. All eight US Navy battleships were damaged, with four sunk. When the smoke began to clear, 2,403 Americans were dead, 1,178 others wounded. Japanese losses were light: twenty-nine aircraft and five midget submarines destroyed, sixty-four servicemen killed, and one Japanese man captured. President Roosevelt declared war on Japan the following day, proclaiming December 7, 1941 "a date which will live in infamy."

Weeks before, the Pacific Fleet Band had been gathering in Honolulu for a month-long tournament to determine the best Navy musicians. The last round of the elimination tournament was scheduled, unknowingly, for the evening of December 6th. The Arizona band was in first place but did not compete that night. The following morning, the Nevada band rose to play Morning Colors, the melody drifting across the harbor. While they played, the Japanese attack began. The entire Arizona band at their battle stations were among those killed in the attack. The band was posthumously declared the tournament winners.

Many say America lost its innocence that day. My father was placed on ready alert at Howard, and my mother and my sister returned to the US. May the tragedy at Pearl Harbor always remind us of the price of peace.

All Powerful God, bring us a day with no war, no disease, no sorrow. Amen

December 8

NAUGHTY OR NICE?

Every good gift and every perfect gift is from above, coming down from the Father of lights. James 1:17

What's up with parents at Christmas time? We all become like drill sergeants, making our kids toe the line. The other twelve months of the year, moms and dads and grannies and grandpas have other ways of disciplining their offspring. Come December, it's all about being naughty or nice or else! First it was Santa's naughty list. If you're on it, kid, you are doomed. No Christmas presents for you. Just coal in your stocking, or you don't get that electronic gizmo or whatever else we threaten them with. Santa wasn't enough. Now we have the Elf of the Shelf, who according to the website of the same name, "is a cleverly rhymed children's book explaining the story of Santa's scout elves, who are sent to be Santa's eyes and ears at children's homes around the world." You will be pleased to know you can "adopt" your own little snitch, and there is even a *Birthday Elf* if your kid doesn't wise up after December 25. I saw an ad for our Jewish friends: Mensch on a Bench, who guards the Menorah, so maybe that's not so restrictive.

We've come too far from the real meaning of Christmas. Before I was a follower of Jesus, I used to get annoyed when I'd see people put signs out that said, "Happy Birthday, Jesus!" I didn't understand His birthday is really what it's all about. Even Old Saint Nick gets a bad rap, because the original one never had a "Naughty or Nice List." The modern figure of Santa Claus is derived from Saint Nicholas, the historical Greek bishop known for lavishing gifts upon folks without any strings attached.

I think we should start a movement to teach kids being good is a good thing to do and isn't tied in any way to whether or not they "get the goods" at Christmas time or any other special occasion or regular day for that matter. Every good gift comes from God, period.

Father of Lights, thank You for providing us with all we need, abundantly. Amen

December 9

THE JERRY SPRINGER SCHOOL OF MANAGEMENT

Whatever your task, put yourselves into it, as done for the Lord and not for your masters. Colossians 3:23

It was comical, if it hadn't been so sad. Following what I called a "hostile takeover," I had been laid off from a two-year college and was working out my last weeks of employment. As a counselor, I did not usually answer telephones, but the receptionists were swamped, so I picked up a call and helped the person on the line. The next thing I knew, I was called into the vice president's office, where he and the admissions director—a new hire—awaited my arrival. While I sat stunned and silent, the admissions director gave me a ten minute lecture on what my job responsibilities were, not including answering the phone. He was not my superior, and had been there a few weeks to my ten years. The vice-president—part of the "new regime" following the takeover— listened quietly, with his finger touching his lips as if he was willing himself not to comment. Finally, I could stand no more. Speaking to the vice-president, I said, "Are you going to sit here and let this man talk to me like this?" His amazing reply: "I've discovered over the years it is best to let employees work out their differences themselves." *Where did this guy learn his management skills?* When the blood bath was over and I was allowed to leave, I wasted no time in filing a human rights complaint, for which I received a denial on my last day of employment.

As Christians, we sometimes walk a fine line between following the Lord and attempting to work in an imperfect work environment. Paul says we are to work as though for the Lord, and not for our human masters. Employment is a way to serve God and demonstrate how Christ would want us to behave. If a company's policies and procedures aren't being followed—or there are none—it is difficult to know what to do. Galatians 6:4 says we are to "test (our) own work," which "will become a cause for pride." Others' performance is not our concern. It's God's.

O Lord, walk beside us as we work for the good of all, and especially for those of the family of faith. (Galatians 6:10) Amen

December 10

THE ARESNIC SEASON

The wolf shall live with the lamb, the leopard shall lie down with the kid, the calf and the lion and the fatling together, and a little Child shall lead them. **Isaiah 11:6**

In my graduate counseling program, I took a class called Family Dynamics about how families deal with difficult times, like when everyone arrives home and each is trying to get his or her needs met at once. The parents are tired from working all day. The kids have been at school or day care and they want attention. Everyone is hungry and crabby. The professor aptly called this time "The Arsenic Hour." It seems as though everyone is ready to go for the throat until they get fed, rested, clear their heads and settle down.

I think the Holidays have become "The Arsenic Season" in our society. The "season" begins earlier every year, with stores and websites advertising and displaying holiday gifts before the leaves have fallen from the trees. "Holiday gifts" somehow have morphed from socks and underwear to expensive toys and electronics many families cannot afford. I dislike "Black Friday," when the stores offer "the best deals" (and then offer even better deals afterwards), and crowds of people make idiots of themselves camping out in freezing weather to be first in the doors of their favorite "big box" store.

The birth of Christ is *not* a capitalist celebration! *Christmas* originated from the Old English term, *Christ's Mass*, a religious ceremony commemorating the birth of the Savior. It is generally accepted the event occurred around the 25th of December. The phrase *Cristemasse* was first recorded in 1038, the components of the term having both Greek and Hebrew origins. The English term *mass* evolved from the Anglo-Saxon word *maesse*, derived from the Latin *missa*, meaning "to send." So Christmas really *is* about God sending His only Son Jesus Christ into the world to seek and to save the lost. If Christmas seems to feel more like "The Arsenic Season" to us, we need to take a step back and remember its true meaning.

Holy Son of God, we simply celebrate Your coming to save us all. Amen

December 11

MARY DIDN'T LAUGH

And she gave birth to her firstborn Son and wrapped Him in bands of cloth, and laid Him in a manger. Luke 2:7

In Walter Wangerin Jr.'s wonderful work, *The Book of God: The Bible As A Novel,* the author writes, "Mary rode slowly toward Bethlehem. Joseph led the donkey, but Mary's condition controlled its speed, the beast walked with a long bobbing of its head." The animal knew she was uncomfortable. They entered Bethlehem but the enrollment ordered by Herod had begun, and the town was packed with Jews. No rooms to be found—Mary could hardly hold herself upright. She was perspiring. Suddenly, "the donkey shook its head and…shuffled into an easy trot," forcing Joseph to run alongside. *'Joseph, it's time!'* Mary exclaimed. "The donkey…wound around a large inn to the back…a cave…enclosed by a rude wooden gate…Mary gasped…*'It's time!'*" Wangerin's description of exactly how he envisioned Jesus' birth is as dramatic as any Hollywood production. It makes me feel as if I were *there* in that stable with Mary, Joseph, the animals, the angels, the shepherds…and a tiny Baby Who would change the course of history forever.

What a contrast between Mary and Sarah, Abraham's wife, who scoffed God and laughed at the proclamation that she would give birth at her advanced age. Young and innocent, Mary humbly accepted the angel's astounding news, even though it meant she might be stoned to death for an unplanned pregnancy. God said He had heard Sarah laugh, and she denied it. Mary trusted her Lord to do with His servant as He pleased.

In this holiest of seasons, let us seek to be honest and straightforward with our Lord, taking His Word as true and His promises as real. Celebrating Jesus' birth is a joyous occasion about a tiny Child entering this broken world. His birth is a beginning. The end of the story is reason for joy as well.

Jesus, You came into this world like any other human child and lived with broken people to make us whole through You. Thanks be to God for Your unspeakable gift! Amen

December 12

BLOODLESS SURGERY

Then Peter came and said to Him, "Lord, if another member of the church sins against me, how often should I forgive? As many as seven times?" Jesus said to him, "Not seven times, but, I tell you, seventy-seven times." Matthew 18:21-22

"Forgiving is a minor miracle, a bloodless surgery we perform on our spirits." These words from Lewis Smedes' book *Keeping Hope Alive*, remind me of how often we talk about Jesus shedding His blood for us. Yet, many of us have had a difficult time forgiving someone in our lives and have lived with anger, resentment and spiritual exhaustion, sometimes for years. Here is how Smedes says forgiveness happens.

First, we somehow start to see the offender as a "blemished person," similar to ourselves. We are all broken. The Bible says "all have sinned and fall short of the glory of God" (Romans 3:23). It would be a lie for the offended one to say she or he has never "fallen short." Next, we "surrender our precious right to get even." We may want retaliation, to hurt the other person, as we have been hurt. But this only prolongs our own agony.

Last, we "gradually find the will" to stop thinking of the offender in negative terms. Forgiving doesn't mean the wrongdoing never occurred. It just means we have discovered the grace to move on from a place of impasse to one of renewed spiritual growth. Jesus knew that forgiving is the healthier choice. Another famous writer, Ann Landers, wisely said, "Refusing to forgive is like letting the other person live in your head rent free." And who wants that!

This Christmas season, let's remember that Christ came into this world to die—shed His blood—for us. But He also asks each of us to carry forgiveness in our hearts, and that requires no bloodshed.

Gentle Savior, You came as a tiny Child to teach us love and compassion. Stir our hearts to forgive others as You have forgiven us. Help us live out Your grace and humility with others here in this world. Amen

December 13

CHRISTMAS CANDY

Every good and perfect gift is from above, coming down from the Father of the heavenly lights, Who does not change like shifting shadows. **James 1:17**

When my first grandson was tiny, we would drive him around the neighborhood to see all the Christmas lights. He called them "candy" because he had not learned the word "lights." It's an easy mistake. The glittering lights on the trees do look like old fashioned hard candy, the kind kids years ago found in their stockings or in the little paper bags some churches gave out.

It's no wonder children think Christmas is magical. One year when we hosted Christmas for my husband's family, I booked an old time sleigh ride with a huge flat sled and two gigantic black Percheron draft horses. Even though it was only eight degrees Fahrenheit that night, we all wore snowmobile suits and bundled up under heavy quilts. There was a full moon and the horses' breath was visible in the air as they puffed and pulled the big sled. The boy who called the lights "candy" was there, all grown up by then, but we had other little ones on the ride. One of our younger grandsons was afraid of the horses, so our daughter kept him in the warming house. The proprietors brought a miniature horse inside for him to pet. These memories will last forever.

I pray that you have Christmas memories like this. Often, families get caught up in disagreements and differences of opinion, making Christmas difficult instead of joyous. Our Scripture verse today says all good gifts come from God, and He is unchanging. Let's allow His holiness to surround us and guide us through this busy time of year. After all, it's His birthday party, and whatever we plan, He should be at the center of it.

Jesus, we know all good things come from You, whether they are things we can touch or things we see and feel. Grant us Your wonderful peace this Christmas and always. Amen

December 14

THE PARABLE OF THE HOLIDAYS

***Other seed fell into good soil and brought forth grain, growing up and increasing and yielding thirty and sixty and a hundredfold.* Mark 4:8**

In today's parable, Jesus speaks of a farmer sowing seed. The place the seed lands determines how it grows (or doesn't grow). Jesus is not really talking about seed, but about the Word of God being sown in our hearts.

During the modern Christmas season, we are all bombarded by images. Among these images are the "seeds" of God's Word made flesh, the incarnate Christ coming to us as a little Baby. As in Jesus' parable, some "hearers" of the Message may be vaguely aware Christmas is a Christian celebration, but they ignore those signs or totally reject them, and Satan is quick to snatch them away. The second "hearers" are like rocky ground. They recognize what is *not* the true Message of the season, but their thoughts and actions have no depth. They consciously or unconsciously block the Message out. The third "hearer" cannot hang onto the Message because the things of this world—the shopping, the decorating, the entertaining—choke out the message completely.

Can any of us in today's society actually be "good Christmas soil?" Do we even want to avoid all the images around us? After all, giving blesses the giver as much as the receiver, right? It is our heart attitude that matters here. We can, if we are diligent, celebrate Christmas without being totally overwhelmed by how the world views this season. We can determine in our minds and hearts to make Jesus the focus of the season, spend within our means, teach our children all gifts come from God including the Nintendo. And gifts do not have to be tangible. What about a mom asking for the kids to clean up after the meal? That's a gift she'd appreciate. Staying focused on God's greatest Gift can help us keep Christmas holy.

Holy Seed-Sower, sow in our hearts the beauty of giving and receiving Your gifts, not those of this world. Amen

December 15

TALKING BIBLES

Joshua then said to the Israelites, "Draw near and hear the words of the Lord your God." Joshua 3:9

No, I'm not talking about *audio* Bibles to hear through headphones. I'm talking about your *heart, mind, soul and body* hearing the words of the Lord. I know my mind sometimes wanders when I'm reading Scripture, and I'll bet most other people have the same problem. If I want to understand about a particular passage in the Bible, I have to read it with "different eyes." I have to use all my senses, my imagination, my education and life experience. If all else fails, I may need to get out my dictionary and my thesaurus, and look at different translations of the text. Staying focused is paramount, so if my mind does wander, I go back and have another look. It's not easy understanding everything the Bible has to tell us. But it is definitely worth it.

We are blessed to have modern Bibles that provide insights and cross-references and study tips. The internet provides us with instant access to Bible verses in many different formats and interpretations. We can "Google" questions, with caution; there is some pretty whacky information out there. But God's Word can even help us discern the truth. Discussion with other Christians is a great way to explore Scripture. A time-honored method of learning in a new way is to learn something and then go teach it to someone else. When I went through the Bethel Series in the late 70s, two members of another denomination were the "teachers." Ordinary Christians like me, they had gone through the training to teach the course.

In writing these devotions, I have looked for lessons in everyday life (modern parables) and then found a Bible passage which speaks to each lesson. It seems to be the creative process in doing this that makes Scripture talk to me.

Lord, tell us a story! We will listen with our hearts. Amen

December 16

JOYFUL? NOT SO MUCH

But the angel said to them, "Do not be afraid; for see—I am bringing you good news of great joy for all the people. **Luke 2:10**

Christmas isn't the same for everyone. When I was married to my first husband, his daughter from a previous marriage would come to our house to celebrate with us on Christmas Eve. Her dad was not always tactful in the way he described her mother, and it has had a lasting effect on her. She would open all her presents, share in our tradition of a supper of appetizers, and go to sleep in "her" bed in "her" bedroom at our house. The next morning, we would get up and take her to her grandparents' home where she would meet her mother and have a second Christmas. Then, she would hear all the criticism of her father from that side of the family. It got to where my stepdaughter said she hated Christmas because she got shuffled around and listened to her families bash each other. She is happily married now and has four children of her own. She fiercely protects her own family's time together, and they have developed their own meaningful traditions.

Each year, people all over the world dread Christmas, whether due to depression, loneliness, lack of money, estranged family and friends, or all of the above. Because the season is so powerfully presented in modern society, the feelings of sadness may seem magnified. Contrary to a long-held myth, the Center for Disease Control has determined that suicide rates in the U.S. actually *decrease* during the Christmas holidays, perhaps due to caring people reaching out to those who are sad. Showing others they are important to us is a basic value for Christians. When we go out of our way to extend kindness to others, we are showing them Christ's love through ourselves. Remember, the shepherds returned to the dark night to tend their sheep and the wise men rode those camels away by a different path to escape Herod's wrath. In the aftermath of Christmas, the Good News will carry us through.

Jesus, You came for the sad and lonely too. Amen

December 17

JESUS, THE SEQUEL

***And I saw heaven opened, and behold a white horse; and He that sat upon him was called Faithful and True.* Revelation 19:11**

Hollywood loves to produce "sequels," movies that continue a story previously presented. According to empireonline.com, one of the fifty greatest sequels was *Star Wars Episode V: The Empire Strikes Back*. "The best sequels," touts the website, "turn (the original) on its head and change the rules...." *The Empire Strikes Back* takes the series from "popcorn fun to something mythical and able to inspire 30 years (and counting) of utter devotion." Another "hook," they say, is "that dark, unresolved ending."

Christians know we are not going to have a "dark, unresolved ending." Christ will return, upgraded from a donkey to a majestic white horse. We won't know when He is coming, and neither do the angels or Christ Himself, "but only the Father" (Mark 13:32). We need to watch for the signs, but not in a newspaper or over the Internet. After the seven year "Tribulation" period, "the sun and moon will be dark, the stars will fall from heaven and the powers of heaven shall be shaken" (Matthew 4:29).

Christ "will come in the same way as (the disciples) saw Him go into heaven" (Acts 1:11, Zechariah 14:4), yet everyone will see Him. (I believe the mobility impaired will stand on their own two feet to watch the divine spectacle.) Imagine "all the holy angels with Him" (Matthew 25:31). "On His head (will be) many crowns" and "His name is called The Word of God" (Revelation 19:12). The best thing about this "sequel" is we are part of the cast: we get to watch it all unfold, and then we go home with the Star. There won't be any reviews because the world as we know it will be "turned on its head." This story has endured over two thousand years with millions of "utterly devoted" followers. Get your popcorn ready and enjoy the show!

Faithful and True Lord, we look forward to Your return. Keep us ever mindful of Your magnificence. Amen

December 18

TWICE THE JOY!

***Then the seven angels who had the seven trumpets prepared to sound them.* Revelations 8:6**

When you hear the old hymn, "Joy to the World," what do you think of? Most people think of the fluffy angels on Christmas Eve coming to sing to the frightened shepherds, to tell them the Good News of Jesus' birth. After the shepherds picked themselves up off the ground, the angels told them, "Today in the town of David a Savior has been born to you; He is the Messiah, the Lord. This will be a sign to you: You will find a Baby wrapped in cloths and lying in a manger" (Luke 2:11-12). We all know the words: "Joy to the world/The Lord has come/Let earth receive her King." But did you know the song was not written as a Christmas carol?

Remember, the Bible speaks of Christ coming as a Baby, but then He comes again in the Book of Revelation. English hymn writer Isaac Watts based "Joy to the World" on the second half of Psalm 98. The English Standard Version Study Bible explains, "The Psalm and (Watts') hymn (is) associated with Christmas...this is not inappropriate, provided it is clear the coming of Jesus...(bringing) light to the gentiles (establishes) the connection." "Joy to the World" was written to glorify Christ's triumphant return at the end of the age, rather than in celebration of His birth. It is Christ's "universal kingship" which is the focus of both Psalm 98 and Watts' famous song. Interestingly, the melody was arranged by Lowell Mason from an older melody that sounds a lot like parts of Handel's "Messiah." Some of the specific lyrics appear in "Messiah," but the tune is not all Handel's work. "Joy to the World" is the most-published hymn in North America.

So this Christmas, when you hear "Joy to the World," be reminded that Christ's birth ushered in this age, and His second coming will usher us into a new heaven and a new earth (Revelation 21:1).

Let every heart prepare Him room, O God! Amen

December 19

WAIT 'TILL YOUR FATHER GETS HOME

An angel of the Lord appeared to him in a dream and said, "Joseph, son of David, do not be afraid to take Mary as your wife, for the Child conceived in her is from the Holy Spirit." Matthew 1:20

Because of my "kinship" with Joseph as a stepparent, I think of him often. After the initial hoopla of Jesus' birth was over, he and Mary planned to take their son back to Nazareth. But following the secret departure of the wise men, Joseph got another surprise visit from an angel. This time, he was told, "Get up, take the child and his mother, and flee to Egypt, and remain there until I tell you; for Herod is about to search for the child, to destroy him" (Matthew 2:13). As the young parents were getting their Baby to safety, Herod was busy killing off all those other babies left behind. I've often wondered what Mary and Joseph thought about the death of the "holy innocents," but by this time, they must have gotten the message that all these goings-on were part of God's plan.

When Herod died, the angel was back. Now the holy family was to return to Israel, but the new ruler, Archelaus , was just as bad as Herod. So Joseph decided they should make their home in the town of Nazareth, in the district of Galilee (Matthew 2:19-23). Jesus "grew and became strong, filled with wisdom; and the favor of God was upon Him" (Luke 2:40). Did he get His wisdom only from God, or did Joseph have a hand in it too? Was Jesus a perfect Kid, as we would imagine, or did He sometimes forget and use His super powers to play pranks on His friends? And how in the world did Joseph enter into the discipline of Jesus, if He had needed any? Did Mary ever say, "Just wait 'till your father gets home," and Joseph was standing right there? Awkward! All we know is God must have thought Joseph was pretty special to have given him charge of His Child in this life. It makes me proud to be a stepparent too.

Jesus, thank You for loving people enough to have them as Your earthly parents. Amen

December 20

NO PLACE FOR YOU

I know that you are descendants of Abraham; yet you look for an opportunity to kill Me, because there is no place in you for My Word. **John 8:37**

A poignant part of the Christmas story is when Joseph and Mary find no room at the inn because of the crowds in Bethlehem. Both the expectant parents must have been devastated there was no place for Mary to give birth except a stable. This scene has been used for generations of a reminder the Messiah came in such a humble way, as a Servant. Even though He is rightfully the King of the universe, His birth was a lowly one carrying a message of sacrifice from the very beginning of His earthly life.

What a contrast between Jesus' delivery into this world and the modern "birthing centers" hospitals now offer! Today's expectant parents can look forward to five star accommodations to welcome their little ones into this life. Jesus' birth was not untypical for many babies born during His time, but parents in advanced countries today would be aghast if they had to face similar conditions. Even being born in a taxi cab doesn't seem so bad!

There is another time in the Bible where the "grown-up" Jesus is speaking to the Jews who actually believed in Him as the Son of God. He told them, "If you continue in My word, you are truly My disciples; and you will know the truth, and the truth will make you free" (John 8:31-32). These Jews were insulted because, they said, they were descendants of Abraham and had never been slaves. They didn't need to be freed (v. 33). Jesus replied, "If the Son makes you free, you will be free indeed" (v. 36). In other words, if Jesus says you are free now, then you'd better believe you were a slave to *something* before! Jesus continued, "I know you are descendants of Abraham; yet you look for an opportunity to kill Me, because there is no place in you for My Word." Just like Mary and Joseph were turned away from the inn, some people have no place in their hearts for God either.

Jesus, prepare our hearts to accept You. Amen

December 21

CHRISTMAS PRESENCE

All the believers were together and had everything in common.
Acts 2:44

There is a story about a grumpy old man whose wife died. After the funeral, he sat on his porch all day long alone. Many neighbors went to visit, bringing food and saying all the "right" things. The man just sat there and never even acknowledged the people who came. Everyone said he was impossible to get to know. Then one day, a little boy who lived next door went over and sat down on the porch floor next to the man. The boy was there for hours. Everyone could see they were talking but no one wanted to go see what they spoke about. When the little boy came home, his mother asked him, "What did you say to him?" The little boy said, "Not much. I just helped him cry."

My friend and mentor Bob Albers speaks of "the ministry of presence," the important task of just being there for someone who needs us. Being available for those in need is a year-round ministry, and the Christmas season is a heightened time to practice this. The hustle and bustle of Christmas, plus trying to stay on top of "normal" activities can be overwhelming for some. Finding time for our own "down time" is hard enough without having to think about what everyone else needs. But it is in the example of the little boy in today's story we find the key: simply *being there* for others. We don't necessarily have to *do* anything. We just have to demonstrate we are *with* the person who needs our companionship and caring. We don't even need to be with the person physically, if that's not possible. Any member of the armed forces serving away from home at Christmastime will tell you how much it means to receive "care packages," cards, letters, and emails. Communicating is even easier with all the electronic methods of communication we are blessed with today. Christmas is about the gift God gave us, the "present" of Jesus Christ His only Son. It's also about Christ's "ministry of presence" among us.

Gracious Lord, thank You for coming to live on earth and show us the way to salvation. Amen

December 22

POPE AND CIRCUMSTANCE

They took palm branches and went out to meet Him, shouting, "Hosanna!" "Blessed is He who comes in the name of the Lord!" "Blessed is the King of Israel!" John 12:13

Pope Francis visited the United States in September, 2015. His humble manner was apparent from the moment he stepped off "Shepherd One." President and Mrs. Obamas' unprecedented personal greeting of the pontiff was a sign of the high respect afforded him during his visit to our powerful and well-to-do nation during a time of economic, social, and political turmoil. The Pope's visit was a security nightmare, but Francis seemed oblivious to all the fuss. He exited the plane carrying his own valise, reported to contain a razor, a breviary (prayer book), an appointment book and a book to read. When he wasn't riding in his open-air, Fiat-Chrysler-made Jeep Wrangler "Popemobile," he was ferried around in an ordinary Italian-built Fiat. The Pope insisted on foregoing the bullet-proof glass bubble atop the Jeep, to be closer to the people. No small task for his security guards.

ABC News reported the pontiff brought about thirty people with him, including Vatican clergy and press. Although the Pope speaks relatively good English, Monsignor Mark Miles served as interpreter for him when the message got tricky. Also accompanying him were seventy-six accredited journalists from all over the world. Pope Francis stayed at the Apostolic Nunciature of the Holy See, better known as the "Vatican Embassy," nice accommodations but not as opulent as one might imagine.

Pope Francis is perhaps the best-loved leader of the Catholic Church in modern times. To his credit, he sincerely tries to keep things simple, honest and straightforward. The accompanying show of magnificence is in stark contrast to the way the Christ lived and moved and conducted Himself while in this world. I am quite sure this humble pope has considered how different his life style is than the Man Whom he represents.

Lord Jesus, thank You for wise and humble religious leaders. Amen

December 23

I DIG CHRISTMAS!

Others, like seed sown on good soil, hear the Word, accept it, and produce a crop—some thirty, some sixty, some a hundred times what was sown. **Mark 4:20**

Oh, it's *so easy* to love Christmas, isn't it? We wait all year and then the magic begins to weave its way into our minds and hearts. We shop for just the right gift for all the people on our list, and we rejoice when we find that perfect item. And, we gleefully anticipate what others will choose for us. Maybe we still even make a list so we won't get stuck with something we don't care for or won't use. The food at Christmas is like no other time of the year. We make special dishes and baked goods and candies, nibbling as we go. The music carries us to a vision of happy families and joyous reunions. The sights, sounds, and smells of the season captivate our senses and leave us almost speechless.

Do they really? Or have we become so accustomed to Christmas being a "big deal" that we just accept what the world says and go along with it? Sometimes all the world can offer us is a false idea of what will make us happy. We say we love to give and get gifts, but are we ready to accept the best Gift of all into our hearts and our lives? The gift of Christ's love, grace and redemption is not like a fancy sweater which will eventually wear out or go out of style. It's not a food gift we eat and then it's gone, and it's not a monetary gift that we spend on some frivolous item. Christ's gift to us is *alive* and it lives within us for the rest of this life and throughout eternity. He gives us living water so we will never thirst again (John 7:38). Through Him we receive bread unlike any we can bake, the bread of His own body given freely so we might live forgiven (John 6:35). He asks us to be "good soil" that His Word might take root in us and grow and produce more love and grace and forgiveness (Mark 4:20). Let's rejoice this Christmas over the most wonderful gift of all-time: Christ Himself.

Praise You, Lord! You are our Christmas gift. Amen

December 24

CHRISTMAS GRACE

An angel of the Lord appeared to them, and the glory of the Lord shone around them. Luke 2:9

Around the corner and down the hall of the care center. Knock and enter in one smooth motion. My mother sits in her usual, dented spot on the love seat, her accoutrements—tissues, lip balm, manicure scissors, water—around her like sentinels. She is playing solitaire and she has forgotten it is Christmas Eve, that we are going to candlelight services. That information is locked away, behind the little slot in her head where she puts the things I tell her these days. No matter. We change her stained blouse, fluff her hair, and we are off on a snow globe drive with my husband Patrick at the wheel.

How frail she looks, as we enter church. She peers out at me from under her hooded coat with the same chiseled features I saw the day before. The same watery eyes and pointed nose and tight little frown. I say a silent prayer she won't be crabby... We have come early to herd her into the chapel without incident. "Merry Christmas!" says the custodian. She removes her hood and flashes a brilliant smile. "Merry Christmas to you too!" What's this? In the short drive from the care center, my normally impossible mother has been transformed. She is friendly to all, does not complain once during the lengthy service, smiles at children, even sings the songs as best she is able.

It was a magic night, a Christmas miracle. When the angels came to the shepherds on that Holy night so long ago, they sang, "Glory to God in the highest heaven, and on earth peace to those on whom His favor rests" (Luke 2:13-14). God's favor seemed to be resting on my ninety-six year old mother that Christmas Eve. Her entire adult existence had been scarred with pain, sorrow, depression and addiction. It was the first time in my life I saw her filled with natural joy. Maybe it was the dementia, but I prefer to believe the Holy Spirit touched my mother, briefly giving her a peace that passes all understanding.

Jesus, thank You for the miracle of Your birth. Amen

December 25

ABUNDANT LOVE

I have been crucified with Christ; and it is no longer I who live, but it is Christ who lives in me. And the life I now live in the flesh I live by faith in the Son of God, Who loved me and gave Himself for me.
Galatians 2:19-20

Why would we want to be reminded of Christ's crucifixion on Christmas Day? Why, when we're in the middle of the glow of our Lord's birth, surrounded by images of joy and glad tidings, would thinking about the awful thing that happened to Him be important? Because Christ's birth reminds us God keeps His promises, all of His promises, including the one to send a Savior to save the world. No one knew, before the first Christmas Eve, that God's promise would come in the form of the Baby Jesus. Only a few knew what this Baby's birth meant that night: His earthly parents, a few unsuspecting shepherds, some "wise men from the east" (Matthew 2:1). Even the inn keeper who turned the expectant parents away didn't realize he was refusing lodging to the King of the universe. Bethlehem was full of people who didn't know Who Jesus was, and it would be three decades before the word really started to get around.

But as we gaze on the little Baby in the manger and eat our turkey and dressing, we must remember this Child was born to die. He was sent here to bring us the Good News of God's abundant love and unquenchable grace. He knew from the beginning He would die a horrible death to prove to all of us He could—and did—conquer death, rose from the grave, and went back to sit at the right hand of the Father. That was His mission, and He carried it out willingly. Jesus means "God saves," and Immanuel means "God is with us." He was and is both Savior to the world and living among us still.

Your love, O Lord, is everlasting. Amen

December 26

PUTTING JESUS AWAY

***The fruit of the Spirit is love, joy, peace, patience, kindness, goodness, faithfulness, gentleness, and self-control.* Galatians 5:22-23**

A little boy observed his mother taking the Christmas storage boxes out of the closet on December 26. "Is it time to put Jesus away?" he asked innocently. What can we say to a child who thinks Jesus is just a plastic doll we place in a toy manger once a year? Maybe we could leave that display out year round. Or at least attempt to have other displays of what we believe visible for children to see at times other than Christmas.

The best display we have of Christ on any given day is ourselves. If others, especially children, see us acting out Christ's love, they are seeing Christ Himself. Do we deliberately try to be a caring person to others? That's love (Romans 12:9). Can we maintain a pleasant attitude no matter what is going on in our lives? That's joy (Psalm 100). Do we preserve tranquility when the sky appears to be falling down around us? That's peace (Proverbs 16:7). Patience is the ability to deal with life's trying moments and people without wanting to lambaste others (Psalm 37:1). Kindness sees ways to help or encourage others if there isn't much we can practically do for them. The spiritual fruit of goodness reflects the goodness of our Lord (2 Peter 1:3). It may mean doing what's right even if it initially hurts someone. It takes integrity to practice faithfulness, like God keeping His promises to us (Joshua 21:45). Gentleness means living within God's peace (Philippians 4:7). Self-control is actually letting go of things that are harmful, and giving those things to God for safe-keeping (John 5:14).

God will produce His fruit in and from us if we follow His lead. He's also the one who convicts us if we miss the mark, and He offers us forgiveness. Let's don't put the Baby Jesus away this year. Let's carry Him around with us, on our faces and in our hearts and minds.

Help me walk Your way every day, Lord. Amen

December 27

JESUS AND THE VIDEO GAME

Here is a trustworthy saying that deserves full acceptance: Christ Jesus came into the world to save sinners—of whom I am the worst.
1 Timothy 1:15

On the website 2knowthyself.com, a list of reasons people play video games begins with the rush they get from saving the world. They actually *feel* the emotions of the hero they are controlling. Other reasons given for the popularity of electronic gaming include problem solving, self-esteem boost, stress relief, and increase in dopamine levels in the brain. Dopamine is the chemical which causes excitement. The player may have to do all sorts of pseudo-frightening things to score in the game, and many of the games are about conquering evil foe and savings damsels in distress. Just like in the old time fairy tales. And, like the fairy tales in a book, the video game player can stop playing the game at any time and return to the real, although perhaps no less dangerous, world.

In a sense, when Jesus came into this world as a tiny Baby, He was entering into a sort of video game. There were many evil foes to fight and He had quite a few damsels in distress to save, along with many men in distress too. In fact, Jesus came to find and save *all of us* from ourselves, from our sin nature (John 3:16-17). The only thing was, Jesus couldn't just turn off the video game and leave the scene. He was here for the long haul, which only lasted about thirty-three years, in one sense. But in another sense, it's lasting longer than that because Jesus is with us all until the end of this age (Matthew 28:20). Jesus is not playing games; He truly is "the way, the truth, and the life" (John 14:6). He is a better teacher than a video game at problem solving, stress relief, and boosting self-esteem. Being in a relationship with Jesus is a rush in itself. He is the Super Hero, and He is in control all the time, throughout eternity. No, Jesus never puts down the joy stick. He is with us always.

We thank You, Lord, that You have vanquished all the foes in this world and the next. Amen

December 28

A TINY CHRISTMAS TREE

Therefore if you have any encouragement from being united with Christ, if any comfort from his love, if any common sharing in the Spirit, if any tenderness and compassion, then make my joy complete by being like-minded, having the same love, being one in spirit and of one mind. Rather, in humility value others above yourselves, not looking to your own interests but each of you to the interests of the others. **Philippians 2:1-4**

Ramona is one of my best friends, a member of the Bible study I lead, a prayer warrior and the most patient of us all. She went in for a routine outpatient test but something wasn't right. She landed in the hospital having emergency surgery, and she was alone. A widow, she lived with her son, and he was out of town. She called and I went to the hospital to see her. Following her surgery, she was transferred to a rehab facility. It was right before Christmas, and she was told she had to achieve a certain level of independence before she could return home. As Christmas Eve grew closer, she feared she would be stuck in rehab for this most sacred of holidays.

As I was leaving to go visit Ramona, I thought, "What can I bring her to cheer her up?" I spotted the miniature Christmas tree I had made for my mother before she passed away. It was a small craft tree, about a foot high, with miniature lights, a garland of tiny gum drops, and a couple dozen petite ornaments, topped off with a shiny gold star. I picked up the tree and wrapped it carefully in tissue paper, with a tag bearing Ramona's name.

Ramona was thrilled with her little tree. She absolutely beamed when I brought it in and set it up in her room. She told me later every person who came in to her room remarked how sweet that tiny tree was. She did make it home by Christmas Eve, although she was too weak to come to candlelight services. But she said the gift of that little tree brightened her Christmas like no other.

Lord, help us remember how much a simple gift from the heart can lift someone else's spirits. Amen

December 29

THE LIGHT IN THE DARKNESS

The light shines in the darkness but the darkness has not understood it. John 1:5

Why doesn't the Gospel of John begin with the traditional story of Jesus' birth? John opens with these words: "In the beginning was the Word, and the Word was with God, and the Word was God. He was with God in the beginning. Through Him all things were made; without Him nothing was made that has been made. In Him was life, and that life was the light of all mankind. The light shines in the darkness, and the darkness has not overcome it" (John 1:1-5). On second glance, this is just another version of Christ coming to live in this world. Mary isn't mentioned, nor are Joseph, the shepherds, the wise men, or any of the other church Christmas play actors. But it is clear in John's Gospel Jesus is the Word, He is One with God, He came from God. It is obvious even though Jesus came down into this world to shed light—His marvelous Light—not everybody "got" this. Many versions of the Bible say "the darkness has not overcome it," which is another way of saying people missed the whole point of Jesus coming.

To non-believers, it must be unclear what we are celebrating. Oh, most adults know what Christianity is: we believe Jesus Christ was and is the Son of God Who came to earth to live among us, He was hung on a tree and murdered, He came back to life and promises believers eternal life. But when they see the blaring secular images that are all around us from Halloween until the New Year, do they think we are a fraud? That the legend we have told all those years contained in a Book we swear is true is just that, a legend? How can they know what it means to believe if they have not been shown? What do our words and actions tell them about this faith to which we cling so ferociously? Let us seek counsel from our God to go forth from this day until our last, speaking, acting, showing the Love we know is real, until there can be no doubt among all humankind.

Triune God, ignite in us the power to show, not just tell, our faith. Amen

December 30

AURORA BOREALIS

He gave a command to the skies above and opened the doors of the heavens. **Psalm 78:23**

Living in the northern part of the United States it is often possible to see the Northern Lights, or the Aurora Borealis, on clear, cold winter nights. According to the Northern Lights Centre's website, "The bright dancing lights…are actually collisions between electrically charged particles from the sun that enter the earth's atmosphere….seen above the magnetic poles of the northern and southern hemispheres. They are known as 'Aurora Borealis' in the north and 'Aurora Australis' in the south….(They) appear in many colors….pale green and pink are the most common. Shades of red, yellow, green, blue, and violet have been reported. The lights appear (as) patches or scattered clouds of light to streamers, arcs, rippling curtains or shooting rays that light up the sky with an eerie glow." The night I saw this amazing light display driving on dark country roads, massive swaths of iridescent lime green shimmered across the sky. The show continued for about forty-five minutes and then faded, eventually disappearing altogether.

The people of Medieval Europe believed the Auroras were signs from God. The Cree Indians called them "Dancing Spirits." Indigenous Australian tribes believed they were spirits of the dead. A noteworthy sighting of the Northern Lights was after the Battle of Fredericksburg during the America Civil War. The lights could be seen from the battlefield that night, a rare occurrence as far south as Virginia. The Confederate Army took it as a sign God was on their side, and a famous painting, "Aurora Borealis," by Frederic Edwin Church is said to represent that conflict.

To see the entire sky light up with glistening hues makes me think of God at work with His mighty paintbrush, giving us a glimpse of heaven and one more reason to be in awe of Him.

Great Spirit, You entertain us with Your majesty and cause us to fall down in worship. Amen

December 31

CHASED BY THE LORD

God is my helper; the Lord is the upholder of my life. **Psalm 54:4**

What a joy this year has been! Recently, I sat bolt upright in bed at 4:30 a.m. asking myself, "Where are You, God, and what have You done with my life?" But the ideas for these devotions just kept coming. Countless people wrote from around the world, called, stopped me at church, to tell me I was doing a wonderful thing. Wonderful? I just wrote four hundred words every day for the past year. What's so wonderful about that? At her peak, Thornbirds author Colleen McCullough wrote 15,000 to 30,000 words a day on an electric typewriter. And I thought I had no life apart from writing.

But I was writing for God and He is Life. God held the carrot in front of my nose, and I never tired of going after it. Minnesota's award winning nature photographer Jim Brandenburg traveled the world for 25 years with National Geographic, often taking up to 300 rolls of film to render a few choices for publishing. Brandenburg always felt "increasingly dissatisfied" with his art, and in 1994 he began a personal project, limiting himself to taking only one shot per day between September and December. Sometimes he swore he'd go home without that one quintessential photograph for a particular day. But the "shot" always showed up. The results appear in his beautiful book, *Chased by the Light* (Northwood Press, 1998).

My ideas for devotional posts burgeoned to where I had several hundred on my list, but often I would begin one and it seemed to go nowhere. God was faithful, however, and where one "literary window" seemed to close, a door would be flung wide and I'd be off writing again. That's not to say each entry is perfect; far from it. But with a daily writing project, I never had much time to ruminate and revise, pontificate and purge. I just had to get it out there. And God delivered.

Thank You, Father, for being my partner in this project. Thank You too for my wonderful, faithful readers. Amen

SUPPORTING SAINTS

March 8	Trudy Baltazar, *A Road to Freedom: Strangers Restore Justice for an Innocent Man*
March 16	Stephanie Landsem, *The Living Water Series: The Well, The Thief,* and *The Tomb*
April 11	Mary Treacey O'Keefe *Meant-to-Be Moments: Discovering What We Are Called to Do and Be*
April 23	Zach Sobiech's song "Clouds" can be viewed at https://www.youtube.com/watch?v=3HtCXgo4fvU
	Laura Sobiech, *Fly A Little Higher*
April 25	Alice Hansche Mortenson, "I Needed the Quiet"
June 24	Betty Liedtke, http://findyourburiedtreasure.com/uganda
July 22	Ruth Bachman, *Growing Through the Narrow Spots*
July 24	Catherine Plantenberg, www.bestlightimage.biz
August 11	Kathi Holmes, *I Stand With Courage: One Woman's Journey to Conquer Paralysis*
August 13	Amy Zellmer, Traumatic Brain Injury Newsletter: http://myemail.constantcontact.com/TBI-Awareness-Newsletter.html?soid=1102026611199&aid=b3mmk_sAKvs
September 4	Caryn Sullivan, *Bitter or Better?*

September 5   Gloria VanDemmeltraadt, *Darkness In Paradise, Memories of Onno VanDemmeltraadt from His Youth in Indonesia during WWII*

September 13   Katie Sluss is a 15 year old whose family are active members or our church. I had the pleasure of being her mentor for her confirmation class. Katie is bright, articulate, and well-able to express herself. She models Christ in her interactions with her peers and with adults.

October 5   Stephanie Sorensen, *Ma Doula: A Story Tour of Birth*

October 11   Nada Giordana is the author of three books, *No Thank You, I'd Rather Be Myself*, *Thinking Skinny*, and *Reinventing New Chapters in Your Life at Any Age*

October 17   Carole Lewis, *Give God a Year, Change Your Life Forever*

October 31   Diane Keyes, *Spirit of the Snow People* and *This Sold House: Staging Your Home to Sell in Today's Market*

November 11   Read about the author's aunt, Ethel (Sally) Blaine Millett and the Angels of Bataan: *We Band of Angels* by Elizabeth Norman

November 25   Bill Elliston, http://www.ellistoncoaching.com/

ABOUT THE AUTHOR

Meg Corrigan is a retired college counselor, author, speaker, trainer and sexual assault survivor. Her memoir, *Then I Am Strong: Moving From My Mother's Daughter to God's Child* (2010, Create Space) chronicles her childhood with an alcoholic mother, co-dependent father, and caring older sister. At age twenty-five, Meg was sexually assaulted at gunpoint and would have been left for dead. God's miraculous rescue of her from the hands of her assailant was to change the course of her life forever.

Following the assault and the unconscionable treatment she received from law enforcement and medical personnel, Meg ran away with the circus. Well, not really the circus, but a travelling Hawaiian show band. Meg's second book, *Perils of a Polynesian Percussionist* (2014, Create Space) is a novel based on the years she played percussion for that group.

God had plans for Meg, pursuing her until she finally gave in and said, "Okay, I'm Yours." She now speaks to churches, civic groups, college students, mental health professionals and law enforcement personnel, as well as youth in juvenile facilities, about her journey to healing and wholeness. She conveys a powerful message of hope in the darkest hours, and she credits her resilience to the grace of God.

Meg loves writing, horses, dogs, gardening, and being out of doors. She lives in Lake Elmo, Minnesota with her husband, Patrick, who has introduced her to motorcycle riding and bass fishing. Meg has never given birth, but she gained ten pounds with each of her children, one adopted daughter and three stepdaughters. The girls have given Meg and Patrick ten exceptional grandchildren, and a great-grandchild is on the way at this writing.

For more information about Meg Blaine Corrigan, or to contact her about her speaking availability, please go to her website www.MegCorrigan.com .
Her books are available at www.Amazon.com .

Made in the USA
Middletown, DE
21 October 2015